Chrystia Freeland was the Moscow bureau chief for the *Financial Times* from January 1995 to August 1998. Before that, she spent several years reporting on Ukraine and Eastern Europe for the *FT*. She has a BA in History and Literature from Harvard University and a Master's of Studies in Slavonic Studies from Oxford, where she attended on a Rhodes scholarship. Chrystia Freeland was born in Peace River, Alberta, Canada in 1968.

SALE OF THE CENTURY

The Inside Story of the
Second Russian Revolution

Chrystia Freeland

ABACUS

First published in Great Britain by
Little, Brown and Company in 2000
This revised paperback edition published by Abacus in 2005
Reprinted 2006, 2007, 2008, 2009, 2010, 2011, 2012, 2013, 2014

A CIP catalogue record for this book
is available from the British Library.

ISBN 978-0-349-11260-2

Typeset in Berkeley by M Rules
Printed and bound in Great Britain by
Clays Ltd, St Ives plc

Papers used by Abacus are from well-managed forests
and other responsible sources.

MIX
Paper from
responsible sources
FSC   FSC® C104740
www.fsc.org

Abacus
An imprint of
Little, Brown Book Group
100 Victoria Embankment
London EC4Y 0DY

An Hachette UK Company
www.hachette.co.uk

www.littlebrown.co.uk

To Graham and Natalka

Contents

Dramatis Personae

The Young Reformers

Pyotr Aven – Smooth English-speaker who was one of the first young reformers to make contacts in the West. Became an oligarch himself in partnership with Mikhail Friedman.

Boris Brevnov – Nizhny Novgorod banker and protégé of Nemtsov who was loosely allied with the young reformers.

Anatoly Chubais – St Petersburg economist who pushed through mass privatisation and was the administratively gifted iron general of the group.

Arkady Evstafiev – Former journalist who became Chubais' loyal spokesman and aide.

Yegor Gaidar – Brilliant Moscow red intelligentsia scion who was the thinker of the group.

Konstantin Kagalovsky – Moscow economist who represented the group at the IMF before going to work for one of the oligarchs.

Sergei Kiriyenko – Nizhny Novgorod businessman and Nemtsov protégé who was loosely allied with the young reformers and became prime minister.

Alfred Kokh – St Petersburg economist who worked on mass privatisation and oversaw the controversial loans-for-shares programme.

Boris Nemtsov – Governor of Nizhny Novgorod and later first deputy prime minister who was loosely affiliated with the young reformers.

Dmitry Vasiliev – St Petersburg economist who was Chubais' first lieutenant of privatisation and then became head of the Federal Security Commission, the stock-market watchdog.

Sergei Vasiliev – Talented economist and administrator, holding a number of senior civil service jobs, who tried to push the reforms through the apparat.

Aleksei Ulyukaev – Moscow economist who worked closely with Gaidar both in government and in Gaidar's economic institute.

The Party of War

Mikhail Barsukov – Head of the FSB, the revamped KGB.

Aleksandr Korzhakov – Yeltsin's confidant and bodyguard who became the politically influential chief of his Kremlin security force.

Oleg Soskovets – Former factory boss who became deputy prime minister and led the hard-line party of war faction in the Kremlin.

Shamil Tarpishchev – Yeltsin's tennis coach and head of the National Sports Fund, a leading loophole-economy business.

The Family

Roman Abramovich – Business partner of Boris Berezovsky and influential Kremlin wheeler-dealer.

Tatyana Dyachenko – Yeltsin's younger daughter and adviser.

Valentin Yumashev – Yeltsin's ghostwriter who rose to become his chief-of-staff.

The Oligarchs

Alfa Group

Pyotr Aven – Former young reformer who joined the group early on.
Mikhail Friedman – Physicist and wheeler-dealer from western Ukraine
who founded the group.

Inkombank

Vladimir Vinogradov – Founder of the banking group and junior oligarch.

Logovaz/Sibneft Group

Roman Abramovich – Secretive businessman and behind-the-scenes
politician with excellent links to the Yeltsin family.
Boris Berezovsky – Former mathematician turned lobbyist *par excellence* who was involved in a series of firms ranging from the Logovaz
car dealership to the Sibneft oil company.

Menatep/Yukos

Konstantin Kagalovsky – Former young reformer who went to work for
the group, playing a key role in the loans-for-shares privatisation of
Yukos, a Siberian oil company.
Mikhail Khodorkovsky – Founder of the banking and oil group.
Leonid Nevzlin – One of Khodorkovsky's earliest partners and the chief
lobbyist of the group.
Vasily Shakhnovsky – Former Moscow City chief-of-staff who came to
work for the group.

Most Group

Aleksandr (Sasha) Bekker – Investigative reporter known as the $100m
journalist for uncovering a story about Soskovets while he was working for Gusinsky's *Segodnya* newspaper.
Vladimir Gusinsky – The flamboyant theatre director who founded the
Most media empire.

Yevgeny Kisiliev – NTV anchor and founding partner.

Mikhail Leontiev – Journalist and friend of Gusinsky who helped persuade him to enter the media business.

Igor Malashenko – TV executive who helped found the Most group's NTV private television station.

Sergei Zverev – Well-connected lobbyist who was a senior Most executive and later went to work in the Kremlin.

Oneximbank/Interros Group

Boris Jordan – Russian–American investment banker who formed a partnership with Potanin. Worked closely with New Zealander Stephen Jennings and Russian–American Leonid Rozhetskin.

Vladimir Potanin – Former Soviet trade high-flyer who founded the group.

Mikhail Prokherev – A well-trained banker who oversaw the development of the banking arm of the business.

Stolichny/SBS Agro Group

Aleksandr Smolensky – Founder of the banking group that was devastated by the crash of 1998.

The Red Barons Who Became Oligarchs

Gazprom

Viktor Chernomyrdin – Soviet minister who took Gazprom private. Yeltsin's longest serving prime minister.

Rem Vyakhirev – Chernomyrdin's ally and senior company executive.

Lukoil

Vagit Alekperov – Smart Azeri and Soviet-era oil executive who pulled together Russia's leading oil company.

Moscow City/Sistema

Yuri Luzhkov – The mayor of Moscow.

Vasily Shakhnovsky – Luzhkov's talented chief-of-staff who went to work for Menatep/Yukos.

Vladimir Yevtushenkov – Luzhkov's confidant and head of Sistema, the powerful quasi-private business closely affiliated with the city government.

SALE OF THE CENTURY

PROLOGUE

ON THE FIRST day of my four-year posting to Moscow, I drove to the Kazan railway station to pick up the unknown 10-year-old who would become my new brother.

It was just before Christmas, one of the shortest days of the year, and even at 8 a.m. the Moscow sky was pitch-black. As I made my way through the dark city, I was terrified. It seemed to be such an enormous thing – to meet a young stranger, announce myself as his new sister and, less than 24 hours later, to whisk him away to a small Canadian town almost exactly half-way across the world.

My mood did not lift as I walked across the dirty slush into the station. No Canadian can legitimately complain about Moscow weather, but the Russian capital's winter pavements are positively evil. The chemicals the city uses to melt the snow are so corrosive that dogs refuse to walk on them, lest they burn up their paws, and in the spring thaw electric tram-lines sometimes explode into small blazes as the fumes from the ground below eat away their external insulation.

From the street, the Kazan station is gorgeous, a glamorous bejewelled cathedral for the iron work-horses of the proletariat. But inside, like all Russian railway stations, it is a Brueghelesque scene of grimy anarchy. Crippled beggars crowd the steps; bad-tempered, machine-gun-toting policemen guard the entrance to keep out the homeless; and exhausted, sweaty passengers, wearing the tracksuits and bulky long underwear which are the uniform of the Russian train traveller, doze on top of the enormous bundles of Moscow goods they will cart home to Siberia or the Far East in marathon railway journeys.

Bumping and shoving, I ploughed my way to the arrival platform of the train from Kazan, a city some 450 miles east of Moscow and about 80 miles southeast of Yoshkar Ola, my new brother's native town. After a few minutes, I spotted a youngish Russian man striding towards me, gripping the hand of a girl of about five on one side and a boy of about three on the other. Next to them, walking alone, was a small, crumpled-looking, dark-haired boy.

Could this be the children from the orphanage with their baby-broker, as my father had dubbed the sharp Russian entrepreneurs who made a business out of finding pretty white babies for childless Westerners? It was. I held out my hand and introduced myself to the little boy, hoping my voice sounded gentle and friendly.

'Hi, I'm Chrystia, your new sister.'

I imagined that Adik, the 10-year-old whom my father and step-mother were adopting, must be scared to death. A new and strange life was beginning in a faraway, foreign-speaking country, and, for him, I was its first emissary. But both Adik and the baby-broker were pro-foundly nonchalant. Adik gingerly took my hand. The man said hello and goodbye in one breath and marched off to deliver his other charges. The child was mine now, at least until I got him home to Peace River, Alberta.

He was remarkably – disturbingly – easy to take care of. Adik ate what was put on his plate, fastidiously hung up his coat and took off his snowy shoes whenever we entered a building and spoke only when spoken to – a cowed, well-behaved stoic, like Anne before she was liberated from her institution and delivered to Green Gables. He didn't make small talk, but as the day progressed I occasionally cap-tured a glimpse of the deprivation and isolation of his orphanage childhood.

The first shock was his luggage. When we had turned to leave the station, I had asked him where we should go to fetch his suitcases. 'It's here,' he said, raising the small plastic shopping bag in his right hand.

In it were all his worldly goods: a half-dozen dry crackers, a pair of tattered slippers and a storybook whose pages I would later discover guarded the pictures of Adik's two best friends.

From what I knew of Adik's background, I shouldn't have been surprised. His mother, who was still alive, had been one of millions who managed to fall through the cracks in the Soviet socialist safety-net. Usually drunk, and only occasionally employed, she had borne three children – of whom Adik was the eldest – to three different fathers. Often, the children had been left alone for weeks at a time, with Adik forced to forage in the streets to feed his infant sisters. Sometimes his mother's boyfriends would beat her and once Adik had tried to intercede to protect her from a lover's knife. Finally, social services stepped in and the children were placed in a local orphanage. Adik's two sisters had been adopted a few months earlier by my stepmother's childless younger sister, my father, a farmer with four daughters but no son, had agreed to take Adik rather than leave him alone in Russia, forever parted from his siblings.

It seemed impossible not to pity the survivor of such a brutal childhood, yet on that first day in Moscow I seemed to be the only one who felt sorry for Adik. At the *Financial Times* bureau, our office manager and research assistant cooed and clucked over him with the wonderful solicitousness Russians have for all children. The main talking point, though, was Adik's incredible good fortune.

'Tell your father he should adopt me next and bring me to Canada,' Katya, the Russian journalist who worked as our researcher, told me.

Adik thought he was lucky, too. The paperwork on the adoption had taken an agonisingly long time to complete and while he waited in Yoshkar-ola the other children had taunted him. Foreigners never adopted children over five, they all knew, especially not dark-haired boys with the slightly slanty eyes of some Tatar ancestor. It was all an elaborate hoax: Adik would never reach mythical Canada. A week earlier, Adik had had the last laugh. A pick-up date in Moscow had been set; he was definitely leaving. At the small party held to celebrate his escape, the sceptical friends began to beg – could he please ask his new family to adopt them, too?

That evening, Adik and I shared a supper of peanut-butter and jelly sandwiches with Jacob, the 7-year-old son of the British friends in whose apartment we were spending our one night in Moscow. Jacob's parents were both away, so it was just the three of us. Adik was astonished that Jacob – a boy with the good fortune to be born in the West – was now living in wretched Russia.

'But if you're English, then why do you live here?' an uncomprehending Adik asked Jacob. 'I'm Russian, but I'm taking a plane to Canada tomorrow morning and I'm never coming back.'

A defeated-looking Jacob knew exactly what Adik meant. With a small child's gravity, he explained his predicament: 'My mummy and daddy have jobs here, so I have to live with them in Moscow. But they've promised me that next year we're leaving, too.'

Adik tried to be sympathetic, but I could see that he was still feeling both puzzled and rather superior. Why would anyone who didn't have to do so live in Russia? He was smart enough to be getting out the very next day.

With that kind of attitude our marathon journey to the Canadian north-west was bound to be easy. By 9 a.m. the next morning, we had already run Adik's new documents through the usually unforgiving gauntlet of Sheremetyevo airport customs control. The ordinarily surly border guard smiled us through, wishing Adik good luck and saying she wished she was moving to Canada too.

It was still before 10 o'clock, but I decided I needed to fortify myself. We headed to the bar, where Adik drank a Coke and I had a beer and a cigarette. The latter was a guilty secret from my family, so I instructed Adik to lie on my behalf.

'Of course,' he said. 'But you really should stop smoking. I used to smoke too, but I quit last year.' It turned out that the young hedonist had also drunk vodka, but he had kicked that habit as well. Apparently his gang at the orphanage believed that nicotine and alcohol stunted one's growth and Adik, quite small for his age, thought he needed all the height he could get.

Then we were in Alberta, and Adik's new life began. It must have been a terrific struggle to adapt. Adik spoke just a half-dozen words of English and, once my two-week Christmas break was over, he was left with a family which spoke no Russian.

His salvation was hockey, the language of skates and pucks that Canada and Russia both speak fluently. One of his first English words was 'ice'. That's what he would mumble down the telephone line to my grandfather – the family chauffeur – when he wanted to be driven to the outdoor rink a few miles from our home to practise. 'Big ice' meant he wanted to go to the more serious, larger indoor rink in town.

Within a year, Adik had become Canadian. The meek and almost painfully well-behaved little Russian boy had been replaced by an outspoken, occasionally obnoxious Canadian kid, addicted to computer games, snow-boarding and dissonant Seattle bands. He hated talking about his Russian childhood and, despite my family's hope that he would grow up bilingual, pretended to have forgotten Russian altogether.

I managed to trick him into conceding a link to his native land only once. 'Pavel Bure [the Russian hockey star who now played for the Vancouver Canucks] can't play hockey,' I teased, speaking in Russian.

Adik, who had feigned misunderstanding of dozens of more innocent forays into his mother tongue, could not endure this insult to his idol.

'He can so, stupid,' he shouted back, then broke into a broad grin and a riot of laughter when he realised he had given the game away. But Adik wouldn't be lured into speaking any more Russian: 'I'm Canadian now, this is my new home.'

In leaving Russia with a smile on his face, my new brother joined a sad but enduring national tradition. As early as the fourteenth century, the Russian urge to escape had been so powerful that the Muscovite princes began to restrict their nobles' right to travel abroad. When the Marquis de Custine, a perceptive French writer, visited Russia in the early nineteenth century, things were no better. Departing aristocrats, he noticed, had a gay and carefree air, like birds released from their cages or schoolboys off on holiday. But on their way home those same Russians were gloomy, worried and mute. For the Marquis, who had gone to Russia a determined supporter of its autocratic system but left a fervent constitutionalist, the conclusion was obvious: 'A country which they quitted with so much joy and to which they return with so much regret is a bad country.'

Heartily in agreement with the Marquis, my own family had been part of a later exodus. During the Second World War, my maternal grandparents fled western Ukraine, careful always to stay a few miles west of the invading Soviet Red Army. Their dangerous and gruelling escape was the best decision they ever made. Many of the brothers, sisters and cousins who stayed behind either died in the war or spent the decade after it imprisoned in Stalinist labour camps.

Yet, to Adik's surprise and my grandmother's dismay, two weeks after escorting my new brother to Canada I flew back to Moscow, swimming against the tide of history and my family's personal experience. And unlike de Custine's aristocrats, I crossed the border cheerful and optimistic about the Russia which awaited me.

I was no stranger to the devastating and impoverished legacy which tsarism and communism had bequeathed to Russia: my grandparents' passionate anti-communism and the four years in the late 1980s and early 1990s I had spent living in Ukraine and travelling frequently to Russia ensured that. But the Russia I moved to at the end of 1994 seemed to be a new and happier beast, in the midst of moulting its Soviet carapace and revealing a tender but viable democratic polity and capitalist economy beneath.

Once sullen and oppressed, with muttering queues for forlorn sausage on its lonely pavements and furtive conversations in its kitchens, Moscow suddenly had become a boom town, with English-language neon screaming from its skyline, energetic traders hustling in its streets and breathtakingly beautiful, bejewelled girls crowding into its bars and night-clubs. Russians were freer than they had been for a millennium to speak and vote, trade and profit, and they seemed to be taking to their new liberties with as much enthusiasm as nineteenth-century nobles and generations of emigrants had embraced those same freedoms in the West.

My job as Moscow bureau chief for the *Financial Times* promised to give me a front-row view of the country's wild ride from communism to capitalism. The very fact that the country was travelling down that road was inspirational. The frequent bumps and periodic slips into reverse gear were no more than anyone had expected. But, over the next four years, as I watched Russia's jostling progress, I came to fear that the country was taking a wrong turn. This is the bitter-sweet tale of Russia's hopeful journey to capitalism and of how and why it lost the map. It is the story of Russia's capitalist revolution and of how that revolution was betrayed. By the time I left, I could imagine Adik saying, 'I could have told you so.'

1

EVERYTHING MARX TOLD US
ABOUT CAPITALISM WAS TRUE

RUSSIA IS A land of icons. They preside over every Orthodox home, are held over the heads of each marrying couple and sanctify every death. The icons of old Russia were so powerful that the Bolsheviks systematically destroyed them, with fire and wrecking balls, and created their own – stylised portraits of Lenin, Marx and Stalin which dominated every public space and glowered into the offices of the faithful and the cautious. The Soviet era had its secret icons, too: the brave crucifixes shaped out of mouldy bread by defiant gulag prisoners; the officially retouched photographs in which a phantom hand or a forgotten hat bore silent witness to the children the revolution had devoured.

As it struggled to shake off communism Russia needed a new icon, one of resurrection, and on 19 August 1991 it acquired one. That morning in Moscow dawned bright and beautiful, cast in the cerulean blues and rich golds favoured by the Byzantine painters who had brought the first icons to the eastern Slavs. At midday Boris Yeltsin strode out of the White House, the hulking Russian parliament building on the banks of the Moskva river, into a mêlée of soldiers and demonstrators. He was hot and nervous: the bullet-proof vest he wore under his brown suit was heavy and uncomfortable; the intense summer sun forced his eyes into a squint. But he could still see the tanks surrounding the Russian parliament and they seemed both absurd and horribly real. They had been ordered there by a cabal of communist hard-liners in order to crush the liberal reforms which had transformed the Soviet Union over the past six years.

Yeltsin, a wily Politburo veteran with a popular touch who had been elected president of the Russian Federation two months earlier, knew the plotters meant business. As Yeltsin recalled in his memoirs, his wife and daughters had kissed him goodbye with tears in their eyes when he left his dacha that morning, knowing it might be for the last time. His drive to the White House, alongside endless columns of tanks rolling into the Soviet capital, had seemed to go on for ever.

But as he looked out at the hundreds of Muscovites who had flocked to his office to defend democracy, Yeltsin took heart. The protestors were Soviet citizens, beaten into cowardly obedience by 70 years of dictatorship, yet they seemed unafraid of the tanks or of the punishments the victorious hard-liners might mete out the next day. Yeltsin's fears and reservations suddenly vanished and he felt utterly confident, absolutely at one with his people. He knew, with a prophet's certainty, that the coup would fail. Yeltsin dived into the crowd, clambered on to a tank and, his voice breaking with the effort to project itself to all of Russia, declared the coup illegal. That moment, that image, became the New Russia's first icon. In it, Russia and the world saw the birth of a new nation with the courage to defy authoritarian zealots, where peaceful demonstrators could overcome tanks, one finally ready to claim the freedom and prosperity that so many Russians saw as their long-denied European birthright.

Seven years less two days later, on August 17, 1998, the White House was again the backdrop for a defining moment in Russian history. But this time Yeltsin, who had opened Russia's post-communist drama with such bravura, was in the wings, secluded in one of the country dachas where he had taken to spending more and more of his presidency. It was deepest night rather than blazing midday, and this White House scene was played out in secret by a small, close-knit group of powerbrokers. Again the White House was surrounded by armed men, only this time they were soldiers of fortune, wearing expensive black leather, and instead of tanks they piloted dark armoured Jeeps and Mercedes, outfitted with police-style blue-flashing lights and privileged plates, nicknamed 'killer' licences, which permitted a total disregard of highway traffic laws.

The owners of those cars were the oligarchs, Russia's unofficial capitalist Politburo. Over the past few years they had schemed and plotted their way to wealth and power. Now they were closeted with a handful of cabinet ministers and central bank officials, struggling against a threat to Russia's new order which was less concrete than the hardliners' tanks had been seven years earlier, but just as menacing – the invisible hand of the market.

Just after midnight, wearing blue jeans and faces puffy from 48 hours of panic, the oligarchs shuffled into the grand echoing office of Russia's novice prime minister, Sergei Kiriyenko. Overlooking the square from which Yeltsin had shouted his defiance, Kiriyenko – eyes downcast, speaking in a clipped monotone – conceded defeat. In a few hours, the Russian government would devalue the rouble, default on its domestic treasury bills and announce a moratorium on the repayment of foreign commercial debt.

That nocturnal meeting never crystallised into one memorable image: there were no cameras or film crews at the private wake which Russia's elite held for the economy it had created and destroyed. But the gathering became a turning point for the new Russia. On the outsized Russian Richter scale of disaster, the financial meltdown was a survivable tremor, a 4 or 5 compared with the tragedies of civil war and Stalinist purges. (In the medium term, devaluation even turned out to strengthen some sectors of the Russian economy.) But measured against Yeltsin's iconic promise, it was a tragedy. Instead of the prosperous market and thriving democracy Russians had dared to hope for seven years earlier, their version of capitalism was limping and corrupt, their politics dominated by Kremlin cliques and a lackeyish media. Russia had freed itself from communism but not from the communist legacy; it had constructed its own capitalist system, only to discover it had built the wrong kind.

The $110 Rose

In the first few years, it seemed as if the capitalist revolution was going to work. The image of Yeltsin standing up for democracy was a strong icon, perhaps strong enough to sway the president himself. In keeping with the bold spirit of that moment, in the autumn of 1991 he chose a radical economic policy and a brave young team to implement it. The group, who would become known as the 'young reformers', were communists by birth and politically conservative by inclination, but their economic plans were as ambitious as any dissident could wish. With an electric combination of liberalising measures – shock therapy – and the most ambitious privatisation programme the world had ever known, they hoped to jolt Russia out of communism and straight into capitalism.

They faced a powerful chorus of nay-sayers, proponents of more gradual change who argued that Russians were culturally unready and spiritually unsuited for capitalism, that 70 years of communism must be undone with slow, incremental steps, that their radical programme would shock the country into famine or civil war or worse. But, with their president behind them and an almost Bolshevik conviction that they were right, the young reformers were unstoppable. Half-measures could never bridge the chasm between communism and capitalism, they liked to say; the only way to cross it was with a single jump.

So Russia leaped, and appeared to arrive on the other side intact. As naturally as a bear shakes off his winter hibernation, Russia cast off nearly a century of communism and threw itself into a riot of buying and selling, of hustling and scheming, of trying to make a fortune in the new world in which everything suddenly seemed possible.

In Moscow, the boom town of this eastern Klondike, the world's entire capitalist cornucopia seemed to be for sale. The local Mercedes dealership was one of the busiest in the world. Couturiers, especially the flashier ones like Versace, rushed to open boutiques. Even in the godforsaken provinces with their dirt roads, horse-drawn wagons and a misery that seemed almost medieval, the capitalist revolution swept in. Hard-scrabble Siberian settlements, whose children had once known of bananas only from story books and whose women had been swaddled in faded head-kerchiefs and ugly felt boots, magically discovered kiwi fruits and dangerous-looking stiletto heels in newly opened local kiosks, the cement still damp on their freshly laid brick walls.

After seven decades of communism, when the nomenklatura had been careful to hide its perks from the queuing comrade workers, the profusion of covetable things was as thrilling for Russians as a toddler's first Christmas. They took to it with the same joyous, unselfconscious greed with which my adopted brother Adik grabbed the Nintendo gameboy and new hockey skates waiting for him when he arrived in Canada. One of the best places in Moscow to watch them was Serebryany Vek, a restaurant housed in the *fin-de-siècle* splendour of what had been the Tsentralnaya bath-house, a short walk from the Bolshoi Theatre.

Serebryany Vek was a magnet for Moscow's nouveaux riches. They came for the mountains of caviar, the chandeliered ceilings and the deferential waiters who allowed them to imagine they were pampered aristocrats reliving the last days of the last tsar. But mostly, they came for the auction which started every night at around midnight. After the gypsy dancers had performed their impassioned dips and a Russian cabaret singer had belted out a few kitschy Soviet love songs, a slender brunette in a sequinned scarlet dress walked on to the stage holding a single, perfectly ordinary red rose. Then the bidding began. A few minutes later, on the night I visited, the flower had been sold for $110 and a proud man in his mid-thirties presented it to the immaculately groomed Slavic Valkyrie at his side.

It could have been a nauseating moment, and when I thought about the pensioners and laid-off workers begging in the urine-splashed, ice-covered underpasses nearby, it was. But there was something glorious about it, too. The man in the suit that was a little too shiny and the tie that was a bit too wide bought that rose just because he *could*. Because there was no central planner, no head of his factory Communist Party cell, no stern censor of morality in the workers' state, to tell him not to. He bought it because after a lifetime of standing in line for milk and sausage, of greasing black-market palms to get a pair of blue jeans, of waiting 10 years for a telephone line and 15 years for a lemon of a Lada, money finally meant something – and he could use it to buy whatever he wanted. $110 might be a lot to spend for a wilting flower, but as a middle finger to the USSR, a public 'Fuck You!' to communism, it came pretty cheap.

But the real excitement was that Russia had become capitalism's newest frontier and anyone willing to move fast enough, work hard enough and adapt often enough could claim his homestead. By 1996, more than 80 per cent of Russian industry was at least partially in private hands, a higher proportion than in parts of western Europe. By 1994, Russia had 40 million shareholders – more than half the number in the stock-crazy United States. Russia's young market economy was rough, wild and injust, more than a little bit like the American Wild West with which Russians hopefully compared their country. But, like nineteenth-century America, Russia seemed to have become a land of opportunity where, with a little luck and a lot of elbow grease, anyone could make his fortune.

My friend Sveta's husband, Mikhail, made his first $2m in just 72 hours in January 1992, the first month of Russia's market revolution. Thrown into capitalism, but lacking almost every institution it takes to make capitalism work – banks, payment systems, effectively functioning markets – Russia in those days was an arbitrage trader's wet dream, a country of so much incomplete information and so many mismatched markets that for a few heady months it felt as if anyone with a few connections and a nose for a deal could get rich. Mikhail made his windfall on one of those mismatches, pocketing the 10 per cent difference between the official rouble/dollar exchange rate and the market one when he arranged the transfer of $20m worth of roubles to a Western bank account for a Russian diamond producer.

Other Russians were prospering, and helping to build up a whole new economic system in the process, in less glamorous ways. Ilya Kolerov, a dreamy philosophy student with an interest in Buddhism, dropped his classes for a few years to found Moscow's first private chain of gas stations. In Novoy Urengoi, a loveless oil town north of the Arctic Circle, Maria Belova opened a cheerful café which did a roaring business with the tool-pushers and rough-necks stranded at the airport in the frequent winter blizzards. Dmitry Zimin, a chain-smoking engineer who had worked on Russia's anti-aircraft radar defence system, set up one of the country's leading mobile telephone networks.

The possibilities in the New Russia seemed so limitless that, before long, Western adventurers started to get in on the action too. For centuries, Russia had been a place from which anyone with brains, ambition and money escaped. Now, talented well-heeled foreigners were actually clamouring to get in. 'Russia is one of the greatest opportunities of the decade,' Boris Jordan – a 28-year-old American investment banker who was one of the leaders, and cheerleaders, of the Western invasion – told me in 1994. 'I just don't understand why everyone else isn't coming here.'

Most encouraging of all, a few years into the capitalist transformation, the red directors – the barons of the Soviet system who were initially among the fiercest opponents of the reform drive – had accepted – even embraced – the new order. Some of them went further still, deciding they were ready to compete with the real capitalists, the Western ones, head-to-head.

'The seven sisters should look out, because in ten years they will have a brother,' Vagit Alekperov – the astute Azeri who had created Lukoil, Russia's largest oil company, out of the pell-mell privatisation of the oil sector – predicted in 1994. 'If only we had begun in 1978, before things went to pieces in Russia, by now we would be the biggest oil company in the world.'

Marx Was Right

Sadly, Alekperov turned out to be wrong. When I first interviewed him in 1994, with Western investment beginning to flood in and the Moscow stock market about to boom, the oilman's boast was just about believable. By 2000, it had become ridiculous. Lukoil's market capitalisation had been beaten back to $9.6 billion, not quite enough to buy 2 per cent of Microsoft or less than 4 per cent of Western oil giant Exxon Mobile. The seven sisters (now reduced to five by mega-mergers in the sector) had nothing to worry about.

And Alekperov was one of the lucky ones. Boris Jordan, once dubbed the tsar of Russian capital markets for his foresight, was now called much less flattering names by the armies of pinstriped investors he had helped lure to Moscow, including his former employers at Credit Suisse First Boston, the international investment bank which wrote off $1.3 billion in Russia in 1998, wiping out its global profits for the year. After being attacked by gangland toughs Kolerov, the gas-pump pioneer, decided it would be safest to sell out; Zimin, the mobile phone entrepreneur, had lost nearly $30m in the crash of 1998 and been forced to lay off 200 workers; even Sveta's husband's instant $2m had vanished, pilfered away on stupid investments and insistent racketeers.

'That is what those times were like,' Sveta told me with a sigh. 'Money was very easy to make, but it was also very easy to lose.'

By the end of 1999, the Russian economy had shrunk to just over half its size a decade earlier. Russia, which just a few years earlier had counted itself a superpower, now produced less than Belgium and only 25 per cent more than nearby Poland.

The country's social and economic infrastructure, rudimentary but functional in the Soviet era, was collapsing. Schools and hospitals were regularly shut down in wildcat strikes by teachers and doctors who were not paid for months at a time; power blackouts and water shortages became commonplace, reaching even into strategic sites like nuclear submarine bases and humanitarian ones such as operating theatres; in 1994 the average male life expectancy had shrunk to 58 years, lower than anywhere else on the globe apart from sub-Saharan Africa.

The only people prospering in the New Russia seemed to be a narrow layer of the super-rich. By 1999, the top 10 per cent of the population owned half of the nation's wealth, while the bottom 40 per cent owned less than a fifth. Between 30 and 40 million people lived below the poverty line, defined as a miserly $30 a month. Russia's new capitalist elite had grown dizzyingly rich in a remarkably short time, but it had done so without lifting the rest of the country up with it. Its fortunes were not based on new technologies, more efficient services or more productive factories. Instead, they were built by capturing pieces of the collapsing Soviet state: the country's oilfields and nickel mines, its television channels and export permits and even the government's bank accounts. And once Russia's home-grown capitalist conquistadors had secured their loot, they whisked it away to safer havens abroad as quickly as they could. Between 1991 and 1999, experts estimated that between $100bn and $150bn in flight capital left Russia.

Russia had created a market economy, but of a distorted kind. With its ten-year economic depression, dying and increasingly deprived underclass and extravagant and parasitic elite, Russia had become a kind of capitalist dystopia, a Soviet ideologue's lurid fantasy of life in what they used to call the 'rotting West'. As one sardonic Russian friend confided: 'Everything Marx told us about communism was false. But it turns out that everything he told us about capitalism was true.'

Russians had hoped for something so much better. When they rallied around Yeltsin in 1991, Russians were not voting for an explicit set of economic policies, but they were voting for a clear economic idea. After a century of messianic leaders bent on ruling the world and burying the West, all Russians wanted now was – as they put it with touching modesty – to be a 'normal' country. They wanted a little bit of the prosperity, the freedom and the opportunity which they had started to see on the foreign programmes on their television screens and in the simple consumer conveniences like tampons and canned foods which had arrived on their shop shelves. They wanted what we had. So, what went wrong?

Forty Years in the Desert

Part of the problem was where Russia began. A few days of bravery in August 1991 were not enough to wipe out the legacy of 70 years of communism and centuries of authoritarianism before that. Russia's most poisonous inheritance was the lack of civil society. Even under tsarism, Russian civil institutions had been notoriously underdeveloped. Under the Bolsheviks, they were systematically destroyed: opposition political parties were banned, the press was severely censored, religion was suppressed and trade unions became arms of the Communist Party. Even the most basic unit of social organisation, the family, was undermined as children were encouraged to inform on their parents and wives were urged to betray husbands. The result was a state without a society, a country of alienated individuals ruthlessly trained to fear one another. In this atomised community, social interaction was governed by a Soviet perversion of the Golden Rule: inform on your neighbour because he is certain to inform on you.

Jadwiga Malewicz, a plump Soviet matron with watery blue eyes and the ghost-white skin of the far north, is living proof of just how indelibly that nasty morality was imprinted on the soul of every Soviet. In 1937, as a teenage girl, she was sent to one of Stalin's gulags for the ten-year term which other prisoners described as 'a children's sentence' because, by the warped standards of the time, it was so mild. Half a century later, Malewicz told Angus McQueen, a British documentary film maker, the worst thing the gulag had done to her.

Early in her sentence, Malewicz had taken pity on one of her fellow-prisoners. Stop working so hard, she warned the girl, otherwise you'll kill yourself. Someone overheard that advice and Malewicz was sent to a freezing punishment cell, its bars open to the Arctic snows outside.

Rationed to just one piece of bread a day, she was kept there for ten days.

'I nearly died,' Malewicz told McQueen. Then, her face twisted with a hard contempt for her fellow-Russians and maybe even for herself, she made a confession: 'After that, I no longer trusted anyone. I have never done a good deed since then.' In a terrible inversion of the Tin Man's visit to Oz, she left the gulag alive but without a heart.

Capitalism is often described as heartless; yet, as Russia discovered, it is remarkably hard to build it out of a society of Tin Men. The impersonal market is actually a sensitive organic system, hugely dependent on trust between its participants. But by the time Russia got around to creating capitalism, most of its citizens, like Malewicz, had been trained into suspicion.

They had also been trained into obedience, the second big millstone Russia inherited from the Soviet Union. In other parts of the sprawling Soviet empire, enough fragments of civil society and a sufficiently strong spirit of independence had survived to foster a powerful dissident movement. When communist governments fell in Poland, Hungary and Czechoslovakia, a well-organised opposition with a robust social base took over.

But in Russia, where the communist straitjacket had been yanked tighter and worn longer, the new regime was the old one. When he stood on the tank, Yeltsin was defying his former colleagues. Like the leaders of the putsch, Yeltsin too had been a loyal apparatchik, climbing up the party ladder to the illustrious post of candidate member of the Politburo. He staffed his new government with the same kind of people: former Soviet cabinet ministers, ex-members of the Central Committee, provincial Communist Party first secretaries. Themselves shaped by the Soviet system, was it any surprise that when it came to creating capitalism, Yeltsin and his comrades could do no better than a Marxist parody of it?

Not to Sergei Kovalyev, a former dissident and member of parliament who became the uncompromising conscience of Russia's democratic movement:

After all, we didn't pick a [Nelson] Mandela or a [Vaclav] Havel as our president [Kovalyev told me]. We chose a provincial Communist Party first secretary. That is what we wanted and that is what we got.

He is in his sixties and it is late for him to re-educate himself. He has learned a lot, considering his background, but everyone has a limit. And when Yeltsin reaches that limit he falls back on his life experience, which is as a standard Communist Party functionary, who had a wildly successful party career.

Struggling to escape communism, but doomed by its communist past to recreate it, Russia was caught in a classic Catch-22. Kakha Bendukidze, a roly-poly biologist-turned-entrepreneur with a shiny bald pate and a lilting voice, believed the best parallel was with the Israelites just after their escape from Egypt. Like the Russians in 1991, at that moment the Jewish people had cast off the Pharoah's shackles but not the slavish habits they had learned in captivity. Russia's only true solution, Bendukidze believed, was Moses' one: the people needed to spend 40 years in the desert so that the old generation could die off and a new, liberated one could be born.

'Unfortunately, there is no desert big enough for all of Russia,' Bendukidze concluded sadly. 'And we have no other people but ourselves. So, with our slaves' hearts we must do the best we can.'

A Licence to Break the Law

Another problem was Russia's collapsing state. The USSR had been one of the most authoritarian, centralised regimes in the world. But its system of control – its source of discipline, information and unifying ideology – had not been the official government structures. Instead, the spine of the Soviet state had been the Communist Party. When Yeltsin outlawed the party and tore it out of political power, he also broke the backbone of his new state. Once again, Marx had turned out to be almost right when he predicted that the state would wither away under communism. Well, the Russian state had withered away all right, but only after the country began its capitalist revolution.

By 1999, the power of the central government had shrunk so much that Sergei Zverev, a businessman and former presidential aide, admitted to me that the only territory Yeltsin really controlled was the Kremlin itself.

'It's like Vatican City. This little fortress has become the only part of

Russia Yeltsin rules,' explained Zverev, a short, powerful man with the best Rolodex in Russia. 'All he can do now is fire prime ministers and change his chiefs of staff.'

Signs of the state's incapacity were everywhere. In war-torn Chechnya, Russia soldiers were so ill-disciplined, so poorly provisioned and had such low morale that they sold their weapons to their enemies, the Chechen fighters. In Tver, a once gracious city in central Russia's agricultural heartland, the rule of law had become so flimsy that uniformed men – a modern version of the private brigands who roamed Europe in the Middle Ages – blocked the highways into town and required tribute from each entering car. In all of provincial Russia, regional governors and businesses refused to surrender tax revenues to a central government which had lost the power to either coerce or cajole them. And in Moscow, thousands of apparatchiks supplemented their meagre official salaries by going onto the payroll of private companies, becoming the employees of outside masters as well as the servants of the state.

The government became so weak that even the law could be bought and sold. There were thousands of examples of the weakness of the Russian justice system – murders covered up, multi-million-dollar court cases won by the party with the best connections or the fattest cheque-book – but the one that struck me most vividly was more trivial and more personal.

Tall, bearded and barrel-chested, Leonid was a well-connected St Petersburger who ran one of his city's leading insurance companies. He agreed to talk to me about his lifestyle to help me understand the culture of the *Novye Russkyi*, Russia's exuberant new business class. As he ticked off the talismans which marked his new tribe – the $100,000 wrist-watch, the armoured Jeep and Mercedes, with a Hummer on order, the young wife and younger mistress, the holidays on the Côte d'Azur and in the Swiss Alps – I felt a flicker of *Hello!*-magazine salacious interest, but no real surprise.

Then he pulled out the one status symbol I had never heard of. A thin laminated piece of paper, just a little larger than a credit card, it bore the official stamp of the Ministry of the Interior and the signature of a deputy minister. That small, unprepossessing rectangle lifted its bearer literally above the law. With it, Leonid could do anything he wanted on the road or in the streets. Ordinary traffic police or boys on the beat had no right to detain him or even ask for I.D. Leonid wouldn't tell me how much the permit had cost, but he did say it was the most valuable thing he owned. I found myself thinking of James Bond. Her Majesty's Government had granted 007 a licence to kill, but that was in the service of the state. Leonid had been given something more absurd, and more troubling: a private licence to break the law.

Not that Leonid had many philosophical objections to his special pass. For him, it was one of the perks of living in a withering state. And it was not the only one. For Russia's richest, best-connected business-men, an enfeebled state offered many advantages: a weak internal revenue service meant taxes could be evaded; bent judges meant investors could be fleeced; malleable civil servants meant that extremely lucrative government contracts could be won.

But the price of these benefits was high – high enough to kill, or at least cripple, many of the country's businesses. Without a functioning federal state, Russia developed a kind of Hobbesian capitalism, red in tooth and claw, in which big businesses preyed on smaller ones and apparatchiks and racketeers preyed on everyone.

Just how fragile that sort of market economy was I discovered in 1993, on a trip to Yekaterinburg, the broad-shouldered, straight-talking capital of the Urals region which was Russia's industrial heartland and Yeltsin's home base. There I met Vladimir, a 36-year-old defence engi-neer turned computer importer, just the type of intelligent, energetic entrepreneur the New Russia needed if its capitalist revolution was to succeed. Sales were brisk and profits were high, Vladimir told me, but he didn't think it would last. His dearest dream was to send his children to college in the United States. When I asked him why, he fished into a drawer and pulled out a gun. 'This is how we enforce contracts here,' he told me, thumping the pistol on the table. 'I don't think that's a very good way to build a stable business.'

The End of History

The early days of Russia's second revolution were heavy with a kind of double-or-quits fatalism, a feeling that either everything would end in disaster or that Russia would safely arrive at capitalism's salubrious shores. It was, after all, the End of History – a moment when so many

Western thinkers, intoxicated by the collapse of the Soviet bloc, began to imagine that the rules of politics and economics were as immutable as those of physics and that the rest of the world would now inevitably converge towards the American model of free market capitalism. This triumphant new faith was not so very different from the Marxist certainty that all economies would eventually graduate to communism, and so for the Russians, too, it made a sort of instinctive sense. This belief was at the heart of the young reformers' economic programme; it was Boris Yeltsin's political credo; even Washington D.C. framed its Russian policy around this central vision.

But while everyone watched the road from communism to capitalism and anxiously measured how much progress Russia had made, Moscow quietly slipped off on to another track, creating an economy which was private but not productive, where there were markets but ones which were rigged. Many road-blocks forced Russia on to its fatal detour, and most of them – like the communist legacy and the withering state – were unavoidable. But at one crucial moment, the Kremlin consciously and of its own free will took a disastrously wrong turn. As we shall see, that moment came when the government made a private pact with a group of upstart capitalist entrepreneurs who became known as the oligarchs. The deal enriched the oligarchs and ensured Yeltsin's re-election in 1996.

It also turned out to be a Faustian bargain, laying a corrupt inegalitarian foundation for everything that came after it. In a way, it was Russian capitalism's original sin. Thereafter, the Russian market economy was irredeemably warped, its government unquestionably corrupt. The challenge was no longer to dismantle communism or to create capitalism; it was to fix a capitalist system which was broken. It is time to return to the beginning and see how it all went wrong.

2

STORMING THE BASTILLE

EVERY REVOLUTION HAS its Bastille Day, the moment when the rebels finally breach the inner sanctum of the old regime. For Russia's capitalist revolutionaries, that moment came in early November 1991 when Yegor Gaidar, the new deputy prime minister and arch market reformer, walked into the offices of Gosplan, the headquarters of the Soviet central planning system.

It was unseasonably cold. Already, there was snow in the pine forests outside the capital and the premature autumnal chill made the hulking grey Gosplan building in central Moscow, designed by Stalin's architects to humble its visitors, feel even more forbidding than usual. This was communism's economic fortress and Gaidar arrived like the interloper he was – with a policeman at his side and the presidential decree appointing him stuffed like a pistol in his pocket.

I'm being insolent, of course, Gaidar admitted to himself, and as he later recalled in his memoirs. It was his first day on the job. His desk was still bare and his telephones had been connected only a few hours earlier. Yet here he was, already penetrating the holiest of holies, the Vatican City of the centrally planned system, and delivering the news that he, Russia's most ardent capitalist revolutionary, was now in charge of the temple.

Short, round-faced and balding, with soft eyes and an impish grin, physically Gaidar may well have been the least intimidating man in Russia. But for the comrades at Gosplan he was as terrifying an apparition as Lenin had been to Russia's aristocrats, and represented a change of the same horrifying proportions. Surveying the faces in the room, Gaidar saw caution, disorientation and naked fear. Some of the apparatchiks, he thought, seemed to want to ask who the hell this young pipsqueak economist was, and how he had suddenly been given the right to take over the huge Soviet central planning machine – with the express intention of dismantling it.

Sometimes, Gaidar asked himself the same question. Just the day before he had been an academic economist, someone who advised rulers but never had to take the hard decisions, or implement them, himself. All that had changed on 5 November, with a telephone call from the Kremlin appointing him Yeltsin's economic supremo. Some men would have felt elation, others a gladiator's pride at having beaten the other contenders. But Gaidar just felt shocked. Intellectually, he had known the call was coming: after weeks of dithering it had become clear that Yeltsin was in a daring mood and would appoint Gaidar and his team – the country's most radical advocates of market reform – to try to rescue Russia's economy.

Even so, when the phone finally rang Gaidar felt as if he had been hit by lightning. Suddenly, he realised, his life had been sundered into a 'before' and 'after', he had been transformed from a thinker to a doer, and the full weight of Russia's future had been thrust on to his sloping professorial shoulders. Gaidar and his colleagues had long dreamed of the moment when they would march into Gosplan and begin tearing it apart. Now it had finally come, and they were terrified. Looking back on it a decade later, they would realise that probably they had not been scared enough.

In one way or another, Gaidar had been preparing for that moment all his life. The man who would one day demolish the communist economy was born in 1956 into a family which was the nearest thing the Soviet Union had to royalty. His paternal grandfather, Arkady Gaidar, was one of the folk heroes of the Bolshevik revolution, a provincial schoolteacher's son who joined the revolutionary Red Army at 14 and went on to write children's stories after the communist victory. A Soviet cross between Paul Revere and Dr Seuss, Arkady left his grandson a surname to conjure with: years later, Yeltsin would admit that the 'magic' of the Gaidar name had influenced his choice of ministers.

Ironically, this privileged red intelligentsia background – at the heart of the communist system, but slightly alienated from it – proved to be the Soviet Union's most salubrious breeding ground for a future capitalist rebel. Thanks to his family's nomenklatura perks and their foreign postings in countries like Cuba and Yugoslavia, the young Yegor had access to books which could get an ordinary Soviet citizen sent to the gulags.

The New Class, by Milovan Djilas – a founder of socialist Yugoslavia whose criticisms of the regime would inspire a whole generation of eastern European dissidents and reformers – helped the teenage Gaidar to understand the failings of the Soviet system. Then, while still in high school, he began a careful study of the capitalist alternative. Gaidar's older brother gave him two volumes of Adam Smith – 'my favourite book for a decade'. Another powerful influence was American economist Paul Samuelson's lucid textbook which became the bible for Russia's young reformers.

Gaidar's subversive economic education continued at Moscow State University, the Soviet Union's most prestigious academy. There, in the 'special access' stacks he read his way through the Western economic classics – Ricardo, Mill, Keynes, Friedman – becoming ever more critical of the centrally planned economy. By the early 1980s, Gaidar, who had gone on to graduate studies in economics, reached the inevitable and radical conclusion: the Soviet economy was in a deep crisis, and only capitalism could save it.

In 1986, he took his first big step towards acting on those convictions. In late August, he and a group of like-minded economists gathered at Zmeynaya Gora, literally Snake Hill – a shabby sanatorium outside the city still known as Leningrad – to hold an economic seminar. During that long weekend in the pine forests, Gaidar and his friends coalesced into a formidable political team: the young reformers.

'It was our first quasi-legal economic seminar, where, for the first time, all the future young reformers met,' Sergei Vasiliev, one of the participants, told me. A slender, neat man with close-cropped grey hair and glasses, Vasiliev had a charming manner, a deep knowledge of economics and a sure judgement which made him one of the young reformers' most effective political operators.

For the participants, the meeting at Zmeynaya Gora was like the Bretton Woods conference and Woodstock rolled into one. They debated serious, clandestine economic theories, but they also drank vodka, lit bonfires and sang songs. They were profoundly, unapologetically geeky: with their hideous bottle-thick glasses, polyester suits and laboured equations, even Bill Gates would have seemed trendy by comparison. But they also had a light-heartedness, an almost childish gaiety perhaps stemming from their sureness of purpose, which Gaidar at least would retain even after the collapse of much of the market economy he had so painstakingly constructed.

Part of the reason their meeting was so electric was the wider spirit of change then sweeping across the USSR. A year earlier, the young reformist Mikhail Gorbachev had become General Secretary and was starting to loosen the Soviet straitjacket. Once banned books were being published, discussion groups were being formed and public demonstrations contemplated.

The young reformers were carried along by this national awakening, but they were not wholly part of it. Most of Russia's intelligentsia was interested in political change; the young reformers focused on economics. Many Russian liberals thought that mass political action – public demonstrations and, later, mobilising a protest vote at the ballot boxes – was the way to transform the country; the young reformers preferred to focus on back-room lobbying. They didn't really care who ruled the country, just what economic policies the rulers adopted.

What distinguished them most of all was their extreme seriousness and self-confidence. In 1986, everyone in Russia was cooking shashliks with his friends around a bonfire and talking about the ways in which the Soviet Union must change. Gaidar and his gang were among the few who had the chutzpah to believe their plans would actually make a difference. They had the rare ability – shared by revolutionary leaders and megalomaniacs alike – to have utter faith in their power to alter the course of history.

The young reformers' absolute belief in the importance of their ideas – and of themselves – was captured by the tragi-comic speech Gaidar delivered at their closing lunch at Zmeynaya Gora. The seminar which had just concluded, he explained, had only two possible outcomes.

One was that the group gathered in the fly-ridden canteen would soon be running the Soviet economy and steering the country from communism to capitalism. Gaidar predicted which post each of the assembled economists would hold, later congratulating himself on his prescience for having foreseen the crucial role which Anatoly Chubais, an energetic red-head from Leningrad, would play as an administrator and organiser.

The other scenario was much bleaker: the Soviet Union would plunge into a new Ice Age of repression and the young reformers would be sent to the gulags for their subversive theorising. Gaidar detailed this outcome with as much precision as the first, specifying the prison term which each participant in the Zmeynaya Gora seminar would serve. His speculation seemed worryingly plausible. Already one of the young reformers, Konstantin Kagalovsky, had been subject to a month-long KGB interrogation because of a technical economic paper he had written to amuse himself while carrying out his military service near the Chinese border.

There was, of course, a third alternative – that the young reformers' theories would remain just that, never having any impact beyond the Zmeynaya Gora seminar room. Gaidar didn't even entertain that possibility, and he proved to be right.

From 1986 to 1991, Gaidar and his group pursued the goals they had set themselves at Zmeynaya Gora, where they took to meeting every summer. They systematically recruited the country's brightest and most radical economists to join their team. They began to map out a detailed market reform plan. And, believing as they did in revolution from above, they tried to find a way to persuade the Politburo to adopt their programme.

Even under Gorbachev, lobbying the Soviet state was a tricky affair. The young reformers' ideas were too radical to publish or to publicly discuss, except in the most veiled form. The USSR still had no elected politicians or independent civic organisations which might be persuaded to champion the reformers' cause. Instead, Gaidar tried to use the subtler channels the Soviet establishment had developed to allow at least a few new ideas to flow to the top. He wrote letters to Gorbachev, asking trusted members of the general secretary's inner circle to deliver them. He tried to influence the more liberal members of the Central Committee, the Soviet Union's political elite, hoping they would in turn win over the Kremlin.

Even for so well connected a communist as Gaidar, it was a frustrating, time-consuming and uncertain process. But then the young reformers had an unexpected breakthrough. In a Gorbachev-inspired mini-coup, Otto Latsis, an old friend of the Gaidar family and a veteran rebel, was appointed deputy editor of *Kommunist*, the ideological journal of the Communist Party and one of the country's most influential shapers of elite opinion. Latsis tapped Gaidar as his economics editor. After knocking fruitlessly at the Politburo's door, suddenly Gaidar was handed the party's most powerful philosophical tribune.

It was, of course, an absurd decision. Here was Gaidar, an ardent capitalist, a fan of F. A. Hayek and Milton Friedman, a man who thought the welfare state in western Europe was far too large and would have voted for Ronald Reagan, shaping the economic ideology of the Communist Party of the Soviet Union. It was like asking a crusading atheist to write a new catechism for the Vatican. If anyone still needed a sign that the Soviet nomenklatura no longer believed its own rhetoric, Gaidar's appointment offered precisely that.

Thanks to Latsis, the pages of *Kommunist* became an invaluable political beachhead for Gaidar and his team. As the ultimate arbiter of political correctness, a kind of official conscience of the Communist Party, the journal was above government censors. Gaidar and the young reformers could publish exactly what they wanted, and they used *Kommunist* to introduce a whole new language and way of thinking to the discourse about the Soviet economy.

'*Kommunist* became a sort of ice-breaker,' Aleksei Ulyukaev, one of the young reformers, recalled. 'We introduced concepts like "budget deficit" and "inflation", which had been unknown to official Soviet economic thinking.' A tall, genial man who looked a bit like an over-sized teddy bear and larded his conversation with quotations from the Russian classics, Ulyukaev would become Gaidar's most loyal lieutenant. Years later, he told me quite matter-of-factly that he loved Gaidar. In the late 1980s, he joined his friend at *Kommunist*, just as over the next decade he would faithfully follow him into and out of government.

A second advantage was that the journal's ideological irreproacha-
bility could also be extended to shield other young reformers less
securely ensconced in the heart of the Russian establishment. That was
crucial, because by 1987 the local KGB had begun to express an
unhealthy interest in the work of the Leningrad branch of the group.
Sergei Vasiliev was called in for questioning, but was saved by Gaidar's
communist status.

From the bully pulpit of *Kommunist*'s densely printed pages, the
young reformers began to wade into some of the major economic battles of the day. But the real prize was not only to influence specific
economic decisions; it was to launch a comprehensive market reform
programme in the Soviet Union before it was too late.

The vicissitudes of Soviet politics, however, seemed to conspire
against the young reformers. Gorbachev appeared to have the right
political outlook, but he was too indecisive. The conservative faction of
the Communist Party of the Soviet Union (CPSU) continued to plot
ways of returning the country to a more orthodox course. Yeltsin,
forced to resign from the Politburo in 1988, reappeared in 1990 as a
populist but unpredictable force, and became a further distraction for
the Kremlin. And all of these Moscow manoeuvrings took place against
the backdrop of the Soviet economic time-bomb, which the young
reformers were certain was ticking off its final hours before blowing the
communist system apart.

Ordinary life, hardly luxurious in the sclerotic Brezhnev era, became
truly miserable. Sugar, milk and meat were sold only through ration
cards. Miners went on strike because it was impossible to buy, beg or
steal the soap they needed to wash off 12 hours of sweat and coal-dust.
The worst sign of all, Ulyukaev remembered, was when consumer
goods started disappearing not just from perennially hard-scrabble
provincial towns, but from the exclusive capital city stores reserved for
the Moscow nomenklatura: 'Gradually, things vanished from the special
stores, too. The apotheosis was in August 1991, when they started to
sell millet in the special stores. The raw grains – you could make a sort
of millet gruel out of them. They came in two-kilogram packets. That
was the condition of the regime.' Once wheat gruel became a perk
reserved for the Soviet Union's most privileged caste, it was clear the
regime was doomed.

Wretched though it was, the Soviet Union in 1991 was of course a veritable Eden compared with the starving abattoir my grandmother's generation had experienced or the post-war austerity which middle-aged Russians had survived in their childhoods. Yet to everyone who lived in the USSR at the time, the deprivations of 1991 felt particularly, dangerously severe. After all, social sentiment is not a straightforward scientific function of standard of living; it is a far more delicate interplay of expectations with reality. The most perilous moment, as de Tocqueville had observed in his reflections on the French revolution, was not when people were the poorest, but when their expectations of significant improvement were frustrated.

'Throughout 1991, I had the personal impression that a catastrophe was happening,' Ulyukaev recalled. 'It was clear that everything was falling apart. As to what would happen next – who knew? Maybe there would be a military coup, a dictatorship and so forth. It was a terrible feeling.'

Gorbachev, too, sensed the coming catastrophe. But, to the dismay of Russian liberals, he responded to the mounting crisis with a sharp shift to the right. As Gorbachev reverted to the hawks, the young reformers' last hope of reforming the Soviet Union from above seemed to evaporate. The obvious alternative was Yeltsin. Yet the young reformers were slow to defect to the camp of the charismatic pretender. 'There are certain honest rules of the game,' Ulyukaev explained to me. 'If you are working for Gorbachev, it is not decent to work for someone else at the same time.'

Along with their moral commitment to Gorbachev, Gaidar and his associates felt an instinctive aversion to Yeltsin's rougher, earthier style. To Ulyukaev, in 1990, Yeltsin seemed to be a populist, and a dangerous one at that: 'He didn't know what economics was, he didn't know what democracy was. If the right people take him by the right hand, then he will do the right thing. But if someone whispers the wrong thing into his left ear, then he will do the wrong thing. We turned out to be the ones who explained the truth to him, but who could have predicted that?'

Honour-bound to an increasingly impotent and directionless Gorbachev, convinced that the Soviet Union was on the brink of a catastrophe, the young reformers spent the first half of 1991 on the sidelines, anxiously watching and waiting. And yet, with the intellectual self-confidence which was their hallmark both in and out of government, in some not too secret corner of their hearts they still believed that before long they would be running the Russian economy. Eventually someone would emerge as Russia's paramount leader. When that day came, the country's new tsar would need someone to sort out its ailing economy. They were the smartest economists. They had the best plan. The new chief's choice would be obvious.

Their iron confidence was on display on 16 June, Chubais' birthday, just two months before the attempted hard-line coup. That day Gaidar happened to be on a business trip to the city still known as Leningrad. As always, he called in at the exquisite Mariinsky Palace, which for a time housed the mayor's office, and paid a visit to the Leningrad branch of the young reformers. The group, which included Sergei Vasiliev and Chubais, the birthday boy, fell into a half-serious debate about which cabinet portfolios each of them would assume when the inevitable call came to form the next Russian government. The key question was who would be the prime minister.

Even then, the young reformers realised it was a tricky, possibly crippling, issue. The difficulty was not that they lacked intellectual oomph; with his photographic memory and gift for explaining complex economic problems in terms even Yeltsin could understand, Gaidar was widely acknowledged to be one of the smartest Russians of his generation. Nor were they short of talented organisers; Chubais was already renowned for the administrative skills which would later blossom into something approaching genius. The rub was that a truly effective market reformer needed to combine these two talents and in Russia, unfortunately, they had been doled out to two separate men. Elizabeth Bennett memorably complained of two of her suitors that only between them did they have enough virtues to make one good man. Russia faced a similar dilemma: only a synthesis of Gaidar and Chubais would have all the qualities a Russian prime minister needed.

'Obviously, it will be Chubais,' Gaidar insisted. 'Chubais is a strong organiser, he must run the government.'

Chubais demurred: 'Of course, I may be a good organiser, but it is Gaidar who is the recognised economic authority. That means that Gaidar must be in charge.'

Sergei Vasiliev, who later recanted the discussion to me, said it was 'half in jest' – but it would prove to be prophetic. In less than four months, Gaidar, freshly appointed deputy prime minister and minister

of finance, would be storming the Soviet economic Bastille. Five years
after they first gathered at Zmeynaya Gora, his dream scenario had
come true.

This was an incredible opportunity – and a terrifying one. When
Gaidar's father – tanned and relaxed after a holiday on the Crimean
peninsula which, in just a few months, would become part of a foreign
country – returned to Moscow and learned of his son's elevation, the
horror on his face was visible. Timur Gaidar's father had given his soul
and ultimately his life to a revolution which had gone wrong. Now his
son was starting a second revolution, one which hoped to undo the
damage of the first. This time, would the Gaidar family finally get it
right? 'If you are certain there is no other alternative,' a half-frightened,
half-exulting Timur told his son, 'then just do what you can.'

Just do what you can. Do your best. Such a universal paternal
instruction, but such a treacherously vague one. Is it ever possible to do
everything you can? Is it ever possible to know if you have? Over the
next few years, it was a question Timur's son would ask himself often,
and his usual answer would be that he had done most of what he could
do, but not everything. The real, much bigger, issue was whether what
he had done, Gaidar's best shot, was good enough for Russia. The jury
is still out on that one.

In 1991, Gaidar still had no idea of what he could do, of what would
prove to be possible. All he could know was what he thought needed to
be done. And on this point, as usual, he was utterly confident he had
the right answer.

In the late 1980s and early 1990s, the Soviet bloc and indeed the
entire world had been engrossed in a debate over how to reform centrally planned economies. Initially, the argument had been about what
sort of economy the countries of the Warsaw Pact should build to
replace communism. Should they opt for softer, Swedish-style social
democracy, or was the aggressively entrepreneurial US version of capitalism more desirable?

In academia this debate still rages, but before long the actual practitioners of market reforms in Warsaw, Budapest and Moscow realised
that it was, well . . . academic. Arguing over the finer details of what
kind of a market system they hoped to build while their economies

were still stuck in sclerotic central planning was rather like demanding that a starving refugee choose between Chinese and French cuisine. It simply wasn't relevant. Communist countries first had to build the most rudimentary foundations of a market economy. There would be plenty of time later on to decide on the details of interior decor.

The real question was how to lay those foundations – and here another, more heated, argument erupted. Some economists believed the best way to shift from central planning to the market was a gradual remodelling of the communist edifice until, one day, it had been transformed into a capitalist one. But others thought that approach was painfully prolonged at best, impossible at worst. The only viable solution, they argued, was first to demolish the communist structure and then to erect a market economy on the cleared site. This radical approach came to be known as shock therapy – although its advocates have always protested the gratuitous cruelty of the name – and Gaidar was one of its most passionate adherents.

Gaidar had always realised that the Soviet system was so far gone that even shock therapy might not be enough to revive it. But it wasn't until he became a government minister that he appreciated quite how difficult his job would be. The first disturbing revelation was how completely the old system had collapsed. The young reformers had long ago dismissed the Soviet economy as bankrupt. Now, looking from the inside, the situation seemed even worse. The country, Gaidar feared, was in real danger of a famine.

A second complication was the political chaos. The failed coup had deeply discredited the Soviet Union, but it was not yet clear if the Russian Federation would have the stamina to take its place. The political uncertainty was only resolved in December, when the Soviet Union was formally dissolved. Until then the Soviet and Russia government structures were in constant conflict, a stalemate which meant that the laws of neither entity had any real authority. Even after the formal burial of the USSR the fledgling Russian government remained shaky. Russia was not only shifting from communism to capitalism, it was building a whole new state.

A third, related problem was the amorphous rouble zone. The Soviet empire was dissolved at the end of 1991, but the Soviet currency remained in circulation. Fifteen new countries had emerged, each with its own government. But they all shared the Soviet rouble, and the central bank in each republic had the effective authority to print as many roubles as it liked by issuing credits. As P. J. O'Rourke put it, Russia was like a man with fourteen pissed-off ex-wives, each of whom still had a credit card billed to his account.

The circumstances were daunting. Yet, paradoxically, the severity of Russia's problems served only to steel Gaidar's nerves. The worse things were, he believed, the more urgently the country needed his bitter brand of market medicine.

And so, on 2 January 1992, less than two months after joining the Yeltsin administration, Gaidar and the young reformers hooked up their market electrodes to the frail body of the Russian economy. To calm his nerves on the eve of Russia's economic big bang, Gaidar took his first night off since accepting Yeltsin's invitation to join the cabinet. With his wife, Masha, he went to a birthday party in the home of one of his close friends, Viktor Yaroshenko, a Moscow writer. There is nothing the Russian intelligentsia loves to do more than to talk and that is what Gaidar and his friends did, late into the night, touching on every subject imaginable except the one that privately preoccupied them all: the daring, terrifying economic experiment which their friend Yegor was going to launch the next day.

The first jolt began to zing through the country even as the old gang exchanged friendly verbal feints and parries in Yarshenko's crowded apartment. At the stroke of midnight, prices, which had been under state control for most of the Soviet era, were freed. There were major exceptions: prices for energy, fuel, transport, communications and certain staple foods were to remain temporarily under government regulation. With hindsight, Gaidar would regret even these compromises, seeing his half-measures as a major cause of Russia's continuing economic malaise.

But at the time, even this partial price liberalisation felt breathtakingly radical. More bold measures swiftly followed. To help put food back on shop shelves, after 70 years of autarky all import barriers were temporarily lifted. To help stimulate the moribund Soviet consumer sector, private retail trade – previously a crime known as *spekulatsia* and punishable by a prison sentence – was liberalised. A country which for decades had known only the enforced stability of communism was suddenly strapped on to the wildest roller-coaster capitalism had to offer.

Prices doubled, tripled, quadrupled. Savings painstakingly hoarded over a lifetime were wiped out. And, at least for the first few days, none of the promised benefits of shock therapy seemed to materialise. The shop shelves were still empty, the queues were still long, consumer goods that were commonplace in the West, like toothpaste or toilet paper, remained a rarity. Intellectually, Gaidar realised that the results would not be immediate. Yet, as political rivals and an anxious media rushed to declare the reforms an overnight disaster – headlines like 'Five days on it is clear the liberalisation is a failure' were standard fare – he began nervously to study his daily status reports from across the country, hoping for a sign, any sign that the nation was twitching into economic life.

That sign came on a crisp but freezing-cold January morning, the day after Yeltsin signed the decree liberating retail trade. Riding in his chauffeured black Volga to his office in Staraya Ploshchad, a block of dark granite buildings in central Moscow which was once the home of the all-powerful Central Committee of the Communist Party, Gaidar passed through the Lubyanka traffic circle, the busy intersection in front of the headquarters of the revamped KGB.

Incongruously enough, the other side of the Lubyanka was domi-nated by Detsky Mir, or Children's World, a vast children's department store that was a sort of glum Soviet equivalent of Toys 'Я' Us. As his clunky car rumbled past, Gaidar saw a huge queue of people milling around on the pavement outside the store. It was a familiar sight and a depressing one. The shortage economy must still be firmly in place if people were lining up in the sub-zero weather to buy children's toys.

But then Gaidar looked more closely at the crowd and his heart soared. These were not shoppers, they were sellers. Holding a few packs of cigarettes, some canned vegetables grown that summer in their dacha plots, a bottle of vodka, or some outgrown children's clothes, they had come to Moscow's busiest shopping street to try to peddle their humble possessions. Like protective body armour, or some superstitious reli-gious talisman, each novice trader had carefully clipped out the presidential decree on free retail trade and pinned it to her heavy winter coat. Arrogant policemen or irate apparatchiks might try to harass the would-be merchants, but they knew they had the president on their side.

For Gaidar, the traders were a revelation. After days of worry, here at last was concrete evidence that Russia's market economy had been born. It was messy, it was shabby, it was amateur, but it was there. 'Not aesthetic? Not seemly? Not civilised? I admit it,' he later reflected in his memoirs. 'But newborn infants are not beauties when they first appear in the world. Only the parents can see what a gorgeous person will, in time, grow out of that crumpled red creature. If I had had doubts before about whether the entrepreneurial spirit of the Russian people had survived seventy years of communism, on that day they vanished for good.'

The reaction was vintage Gaidar, a moment which captured both his strengths as a leader and the weaknesses which ultimately undermined him and his reforms. Gaidar's greatest strength, and that of the young reformers he led, was their vision. Some politicians were so overwhelmed by Russia's tragic history and current misery that they found it impossible to conceive of a freer, more prosperous future or to think beyond averting the next disaster – but not Gaidar. It took a rare, imaginative gift to see those shivering, huddled masses outside Detsky Mir as the harbingers of an entrepreneurial revival. But like the Silicon Valley entrepreneur who knows, just *knows* that no matter what the previous setbacks, the next start-up will make him a billionaire, Gaidar never stopped believing that the capitalist revolution would succeed.

Yet Gaidar's tunnel vision was also a weakness. It allowed him to foresee Russia's bright future, but sometimes it blinded him to the miserable present. Unemployment wasn't a problem, it was a welcome sign of structural change. The same went for bankruptcy and sharply curtailed social services. Even the hard-hearted number-crunchers at the IMF admitted to me that occasionally they were stunned by the young reformers' ability to dismiss their country's current suffering as the unavoidable price of future prosperity. This attitude meant that Gaidar and his group were often accused of being unfeeling, bloodless technocrats – but that wasn't quite right. Many of them cared deeply about the Russian people, it was just that they believed – in fact, they knew! – that pain today would bring gain tomorrow.

At its best, the young reformers' iron faith in their ideas was heroic, and necessary. But at its worst, it was dangerous. It wasn't only Silicon Valley pioneers who shared the reformers' absolute commitment to their cause. Dictators and religious zealots and imperial invaders have the same Machiavellian belief in the righteousness of their mission. So, for that matter, did the Bolsheviks.

'It is a Leninist morality, absolutely, that is exactly what it is,' Latsis sadly explained to me years later. 'They have the same belief that they can allow themselves to do anything they like because the end justifies the means.' The young reformers did not disagree. Ulyukaev once even likened the aggressive reform drive of early 1992 to 'Lenin's red-guard attack on capital'.

Maybe a new band of Bolsheviks was precisely what Russia needed. Maybe only a Leninist zeal and ruthlessness could undo the damage Lenin's revolution had wrought. But maybe not. Ultimately, the Bolsheviks' faith and fervour perverted the ideals in whose name they had fought. In the end, something not so different happened to the young reformers.

In one crucial way, though, Gaidar and the young reformers could not have been more different from Lenin and his revolutionary party. Lenin understood power. His first and perpetual priority was to seize control of the state and of all of its institutions. By comparison, the young reformers were dilettantes.

You might call them McKinsey revolutionaries. Management consultants are the smart-alec outsiders who come in with their revolutionary ideas hoping to transform a company in a few weeks or months. They are not the dogged businessmen who've built up the firm – with elbow grease and 24-hour days and attention to a million tedious details – in the first place. Gaidar and the young reformers took something of the same attitude towards transforming Russia. They had the master-plan, but they weren't really interested in the mundane, messy work of winning the political power necessary to implement it. The result was that they were ultimately never more than salaried advisers always at the mercy of the man who hired them. Most of the time, that man was Yeltsin and he could be a nightmare of a boss. For one thing, as Ulyukaev had suspected from the outset, Yeltsin never really understood market economics. He chose Gaidar because he was in a revolutionary mood and because his name conjured up warm childhood memories. But Yeltsin never seemed fully to comprehend what the young economist, who became acting prime minister in June 1992, was trying, with so much agony, to create. He looked at the squalling baby and, a lot of the time, that was all that he saw. As the management consultants say, Yeltsin was never totally on message.

There were a million different small signs that the young reformers had failed to bring Yeltsin fully on board, ranging from the president's schizophrenic cabinet shuffles, to his policy zig-zags, to his erratic public pronouncements. Perhaps the most revealing was the story which Boris Nemtsov – an important regional ally of the young reformers who would himself one day become a deputy prime minister – told me about his encounter with Yeltsin just a few days after Russia's market transition began.

Young, tousle-haired and charismatic, Nemtsov was an instant favourite in the president's court. The Kremlin chief liked the 32-year-old physicist so much that in the aftermath of the failed August coup, when personal loyalty and anti-communist sentiment were at a premium, he appointed him governor of Nizhny Novgorod, an important scientific and industrial province 250 miles east of Moscow. In a nation accustomed to geriatric leaders, it was an iconoclastic choice and Yeltsin promised to visit his protégé in a few weeks time to see how he was managing.

True to his word, on 9 January 1992, seven days after Gaidar's price liberalisation, Yeltsin travelled to Nizhny Novgorod. The city, traditionally one of Russia's most prosperous, was in an uproar over the drastic price rises. 'It was a total madness. Prices had increased six-fold,' Nemtsov recalled.

In those days a master of populist, flesh-pressing politics, Yeltsin insisted on walking around the town centre to discover first-hand how his electorate was responding to shock therapy. Theoretically, of course, the president realised that the sudden escalation of prices was difficult for ordinary Russians to bear. But his pampered Moscow life of chauffeurs, bodyguards and sycophantic functionaries had shielded the Kremlin chief from the full fury of the public reaction. In the shops of Nizhny Novgorod, it came rushing in on him with a vengeance. 'We went into a grocery store,' Nemtsov recalled, 'and the old ladies all threw themselves at him and began to shout, "How can this be? Why are the prices so high?"'

Their anger horrified Yeltsin, who just a few months before had been the nation's heroic defender from a hard-line putsch, received rapturously wherever he went. Alarmed, the president responded with the authoritarianism that had become instinctive after a career spent climbing the Communist Party ladder. 'He commanded – First, lower the prices immediately! Second – Find out who is the director of the neighbourhood milk-trading association!' Nemtsov said.

Nemtsov tried to explain to the president that prices could no longer be dictated by Kremlin decree: that, after all, had been the whole point of the price liberalisation. Moreover it was, he gently pointed out, none of the government's business who ran the local milk-trading firm. Like most of the small businesses in Nizhny Novgorod, it had already been transformed into a joint-stock company and was no longer directly owned or controlled by the state. Yeltsin was having none of it: under his furious supervision, the price of butter was lowered by more than 25 per cent, from 207 roubles to 150 roubles a kilogram. The president didn't stop there. As he left the shop he told Nemtsov that the director, the man who was so greedily gouging little old ladies, must be fired at once.

Nemtsov decided to resort to the stratagem of every wise Russian apparatchik when confronted with an insistent but irrational boss. He heard the president out, nodding in apparent obedience, while privately vowing to let the matter drop. The governor spent the rest of the day squiring Yeltsin around the Nizhny Novgorod region and, that evening, accompanied him to the steps of his Kremlin jet. With the president safely in the air and the milk shop long forgotten, Nemtsov and his aides sat down to a vodka-enhanced celebration of their first, stressful presidential visit. The toasts had barely begun when Nemtsov's special *vertushka* telephone connected to the Kremlin rang. 'What could it be?' a perturbed Nemtsov asked himself. 'He just left and already he's calling?'

He picked up the phone only to hear a barked greeting from Yeltsin which was half-question, half-command: 'Have you fired Zakunin [the manager of the grocery store] yet? Fire him!' So explicit a presidential order could not be tactfully evaded, no matter what the legalities of private ownership and price liberalisation. So, although it was already close to midnight, Nemtsov summoned his chauffeur and returned to his office in the lovely medieval kremlin, or fortress, at the centre of Nizhny Novgorod. When he arrived there, he summoned the hapless Zakunin to join him and explained the president's unfortunate obsession.

Zakunin understood his predicament at once. Laws were one thing, but the will of the Kremlin was something altogether different and more important. 'He understood everything, he was an old party man,' Nemtsov explained. While Nemtsov watched, Zakunin wrote a letter of resignation. The governor signed it. The nefarious Zakunin – whose only crime had been to obey the new rules of Russia's nascent market economy – lost his job. 'And thus,' Nemtsov ruefully concluded when he recounted the tale several years later, 'began the epoch of liberal reforms.'

For the luckless Zakunin, Yeltsin's misunderstanding of the basic principles of capitalism had little long-term effect. Within a few months, once the president's mind was safely occupied by other matters, Zakunin returned to a powerful job in the Nizhny Novgorod milk trade. The episode became a long-running joke between him and his young governor. But for the young reformers, and for Russia's capitalist transition as a whole, Yeltsin's conceptual confusion had far more serious consequences. At dozens of crucial moments, Yeltsin deployed his formidable political skills and authority in defence of the young reformers – not least by appointing them in the first place. Yet he was never able to fully unlearn his communist instincts or to comprehend the essential logic of the transformation which they launched. As a result, his support was never absolute and it was never predictable. Every once in a while, sometimes just when the young reformers needed him most, Yeltsin would revert to Soviet type.

Even when the boss is on side, management consultants have to do battle with their client's middle managers, the entrenched old guard which knows change threatens its power and position – in this case the apparatchiks, the army of bureaucrats who ran the creaky machinery of government Russia inherited from the USSR. Ideologically, many apparatchiks were commited communists; as Soviet government officials, adherence to the reigning ideology was part of the job. By nature the apparat, a punctilious culture of bureaucratic memos and carefully observed hierarchies, was also instinctively hostile to the free-wheeling, rather unworldly spirit of the young egg-head economists. Most important of all, the apparatchiks had a vested interest in tripping up the young reformers. The Gaidar team's self-declared mission was to dismantle the command economy; the apparatchiks' job was to run it.

And so, with a million camouflaged bureaucratic trip-wires, the apparat set about sabotaging the reformist ministers who were, temporarily they believed, their bosses. One of the most astute observers of this partisan war being waged in the red-carpeted corridors of the Russian government was Sergei Kovalyev, the white-haired, silver-toothed and thick-spectacled former dissident who became a kind of father-confessor figure for the young reformers.

In the Soviet era, Kovalyev had fought his moral battle against the naked face of communist power – KGB interrogators and Siberian prison-camp jailers. When the young reformers came to power in late 1991, he dared to hope that struggle was over. But as his youthful friends began to try to implement their reforms, he gradually realised that the old fight was still raging, only it had moved underground. One day, he told me the story he thought best illustrated just how devious and entrenched the Soviet bureaucracy still was, and how vulnerable Gaidar remained to its attacks.

From the outset, Kovalyev explained, Gaidar had realised that controlling the apparat would be one of his greatest challenges. So he decided to ask the president to appoint someone from his own team, Aleksei Golovkov, a tough organiser whose loyalty was absolute, to head the government apparat. Yeltsin sighed grumpily when Gaidar proposed his unorthodox candidate, but he agreed and the decree was duly signed. It was then that the intrigue began. The signed decree disappeared and, without a piece of paper with the presidential seal and signature, Golovkov could not officially begin doing his job. The situation was ridiculous, untenable and so, after a week of demanding that the apparatchiks find the lost decree, Gaidar had no choice but to go back to the president.

'Sign this please,' he asked. 'It's a copy of the decree. The original has been lost.'

According to Kovalyev, Yeltsin was furious: 'He made an unhappy face, banged his fists on the table and stamped his feet on the floor and shouted – "What do you mean, the decree is lost? Am I the president or not? Go search for it immediately! A presidential decree cannot be lost!"'

Embarrassed, Gaidar initiated a further search. It was equally fruitless. After a few more days, another trembling delegation from the young reformers' camp went back to see Yeltsin to petition him again to sign a copy of the original decree. After another and even more furious round of banging, stomping and shouting, the president agreed.

Then the second decree, extracted from the president with so much effort, vanished just like the first. This time, after another round of searching and presidential cursing, the second decree was found. But by that time, two months had passed. When Golovkov finally arrived to run the apparat, it was too late for him to appoint his own team. All the jobs had been filled; and the people who filled them were same ones who had always been there – the old Soviet apparatchiks. 'He [Golovkov] was the boss, but all he could do was come in and sit in the sole unoccupied seat,' Kovalyev explained.

It was an instructive story of all the trivial but vital ways in which the apparat could put spokes in the wheels of a leader it did not like. But it did not end there. I was not the only person Kovalyev decided to alert to the machinations of the bureaucracy. The episode seemed so symptomatic and so worrying that Kovalyev decided he must bring it to the attention of the president himself.

Kovalyev got his chance in late 1993 when the Presidential Council, an elite group of government advisers, convened around a vast circular table in one of the grand, echoing rooms of the Kremlin. All the players in the saga of the lost decree were there – Yeltsin, Gaidar and Viktor Ilyushin, the president's chief of staff. In an impulsive break from the official programme, Kovalyev abandoned the text of his prepared speech about reforming the KGB and instead recounted the story of the lost decree to what must have been the most powerful audience in all of Russia.

As he spoke, Kovalyev nervously kept his eyes fixed on the president, afraid that at any moment he might be furiously contradicted. But Yeltsin listened in silence with a poker face, which Kovalyev took as implicit confirmation that his story was true. Emboldened, Kovalyev concluded his account with an impassioned plea: 'Boris Nikolaevich [Yeltsin], you must understand that this cannot be allowed. If you are the *khozain*, the boss, how can you permit yourself not to seek out the bastard who allowed himself to lose your decree? If things of this sort are allowed to take place, then you are no longer the *khozain* of the country. The *khozain* is your little apparatchik, the one who does these things with your documents.'

By now, Kovalyev was on an adrenelin high. Astonished and quite pleased by his own audacity, he waited for the president to respond. But Yeltsin was as impassive as ever. Stony-faced and speaking in a mono-tone, he solemnly thanked Kovalyev for his 'extraordinarily interesting' remarks and the meeting went on. Kovalyev was dumbfounded. If his story was false, surely the president would have rudely contradicted him? But if it was true, why wasn't Yeltsin as horrified as he was? Still worrying over the episode, one day Kovalyev decided to ask Gaidar about it directly. 'You laid out the sequence of events with great accu-racy,' Gaidar assured his friend, then offered a pithy explanation: 'For some reason, Yeltsin really didn't want Golovkov to get the job.'

Suddenly, the whole confusing picture fell into place. Yeltsin wasn't horrified by Kovalyev's story for one very good reason, and that reason was that it was he who had ordered the decree to be lost in the first place. He didn't want to give the job to Golovkov, but also he didn't want to openly rebuff Gaidar. So he signed the decree, and then told his apparatchiks to 'lose' it – twice.

Kovalyev believed the episode evoked in miniature crucial truths about the nature of the Soviet apparat, Yeltsin's philosophy of gover-nance and the difficulties the young reformers faced while working in such an alien system:

> You and I have never worked in the CPSU, but our president, the cunning old party fox, has. You don't have to quarrel with your prime minister about this or that decision, all you have to do is change it at the level of the apparat. There are always small technical changes, which can mean much more than the principled decision. The most radical step can be stopped, drowned in a mass of trivia and, on the contrary, you can achieve almost anything without taking any prin-cipled decisions, but simply through a number of technical steps. Yeltsin understands that perfectly. Gaidar, I think, understood it only a little bit. And I had no idea at all.

Cadres, as Stalin observed and every Soviet schoolchild was once taught, determine everything. This lesson, and countless other bureau-cratic manoeuvres, had been learned perfectly by an apparat for which, just a generation earlier, the price of a mistake could be death. Gaidar and the young reformers were up against thousands of these masters of guile, and their only source of support was a president who belonged at least as much to the murky universe of the apparat as he did to their vision of a new Russia.

There was one way in which the young reformers could become more than McKinsey revolutionaries and liberate themselves from both the whims of the president and the guile of the apparat. The solution was to build up their own independent power base. Lenin had acquired power by seizing it, and then ruthlessly suppressing all dissent. The young reformers had neither the will, nor the means, to do that. But, if they chose, they could try to get power in the modern democratic way by appealing to the millions of ordinary Russians whose lives would be improved by a successful shift to a market economy. They could try to forge a broad, national constituency which supported reforms. They could, if they really worked at it, create their own political party.

A few months after Gaidar began his capitalist revolution, a wise neighbour advised him to do precisely that. In the spring of 1992, the Russian leader made an official visit to Prague where he met Vaclav Klaus, then the Czech minister of finance and at the time seen as the most successful of all the former communist market reformers.

In their first private conversation, Gaidar, wholly absorbed by the dramatic economic change he was spearheading, let loose a fusillade of statistics. Klaus listened patiently for a while, then abruptly interrupted. Inflation figures and measures of money supply were all well and good, he told his younger colleague, but ultimately the fate of Russia's capitalist revolution would be determined by the political talents of its authors, not by their technical prowess.

'If you fail to create a political base to support market reforms, then you will forever be the hostages of those who invited you into government and of their unexpected political manoeuvres,' Klaus warned. 'They can very easily destroy everything that you are doing and hope to do. Your most important task is to consolidate the political forces which can become a base for the reforms you are implementing.'

Klaus was blunt, even pushy, as he delivered his lecture. Across the former Warsaw Pact, the Czech minister was admired but he was also loathed. He was Mitteleuropa's Margaret Thatcher, convinced he was right to the point of arrogance.

'How often do you speak to large auditoriums, to the public? How often do you explain what you are doing?' Klaus demanded. When Gaidar protested that he was just too busy, the Czech pounced. He himself always found the time, he insisted, speaking in public and appearing on television several times a week. Gaidar ought to start doing the same. The Polish reformers had ignored Klaus' advice and now they were losing power. If Gaidar didn't watch out, Klaus warned, the same thing would happen to him.

Klaus' impassioned counsel made a huge impression on Gaidar. It was unexpected, it was important and it was very worrying. Apolitical by inclination, the young reformers had launched Russia's most radical political transformation as technocrats, not as politicians. Theirs was a revolution waged in isolated government dachas and hectic cabinet meetings; it was not conducted through public debates, television interviews or mass demonstrations. They dismissed public relations as a trivial distraction. The only thing that mattered was to act.

Before long, the young reformers realised this ivory tower approach was untenable. By the spring of 1993, a year after his conversation with Klaus, Gaidar had become a leading figure among democratic political activists. A few months later they chose him, rather than other more overtly political pretenders, to head Russia's Choice, the most powerful democratic party at the time.

Yet even as the young reformers became more involved in public politics, it remained their Achilles heel. In the December 1993 parliamentary elections, when Gaidar was first deputy prime minister and his party enjoyed the backing of the machinery of state, Russia's Choice did worse than expected, allowing Vladimir Zhirinovsky's extremist nationalists to come in in first place. By the time Russia next went to the polls in parliamentary elections in 1995, Russia's Choice had become so weak that it failed to top the 5 per cent barrier which would have granted it seats through proportional representation. A year later, their political weakness would force the young reformers into what many eventually would judge to be their gravest error – the strategic alliance they formed with the oligarchs, the group of powerful newly minted Russian businessmen, to keep the communists out of the Kremlin.

Even when the young reformers made something of a political comeback – winning nearly 9 per cent of the vote in the December 1999 parliamentary elections – it was on the coat-tails of yet another strongman, Vladimir Putin, then the prime minister. In an uncomfortable echo of their relationship with his mentor, Yeltsin, the young reformers enthusiastically backed Putin and his brutal war in Chechnya, hoping he would eventually repay them by sponsoring a new wave of economic reform. Yet again, the young reformers bet their future on the fate of a powerful and enigmatic Kremlin chief. Yet again, they sacrificed their private liberal principles for the sake of their public economic goals. And, yet again, they had no guarantee that once he was securely in power their man would implement their policies.

So why did these brilliant, energetic young economists prove to be such lacklustre politicians? Partly because they never tried hard enough and they started too late. But it was also simpler than that. These self-confessed 'egg-heads', reared in the sheltered world of the red intelligentsia, just weren't cut out to be democratic politicians. In his memoirs, Gaidar admitted as much: 'The role of a democratic leader was absolutely uncomfortable for me, it was internally not my own.'

His friends say he was too decent for the slime and scandal of post-Soviet politics. His critics say he was too soft. Both are probably right. In a passage in his autobiography which is both touching and worrying, Gaidar describes with great concern how the political rough-and-tumble was deeply distressing for his mother. Her precious son had always been a complete success. Now, suddenly, there came a 'mass of unpleasantness, hatred'. Gentle and thoughtful man that he is, Gaidar was horrified to be a source of maternal anxiety: 'I tried to carve out free moments to call her, to calm her down.'

Gaidar's concern was laudable, but it bespoke a sensitivity which few politicians – not to mention Russian ones, in the throes of a revolution – could afford. Just as the young reformers often found themselves out-manoeuvred by apparatchiks willing to stoop to a cunning they would not permit themselves, so they found themselves out-punched by politicians cut from a rougher psychological cloth: including the man who gave them their big political break. Yeltsin had appointed the young reformers, but as a man and a politician he was their antithesis. Crude, mercurical and intuitive, Yeltsin was the sort of larger-than-life leader who once stood up the Irish prime minister because he was too drunk to get off his airplane, won a conflict with parliament by sending in his tanks and tried to resolve a dispute with separatist Chechnya by sending in his army.

Unsuccessful in building a political power base of their own, the reformers were at the mercy of their tough, volatile president. And for Yeltsin, as one Kremlin courtier put it, 'power was his love, his passion, his mistress'. Once market reforms threatened to jeopardise Yeltsin's grip on power, the reformers had to go: as early as May 1992, the Kremlin chief began to withdraw his support and by the end of 1992, Gaidar was forced to resign from his post as acting prime minister.

His departure did not mark an end to the reformers' role in government: Gaidar briefly returned in 1993, Chubais and his privatisation programme chugged along until 1996; in 1997 Chubais returned to cabinet for nearly a year; in 1998, Sergei Kiriyenko, a protégé of the young reformers, briefly served as prime minister; and in 2000, Putin, the acting president, began to rely on the young reformers for some economic advice. But the young reformers would never again enjoy the almost total control of the government they had had in the first few months. Their periods in office would be intermittent, their cabinet colleagues would often be hostile to their politics and, even when they were in power, their effectiveness would depend totally on the yo-yo of presidential favour. They were always McKinsey Revolutionaries, and whenever the boss fired them, their project had to be put on hold.

3

THE IRON GENERAL
PRIVATISES RUSSIA

IT IS HARD to convey quite how much most Russians hate Chubais who, even more than Gaidar, has come to personify the country's flawed capitalist revolution. The red-headed St Petersburger was the young reformers' enforcer, the iron general who translated Gaidar's dreams into action and hung on to political power long after his gentler comrades had been forced out. Without Chubais, Russia's capitalist revolution would probably have petered out before it had properly begun. And for that, some Russians will never forgive him. Think of how the British must have felt about Hitler during the Blitz, or how the Bosnian Muslims feel about Milosevic. Of course Chubais is no bloodthirsty tyrant, but still, many, Russians revile him as if he were. What makes it worse is that Chubais is a Russian and his countrymen despise him with the particular vehemence people reserve for their nearest and dearest. Russians loathe Chubais intimately, personally. For them, hating Chubais has become part of the daily fabric of life.

If they could, most Russians would probably like to tell Chubais himself how much they despise him, to his face, every day. Since that's impossible, they find other ways to express a rage that smoulders on, and on. A couple of years ago, a stray cat moved into the courtyard in front of a Moscow friend's apartment block. The creature was ginger-haired, like Chubais, so that is what the neighbours named him. Any time anyone passed the poor animal, they would give him a vicious kick: Take that, Chubais! And that, and that!

Like the cat, my friend Leonid is a red-head. In his mid-twenties, he's smart and well-educated and he still hasn't quite decided what to do with himself. When he asked a favourite former boss for advice, his mentor told Leonid there was one career that was out of the question: politics. The reason: Chubais had given the whole country an 'allergy' to red-heads and Leonid would be an old man before the nation got over it. These people aren't laid-off factory workers or provincial pensioners still clinging to their party cards. They are rich, sophisticated Moscow insiders, people who attend the same cocktail parties Chubais is invited to, the friends of his friends. Chubais isn't hated only by the people who should hate him, those who were inevitably going to come out on the losing side of market reforms. He's also hated by many of the people who should love him, by the winners who think they should have won more or who worry that there are too many losers in the country for their winnings to be secure.

Yet there are also people who love Chubais, and what they lack in numbers they make up for in passion. Some of his biggest fans are foreigners. One senior World Bank official once told me, straight-faced, that Chubais was a demi-god. That admiration was so widely shared among Western policy-makers that for a long time it was an article of faith in Moscow that all it took to get money from the IMF was to buy Chubais a plane ticket to Washington.

A few Russians are crazy about him, too. A small band of liberals sees Chubais as an almost Christ-like figure, crucified for his country's sins, but certain to be resurrected in glory. They don't think that day is very far off, either. One Chubais supporter told me confidently that if he was not elected president in 2004, he definitely would be in 2008. Even if Chubais doesn't get his earthly reward, his admirers believe history will be kind to him. I don't care what they all say about Chubais now, a Siberian entrepreneur told me, one day, there will be a statue of him in every town in Russia.

Chubais is loved in a more personal sense, as well. He is loyal to a fault, defending colleagues and subordinates even when it damaged his own position or when it was clear they were corrupt. Gaidar found

Chubais to be such a faithful friend, respecting him equally whether he was in government or not, that in his honour he invented a new unit of measurement, a 'chub', the emotional equivalent of pounds or miles, to quantify personal loyalty.

Powerful and contradictory, the rich Chubais mythology is like radio static, making it almost impossible to tune into the 'real' man. A few basic facts, at least, are not in dispute. Chubais is tall, with a face which might be forgettable if it belonged to a different man. His features are regular, but a bit rough, like a drawing which is not quite finished. Naturally skinny, the years in Moscow have thickened his waist and created jowls. The famous red hair is not a true burnished copper but a darker, dirtier colour. He doesn't have the Scottish red-head's translucent complexion and prominent freckles, either. Instead, his skin is a very Russian, mortician's off-white, turning bright pink when he's angry or excited.

Compared with Gaidar, Chubais' background was relatively humble. The son of a professional soldier, Chubais was born in 1955 in a small town in Belarus, one of the most forlorn corners of the Soviet Union. In 1986 – the year the young reformers coalesced as a group – he was an assistant professor at the Leningrad Institute of Engineering and Economics, a respectable but not quite first-rate institute. 'As an economist, Gaidar was head and shoulders above Chubais,' Sergei Vasiliev, one of the young reformers, told me. 'Chubais does not have a good economic education. He has read little in English.'

But, from the very beginning, Chubais shone as an organiser. It was he who initiated the young reformers' systematic campaign to find and recruit other up-and-coming market economists. He also tried to pull the young reformers into the wider political ferment of the time. In Leningrad, Chubais was active in local political discussion groups, the unfocused but lively proto-political parties of the late 1980s. When the Soviet Union's first free elections propelled this early wave of activists into local government, Chubais was part of the incoming tide, swiftly rising to prominence in the Leningrad city administration.

Even as he pursued these early political enthusiasms, Chubais displayed the one defining quality which would make him the most successful of the young reformers, and ultimately the most tragic – his iron will. Many of the other young reformers, including Gaidar, were reluctant refugees from academe, uncomfortable with the sadism and deceit of high politics à la Russe. Not Chubais. As one admiring Wall Street fund manager put it: 'The guy's got the biggest balls in the whole damn country.' A Russian journalist famously compared him to Marshall Zhukov: like the World War Two general, Chubais would do anything to achieve his goal, even if he had to walk over dead bodies to do it.

In Russia's hard-edged political culture, a world in which the Kremlin chief had been known to play spoons on the heads of neighbouring presidents and where screaming at subordinates is the routine way of getting things done, Chubais' iron nerve served him well. When he picked a fight, or was cornered into one, he usually triumphed. Increasingly, as his pugnacious talents became more widely known, other politicians deemed it wisest simply to avoid confrontations with him altogether.

As Sergei Karaganov, a sometime Kremlin adviser and influential political scientist, explained: 'I would go into a fight with any Russian except Yeltsin and Chubais. The way to win a fight in Russia is to never give in and always to escalate the conflict. That is what I do, but Chubais does it better.'

Chubais' first big fight was mass privatisation and he approached it with his usual single-minded determination. To other reformist economists in the early 1990s, privatisation seemed to be a social and political minefield. The long-term objective was clear enough: in order to create an efficient, competitive market economy, many of the assets accumulated by the communist state should be transferred to private owners.

But achieving that goal seemed to be fraught with dangers. Some reformers in eastern Europe agonised over the justice of privatisation, anxious that state property which belonged to the entire citizenry might be captured by a small minority. Others were more concerned about making sure the privatised companies went to the most able new owners, people with the money and the know-how to restructure communist behemoths into effective market competitors. A third group worried about how to synchronise privatisation with the wider reform effort: privatising too slowly might mean the market economy never got off the ground, but privatising too fast threatened to create private businesses which were unable to function properly because a capitalist infrastructure had not yet been created.

Even in gung-ho Poland, whose radical reformers had pioneered shock therapy in 1990, these fears were powerful enough to postpone the privatisation process for years. But they didn't stop Chubais. He understood the complex questions privatisation raised and the varying objectives it could be used to achieve. However, with the ruthless focus which was his hallmark, he almost immediately identified a single, overriding goal: to transfer as much property, as quickly as possible, from the state sector into private control. Other possible consequences of privatisation would certainly be desirable. It would be nice if privatised firms quickly restructured and became more efficient than those which were state-owned. Social justice, a fair division of the property accumulated under 70 years of Soviet rule, would not be a bad thing. And Chubais certainly was not averse to filling the disastrously empty state coffers with privatisation revenues. But all of these potential benefits were secondary, and sacrificeable, in pursuit of the central objective.

His central mission was as much political as it was economic. By swiftly shifting ownership from the state to individuals, Chubais set out permanently to break the back of the all-powerful Soviet bureaucracy and create an instant constituency – the new private owners – willing to fight for the capitalist revolution. His philosophy was what one government adviser described as 'reverse Marxism': just as the Bolsheviks had built communism by transferring the means of production from private owners to the state, so he believed that his central mission must be to undo that transformation, and return the property to private owners, in the quickest way he could.

In Russia, things always seem to happen at the last minute. The revolutionary privatisation programme was no exception. Having reluctantly accepted the prickly job, Chubais hurriedly began to assemble a team. The first call went out to Dmitry Vasiliev, an old friend and colleague of his in St Petersburg.

A thin, gawky man with the bottle-thick glasses and stern manner of an old-fashioned Russian *intelligent*, Vasiliev was an obvious choice. A year earlier, when Chubais and his team joined the St Petersburg city administration, Vasiliev had been press-ganged into making privatisation, seen then as 'dirty, trivial work', his speciality. Now, Chubais was in charge of privatising the entire country and he wanted Vasiliev to be his deputy.

Vasiliev learned of his sudden elevation on 8 November 1991, just a few days after Yeltsin signed the decree appointing Gaidar deputy prime minister. That night the telephone in Vasiliev's St Petersburg apartment rang. It was Mariya Vishnevskaya, Chubais' second wife and a respected economist in her own right. Chubais was in Moscow meeting the new deputy prime minister, she said, and he wanted Vasiliev to prepare a draft privatisation plan within 24 hours.

Vasiliev was flabbergasted. Events in the capital city were moving so fast that the St Petersburg contingent of the young reformers had not yet grasped that the group was now in charge of the government. But, having absorbed the rather daunting idea that he would be the author of the nationwide privatisation programme, Vasiliev sat down to work.

'In a day I wrote down the principal ideas on three sheets of paper,' he told me. 'That's the only way such programmes get written. Either you write them quickly, or you don't write them at all.'

A day later, Vasiliev was in Moscow with Chubais at building No. 21 on the Novyi Arbat boulevard, one of a row of monumental Stalinist skyscrapers designed to look like open books. The two friends, who were soon joined by a few other young reformers from St Petersburg, started from absolute zero. Whereas Gaidar, just a fifteen-minute walk away in another set of forbidding government office blocks, was struggling to bring the Soviet-era apparat under control, there was – by definition – no communist institution for the privatisers to take over.

At first, the lack of a pre-existing infrastructure seemed to make a job that was already hard even more difficult. But, in the long run, that blank slate would turn out to be one of the privatisers' greatest assets. While the rest of the young reformers fought against a current of 'lost' decrees and sabotage within the ministries ostensibly under their control, Chubais and his team were building the State Privatisation Committee, known as the GKI – an acronym for its Russian title, Gosudarstvennyi Kommitet Imushchestva – from the ground up. Within a year, the GKI had offices in each of Russia's 89 regions and local branches in hundreds of other towns and cities. Staffed by Chubais' hand-picked army of intensely loyal, ideologically committed officials, it swiftly became Russia's most effective reform machine. In many ways, the tragedy of the young reformers was that they managed to build only one GKI. But it took an organiser with the administrative talents of Chubais to create the GKI, and there was only one Chubais in the reform team.

Chubais' skill in institution-building stemmed in part from his talent for attracting smart people and his willingness to give them free rein to do their job. At the GKI, Vasiliev and the team of specialists he assembled became the chief engine of ideas and the workshop for the crucial and time-consuming job of drafting legislation to put the ideas into practice. Chubais confined himself to supervising the overall thrust of the privatisation programme and to the tricky job of winning political approval for the plan.

While Chubais began feverish negotiations to win political support for a mass sell-off of state property, his team launched a furious effort to prepare a full-blooded privatisation programme. As they sat in their fur hats and greatcoats in unheated offices, picking out their ideas on ancient manual Soviet typewriters, the privatisers felt they were making history.

'At the start, we didn't have a single employee, not even a secretary. We didn't have any equipment, not even a fax machine. And in those conditions, in just a month and a half, we had to write a comprehensive privatisation programme, we had to write twenty normative laws,' recalled Vasiliev, who grew so thin during his first frenetic weeks in government that when his wife came to visit from St Petersburg she didn't recognise him. 'It was a really romantic period. We knew that the economic situation was catastrophic and we were working for the future. We knew that what we were doing had to be done.'

While the team at the GKI was still debating the finer points of privatisation and doing the laborious work of drafting dozens of laws and regulations, Russia's shock therapy market reforms got started with a bang. The disastrous state of the public finances, and the mounting food shortages meant that the young reformers had to launch their radical macro-economic stabilisation programme almost immediately. Privatisation could afford a slightly slower start.

But not much slower. Constantly fearful that the window of political opportunity would slam shut, Chubais was anxious to begin transferring property away from the state and into the hands of private owners as soon as possible. By the spring of 1992, the privatisers had a draft plan and Chubais began the gargantuan task of steering it through the Soviet-era parliament, the Supreme Soviet.

Selected under only quasi-democratic laws in 1989, the Supreme Soviet was dominated by the elite of the *ancien régime*, high-ranking former party officials and directors of the country's largest enterprises. After a few months of shock therapy, many of them realised that Gaidar had launched a revolution and they were now the class enemy. They began to plot a revanche which would ultimately culminate in an armed and bloody confrontation between the Kremlin and parliament eighteen months later.

Yet Chubais needed their support to translate Vasiliev's plans into binding legislation. To win the backing of the recalcitrant parliamentarians, Chubais agreed to the huge political and economic compromise at the heart of Russia's mass privatisation.

The Bolsheviks had enforced the last big transfer of property rights in Russia at gunpoint. Chubais and his band of capitalist revolutionaries had neither the will nor the means to do that. Instead, they needed to win the backing of those who already effectively controlled Russia's thousands of enterprises – the managers and workers of each company. To do so, the privatisers had been prepared from the very outset to offer attractive sweeteners, granting workers and managers up to 40 per cent of the shares in their firms.

It was the most generous provision for company insiders which any privatisation ever attempted in the world had offered; but in the increasingly polarised political atmosphere of the spring of 1992, it was not enough. Soviet-era ministries, at first stunned by the speed with which the young reformers had struck, were beginning to regroup. If Chubais wanted to get the privatisation programme through parliament, he had to act fast.

So, he cut a deal which effectively made the Soviet-era factory directors the capitalist elite of the new Russia. In consultation with the Supreme Soviet, the GKI also agreed to offer a second privatisation scheme. Known as option 2, the compromise allowed workers and managers to buy 51 per cent of the voting shares in their company at a nominal price. It was a huge concession, one the privatisers granted with great reluctance and only as a necessary evil.

Vasiliev, who would later go on to found and head the Federal

Securities Commission, Russia's stock-market watchdog, believed many of the deformations of the country's young capitalism – the continued dominance of incompetent Soviet-era managers, the persistent abuse of minority shareholders by company insiders, the failure of real owners, interested in profit-making rather than rent-seeking, to emerge in many companies – could be traced to this early decision. 'In order to save the privatisation programme, we had to agree,' Vasiliev told me years later. 'Clearly, it was undesirable and gave rise to problems I am trying to untangle to this day.'

But the bitter side-effects were tomorrow's problems. On 11 June 1992, the day when the Supreme Soviet finally ratified the privatisation plan, Chubais and his team rejoiced. In the face of an increasingly hostile political climate, one which had begun to stymie the macro-economic reforms that began the year so boldly, the privatisers had persuaded the Soviet-era legislature to sign the death warrant of the economic system which had created it.

Having agreed on who Russia's companies would be sold to, the privatisers had to decide what they would be sold for. Their initial bias was towards cash privatisation: selling state property for money would help solve the country's chronic budget shortfalls and soak up the pools of excess cash, known as the monetary overhang, which had been created by the shortage of anything anyone wanted to buy in the Soviet era. However, while cash privatisation was, in Vasiliev's words, 'theoretically very beautiful', in practice it swiftly began to seem both untenable and politically dangerous.

'Price liberalisation had destroyed everyone's savings,' Vasiliev said. 'There was no money any more. That realisation led us to the conclusion that cash privatisation would lead to a cataclysm. A very narrow group of people would buy the whole economy. That would provoke the deep-seated envy of the Russian people and could spark a social upheaval.'

Instead, the young reformers opted for a scheme designed to maximise public support for the grand sell-off: the Soviet Union's patrimony would in effect be given directly to the Russian people. Voucher privatisation, announced by Yeltsin on 19 August 1992, exactly one year after he had climbed on top of the tank in front of the White House, proved to be a stroke of populist genius. Every Russian born by 2 September 1992 – Chubais moved the cut-off date forward from

1 September so that Olga Kokh, the newborn daughter of Alfred, one of the St Petersburg privatisers, would qualify – was given a voucher with a face value of 10,000 roubles, then worth about $25. Vouchers were a currency with which workers could pay the nominal fee required to buy their reserved shares in their enterprises; they could be used to buy stakes in companies that would be sold in public auctions, they could be invested in voucher mutual funds, or they could be traded on the street for anything from US dollars to a bottle of vodka.

Later, the vouchers would become a target for popular dissatisfaction with the reform programme, as people complained that the vouchers, like the market economy as a whole, had failed to transform their lives. But in the crucial early months of privatisation, they won the young reformers their most muscular constituency: the 144 million Russians who took the trouble to go to their local branch of Sberbank, the state savings bank, and pay a nominal fee of 25 roubles (less than 10 cents at prevailing exchange rates) to collect their voucher. With their vouchers in hand, millions of ordinary Russians became an automatic lobby group, pushing for privatisation to go ahead and give their pieces of paper real value.

'We created a situation in which the people demanded – privatise the property we can buy with this voucher,' Vasiliev explained. 'We created a process which was irreversible.'

The vouchers also stimulated the creation of a securities market. Freely tradeable, they almost immediately awoke the entrepreneurial instinct which had been hibernating in Russian souls for 70 years. In the opinion of one of the American pioneers of the Russian capital markets, the vouchers became 'the most liquid security in the world'. Street kiosks, whose briskest business was in vodka and cigarettes, began a robust trade in vouchers as well. Young hustlers went from door to door, buying up spare vouchers. Soon, vouchers were being traded in huge blocks on the nascent commodities exchanges through-out Russia. On the Russian Commodity and Raw Materials Exchange, then the largest bourse in Moscow, the daily turn-over in vouchers quickly reached the dollar equivalent of $1m. By the end of the auctions in the summer of 1994, the daily volume sometimes exceeded $10m.

With the privatisation programme approved and the vouchers dis-tributed, by the autumn of 1992 the young reformers were ready to begin mass privatisation. The only problem was within the national

political establishment, where hard-line communists and the industrial elite were preparing a united challenge to the young reformers and
their market revolution. It looked as if Gaidar would be fired by the legislature by the end of the year, and most of his team would probably be
forced out with him. In what would come to be a classic Chubais
manoeuvre, faced with growing political opposition at home, he turned
to the West for help.

By the end of the decade, Chubais' reliance on Western advisers,
Western aid money and Western political support would seem to be a
disastrous miscalculation for both sides. Propped up by the West,
Chubais never bothered to build up a grass-roots domestic political
constituency and found himself caricatured as a foreign agent in his
own land. Closely associated with Chubais, Western governments and
aid agencies were seduced into backing people rather than policies and
found themselves tainted by the corruption which became the young
reformers' darkest legacy to Russia.

But at the time, the alliance seemed as natural, and as moral, as
Western support for Soviet dissidents had been a few years earlier. The
evil empire was gone, but its ideological battle-lines lingered; the strug-
gle to defeat communism had now shifted to the economy. Chubais and
Gaidar were identified as the good guys just as surely as Sakharov and
Solzhenitsyn had been in the previous, political round of fighting.

Western governments had even set up a brand-new aid agency, the
European Bank for Reconstruction and Development (EBRD), whose
express purpose was to help the countries of what had been the Soviet
bloc shift to capitalism. As Chubais desparately scrambled to set mass
privatisation in motion before the young reformers were sacked, the
EBRD was the natural place to turn to for assistance.

Charlie Ryan, a young American EBRD official who would later
found his own investment bank in Moscow, recalled: 'In October '92 he
[Chubais] made a frantic call to the EBRD saying – look, we have not
done a single voucher privatisation. We have to do a voucher privatisation before Yeltsin appoints a new prime minister or the whole thing
will collapse.'

The EBRD was delighted to help, but it was eager to get Western
commercial banks involved in Russia too. In particular, the EBRD
wanted to tempt Credit Suisse First Boston, the Swiss-American investment bank which had played a crucial role in the development of

capital markets in eastern Europe, into the Russian market. There was just one problem – Hans-Jorg Rudloff, the 52-year old German banker and pioneer of the eurobond market who had led CSFB's pioneering foray to the East, was fiercely hostile towards the Russian government.

His animosity dated back to earlier in the year when he and his Russia team bid to become the GKI's chief privatisation advisers. By then, Rudloff was a legendary figure in eastern Europe, accustomed to red-carpet treatment from the presidents and prime ministers whose young economies he had played such a crucial role in creating. The Russians, however, gave Rudloff the brush-off: the CSFB proposal was rejected and, according to Ryan, Chubais added insult to injury by walking out of the bank's elaborate presentation after the first fifteen minutes.

'Rudloff has a fit,' Ryan recalled. 'He takes his private jet back to Switzerland then he declares he would never go back to Russia.' According to an internal CSFB report, 'Rudloff questioned whether the firm should ever again compete for an assignment for the Russian government.'

The EBRD officials decided that the voucher privatisation was an ideal opportunity to try to lure Rudloff and CSFB back to Moscow. If Rudloff would agree to advise Chubais on Russia's first voucher privatisation, the EBRD would cover his expenses. CSFB would get a head start in the Russian market – and Western taxpayers would foot the bill. It was too good a deal even for Rudloff to resist.

In more ways than one, CSFB's involvement in the first voucher auctions would prove a turning point. The auctions themselves were, of course, crucial. CSFB became the dominant Western investment bank in Russia's mass privatisation, eventually handling 1 out of every 10 vouchers issued in the entire country. Moreover, the project was the Moscow debut of two Western investment bankers who would play a central role in the tumultuous development of Russia's market economy over the next decade: Boris Jordan and Stephen Jennings.

In the not-too-distant future, the involvement of highly paid Western consultants like Jordan and Jennings would become fiercely controversial. Russian nationalists would accuse the West of insinuating its own henchmen into the reform process in a nefarious attempt to destroy the economy of its erstwhile Cold War adversary. Other critics, both in Russia and the West, would claim that the Western advisers had been overpaid and that many later used their Russian government contacts to their fullest advantage. But the Russians who faced the formidable task of privatising the Soviet economy have no doubt that their foreign advisers played a crucial role.

'Of course, they earned money,' Vasiliev said. '[Western] people could not work on the sort of money that we earned here. If you don't take bribes it is very difficult. You can say what you like about Boris [Jordan] – and some people criticise him – but his energy is simply fantastic. He is a motor-man.'

The motor-man was just 26 years old when he came to Moscow in the autumn of 1992 to be co-head, with Jennings, of CSFB's Russia office, and he was the more flamboyant member of the pair. Tall, fair-haired and baby-faced, Jordan had the wide-eyed look of those dazed aristocrats you sometimes see in *fin-de-siècle* portraits of Imperial Russian high society. The resemblance was fitting enough: Jordan was the grandson of blue-blooded White Russians who fled their homeland after the Bolshevik revolution. Arriving in New York via Paris, they joined an émigré community which was defiantly a culture in exile rather than a dissolving morsel in the American melting-pot. Boris grew up dreaming of becoming a Cold War warrior and using all the might of his American birth country to liberate the land to which he felt he really belonged.

'I was going to become a diplomat and play a role in breaking up communism and bringing back the Russia of old, but using the United States as a tool,' he recalled.

But by the time Jordan reached Russia, communism had already collapsed. With the energy and shark-like ambition he had learned during an apprenticeship working on some of the sharper deals of the 1980s greed-is-good Wall Street, Jordan threw himself into the next best thing. He couldn't be a Cold War warrior, so he decided to become a free market one instead.

Stephen Jennings, his co-head, was a subtler man; 32 years old when he arrived in Russia, he was an investment banker straight out of central casting: tall, dark and handsome, a skilful rugby player, always wearing the whitest shirt and the most conservative suit in the room. By 1992, the native New Zealander was a veteran of privatisations: he had been closely involved in New Zealand's radical market reforms in the 1980s, then branched out to privatisations in Australia, Spain and eastern Europe.

Jennings had no particular passion for Russia and, indeed, even after almost a decade in the country he admitted to barely speaking the language. But he loved the thrill of working in countries in the throes of systemic change, and he was a true believer in the power of free markets. When CSFB asked him to move to Moscow and participate in the world's biggest capitalist revolution, he jumped at the chance.

For Jennings, the small, united and ideologically zealous band of young reformers he met at the GKI was reminiscent of the teams of free marketeers he had worked with in the Antipodes and Europe. But while the Russian privatisers seemed to share the passionate intensity of the free market evangelists of the West, the task they faced was far more daunting and their resources far more scarce. On 29 October, Rudloff received a letter from Chubais, inviting CSFB to submit a plan for conducting Russia's pilot voucher auctions. By early December, the GKI wanted them to have sold off at least one company through a voucher privatisation auction.

The timing was crucial because the Seventh Congress of People's Deputies, the full session of the Russian parliament, was scheduled to convene for two weeks, starting on 1 December. The reformers feared – rightly as it turned out – that when it came back from holiday the communist-dominated legislature would sack Gaidar, who by then was acting prime minister. His ouster could put a stop to the entire reform programme. So, to pre-empt the Congress, the reformers were desperate to get their mass privatisation under way with at least one high profile voucher auction before the legislators met.

By 5 November, the GKI had approved CSFB's hastily conceived draft auction plan and tapped the bank to conduct the pilot sales. Jennings, who had only seen snow before on skiing holidays, joined Jordan in Moscow two days later on 7 November – coincidentally the 75th anniversary of the October Revolution. Even though it was a Saturday, and late at night, the CSFB bankers went straight to the GKI to meet with the top members of the Russian government team: Vasiliev; a Harvard-trained Russian economist named Maxim Boiko; and the Harvard lawyer Jonathan Hay. Jennings was impressed by their courage and commitment, but he was horrified at their lack of preparation for auctions that were supposed to be just five weeks away.

The CSFB bankers, drafted for the job just a few days earlier, were winging it as well. 'In typical investment banking fashion you kind of bluffed your way through and made believe that we had some highly developed incredible plans,' Jennings said. Having persuaded the privatisers at the GKI that they knew what they were doing, Jennings and Jordan went back to their hotel rooms. They stayed up most of the night, trying to figure out how on earth they would could sell off a major Russian company in the next month and a half.

First, they had to catch their wolf. The GKI was so woefully under-staffed and underorganised that it did not even know which Russian companies had already been corporatised – the preliminary legal step which a firm had to take before it could be sold off. It took Jordan and Jennings 'about two weeks' of the precious 5 just to get a list of corpo-ratised enterprises. And the news it contained was not good, in Moscow, the nation's nine-million-strong metropolis and home to thou-sands of enterprises, just eight companies had got that far and were thus eligible for privatisation.

The CSFB team began frantically courting the eight firms, trying to find one that would be willing to be the nation's guinea-pig. It was a frustrating task. Some of the factory directors were so reluctant to par-ticipate in this newfangled market experiment that they resorted to the favourite Russian bureaucrat's ploy – they simply refused to schedule meetings. Others would talk, but were unwilling to cooperate.

As the session of the Congress of People's Deputies drew nearer and nearer and the search became ever more desperate, the bankers launched a parallel organisational drive. From a 'war-room' in the Metropol Hotel, Jordan and Jennings coordinated teams of newly hired employees who began planning exactly what they would do once they found a company willing to cooperate.

It was an organisational nightmare. Not only did the auction have to be held quickly, it must be conducted without a single mistake. The whole nation would be watching this pilot privatisation, and critics would be waiting to pounce on any error with cries of corruption or gleefully seize on it as evidence that the reformers' programme was logistically unfeasible. Jordan and Jennings needed instantly to recruit a Russian staff which was hard-working and reliable – two qualities for which the Russian work-force is hardly renowned.

Their response was to try to create systems which were nearly fool-proof and to impose strict discipline on their newly hired staff. 'People were hired on the basis that if they made two mistakes they would go on the spot,' Jennings said. 'That was one of the reasons I was able to have the whole thing work and it ran very smoothly.'

As the administrative machine began to take shape, the search for a company willing to participate narrowed down to the Bolshevik Biscuit Factory, founded in 1855 by a Swiss baker. Bolshevik was an obvious candidate; apart from the poetic justice of its name, it was well-known throughout Russia, had relatively modern production lines and was already being eyed by several major Western consumer-food groups interested in a Russian acquisition.

But the virtues of privatisation were far less apparent to Bolshevik's Soviet-era managers, who were still unfamiliar with the most basic concepts of a market economy. 'We met with Bolshevik and, not surprisingly, they were extremely reluctant to start this crazy experiment,' Jennings said.

Gradually, after dozens of hours of conversation, hundreds of cups of tea and some flirting with Galina Kaplunova, the matronly chief economist and power behind the throne at the factory, the bankers and the GKI officials began to win over the Bolshevik managers. Privatisation, they explained, would free Bolshevik from the interference of the loathed apparatchiks in the central government ministries. It would also give the company access to the Western capital it needed to upgrade its equipment and allow it to attract a strategic foreign investor. Slowly, these arguments started to sink in.

Finally, the Bolshevik managers agreed. On Wednesday 9 December a week into a raucous session of the Congress of People's Deputies, the doors swung open to a cavernous exhibition hall on the Moskva river and a waiting crowd rushed in to buy one of Russia's most famous factories.

In the run-up to the sale, Jennings and Jordan had worked the phones to drum up interest in the burgeoning Western investment banking community. Their colleagues had responded by carting sack-loads of vouchers to the exhibition hall to participate in the auction. Some Russian businessmen got in on the privatisation too – most notably Mikhail Friedman, an aggressive hustler who would eventually become one of the oligarchs. On the day of the privatisation itself, hundreds of Bolshevik employees and their relatives – not to mention Galina and other company managers – flocked to the hall and used their vouchers to buy shares in their company. Mass privatisation in Russia had begun.

The sale of Bolshevik did not come a moment too soon. The next day, as the liberals had feared, the Congress unleashed a fierce attack on Gaidar. By 14 December, Gaidar was fired and Viktor Chernomyrdin, an older Soviet-era industrialist and champion of the gas sector, was Russia's new prime minister.

Gaidar's ouster marked the end of the beginning of Russia's market revolution. Hostility towards the reformers had been mounting for months, but now it was overt and shouted from the very highest levels of government. Shortly after he was appointed, Chernomyrdin went so far as to compare privatisation with Stalin's blood-soaked forced collectivisation of agriculture in the 1930s.

Remarkably, though, privatisation kept chugging along. During the brief window of opportunity in 1992, the GKI had laid the legal foundations and created the administrative momentum for mass privatisation. Together with Chubais' iron will, that was enough to keep the process doggedly moving forward.

There were some close calls, one of which came during the violent clash between the leftist parliament and the Kremlin which erupted in the autumn of 1993. The showdown began on 21 September when Yeltsin ordered the dissolution of parliament and new elections. The parliamentarians refused to leave the White House, at that time the seat of the legislature, provoking a tense two-week siege. On 3 October, the stand-off exploded into street fighting as the hard-line parliamentarians tried to battle their way out of the legislature and their allies tried to capture a few strategic sites in the capital city.

The young reformers were terrified. Most of them spent the day hiding their wives and children in the homes of less prominent friends. Around midnight, they gathered for a meeting in the office of Gaidar, who by then had returned to government for another brief stint as deputy prime minister. All of them were poised for action and a few of them were armed; but, for now, there was nothing to do but wait. Most of the young reformers stayed in Gaidar's office until daybreak, talking, planning or trying to catch some sleep on the uncomfortable government-issue chairs. At any moment they feared that the parliamentary reactionaries, who were already storming the Ostankino television towers in a pitched battle that would cost dozens of lives, might turn their attention to the government offices. 'They could have arrested the whole government. Maybe, in the best case, Chernomyrdin would have managed to escape in his armoured Mercedes, but that's all,' Dmitry Vasiliev told me. 'Most likely, they would simply have shot us all. I will never forget that night, the night of the putsch.'

As it turned out, the hard-liners didn't try to storm the government offices on Staraya Ploshchad; 'as always in revolutions, mistakes were made', Vasiliev observed ruefully. But that day they did overrun a building of almost equal strategic importance: the former COMECON building which had become the mayor's office, a huge skyscraper on the banks of the Moskva river, across from the besieged White House.

When Vasiliev, anxiously pacing Gaidar's office, discovered that the hard-liners were looting the tower block, he panicked. The problem was that in a shabby little room in the basement of the blue and grey high-rise, the GKI had stored 11 million privatisation vouchers, about 7 per cent of the nation's total. The vouchers had already been used and were being stored ahead of disposal. If the hard-liners had found them and put them back into circulation, the entire privatisation programme could have been compromised. Terrified, Vasiliev called Vasily Shakhnovsky, the Moscow mayor's chief of staff, and begged him to send an armed patrol to secure the vouchers, worth about $55m at the going market rate. Shakhnovsky, in the midst of trying to put down an armed revolt, was unable to oblige.

Luckily, the disorganisation of the young reformers, the casualness with which they had simply tossed $55m worth of vouchers (some of them tied together with unused condoms because the GKI couldn't afford imported elastic bands) into the basement of a government building, saved the day. The obscure little room where the vouchers were stored, secured with nothing more than a flimsy wooden door and an ordinary lock, was too modest to attract the rioters' attention. The computers were stolen, the telephones ripped out, even a few light bulbs snatched, but no one noticed the vouchers.

And so, by sheer good fortune, the voucher privatisation programme survived the failed coup. But it was not smooth sailing yet. Initially, the plan had been for mass privatisation to be completed and for the vouchers to expire on 1 January 1994. But as 1993 drew to a close with two-thirds of the vouchers still unused, it was clear that deadline would not be met.

Horrified that their own tough timetable could undermine the entire privatisation process, the young reformers persuaded the president to extend the vouchers for six months, until 1 July 1994. Then they adopted the tried and true hell-for-leather implementation campaign the Soviets had called *shturmirovka*. 'Hand the responsibility over to me and I will devote myself to daily control,' Vasiliev volunteered at a crisis meeting with Chubais and the other privatisers in January 1994. He later told me, 'Every day we checked how many vouchers had been collected across the whole country, how many had been handed over, how the sales were going, where the auctions were taking place. Vasiliev and his team began what he termed a '*davilovka*' using the Soviet word for intense bureaucratic pressure from above. And it worked.

Russian politics had ridden a violent roller-coaster between November 1991, when the privatisers first convened in Moscow, and 1 July 1994, when the vouchers expired. A coup had been launched and suppressed; a referendum and parliamentary elections had been held; Gaidar had dominated the cabinet, been sacked, returned and resigned. Overall, the economy reflected this turbulence – gross domestic product was still contracting sharply, inflation continued to rage at an average 10 per cent a month in 1994, and the rouble was tumbling against the dollar.

Yet, on the privatisation front, Chubais and his team had prevailed. In 1991, when the young reformers came into government, fewer than 1 in 10 Russians were employed by the private sector. Less than three years later, nearly two-thirds of the labour force worked in Russia's 14,000 private or partially privatised companies. Chubais, the iron general of Russia's market revolution, had won his first major campaign.

Over the next few years, whenever the country faced a seemingly insurmountable challenge – reining in runaway inflation in 1995, defeating the communists in the 1996 presidential elections, winning Western financial support in 1998 – Chubais was the man that everyone called on. As Gaidar put it, he became Russia's 'expert in impossible missions'. To many of his allies, and perhaps even to himself, Chubais started to seem invincible. His swagger, which would become more pronounced over the next few years, was already apparent in 1994 when Chubais announced the completion of the voucher scheme.

Succumbing to the temptation to gloat, he described his mass privatisation drive as the first major national programme in Russia since 1917 to be completed on time and to achieve more than it had promised.

A few years on, Chubais' proud claim was already starting to look distinctly tattered. For one thing, while Russia's privatisers were phenomenally successful in their self-proclaimed mission of transferring property to private owners, their performance was far patchier by the one measure which would really count: improving the efficiency and profitability of the privatised companies.

Although Russia became a privately owned economy far more quickly than almost any other former Soviet state, it has been far slower than many of its neighbours to achieve economic growth, a failure which would contribute to the financial crash in 1998. By 1994 most Russian firms were in the hands of private owners, but even by the end of the decade far too many of them were still badly run. Corporate restructuring was not, as the young reformers had hoped, the inevitable and immediate consequence of privatisation – a miscalculation which continues to haunt the Russian economy to this day.

A second drawback to Chubais' reverse-Bolshevik approach was his tolerance of corruption. Intent on getting property into private hands in any way they could, the reformers legalised the capture of state assets by Soviet-era directors. And if managers wanted to grab even more of their companies than they were granted according to the generous provisions of the privatisation programme, the officials at the GKI in Moscow were inclined to turn a blind eye.

Mikhail Berger, a liberal Russian journalist who chronicled each twist and turn in the privatisation programme, believed the young reformers' guiding ethos could be summarised in a catchy slogan – 'Corruption for the sake of Democracy'. It was not an accidental trade-off, but a fully conscious pragmatic choice.

In an interview with me in 1996, Sergei Kovalyev, the former dissident and leading liberal politician, recalled a conversation with Chubais which offered a glimpse of this Machiavellian logic. 'They steal and steal and steal,' Chubais complained of the country's businessmen and their routinely corrupt practices. 'They are stealing absolutely everything and it is impossible to stop them. But let them steal and take their property. They will then become owners and decent administrators of this property.'

Chubais hoped he could craft a programme which would be impervious to the country's widespread corruption, and maybe even take advantage of it. Businessmen's greed would make them privatisation's most effective lobbyists; their corruption would stop once they became real owners. Kovalyev was less sanguine. 'From my point of view this is economic romanticism,' he confessed. 'There is a view that the country will become a market economy and then everything good will follow. Then there will be democracy. In my view it is a very dangerous mistake.'

A few years later, Kovalyev's misgivings would seem painfully prescient. The young reformers' astute political compromises did indeed allow them to achieve their over-arching goal – they created a market economy. But eventually, the corruption and the half-measures they had tolerated for the sake of expediency caught up with them. At the beginning, the ends had justified the means, but before long they would be jeopardised by them.

4

WHO GETS THE LOOT?

FOR THE FIRST few years, Russia's second revolution was about ideas. But once the young reformers had set their revolution in motion from above, a whole new struggle began. Russia's transformation was no longer just an ideological battle, a clash between dissident intellectuals and communist hard-liners. Instead, it became a fight over what all revolutions are ultimately about: Who gets the loot? Who would own the stuff – the rust-belt manufacturers, the Siberian oilfields, the Arctic diamonds – that the Russian state no longer had the will or the power to control?

In most revolutions, the answer to that question is simple; the revolutionaries confiscate the loot from their opponents and give it to their friends. The Jacobins beheaded the old French nobles and handed over their estates to the rising bourgeoisie. The Bolsheviks executed and exiled the Tsarist aristocrats and merchants and transferred their property to the state. Iran's ayatollahs expelled the Shah and his ruling class and nationalised their assets.

But Russia's capitalist revolutionaries were different. They quickly identified their friends and enemies: a new breed of aggressive, ostentatious entrepreneurs, eventually dubbed the New Russians, were the reformers' natural allies, while the old Soviet industrial bosses, known as the red directors, were their instinctive adversaries. Ideally, the reformers would have liked instantly to force out the communist industrial elite and usher in a new capitalist one. But if that wasn't possible, it didn't worry them too much. The main thing was to create a capitalist system: it didn't really matter who the capitalists were. For them, transforming Russia was sort of like writing a computer program. As long as they got the program right – as long as they created the proper capitalist incentive structure – everything else would automatically fall into place.

So the young reformers wrote their program – they set mass privatisation in motion – and then stepped back and let Russia's 147 million citizens fight it out. Most of the time, the struggle was between the red directors and the New Russians. Occasionally, foreign investors tried to get involved too. Always, the battle was about more than one specific plant somewhere out in the southern steppes or a single remote oilfield in the Arctic tundra. Each fight was a fight for dominance of the new Russia. Here are a few stories from the front line.

The Smartest Red Directors of All

The canniest players in the fight for the loot, and the most enduring ones, were the *gazoviki* and the *neftyaniki*, the natural gas and oil executives who managed the vast reserves of fossil fuels with which Russia is endowed. By nature and by experience, they did not seem particularly well adapted to the fledgling market economy; they were red directors, crimson-cheeked, heavy-drinking, fist-thumping princes of the Soviet Union's industrial nomenklatura. Yet somehow, once the dust had settled, the old-school *gazoviki* and *neftyaniki* had emerged as the most successful combatants in the struggle for economic dominance in the new era.

The secret of their phenomenal success was that they had the audacity to apply the basic privatisation principles, which had been designed for a worthless industrial base, to Russia's precious natural resources. The whole idea behind Chubais' privatisation drive was that it didn't really matter if Russia's factories were given away – the important thing was to transfer them to private owners. Where the Soviet rust-belt was concerned, that philosophy made some sense. But there was a world of difference between being given shares in an antiquated steel mill and shares in a vast natural gas-field. That difference was what made the *gazoviki* and *neftyaniki* the most powerful of Russia's new capitalists.

The mightiest of all were the unlikely capitalist duo of Viktor Chernomyrdin and Rem Vyakhirev, two middle-aged former Soviet gas engineers. A heavy-set man with a shaky grasp of Russian syntax and a plodding manner, Chernomyrdin was swiftly dismissed as a nonentity by the quick-witted Moscow intelligentsia when the parliament appointed him prime minister in late 1992, as a compromise replacement for the increasingly unpopular Gaidar. Yet it was the stolid Chernomyrdin who had masterminded the creation of Gazprom, capitalist Russia's dominant company.

As the Soviet cabinet minister for the oil and gas sector in the mid-1980s, he was one of the first industrial apparatchiks to spot how Gorbachev's perestroika might one day transform the country's entire economy. What other red directors saw as a threat, Chernomyrdin turned into an opportunity. In 1989 he brought the whole gas industry into a single company, then still state-owned, and became its chairman. The beauty of his strategy became clear after the young reformers' privatisation drive began to reshape Russian industry.

A massive 15 per cent of Gazprom was sold to the company's employees and management at a nominal rate. Ten per cent was retained by the company itself, 35 per cent sold to domestic investors – generally at closed auctions held in the remote Siberian regions where most natural gas is produced – and a golden 40 per cent stake was retained by the government. The Gazprom executives' power was further enhanced by a trust agreement between the cabinet, led by Chernomyrdin, and Vyakhirev, his former deputy who succeeded him as the head of Gazprom. The deal gave the Gazprom boss the right to manage the state stake and vote on the government's behalf at shareholder meetings. A further, secret agreement, which was later revoked by the state, gave the Gazprom management the option to buy additional shares far below their market value. Vyakhirev also had tremendous authority over the private shareholdings in his company: the Gazprom charter granted the company's management the right to veto all private transactions in the firm's shares.

As the first fuzzy outlines of Russia's post-communist economic landscape began to emerge, Gazprom towered over every other business in the land. It had 360,000 employees and, counting pensioners, family members and sub-contractors, supported an additional 6 million people. Gazprom controlled 30 per cent of the world's known natural gas reserves; it was Russia's single biggest hard-currency earner, and it accounted for about 8 per cent of the country's GDP. In 1996, when a leading Russian financial journal polled the country's top entrepreneurs and economists to determine the nation's most powerful businessmen, there was no contest: Vyakhirev of Gazprom was at the top.

Although the *gazoviki* were probably Russia's most successful capitalists, they were also among the most old-fashioned. Gazprom's biggest nod to the paternalistic traditions of the USSR was the subsidised prices – usually less than a tenth of the world level – at which it sold gas on the domestic market, and its tolerance of huge levels of non-payment by its Russian customers. On the face of it, Gazprom's support for state-controlled, artificially low gas prices seemed bizarre. But in a country where gas was a major source of heating, the chief source of cooking and an important fuel for electricity production, the subsidies gave Gazprom the right to claim, as Vyakhirev did in a conversation with me, that 'we heat and feed all of Russia'.

The political and financial advantages of playing such a role were inestimable. Gazprom was granted a number of generous tax concessions, including tax breaks to build up a special internal stabilisation fund. Although gas exports were regulated by licences and quotas, Gazprom itself was exempt from export tax, some import tariffs and VAT. According to Anders Aslund, a Swedish economist who is one of the company's most informed critics, Gazprom's package of tax breaks amounted to billions of dollars in lost state revenues every year.

These tax concessions, and Gazprom's close relationship with Chernomyrdin's cabinet, prompted many of the young reformers to attack the company as one of the biggest obstacles to the emergence of a liberal, transparent market economy. Western critics were even more virulent. Jeffrey Sachs, the Harvard economist who was one of the intellectual fathers of shock therapy, argued that Gazprom had been 'stolen' from the Russian people. Coming from one of the world's arch market reformers, his proposed solution was shocking: renationalisation followed by a more equitable privatisation of the company.

Unsurprisingly, Vyakhirev turned even more beet-coloured than usual when I put these charges to him. What was good for Gazprom, he insisted heatedly, was good for Russia: the government was absolutely justified in taking special care of its flagship; indeed, it would be folly to do otherwise. His argument, backed by Gazprom's tremendous economic and political muscle, worked. Gazprom shrugged off the young reformers' repeated attempts to curb its power and trim its privileges as languidly as Vyakhirev stubbed out the cigarettes he chain-smoked.

Vyakhirev was confident that Gazprom would endure no matter who Russia's political merry-go-round would spin into the Kremlin next. 'No matter who is in power, they won't start dividing the pipelines or give them to some collective farm,' he told me. 'The system cannot be disturbed. Without Gazprom, there is no Russia.'

This was the kind of ponderous comment which made Vyakhirev and the old-school Gazprom executives seem so out of place in the increasingly Westernised, fast-moving and sophisticated business culture of the new Russia. But two and a half years later, when the new Russian economy came crashing down to earth, I would remember Vyakhirev's words as being more than a little bit prescient. Russia's looming economic collapse would take down many of its newfangled high flyers. But the apparatchiks at Gazprom, who had kept one foot firmly planted in the Soviet past, and used their old-school connections to milk the state more effectively than the most resourceful entrepreneur, were left standing. Rem was right: warts and all, Gazprom really was Russia.

The New Russians Win: Showdown in the Arctic Circle

On a clear blue morning in the middle of February 1996, with the slam of a door that would not quite shut and the whirr of helicopter blades, I was on my way to Gaz-Sala, a remote settlement of 2,000 people north of the Arctic Circle. The only reason why people lived this close to the North Pole was to search for more of Russia's abundant natural gas and oil reserves, and in Gaz-Sala the company which did that was Zapolarneftegazgeologia (ZNGG), a small seismic exploration and drilling enterprise.

For savvy New Russians, companies like ZNGG – known as geologias – were a potential Klondike. The main work they did – geological exploration on contract to the larger companies – was not particularly lucrative. But, thanks to a loophole in Russian legislation, in theory the geologias also had the right to obtain production licences for any oil and gas they discovered on the territory they were chartered to explore. That made the geologias a back door into the Russian oil and gas industry. For those investors smart enough to realise it, the geologias were a way of buying access to potentially millions of dollars' worth of fossil fuels for mere kopeks.

Naturally, like the communist-era managers of all Soviet companies, the directors of the geologias were not keen to surrender their enterprises to outsiders. The remoteness of the Arctic magnified the power every Soviet director enjoyed, making the heads of the geologias more like feudal lords than mere managers. A lifetime spent enduring the hardships of the far north also sharpened their resentment of outsiders who sought to use the privatisation process to win control of companies the directors had come to think of as 'theirs'.

Just getting to Gaz-Sala was a major expedition. I travelled the final leg of my three-day journey with vodka rubbed on my face by anxious fellow-travellers to ward off frostbite and wrapped up in newspapers like a pinata to provide an extra layer of insulation under my coat and boots. When we finally arrived I was astonished, and not just because I had survived the trip. It was one of those absolutely still northern days which are the coldest, but also the most beautiful. The silent and seductive landscape was a world away from the metropolitan grime and big-city politics of Moscow. But even here, at the edge of civilisation, Russia's capitalist revolution was making itself felt.

I began to learn the story of the battle for ZNGG a few hundred metres away from the helicopter landing pad, in the two-storey headquarters of the company which was perched on stilts above the treacherous permafrost. The ramshackle building dominated the sad little street which passed as Gaz-Sala's centre and had the thrown-together, almost intentionally ugly look of most settlements in the far north. Inside I met Joseph Piradashvili, the acting director of ZNGG and the local representative of Kakha Bendukidze, the sharp Moscow-based New Russian entrepreneur who had launched the battle for the company.

A small, energetic man with thick black hair, chocolate-brown eyes, soft hands and the elaborately courteous manners of his native Georgia,

Piradashvili was not the sort of person I had expected to encounter at the edge of the world, at the eye of a corporate war. In what Russians called their 'past life' – meaning life before the collapse of the USSR – Piradashvili had been a theoretical physicist in Tbilisi, an ancient, elegant city of cobblestoned streets and sidewalk cafés. But the disintegration of the Soviet Union had thrust Georgia into civil war and desperate poverty. Piradashvili, in his late thirties and with two children, needed a new job.

So one day in late December 1994, he phoned Bendukidze, a fellow-Georgian and old university buddy, who had hustled his way into business in Moscow producing chemicals for laboratories then had quickly expanded into everything from trading cigarettes to refining oil. Three days after making the call, Piradashvili was putting up posters around Gaz-Sala, part of a team trying to buy enough shares in ZNGG to give Bendukidze majority control.

Oleg Kudrin, the company's pugnacious and hard-drinking red director, put up a powerful defence. He stoked the suspicions of the already sceptical locals, claiming that the outsiders were dangerous Georgian *mafiosi*. Helicopter operators, part of the Soviet industrial establishment in which Kudrin was an influential figure, would not allow Bendukidze's employees to fly with them. When the group chartered their own helicopters, they were refused permission to land. When they finally managed physically to arrive in the town, the two local hotels – both controlled by ZNGG – would not rent them rooms. The best they could do was persuade one sympathetic resident to rent them his three-room apartment – a tight squeeze for 10 men living in isolation for nearly half a year.

By June 1995, the team's tenacity and deep pockets had paid off. Bendukidze's group had bought up over 54 per cent of the enterprise, paying more than a hundred times the initial price for the last few vital shares. Legally, Bendukidze now owned ZNGG. But the fight did not end there. Accustomed by long years of Soviet experience to treating the enterprise he managed as effectively his personal property, Kudrin, like thousands of other red directors, refused to hand over control to an outsider whose only claim to ZNGG was that he had bought it.

One of the most popular and most effective ways of keeping the new owners out was the one Kudrin used against Bendukidze; he refused to enter the outsiders' holdings in the shareholder register. It was a widespread tactic, and before long fund managers in New York and London were complaining about managerial tampering with share-holder registers, warning that the lack of safeguards for investor rights would dissuade many outsiders from bringing their capital to Russia.

Like many Western investors, Bendukidze responded by taking Kudrin to court. Bendukidze won. But, back in Gaz-Sala, the court's ruling had no effect. In a symptom of the weakening of the Russian state, which was felt in thousands of similar cases across the country, the government lacked the muscle to enforce its laws on the ground.

So, Piradashvili took matters into his own hands. On 20 July – one of those endless northern summer days – when Kudrin was out of town Piradashvili and his team, feeling a bit ridiculous, 'like actors in a Western', walked into the ZNGG headquarters and took over the company by force.

These commando-style tactics were the beginning of a surreal three-month stand-off which Piradashvili described as 'like something out of Gogol'. The Bendukidze group held their ground in the managers' office and began to issue a stream of orders. Meanwhile, the old management continued to occupy the rest of the building and issue their own edicts. In practice, the old management still ruled the roost, but they couldn't evict the capitalist cuckoo either.

Like any military siege, the stalemate was both mind-numbingly tense and excruciatingly boring. At one point, Kudrin threatened to shoot the interlopers to force them out of town. To keep themselves amused, the occupiers played computer games. Throughout, Piradashvili and his team knew that all of their telephone conversations with Bendukidze were being bugged. They were on the verge of buying a scrambler when the two men realised it would be cheaper and easier simply to revert to Georgian, their mother-tongue.

The conflict only ended in October, when the brief riotous blooming of the tundra and the midnight sun had already given way to 3-foot snowbanks and lengthening nights. Neither the duelling cowboys in Gaz-Sala nor the ineffectual local courts managed to resolve the struggle. As with so many things in Russia, it was only settled when the power-brokers in Moscow made a deal.

After months of negotiating, Bendukidze reached an agreement with the Moscow financial group that had been backing the red director. The opposition on the ground in Gaz-Sala evaporated.

Bendukidze was now the uncontested owner of what he hoped was an embryonic oil company, and Piradashvili was appointed the enterprise's new manager.

It seemed like a victory for Russia's market revolution. Not only had ZNGG been privatised, but ownership had been transferred to the sort of aggressive entrepreneurs that Chubais hoped would eventually acquire most of Russia's assets. With progressive, Westernised owners and managers like Bendukidze and Piradashvili in charge – men driven by the profit-motive, not the party *diktat* – the young reformers in Moscow were confident the Russian economy would emerge from terminal decline into robust growth.

But up in frozen Gaz-Sala, Piradashvili discovered it was not quite as simple as that. For one thing, during the era of dual power, while the rival directors had duked it out from neighbouring offices, the company had been 'paralysed' and its financial health had deteriorated precipitously.

ZNGG's difficulties were exacerbated by bizarre decisions which Kudrin had taken in his effort to adapt to the strange new economic rules being imposed by the reformers in Moscow. For example, Kudrin had decided to use ZNGG's slender financial reserves to play the stock market. Like so many of Russia's enthusiastic but inexperienced investors, he had been ripped off. Piradashvili and ZNGG were left with his losses.

Another problem for Piradashvili, and the thousands of other New Russian managers across the country, was the corrosive legacy of the Soviet past. Like every enterprise in the Soviet Union, ZNGG had been created and run to suit the needs of the centrally planned economy. These were usually wildly at odds with the market conditions which were gradually coming to predominate. Restructuring ZNGG – and indeed the entire Russian economy – would ultimately prove far harder than privatising it.

For Piradashvili, the hardest thing to do was sacking the hundreds of superfluous workers which the communist system had given managers implicit incentives to employ.

'People come to me with tears in their eyes and beg for their wages and their jobs, and I must be hard and refuse,' he told me. 'I have become like a caricature of the evil capitalists I used to read about in school as a child.'

What made the lay-offs particularly traumatic was the country's paternalistic tradition. Life in the Soviet Union was oppressed and uncomfortable, but the workers' state was true to its communist credo at least in so far as it offered almost all of its citizens the right to a job, however unpleasant or poorly paid. Within a few months, Yeltsin's capitalist revolution had swept away those guarantees and dissolved the savings that might have cushioned people's transition.

The economic deformities of the Soviet era were not Piradashvili's only problem. Russia's new economy, still floating in a limbo between communism and capitalism, imposed its own distortions. The most crippling of them, and the one which would prove the most difficult to unravel, was the web of inter-enterprise debt.

Russia's hulking monopolies, partially privatised behemoths that controlled energy and transport and had no incentive to adapt fully to the market economy, were at the centre of the arrears web. These monopolists, a group which included Gazprom, allowed other enterprises to accumulate huge unpaid arrears to them. Burdened by massive debts, these smaller enterprises were unable to pay one another, or the government, or their workers. That made it difficult for the government to pay its own bills to everyone ranging from pensioners to arms factories, to energy suppliers. The energy and transport monopolists in turn amassed huge debts to the government and to their own suppliers.

For many people, the arrears crisis was a financial bonanza which served as a smokescreen, obscuring the significance of transactions in what was supposed to be a market economy. Behind the veil of arrears, managers could steal from their own companies, pay one another kickbacks, defraud the state and bribe bureaucrats.

But for progressive managers like Piradashvili, the debt-web was a tremendous obstacle in the effort to create profitable, financially transparent companies. When Piradashvili finally took over ZNGG in the autumn of 1995, the company owed Rbs 42bn in back taxes. But it was owed almost three-quarters as much by the government and Gazprom, for which ZNGG worked as a contractor. Because the arrears crisis was as much a political creature as an economic one, these debts had a chimerical nature which made them particularly difficult to manage.

As Piradashvili put it: 'It's a strange sort of debt which can get larger or smaller all by itself. Yeltsin says one thing, or signs some decree in Moscow, and the debt changes.'

For the ordinary people of settlements like Gaz-Sala, Russia's bizarre metastising web of debt had one very practical consequence: wage arrears which meant that salaries were paid months, and in some places years, late. When I travelled to Gaz-Sala I was accompanied by three armed bodyguards carrying a suitcase stuffed with a third of a million dollars' worth of roubles. The injection of cash was part of Piradashvili's effort to reduce ZNGG's wage debt from the Rbs 9bn burden he inherited to Rbs 4bn after our delivery of roubles had been distributed.

After a happy day doling out the money from Moscow, Piradashvili invited me to join him and Vladimir Semianiv, the local policeman, for supper at one of the town's three private restaurants. Stepping into Svetlana's Place was one of the most encouraging moments of my visit.

Warm, clean and cheerfully decorated, with the hearty atmosphere of a Mom and Pop's truck-stop somewhere in the Midwest, Svetlana's Place was an exception to the general gloom of Gaz-Sala. If someone in such a remote town had been enterprising enough to open a restaurant like this, I thought as we sat down, then the outlook for Russian capitalism must be pretty bright.

My optimism did not last for long. Within a few moments vodka and its traditional accompaniments – rye bread, pickles and marinated mushrooms – had arrived, and Vladimir launched into the ritualised lament about the new Russia which I had heard dozens of times over the past few years.

'People here have worked hard all their lives, freezing and finding oil,' Vladimir, a tall, lanky Afghan war veteran with a perky moustache and two gold teeth, declaimed. 'Now, they have all lost their savings overnight. Worst of all, now some people have become very rich, while others have become very poor. I'm surprised we haven't had a public revolt.'

After a second shot of vodka, Vladimir became more poetic and began to embroider on a rhetorical question that was a kind of popular chorus for the people of the far north: 'What I can't understand is how the Arabs in the desert could create for themselves a paradise on earth, while we live in hell. We live on top of a fortune, but we live like beggars.'

It got worse: soon Vladimir was telling me that half the townspeople were alcoholics, that freezing to death in the 5-foot snowbanks after a particularly nasty bender was one of the most common causes of death, and that the settlement's pensioners – who had expected a comfortable retirement on 'the earth' as the people of the Arctic called anywhere south of the permafrost line – had instead become 'prisoners of the north', trapped because their life savings had been devalued by Gaidar's price liberalisation.

To my relief, this pessimistic litany was interrupted by the arrival of our first course: a pinkish slab of a northern fish called shchokur which is rich in vitamins and tasty. Vladimir and Joseph told me that shchokur, eaten in raw, half-frozen slices dipped into a spicy sauce, was 'the ice-cream of the Arctic'.

Introducing a foreigner to a strange local delicacy seemed to lighten the mood and, by the time we got to our fourth shot of vodka, Joseph and Vladimir grew more optimistic. They regaled me with stories of northern hardships fought and mastered. How thick the mosquitos were in the summer, but also how rich the tundra was, for a few precious days, in berries and wild-life. How, in the winter, the snowy landscape and ivory horizon grew so indistinguishable that driving was impossible. But also how – as I would learn when I left the settlement before dawn the next morning – driving by night, with powerful headlights, was a way to outmanoeuvre nature's white-out.

'You can see the people here as prisoners of the north, but that is not the only way to see them,' Joseph said. 'The people here are men who take masculine pride in the brave and difficult work they do. They are women who want to live with their menfolk. It is not just the rejects who are here, but good hard-working people, people who deserve a better life than bad managers have given them. We are here to further our corporate interests, of course, but we also hope that our efforts will lead to an improvement in their lives.'

They were also people, Joseph said, who, like the rest of their countrymen, were taking their first few breaths of freedom. Liberty was unaccustomed, and difficult to adapt to, but it was exhilarating. 'Last year, this town faced a real and difficult choice,' Joseph explained. 'You had to work with us or with Kudrin, the old manager. People here, and in Russia as a whole, are not accustomed to making choices. The whole idea of making choices is difficult, but it is also exciting. This is the victory of Russian democracy. Even here, in a town that appears on no maps, it is being felt and that's why I think democracy has a great future in our country.'

Vladimir agreed: 'Let us have choices, even bad choices, because that is better than no choice at all.'

And, with that, Joseph proposed our fifth and final toast: 'I perfectly understand its defects, but, all the same, let's drink to Russia's new democracy. To freedom!'

The Foreigners Win: Cats, Rats and Beer

A few weeks after joining Joseph in his toast, I was drinking to Russia's future with another group of enterprising company directors in another remote province. The hopes and fears expressed around that heavily laden table were much the same, but these were toasts with one important difference. Our tipple of choice was beer, rather than the more traditional vodka, because the enterprise whose prospects we were rooting for was the Perm Brewery, in the eponymous city in Russia's geographical heartland.

Perm Brewery's initiation into capitalism was a world apart from the physical struggle which raged in Gaz-Sala. For a start, the factory's transition from state control to outside proprietors was a gentle, conciliatory process. And the brewery's new owners didn't just fly in from distant Moscow, they came from New Delhi.

Russia has an ancient and volatile relationship with foreign entrepreneurs. The first eastern Slavic state – Kievan Rus, based in what is now Ukraine – was founded by Scandinavian merchant princes. Some of the younger scions of the trading clan were sent up north, eventually forming what became the first Russian city-states and the country's royal dynasty. The Mongols, bitterly resented for imposing what Russian historians dubbed the 'Tartar Yoke' on medieval Russia, introduced a business relationship with the outside world of a different kind: for two centuries, the Mongol overlords exacted heavy tributes from the Russian princes, constraining the region's social and economic development but also opening up trade routes to the East.

Imperial Russia continued this love-hate relationship with businesses and business ideas from abroad. Peter the Great spent a year as a lowly apprentice in Dutch and English shipyards and imported foreign tradesmen en masse. Yet he also introduced Russia's first comprehensive protective tariff and treated the country's fledgling industrialists, both foreign and native, as vassals, utterly subservient to the will of the tsar. Subsequent Russian rulers, including the Bolsheviks, continued this schizophrenic pattern, seeking to acquire foreign know-how but often rejecting the foreigners themselves.

Boris Yeltsin's Russia exhibited the same ambivalence. On the one hand, the capitalist revolution and its chief architects, the young reformers, were strongly in favour of foreign investment. They knew the moribund Soviet economy needed external capital and know-how to be rebuilt. But, in practice, the new Russian economy was often hostile to foreign investors. A business culture that relied far more on personal ties than on the rule of law tended to automatically discriminate against outsiders. Where 'strategic' sectors of the economy such as the defence industry or natural resources were concerned, the bias became overt, with official restrictions on foreign participation.

These barriers, and the lingering failure of market reforms to deliver economic growth, kept direct foreign investment far below the Russian government's hopes – and below the international norm. Indeed in 1997, the year of the country's strongest economic performance since the collapse of communism, little-league Peru attracted more direct foreign investment than the former Soviet superpower.

But a few adventurous outsiders were undeterred. For these buccaneers, Russia's mass privatisation drive represented, in the words of one American, 'the sale of the century' and they were determined to get in while the bargains lasted. One of them was Shiv Khemka. Like many of the first wave of foreign investors, his family had been doing business with the USSR since the 1950s, when the special relationship between non-aligned India and the Soviet Union was at its apogee. When Russia launched its market revolution, the Khemkas suddenly had an opportunity to build their Soviet-era connections into big business.

Shiv, the eldest son, was delegated to spearhead the family's new Russian campaign. A teetotalling vegetarian with a coffee complexion, a hooked, patrician nose and the plummy accent and almost painfully good manners of his Eton education, Shiv, who was in his mid-twenties when I met him in 1992, seemed disastrously ill-suited for the vodka-slurping, meat-chomping, earthy masculinity of Russia's nascent business culture. But in the spring of 1996, when I joined him on a visit to the Perm Brewery, I discovered a foreign investment which, ever so slowly, seemed to be starting to work.

From the moment in the early 1990s when they decided to focus on the beer business – by 1996 the family owned several Russian breweries and a separate distribution company – the Khemkas owed their survival in Russia's rough young marketplace to two basic tenets: a sensitivity to the political constraints on foreign investment and a boundless faith in the country's economic prospects.

It was thanks to the first principle that the family chose the humble world of beer rather than sexier sectors like oil and gas. Like most out-side investors, the Khemkas were initially attracted to the country's wildly undervalued and easily exportable natural resources. But Shiv's father's old apparatchik friends, many of them powerful figures in the conservative defence industry, warned that foreign investors in such high-profile areas risked becoming the targets of overt nationalist polit-ical attacks or more subtle back-room manoeuvring.

Their second principle, an adamantine confidence in the coming Russian economic boom, narrowed the choice down to beer. Beer has a marginal role in the life of the Russian drinker. With its wimpish 3 or 4 per cent alcohol content, it is treated as it was in medieval Europe as a soft drink rather than a genuine alcoholic beverage. The peak daily consumption of beer is between 6 and 8 a.m. at breakfast time, and in stores it is sold next to the mineral water and Coca Cola.

By contrast, vodka has pride of place as a 'real' drink. Russian drinkers guzzle 83 per cent of the world's vodka, Shiv informed me during our flight to Perm, with the average Russian drinking 2.5 times as much vodka as the total hard liquor consumption of the average American. Consumer-trend specialists predicted that if Russians were to become richer they would adopt Western drinking patterns, switching from vodka to the gentler pleasures of beer. For the optimistic Khemkas, that made beer the perfect choice: it was like buying an option in Russia's future prosperity.

Picking a sector turned out to be the easy part. As the Khemkas started to try to acquire majority stakes in newly privatised Russian breweries like Kakha Bendukidze, they began to clash with entrenched red directors. At one brewery, the director used his majority control of the enterprise to dilute the Khemkas' 20 per cent stake to just 3 per cent, a legerdemain which foreign investors in all branches of the econ-omy would suffer. At another brewery, this time in Siberia, a factory director who initially had welcomed the Khemkas' interest and offered to assist them in buying his brewery decided at the last minute to buy a 51 per cent stake himself.

For Shiv, each of these setbacks was a lesson in the evolving art of Russian capitalism. The Perm Brewery, which the Khemkas acquired in 1999, was a crucial part of the learning process. Although it was the first brewery the Khemkas bought, the Perm Brewery was not an obvious choice. Perm was one of the engine rooms of the Soviet Union's collossal Cold War arms build-up. Until 1989, the city was closed to foreigners and a whopping 70 per cent of the local economy was devoted to military production. When Shiv and I visited in 1996, the legacy of that period was still visible in the dramatic designs which the Mig jets based in the city traced across the skyline every night.

However, in a typical Soviet pattern, heavy spending on the defence sector left few resources for producing consumer goods, including beer. When Shiv first toured the Perm Brewery in 1991, he was horrified: 'It was the biggest disaster I'd ever seen. There were rats running around. There were cats to kill the rats. There was mould hanging from the ceiling like vines. No one was smiling, everyone looked depressed. You needed galoshes to walk around. There were no lights on. It was only operating at 20 per cent capacity, and the beer was undrinkable.'

Not surprisingly, Shiv crossed the brewery off his list. But his technical team urged him to take a second look. Beneath the mould, they said, there was a functional factory. So, the Khemkas began to woo Sergei Mitirev, the Soviet-era director, and the Perm regional government. By June 1993, their efforts paid off and the Khemkas acquired a 75 per cent stake in the Perm Brewery.

Three years later, the brewery's capitalist transformation was well on its way. The walls and floors gleamed with fresh coats of brightly coloured paint, and plants adorned the corridors. Profits and production standards had improved too. Production was up by more than 30 per cent; the shelf-life of Viking, the brewery's beer, had been extended from 5 days to 90 days; the company was in the black.

A key factor in the brewery's metamorphosis was Mitirev's enthusiastic participation. Having been outwitted and double-crossed by red directors at other enterprises, at Perm, the Khemkas set out to co-opt their potential antagonist. Even after their take-over, Mitirev, a jovial red-faced, barrel-chested manager of the old school, still enjoyed all the pomp and circumstance of the old industrial class. He retained his title, his long narrow office the size of some pre-revolutionary ballroom, and an antechamber staffed with two heavily made-up, bored-looking secretaries whose chief occupations seemed to be watching soap operas and humiliating unimportant visitors.

Better still, life with the Khemkas had brought Mitirev a whole new set of perks. He had been taken on tours of state-of-the-art breweries in the West; he and the four other Soviet-era managers of the Khemka breweries were sent on company-sponsored group vacations to the tropics. And Mitirev had been given shadow stock options – bonuses linked to the company's performance – which would probably make him a very wealthy man.

'We honour them, we make sure they are well off, we give them performance-based bonuses,' Shiv explained. 'All of our directors should become millionaires in dollar terms.'

But what the Khemkas were careful not to do was give the old directors any unchecked financial authority. A few doors down from Mitirev's status-symbol office was a cramped room full of foreign men in suits perched over notebook computers. There were no dragon-secretaries guarding the entrance to this room and it lacked the long, rectangular dark wood power-meeting table which no self-respecting Soviet manager can do without. Yet it was here, with the Khemka group's hand-picked team of foreign accountants, that the real power resided.

'We have control of the finances of the company – earlier, there was leakage,' was Shiv's tactful explanation.

Perry Moi, the chief accountant, was less oblique. One example of the 'leakage' which the brewery suffered before tight external financial control was imposed was Mitirev's plan to reface the outside of the plant with granite. It seemed like an absurd gesture – extravagant and impractical – until Moi discovered that the supplier of the overpriced granite was one of the old management's best friends.

Instances like this explain why the Khemkas, like most foreign investors in Russia, quickly learned to distance Soviet-era managers from the money side of their business. But they did so as tactfully as possible. For one thing, Mitirev's technical expertise and knowledge of the company's work-force helped to keep the plant ticking. More crucially, as a former member of the regional nomenklatura Mitirev was plugged into the local establishment. For the Khemkas, his connections were vital, especially when it came to the all-important issue of taxation. Taxes and their cousins, a thicket of government regulations, often determined whether a company turned a profit or made a loss. But the level at which taxes were levied, and the rigour with which regulations were imposed, was more a question of politics than economics.

It was, as Shiv put it, 'a very interactive process'. And in this process of interaction, Mitirev's cooperation was a huge advantage in ensuring that the brewery was still seen as part of the local power structure, rather than a foreign cash-cow to be milked for all the money the provincial authorities could extract.

Mitirev's local contacts also proved useful to the brewery in another respect. Perm's bloated under-employed defence plants hugely complicated the region's efforts to adapt to the market economy; but for the brewery they became a useful local resource. Mitirev and the Khemkas negotiated with a Perm factory which used to produce shells to turn its expertise to building brewing equipment. The results were excellent, and just a fifth of the price of imported machinery.

The Khemkas hoped to do more than harness the expertise of Perm's arms manufacturers. The key to reviving their decrepit brewery – and the Russian economy as a whole – Shiv believed, was to recapture the vigorous sweating enthusiasm that had powered Russia's transformation from European hinterland to Cold War superpower.

'What we have to do is turn the cold war drive to succeed into a business drive,' Shiv told me. 'When you come out to factories like this, and see the change which has been accomplished in just two or three years, you can see that that is beginning to happen. To me, it gives me the feeling that market reforms will work.'

We concluded our visit to the brewery with the obligatory feast, including vegetarian dishes especially prepared for Shiv. Mitirev made the final toast, in the effusive Russian tradition: 'We used to be one of the worst breweries in Russia, and all the defence factories looked down on us. But now we pay our wages on time and when we go to trade fairs we are respected, even feared. Everyone knows Viking beer and everyone knows it comes from Perm. Soon, Russia will get richer and people will drink more Viking.'

We all raised our glasses of the reddish Viking brew – except for Shiv, who toasted the plant's success with mineral water.

The Red Director Wins: The Tsar and God vs the $100 Million Journalist

The Perm Brewery and ZNGG were the kind of local dramas which Gaidar and Chubais had hoped to catalyse when they launched their capitalist revolution. But a far more typical story was the one that was played out in Novosibirsk, the gateway to the Siberian steppes which was dubbed the Russian Chicago when it was founded just over a century ago.

One of the city's chief enterprises was the Novosibirsk Tin Factory, Russia's only tin producer and the biggest plant of its kind in Europe. With 1,300 employees and a product which could be readily exported for hard currency, this factory was one of Novosibirsk's most attractive companies.

But at the Novosibirsk Tin Factory, the capitalist revolution did not bring in the money and know-how of a foreign investor or a New Russian entrepreneur. Instead, privatisation entrenched the position of Aleksandr Dugelny, the factory's Soviet-era red director, transforming him from party comrade to independent capitalist.

Dugelny was not alone. In a survey of 2,000 Russian enterprises, Joseph Blasi, a Rutgers University professor who was part of the team of Western economists advising Chubais and the GKI, concluded that two-thirds of medium and large-sized Russian companies had ended up in the control of their old managers after privatisation. This was the great irony at the heart of Russia's capitalist revolution: thanks to the political compromises which Chubais had made to push through privatisation, the red directors, the aristocrats of the old order, became the biggest beneficiaries of its collapse.

Even though the young reformers had already loaded the legal dice in their favour, many red directors could not resist taking extra liberties, manipulating the power they had enjoyed in the old system so as to give themselves an even greater stake in the companies they managed. For a few months, the Novosibirsk Tin Factory became a national symbol of this sleazier side of nomenklatura privatisation.

It owed its fleeting notoriety to the efforts of one crusader – Sasha Bekker. A small thin man with desperately nerdy Soviet-style glasses, an old-testament beard and the neurotic energy of a Russian Woody Allen, Bekker was a Novosibirsk native who had moved to Moscow in 1983 and become one of the country's leading economic journalists and advocates of market reform. He was also a Rottweiler of a reporter.

In the spring of 1994, Dugelny and his bureaucratic backers had the misfortune to pass onto the radar screen of this reporting fanatic. The injustice at the Novosibirsk Tin Factory became Bekker's personal campaign, and within a few months the factory and its manner of privatisation became a national *cause célèbre*.

'I saw Dugelny as an insult to my ideas of honour, of decency, of patriotism,' Bekker told me. 'He represented all of the people who were preventing us from building a normal economy.' In 1995, Bekker persuaded me to join him on a trip to Novosibirsk to see for myself how the red directors were taking over the new Russia.

Our first encounter was with Anna Gumerova, the former head of the factory's securities department. A pretty 35-year-old brunette, Gumerova was as passionate about the sins of the Novosibirsk Tin Factory as Bekker was. As I struggled to stay awake after our 'red-eye' flight from Moscow, the two crusaders explained what Dugelny had done and how they had tried to stop him.

Just 34 years old when he was appointed director of the tin factory in 1987, Dugelny had been something of a wunderkind. He was popular with the 'workers collective' and was an influential member of the regional establishment; he could, as Gumerova put it – using a Russian colloquialism for the well connected, go to any office in Novosibirsk and 'open the door with his foot'.

He was progressive, too. While other Soviet factory directors were fighting Gorbachev's tentative efforts to introduce market reforms, Dugelny threw himself and his plant into the transformation. Even before the collapse of the Soviet Union, he was chafing to go further. In 1989, he wrote an article in a Novosibirsk magazine complaining that the market transition was not moving swiftly enough. Why were the *kooperators*, the small private businessmen allowed to set up firms in the late 1980s, the only people who were getting rich? Surely the managers of the country's largest factories, like Dugelny himself, should be getting a piece of the action?

Then the Soviet Union fell apart and Dugelny got his chance. He was such an enthusiastic supporter of the privatisation drive that his plant became the first in the vast Novosibirsk region to be sold off. From the point of view of the young reformers in Moscow, that made him one of the rare good guys, a Soviet director who couldn't wait for his factory to be transferred to private hands. 'Dugelny wanted to buy state property as quickly and cheaply as he could,' said Gumerova, who at the time was Dugelny's economic adviser.

There was just one problem. Dugelny was so determined to sell his plant off quickly, and to make sure that he was its new private owner, that he wasn't about to let mere laws slow him down. He systematically undervalued the factory's assets, making it easier to buy it up, and manipulated an 'investment tender' through which part of the plant was sold off, ensuring the stake went to a company to which he was closely connected. Troubled that these measures might be illegal, Gumerova, who was now running the factory's securities programme, began to ask a few awkward questions. But she was young, unconnected and female. No one, least of all Dugelny, took her seriously.

Then Dugelny launched a new campaign to increase his stake in the factory and Gumerova's criticisms became impossible to ignore. As we have seen, Russia's mass privatisation programme granted a generous stake in privatised companies to the rank-and-file labourers who worked there. Dugelny wanted those shares – altogether more than 50 per cent of the company – for himself. To get them, he set up a system of carrots and sticks to cajole workers into selling their shares back to a company fund which he controlled. At the heart of the scheme was a pool of consumer goods, ranging from television sets to stockings, which Dugelny bought using company revenues. Workers were encouraged to trade in their shares for these consumer goods.

Beyond Dugelny's use of company money to increase his own control over the plant, what really infuriated Gumerova were his underhanded tactics. These included not paying factory workers their regular wages so that they had no alternative but to sell their shares to survive. Gumerova began explaining to the factory workers that selling their shares to the company was not their only option. ('To make people real owners, it's not enough just to give them shares, you have to educate them as well,' she believed.) But most of Anna's fellow-employees were still too scared to defy their boss.

'Dugelny had a powerful instrument. He decides who keeps his job and this is especially important in a city like Novosibirsk, when people at so many factories are being fired,' she said. 'At the Novosibirsk Tin Factory, Dugelny was like a tsar and a god.'

By the time I met Gumerova in the spring of 1995, she had been forced out of her job. Dugelny had simply stopped paying her wages until she had had no choice but to leave; she had received anonymous death threats late at night over the telephone; young thugs had warned her to drop her campaign – or else . . . But still Gumerova carried on. Like Bekker, she had begun to see the Novosibirsk Tin Factory as a metaphor for everything that was wrong with Russia's capitalist trans-formation. It was Gumerova, together with two colleagues, who first found Bekker and tipped him off to the story: 'Once he wrote his first article, the state machine began to notice.'

Yana Rogozhina, a Novosibirsk prosecutor, began to pursue Dugelny through the civil courts, ignoring pressure from his friends in the local government and condemnation from market reformers in the media who worried that the furore threatened to block the devel-opment of the new economy. At the same time, the organised crime unit of the local police department started to try to build a criminal case against Dugelny, who they suspected had embezzled profits from the export of the plant's tin. Sergei Afanasiev, a 29-year-old police detective, was in charge of the investigation and his office was our next stop.

The room Afanasiev shared with his partner was on the second floor of a dilapidated fire station. It had all the usual markings of a post-Soviet bureaucrat's habitat – a dusting of paint drifting off the walls, lots of wooden desks crowded into a small space, bulky, ancient tele-phones – but with a cops-and-robbers' edge: a few pistols, resting casually in their holsters, lay on one desk, and a topless pin-up girl gig-gled into the room from a poster in the corner.

Afanasiev matched his slightly louche environment perfectly. He was tall and dark, with the razor-sharp cheekbones and brooding look of the Russian steppe. When he wasn't sucking on a vile locally-made ciga-rette, he was playing with his lighter – a bright red bit of plastic adorned by a drawing of a busty brunette and the word Lolita.

By tracing the trail of metal leaving the Novosibirsk Tin Factory, Afanasiev had found several firms which he alleged Dugelny was using as dummy companies to conceal his profits abroad: one in Lichtenstein, one in Singapore and one in the UK. Afanasiev wasn't surprised by the sordid turn privatisation seemed to have taken. 'The ideas were good on paper, but when they began to be applied in real life they took the Russian path, and we know what that means – Russians steal.' But he was worried by it. His biggest fear was that the current injustices would lay gunpowder trails for future social protests, which is why he was so committed to righting what wrongs he could now.

'My job is necessary to prevent a new social revolt,' Afanasiev told me. 'Already, some nationalist politicians are saying to the people: look boys, you were robbed. It is very sad that our New Russians do not understand this.'

Predictably enough, Afanasiev's bosses in the regional government and in Moscow did not share his zeal. But he was undeterred: 'The time has passed when all it took was a telephone call to stop our work. Look, our country is in an absurd position. We are begging for $6bn from the IMF when twice that amount of money, from places like the tin factory, leaves the country as capital flight every year.'

The next day, I went to see the man Afanasiev was trying to stop: Dugelny. After a day of denunciations, it had been hard to imagine Dugelny as anything but an ogre. Yet, in the flesh, he was charm itself. A vigorous 42-year-old with a thatch of greying hair, he looked modern but not too modern. His sharp suit and mobile telephone distinguished him from those hard-core red directors who still clung to the personal accessories of the Soviet era. But he wasn't suspiciously flashy either, at least not by the over-the-top standards of the New Russians.

His spiel matched his look. Dugelny saw himself as a forward-thinking, reform-minded manager who had had the courage and the insight to support privatisation from the outset. He might have bent a few rules along the way, but so did everyone else. The campaign against him, he believed, was motivated by nothing more noble than envy.

'For other directors, privatisation was a tragedy, for me it was an opportunity,' he told me proudly. 'I made only one mistake – I lived in euphoria about the change in our country, the new developments. I didn't count on the fact that the old mentality of envying and opposing those people who achieve more remains, and that my success would attract enemies.'

Now that those envious enemies had materialised, Dugelny was fighting back. His strongest argument against the policemen, prosecutors and journalists accusing him of privatising the plant illegally was the one which, sotto voce, was being made by some of the young reformers in Moscow. All right, Dugelny said; even if, for the sake of argument, I admit to having broken a few laws, what difference does that make now? The privatisation process is finished and to begin questioning its legality is to open a Pandora's Box of legal and political problems.

'What is the point of all of these court hearings?' Dugelny asked me. 'The factory has been privatised. How would the state benefit if it were renationalised? To do that would be against the interests of society, against the interests of the shareholders and against the interests of the whole new market economy we are trying to create. Since the beginning of all this I've asked – what is our goal? To abide by the letter of the law or to create a prosperous market economy? I ask myself, why did I work so hard when now they are threatening to take it all away from me? Maybe I should just emigrate to the West.'

I listened to Dugelny's arguments with a growing sense of unease. He was probably the greedy bully his opponents had described, but I had a queasy feeling that he might have a point. Enriching red directors like Dugelny had been the political price the young reformers had paid, part of the social compact they had struck with the old Soviet elite. Dugelny was acting within the confines of that unofficial deal. His sins had been venal and, in a country which lost billions of dollars a year in capital flight, if he had pilfered it had been on a relatively petty scale. Dugelny was a rather sordid poster boy for Russia's capitalist revolution – but he was probably an appropriate one.

Eventually, the legal case provoked by Bekker's articles reached the highest stage in the Russian appeal process. When it got there, the courts and the procuracy finally balked. Dugelny and the management of the plant were found guilty of violating several laws, but the federal authorities decided it was too late to do anything about it. The factory management paid a token fine – whittled down to almost nothing by raging inflation – and Dugelny kept his majority stake.

'He is now more entrenched at the plant than ever,' Bekker told me after the final decision. 'He fought like a lion for his property and he won.'

After Bekker's years of fanatical obsession with the factory, I assumed he would be depressed. The red director and his backers had triumphed; it seemed to be a personal defeat for Bekker and a bleak omen for the fate of Russia's market reforms as a whole.

To my surprise, Bekker saw the whole episode as a source of hope: 'It proved to me that Russia is not a lost country. That if a journalist writes an article it can force the most powerful state institutions, like the regional property committee, the procuracy, the civil courts, the ministry of the interior, into action. We turned on the legal machine. It was only at the final stage that we lost.'

Bekker's optimistic spin astonished me. Privatisation had triumphed, but it was increasingly moving out of the control of the young reformers and becoming the province of the old elites. And it had become disconnected from the liberal political revolution – the rule of law, anti-monopoly regulations, shareholder rights – which was vital if the change in ownership was to create a functioning prospering economy.

Before long, Russia's two huge transformations seemed destined to clash. Once ordinary Russians realised that the promised market revolution had effectively been a transfer of assets to the hated apparatchiks, and that those apparatchiks did not seem particularly good at running their new property, how would they vent their ire? Would they use their new political freedoms – the vote and a freer press – to back the young reformers in a push for a second wave of market liberalisation? Or would they turn their backs on liberal reforms, both economic and political? The moment of truth was not far off – parliamentary elections were scheduled for December 1995, and the presidential race in 1996 – and both the Kremlin and the young reformers were beginning to worry that Russia's political revolution would devour its capitalist one.

5

THE LOOPHOLE ECONOMY

ONE WARM AUGUST evening in 1994, I turned on my Moscow television set to discover a remarkable advertisement.

Opening shot: a group of businessmen, sitting in a darkened room and filmed in soft-focus. They all looked haggard and their conversation suggested why – the Russian taxman was eating into their first tentative profits. But wait! Help was on its way. A door flew open and light streamed into the room. 'Your tax problems are over,' a reassuring voice crooned, 'register your company in the republic of Ingushetia and you will be freed from all taxes.'

At first glance, that seductive promise seemed like just one more brand of the snake oil which was so assiduously peddled and so avidly purchased during Russia's initial optimistic embrace of capitalism. After all, 1994 was the peak of Russia's most notorious scam, the MMM investment pyramid, which defrauded more than a million Russians of their life savings before a raid from the black-hooded, machine-gun-toting tax police brought its machinations to a crashing halt.

But obscure little Ingushetia's offer turned out to be genuine. A presidential decree which came into force on 1 July 1994 granted Ingushetia, a small north Caucasus republic, the right to become an *ofshornaya zona*, the newly coined Russian term for offshore tax haven. Only fully privatised companies could register in the Ingush offshore zone, but for those that did, the benefits were tremendous: no local or regional taxes, an 80 per cent reduction in federal taxes, and a 50 per cent cut in regular import and export tariffs.

On the face of it, the Kremlin decree seemed like some bizarre bureaucratic aberration: Why create an offshore zone in the middle of a huge country? Why choose Ingushetia, an a oblong sliver of land, squeezed between two of the fiercest tribes of the smouldering north Caucasus? Maybe some presidential apparatchik had prepared the decree without really understanding the fancy new Western terminology. It wouldn't be the first time.

But, strange as it was, the Ingush *ofshornaya zona* was neither an exception nor a mistake. It was in fact a typical manifestation of one of the most significant, yet most overlooked, sectors of Russia's nascent market economy – the Loophole Economy.

The young reformers and their Western supporters tended to focus on the sort of virtuous economic activity which Russia's capitalist revolution was supposed to create: formerly state-owned manufacturing companies turned around by their new private owners and enterpreneurial start-up firms offering new services, like dry-cleaning or computer software support or banking or restaurants that were actually pleasant to dine in. By 1994, a few of these hoped-for businesses were finally beginning to appear.

But much of the new Russia's hustle and strut was not coming from this kind of productive business activity. Instead, one of the country's most lucrative new business sectors was the Loophole Economy: its entrepreneurs were the people who had mastered the delicate alchemy of transforming the base elements of corruptible bureaucrats and inadequate civil laws into business opportunities. Strange and inconsistent tax exemptions, odd import privileges and precious export quotas were their currency.

Some of Russia's most esteemed institutions and most well-connected politicians were players in the Loophole Economy. The Russian Orthodox Church, which had returned to its traditional role as the national church following the collapse of communism, was granted the right to import alcohol and cigarettes duty-free, and owned a stake in one of the privileged 'special exporters' with the valuable right to sell

Russian oil abroad. The National Sportsmen's Fund (run by Yeltsin's tennis coach) and the Russian hockey league were other unlikely importers of cigarettes and booze. So were a raft of other ostensibly altruistic causes like the Afghan War Veteran's Union, the society of the deaf and a Chernobyl victims' charity.

The tax haven in Ingushetia was another example of the creative, and absolutely legal, scams which thrived in the Loophole Economy. My interest piqued, I decided to investigate. The TV advertisement had already reassured me (and prospective clients) that it was not necessary to travel to remote and occasionally violent Ingushetia to avail oneself of the province's tax perks. Instead, a Moscow telephone number flashed across my TV screen. When I called, I was invited to one of the capital city's most prosperous suburbs – on the leafy and well-maintained boulevard leading out towards Yeltsin's forest dacha – to visit the headquarters of the Bin Financial Group, the sole company empowered by the Ingush government to register companies in the *ofshornaya zona*.

I found a cluster of gleaming white marble buildings set in a grove of fir trees. Stepping inside the largest one, I was instantly up against a gamut of metal detectors and scowling bodyguards. The slightly menacing high security was as ordinary in the Moscow business world as a smiling receptionist in the West. But the waiting room I was ushered into was garish even by New Russian standards. A symphony of gold, crystal and ornate floral designs, it was the sort of thing an 8-year-girl with a princess fantasy and a gold credit card might concoct.

The Barbie Doll decor seemed even more bizarre when I was invited in to meet Mikhail Gutseriev, the 36-year-old inventor of and driving force behind the *ofshornaya zona*. His combination of dark, nearly black hair, an olive complexion and blue-green eyes was typical of the 'people of the mountain turrets' as the Ingush called themselves. More than 6 feet tall and sporting a rogueish moustache, he had the physical heft and mischievous expression that his ancestors must have worn when they conducted their periodic horseback raids into the Russian steppes for hostages and booty.

A century later, Gutseriev was finding his own rich pickings in Russia, but he had refined a more sophisticated raiding strategy. Reclining on a soft leather sofa beneath an ornate pink-glass chandelier, he explained to me how he had created his niche in the Loophole Economy.

He had come up with the idea for an *ofshornaya zona* two years earlier when, in what was standard practice for Russian businessmen, he took advantage of another loophole, Russia's tax treaty with Cyprus. The Mediterranean island's extremely low corporate tax rates attract many companies which register in Cyprus, but then proceed to do almost all of their business in Russia.

'Why should these offshore zones, where me and my friends were putting most of our money, exist only abroad?' Gutseriev asked himself. 'Why not create one here in Russia?'

The young reformers still clinging to jobs in the Russian government could think of plenty of reasons why not. The collapse in revenue collection, which would soon start to jeopardise the state's ability to perform even its most basic functions, had already begun. Capital flight, estimated at between $10bn–$20bn a year, was leaching away much-needed domestic investment and infuriating foreign aid donors. In these circumstances, making it simple and legal to avoid taxes would seem to be the last thing the Kremlin would want to do.

But Gutseriev had grasped the one crucial element upon which the Loophole Economy was constructed: the philanthropical purpose in whose interest the tax exemption or import privilege or export quota was purportedly granted. Gutseriev's inspiration was to capitalise on one of the causes dearest to the Kremlin's heart – the territorial integrity of the Russian Federation.

For most of the people of Ingushetia, their proximity to their ethnic cousins, the embattled Chechens, was costly and often physically dangerous. Yet Gutseriev saw in this unfortunate geography an opportunity. Chechnya's independence drive had made obscure Ingushetia a region of strategic importance to the Kremlin, which was desperate to prevent the Chechen struggle from engulfing the rest of the volatile north Caucasus. Somehow, Gutseriev managed to persuade the Russian government that a rich Ingushetia would be a loyal Ingushetia and that it would take an offshore zone to make Ingushetia rich. 'It's time for everyone in Ingushetia to stop running around with machine-guns and start running around with money,' Gutseriev told the Kremlin. The Kremlin had agreed.

The Ingush economy was still in the doldrums when Gutseriev and I first met, but Russian and foreign businesses had not been slow to grasp the convenience of a home-grown *ofshornaya zona*.

'The demand is absolutely unlimited,' Gutseriev claimed. 'We get between 500 and 600 phone calls a day from all parts of Russia.' The zone, operating out of Bin's Moscow headquarters, offices in several Russian cities and a little-used outpost in Nazran, the hard-scrabble capital of Ingushetia, was already bringing in about $100,000 a day, Gutseriev boasted, and that was just from the $4,000 registration fee which companies had to pay in order to qualify for its tax-protected status.

I suspected there was more than a bit of braggadocio in that figure – after all, the zone had been in business for less than two months, and even in the new Russia revenues of $1m every 10 days represented a lot of money. But, once the scheme got going, I didn't think Gutseriev's grinning expectation of a financial windfall for himself and his province was at all inflated.

Companies registered in the zone were freed from most but not all taxes. Those they were required to pay went directly to Ingushetia and to Bin, rather than to the central government. Over the next two years, Gutseriev predicted the registration fees and taxes would produce at least $1bn, a huge amount of money in a country where the average monthly salary in 1994 was $100. Officially, a massive 10 per cent of that would go to Bin.

Bin's financial gain from the scheme did not stop there. To qualify for the offshore zone's tax breaks, registered companies were required to do all their banking through Gutseriev's Bin Bank. This proviso was bringing in so much money that he could hardly contain his glee. Racing over to his desk, he produced the bank's daily balance sheet and laid it before me with a flourish.

'Rbs 23bn [6.9m pounds sterling at the exchange rate of the time] flowed into our accounts today alone,' he trumpeted. 'And it's like this every single day. We have so much money I don't know what to do with it any more. Perhaps you have some investment suggestions?'

Gutseriev's venture had become so profitable so fast that his chief concern was that Bin and the Ingush offshore zone would become victims of their own success. His voluble account of the scheme's progress was occasionally interrupted as he reminded himself: 'Maybe I shouldn't be telling you any of this because, if people discover how much money we are making, we will be in mortal danger from the *mafia*.'

When I first met Gutseriev in 1994, Ingushetia's *ofshornaya zona* and the other thriving enterprises of the Loophole Economy had barely registered on the political radar of the Russian establishment and its Western allies. Russia was still struggling with the big questions: mass privatisation had just barely been concluded and the government had not yet succeeded in its two year campaign to rein in runaway inflation. Against the backdrop of these vast systemic changes, a few small wrinkles of legislation – here a concession to the war-torn Caucasus, there a perk for some worthy religious cause – seemed trivial.

But over the next few years, the young reformers and the Western donors who had begun underwriting Russia's capitalist transition began to realise that the devil might be in the details. The entrepreneurs of the Loophole Economy were not part of Russia's grand ideological struggle between communism and capitalism. Yet their back-room deals and private scams posed as great a threat to Russia's nascent capitalism as any more direct challenge. Like a thousand wispy weeds, each inconsequential in its own right, the Loophole Economy was imperceptibly taking over the post-communist terrain into which the fledgling market system was trying to set root. The weeds were starving the fragile young Russian state by leaching away the vital nourishment of revenues; the finance ministry estimated that in 1994 alone the government lost up to $5bn in revenue because of tax and duty loopholes. And they were stunting more productive economy activity as well, by grabbing lucrative markets and diverting entrepreneurial energy from other sectors.

Gradually, the campaign to root out the Loophole Economy rose to the top of the political agenda. By the spring of 1995, the IMF – which had become a major player in Russian economy policy – began to demand that the loopholes be closed as a condition of releasing new loans. Grudgingly, the Kremlin agreed. In March, the president's chief economic adviser announced that all tax breaks and import and export tariff exemptions would be revoked.

But the Loophole Economy proved surprisingly resilient. There was no outright political resistance; yet somehow, through some largely invisible lobbying process, it held its ground. The government deadline for revoking the myriad tax exemptions was pushed back from 15 March to 15 May and then to 1 October. The strongest groups, like the National Sports Fund and the Orthodox Church, were granted special delays and even paid compensation by the state.

And, even after the rules came into force for everyone, new weeds found a way of springing up. Fresh loopholes were constantly being created – like the duty-free import channel through neighbouring Belarus – and it would be months before the IMF and the young reformers discovered them.

In late 1996, eighteen months after the Kremlin had promised its crackdown, I decided to track down Gutseriev again to see how he was faring under the tough new regime. I was slightly hesitant. The *ofshornaya zona* seemed such a naked scam – the sort of thing Russians hoped the West would never notice – that I could hardly imagine Gutseriev had welcomed my piss-taking story in the *FT*. He would probably refuse to talk to me, or worse. Crossing my fingers that he would have forgotten all about me, I plunged into a labyrinth of old telephone numbers and surly secretaries. When I finally found Gutseriev, I was in for two surprises: the first was that he was delighted to hear from me.

'Oh yes, yes, the Western journalist, I remember you,' he bellowed down the telephone line. 'We had so many companies, even some Western ones, that contacted us after your story. You must come have supper with us so you can see what we have done.'

The second shock was even greater. Gutseriev was now not only a flourishing Loophole Economy entrepreneur, he was a fairly senior politician serving as one of the three deputy speakers in the Russian parliament. We agreed to meet a few days later at the Bin Club, a restaurant and casino which was his latest venture.

The Bin Club, located on one of the massive 8-lane highways which bisect central Moscow, had the same fantasyland look as the office I had visited two years earlier, but with a slightly more lurid edge. There were gold-plated fixtures in the bathroom and a fountain with frolicking scantily clad marble nymphs in the foyer. Off the corner of the private dining room, I glimpsed two lavishly appointed bedrooms complete with scarlet satin bedspreads, mirrored ceilings and jacuzzis in the corner. 'Those aren't for Western ladies like you,' Gutseriev said with a broad wink as he noticed the direction of my gaze. 'But sometimes we have special guests and they like to be entertained.' This prompted a few nudges and knowing looks between the bodyguards and a Cheshire grin from Gutseriev. As usual, the new Russia seemed to be doing its best to bring to life the tackier moments from the Godfather trilogy. I felt as if I had walked into the scene where Michael catches his slacker brother Fredo consorting with the giggling courtesans of Las Vegas.

Moving swiftly on, I stepped into the gaming room which was dominated by the green baize of a blackjack table and further adorned by two naked gold-plated female busts. Vividly coloured oil paintings of naked women wrapped in furs – just one step up from the tacky garage-sale school of nude Venus on velvet – hung on most of the white walls.

As he showed me around, Gutseriev admitted the casino would soon be closing down to make way for a bar. The problem, he said in the slightly whining tone of a child deprived of its favourite toy, was that Yuri Luzhkov, the all-powerful mayor of Moscow, was trying to corner the market in the capital city's lucrative casino business for himself. Luzhkov had launched a crackdown on those casinos the city government didn't already control and Gutseriev deemed it the better part of valour simply to shut his business down. It had clearly been a painful sacrifice. But then Gutseriev brightened. After all, he explained, casinos were not that prestigious any more – some of his friends had told him that owning one was actually quite vulgar.

At supper, Gutseriev recounted the story of his unlikely venture into politics. The *ofshornaya zona*, excluded from the Kremlin attack on loopholes because of its strategic importance, had really taken off, he said. Even some of the country's most prominent businesses – including Lukoil, Russia's largest oil company, and Logovaz, the car dealership run by Boris Berezovsky, one of the future oligarchs and for a time one of the most powerful men in the nation – had registered branches in Ingushetia.

Indeed, the *ofshornaya zona* had proved so profitable that some of the revenues were actually spilling into Ingushetia itself, as I had noticed on trips through Nazran on my way to cover the war in Chechnya. The dusty provincial city now boasted the Assa, a fancy hotel built and owned by the Bin group. A vast new mosque, surrounded by an oasis of carefully tended grass, was going up near the town centre. It would cost more than $20m to complete, Gutseriev bragged, and Bin was footing most of the bill. And Ingushetia was also the site of another, even bigger construction project, almost breathtaking in its ambition – or its idiocy. The dirt-poor region was building a brand-new capital city, and Gutseriev told me that Bin would play a major part in the construction of the shiny new marble palaces which were being designed to grace it.

But the big money, Gutseriev conceded, was to be made in Russia proper – and that's where Bin was investing 70 per cent of its revenues. He was involved (he told me) in construction in Moscow, the timber export business, a chain of supermarkets and the privileged and profitable export of oil. In building up his Russian holdings, he soon realised what it would take the IMF and G-7 governments two more years to fully comprehend: in Russia's distorted version of capitalism, politics and business were Siamese twins.

'What we have in Russia is not yet a market economy – it is state capitalism,' Gutseriev explained. 'I spent my days working and selling, yet those who had political power had the authority to take my accomplishments away from me. I understood that we in Bin were getting too big to keep on fighting the *chinovniks*: we had to join them.'

In his quest to become a politician, Gutseriev decided to approach the party which had become a byword for its straightforward attitude to selling political posts, the Liberal Democratic Party of Russia (LDPR) – the slightly zany group run by Vladimir Zhirinovsky, Russia's flamboyant ultra-nationalist. The LDPR, which had shocked Russia by coming first in the 1993 parliamentary elections, traded its power for cash without shame or pretence. The leader's press secretary matter-of-factly quoted the prices Zhirinovsky demanded per half-hour of interview time, and it was an open secret that the faction's block vote in parliament could be bought.

Ideologically, though, the LDPR seemed to be a strange home for Gutseriev. The party was proudly racist, raging with particular venom against what Russians called the *chornyi*, or blacks, of the Muslim north Caucasus – a group to which Gutseriev, of course, belonged. But, with the acute antennae he had developed in the Loophole Economy, he sensed that LDPR was a party he could do business with. He was right. In the summer of 1995, a few months ahead of December parliamentary elections, Gutseriev approached the LDPR. The party officials were happy to see him and quickly set up a meeting with Zhirinovsky. 'We immediately found a common language,' Gutseriev recalled.

Gutseriev's profits from the *ofshornaya zona* contributed to that swift mutual comprehension. He paid for LDPR television commercials, posters, pamphlets, campaign transport and 'whatever else was necessary'. On election day, he got his reward when he was placed sixth on the party list, effectively guaranteeing him a seat in parliament thanks to the proportional representation element in the Russian voting system. Once he got to the Duma, the lower house of the Russian parliament, the grateful LDPR made him a deputy speaker.

Gutseriev had taken to his new public position with gusto. His wealth, he insisted, meant that he could refrain from the common practice of using high office to line his pockets: 'When I went to the Duma I already had a Mercedes and a dacha. I didn't need to steal from the government.'

But Gutseriev did want to parlay his political post into something that had become more valuable to him than mere money. He wanted to become a gentleman. His suit was certainly sharper than when we had first met; it was bespoke, he told me proudly, the best the tailors on London's Savile Row could produce. The tobacco in his after-dinner pipe had an equally refined provenance: Gutseriev now bought all his smoking supplies in a little shop off Piccadilly.

He was even trying to mould his body to suit his new image. While I devoured a delicious trout amandine, Gutseriev abstained. He was dieting and had already slimmed down to 85kg from the 107kg which he weighed at his peak. Gutseriev was enthusiastic about his personal improvement plan, but, by the end of the meal he admitted to me that it had its limits. No matter how slim he became or how well he dressed, he knew that in Moscow he would forever be seen as a *chornyi*, a bandit from the Caucasus. But for his two sons, Gutseriev was determined that things would be different. Both were already studying at prep schools in England; next year, he hoped the eldest would be admitted to Eton. They would, he hopefully predicted, be real aristocrats.

A lot of Russia's future was riding on that bet. Gutseriev, with his fly-by-night businesses and a lifestyle caught somewhere between *The Godfather* and *My Fair Lady*, was a quintessential New Russian. Like the yuppies or the slackers in the West, the whole country was intently studying this new social tribe, even creating a new genre of *anekdoty* – the elaborate, wry jokes with which generations had laughed off the indignities of first tsarism, then communism and now raw capitalism. (A sample: When does a New Russian know it's time to buy a new Mercedes? Answer: When the ashtray is full.)

The mocking humour disguised a deeper social anxiety: Were the beefy, none-too-smart and occasionally sadistic apparatchiks who had commanded the USSR to be replaced by this new breed of vulgar gangsters as the nation's post-Soviet ruling class? Did capitalism mean that Russia must submit to the rule of thugs?

Optimists pointed to the robber barons and Western outlaws of the nineteenth-century United States. The Carnegies, the Rockefellers, the Morgans and the California prospectors had been as bent and as barbaric as any New Russian, they argued. But once the first generation had made the family fortune, their descendants could concentrate on becoming genteel. The same thing would happen in Russia, the beleaguered intelligentsia hoped, and the junior generation of Gutserievs at Eton was the sort of thing they took as a sign that they were right.

But for the American parallel to hold true, the Russian economy needed to burst into an era of dynamic growth. That legacy was what had redeemed the robber barons and their progeny in the eyes of future generations and made it really worthwhile to be part of the American elite. Pessimists worried that the distortions in Russia's fledgling economy, the very loopholes which had made Gutseriev rich enough to dream of sending his son to an English public school, might blight the prospects of the nation as a whole.

As one Western businessman told me, when I asked him what he thought of the *ofshornaya zona*: 'It's absurd. If this is allowed to continue, pretty soon no one will formally be left doing business in Russia itself.'

6

THE OLIGARCHS:
THE OUTSIDER, THE APPARATCHIK
AND THE BLUE BLOOD

NOWADAYS, IN THE West, the biggest money is nerdy, so cerebral you can hardly see it. It wears Gap clothes, operates from a featureless cubicle and is so busy working 24/7 on the latest internet IPO that it has very little time left for conspicuous consumption. The seven Russian businessmen known as the oligarchs are a different proposition altogether. To understand them you have to go back a decade to Reaganomics, greed-is-good and the Masters of the Universe for whom bigger was always better, no bonus was ever obscenely large enough and the best CEO was the one who could be convinced to bet everything on an absurdly leveraged management buy-out.

The Russians have the same machismo, the same killer instinct. They think – in fact, they know! – that they are smarter, ballsier, luckier than anyone else. They have the same swagger, the same if-you've-got-it-flaunt-it mentality. The oligarchs wear $100,000 wristwatches and their wives wear $100,000 fur coats. They travel in motorcades of armoured Mercedes and Jeeps, employ small armies of bodyguards and maintain a collection of homes. They spend $1m on a birthday gift for a helpful politician as casually as you or I would send a card to a friend.

Many of Wall Street's Big Swinging Dicks or Silicon Valley's Micro-Midases are richer and exert greater global influence than the oligarchs; but the Russians are tougher and, in a perverse way, more impressive. The thing about the oligarchs, what makes them so cocky and so cruel, is that they are the victors of gladiator's capitalism. In the West, capitalism is a game played with a safety-net. Would-be entrepreneurs who never quite make it rarely suffer anything bleaker than life in the lower middle class. Successful businessmen who break the law, cross the wrong rival or go bankrupt might, in the worst-case scenario, do a little time in a country-club prison.

But in post-communist Russia, trying to become a capitalist was more like being trapped in *Logan's Run*. Like the deadly society in the 1970s science-fiction movie, capitalism in the new Russia was a contest which everyone in the country was forced to enter. In the film, the losers die. In Russia, they were usually left alive but condemned to a life of grinding poverty. And even the lucky few who made it really big and became oligarchs always felt at risk: maybe the communists would storm back into power and execute or imprison the wealthiest businessmen, as the Bolsheviks had done in the Twenties. Perhaps a political enemy would take over the Kremlin and arrange for the arrest – and perhaps a jail-cell heart attack? – of an oligarch he hated. Or maybe a rival businessman would have better luck with that car bomb which, last time, killed the chauffeur and totalled the Mercedes but left the targeted oligarch unscathed. The rich have always been different from you and me, but in Russia the biggest difference was that they were more scared; they were always looking for the emergency exits. As I got to know a few of the oligarchs, the question they asked me most frequently was whether it was easier to emigrate to Canada or the United States. No amount of money and no number of musclemen were ever enough to make them feel safe.

Maybe that perpetual sense of insecurity was behind the biggest difference between the oligarchs and their Western counterparts – the oligarchs weren't just businessmen, eventually they also became politicians. At times their influence was so great that it would not be an exaggeration to call them a type of unofficial capitalist Politburo. Usually, their power was malign. The oligarchs, and the intimate links between their corporate and their political interests, became a metaphor for all the corruption and insider deals which deformed Russia's young capitalism. And they themselves organised the biggest, most distorted insider deal of all.

This chapter, and the next one, tell the stories of the five most important oligarchs during their early years, before in fact they became oligarchs.

The Outsider – Mikhail Friedman

Most of the oligarchs are the business equivalents of Bill Clinton, men born believing they were destined to lead and determined, from the very earliest age, to do whatever it took to make that prophecy come true. Mikhail Friedman is an exception. A stocky man with a sallow complexion, a square-jawed, slightly pudgy face boyish enough to belong to a 12-year-old and an impish grin, he grew up a long way from power and thought that was where he would stay.

Born in 1964, Friedman was raised in Lviv, the beautiful but decaying western Ukrainian city which was only forced into the Soviet Union in 1945 and spent the next five decades desperately trying to pretend the USSR didn't exist. Ukrainian fighters prowled the local forests taking potshots at the Soviets until well into the Fifties and western Ukrainians accounted for nearly a quarter of the USSR's political prisoners. Poland, with its freer speech and relatively vibrant civil society, was only 40 miles away.

In an environment like that, feeling an outsider within the larger Soviet system was the norm. Friedman grew up listening to Radio Liberty broadcasts in the family kitchen and with an almost instinctive awareness of the absurdities of the communist system. People like him naturally gravitated towards the sciences, which demanded less mouthing of political orthodoxies than other disciplines. Luckily, Friedman loved maths and physics and was very good at both.

But Friedman was too much of an outsider to get into the MIT of the Soviet Union, the Moscow Physical-Technical Institute (MPTI). For one thing, he was Jewish and in his experience Soviet anti-Semitism 'was absolutely obvious, no one announced it to your face, but no one ever really bothered to hide it either.' He was also a nobody, the son of obscure provincial engineers without enough *blat*, or connections, to overcome the black-ball of his Jewish origins. After his second application to MPTI was rejected he quickly settled on another, less prestigious Moscow school, the Institute of Steel and Alloys, to avoid being drafted.

Russians termed the early 1980s the years of stagnation, which is a pretty fair description of Friedman's quality of life as an out-of-town student in the Soviet capital. His dormitory was squalid, his student grant enough 'not to starve' but inadequate to buy new clothes regularly, and the height of glamour was a video-machine smuggled into the country by the well-connected papa of a fellow student. The Soviet regime was too senile to be properly totalitarian, but it still had a few repressive teeth left: one of Friedman's classmates was arrested and imprisoned for possessing anti-Soviet literature.

Yet, at least for the intelligentsia, life in the *fin-de-siècle* USSR had its compensations. No one had very much money, but no one had to do very much work either. The result was an entire society which acted as if it had never left college: intense, emotional, time-consuming friendships; endless hours spent drinking tea or vodka and discussing the meaning of life; the avid pursuit of esoteric spiritual or creative interests. If middle-class Russians sometimes seem perversely nostalgic for the Soviet Union, one of the reasons is that the collapse of communism forced them horribly and abruptly to grow up. Even Friedman, one of the biggest winners in the capitalist casino, sometimes can't help but regret the end of those languid years.

'My life was very carefree, just as life was for everyone in the Soviet Union,' Friedman told me. 'Materially, of course, people did not live very well, but no one had to worry about anything. The main thing, what was really intense, was friends, spiritual interests, books. The relations between people were far more open. People did not compete. There was not the same disproportion or envy. People today are far more stressed.'

But even as Friedman enjoyed the mellow life of the late USSR, he was one of the people who inadvertently began to undermine it. With all the free time which the late communist state granted to the intelligentsia, Friedman needed something to do alongside his studies and, almost by accident, he found himself running a quasi-clandestine student business. Thanks in part to the pressure of thousands of small, secretive business schemes like his, in just a few years the slacker lifestyle of the Soviet intelligentsia would be gone.

His first venture was joining the 'theatre *mafia*'. The basic principle was simple: with their abundant free time, Moscow university students queued to buy theatre tickets, then bartered them for whatever they wanted on the black market. The theatre *mafia* had been around long before Friedman's arrival, but he was the first to organise it into what was effectively a proper business. He imposed a clear management structure: every university department had a *komandir*, what Western managers would call a department head. Once a week, the *komandirs* met with Friedman – 'I guess I was like the majority shareholder' – to review their business plans. The scheme even offered a kind of flexitime working schedule for its 150 scholar-employees: if they didn't want to wait in line overnight, students could come to take their places in the queue in the early morning and be paid a half-salary.

Just as the Russian oligarchs would later do, the student entrepreneurs at various Moscow institutes coordinated their activities, creating a kind of theatre ticket cartel. Each theatre was assigned to a specific institute – Friedman had dibs on the popular Satyra, on Mayakovsky Square – and the *komandirs* were careful not to tread on each others' territory.

The theatre *mafia* would prove to be a valuable training ground for Friedman. His first experience of organising a business, it taught him how to operate in the complicated world of barter deals which still dominate much of Russia's fledgling market economy. It also brought Friedman together with most of the partners with whom he would eventually form the Alfa group, the umbrella for his oil, industrial, trading and financial conglomerate.

But in the 1980s, for Friedman, the most valuable result was that it allowed him to buy his way out of forced exile to the dismal Russian hinterland. After graduation, he was assigned to a compulsory three-year industrial posting in an obscure corner of Ryazan, a province in central Russia he describes as 'a cockroach-infested fog'. With the barter points he had accumulated through the theatre *mafia* business, Friedman was able to buy the favour of key officials at his institute: 'For two years I supplied them with various foods, consumer goods, all sorts of things.' Magically, his posting was switched from distant Ryazan, to Elektrostal, a steel mill some 60km outside Moscow.

By then, Friedman had caught the entrepreneurial bug. While nominally working at the mill, he and his friends set up a *kooperativ*, the name for the small private businesses which were legalised in 1987 as part of Gorbachev's tentative embrace of market reforms. Friedman's business ventures were no longer just a student hobby, they were now his full-time adult job.

His parents and friends were horrified. Before long Gorbachev's thaw, like every previous liberalisation, was sure to end in a bloody crackdown and Friedman would be executed or imprisoned. The irony of the situation was that while such misgivings were perfectly reasonable, the wise parents turned out to be wrong and the wild son proved to be right. Starting a private business was risky, but in the topsy-turvy Soviet universe of the late 1980s, not starting one was even riskier. Everything about the Soviet experience had taught people to be cautious, to play it safe. But suddenly, playing it safe was about to become the most dangerous strategy of all.

'In those days, experience played a cruel joke on people,' Friedman told me. 'Life experience contradicted everything that was happening – and it is very difficult to fight with life experience. As a result, many people in those days reacted very passively. Just as they had always gone to their old jobs, so they continued going to them right up until 1994, when they discovered that they had lost everything.'

Friedman was one of the fortunate ones who, half by chance and half by instinct, chose to risk believing in market reforms. His young *kooperativ* tried everything: a courier service, an apartment rental agency, selling Siberian wool shawls, even breeding white mice for laboratories.

Their breakthrough was windows. One day on the metro, Friedman overheard two engineers complaining about the absurdities of central planning. Apparently their institute had funds left over in its official spending allocation, and they needed to use them up or risk having their budget slashed the next year. They also had something they would be happy to spend the money on: washing the accumulated winter grime from their institute's windows. The problem was that their funds were in non-cash roubles, a bizarre Soviet kind of psuedo-money which could be used only in official, business-to-business transactions, not on the street. Their institute didn't know of any such official business that washed windows.

Friedman's *kooperativ* stepped in. Soon business was so good that he convinced his workshop at the steel mill in Elektrostal to begin producing brushes purpose-built for his student brigades of window-washers.

Within a few months, Friedman was earning 10,000 roubles a month, forty times the combined salaries of his parents.

After that, Friedman and his partners became more ambitious and moved into the hugely lucrative import trade, bringing in Western cigarettes, perfume, computers and Xerox machines. Then they hit the big time, exporting oil, a tremendously profitable business given the huge discrepancy between domestic Soviet prices for oil and the going rate on the world market.

Western business schools tell their students that the secret of success is to know your customers. In the late Soviet Union it was to know your apparatchiks. Friedman spent more and more of his time befriending bureaucrats. His favourite story describes what happened when a shipment of his computers was 'arrested' at Sheremetyevo airport. It was missing a vital piece of paperwork – a document which offered assurances that the computers were not being imported for resale. Of course, Friedman admits, that was exactly what his firm intended to do. Nonetheless, they duly supplied the appropriate 'lying' document to the customs officials. Still, customs refused to release the computers.

Finally, Friedman drove out to the airport himself and found the head of the customs department. They spent five hours downing shots of vodka; by the end of the session, the apparatchik was so drunk he had to be carried out of the room, Friedman had heard dozens of stories about 'the glorious victories of the customs service' . . . and he was free to take his computers.

The litres of vodka, battalions of charmed apparatchiks and dozens of creative business ideas eventually bore fruit. By 1991, Friedman and his partners were dollar millionaires. However, their business techniques were still primitive; as Friedman admitted, 'we were absolute savages.' But by the standards of their time and place, they had made it. Although the Soviet Union still existed, 'we were already living in a market economy,' Friedman said. 'We bought at market prices, and we sold at market prices.' They had started to live like capitalists in their personal lives too, taking their holidays on warm, sunny islands abroad, usually Cyprus.

In fact, they were doing so well that when Gorbachev's Politburo appeared to swing back towards reactionary policies in 1991, violently cracking down on democratic protestors in Lithuania, Friedman and his colleagues moved part of their business to Prague as an insurance policy. But by the end of the year the Soviet Union no longer existed, Yeltsin was in power and the young reformers had launched their market revolution.

Ideologically, Friedman sympathised with the new regime, but he was still an outsider. For him, the young reformers, many of them well-connected sons of the nomenklatura, were as distant as if they had been 'citizens of the moon'. In theory, that should not have been a problem: the young reformers were supposed to be building a fair and equitable market economy. But in practice, who you knew still mattered.

So, just as he had befriended the Sheremetyevo customs officer, Friedman looked for a way to get close to the new government. His path was bracingly direct – he simply brought in one of the prominent young reformers, an economist named Pyotr Aven, to an executive position within the Alfa group. Aven was one of the first of the young reformers to cross the line and go into private business. His government connections – together with the shadow economy network Friedman had built up in the Gorbachev era – gave Alfa an entrée into the lucrative Loophole Economy of oil exports.

But even before Aven helped the Alfa team nose its way to the golden trough of government contracts, oil export licences and servicing state bank accounts, Friedman was the first of the oligarchs to spot the other great opportunity: mass privatisation. He owed his head-start to Alfa's detour into Prague in 1991, where the Czechs were pioneering a voucher-based mass privatisation programme. Thanks to his Czech experience, Friedman grasped the potential of the voucher scheme in Russia more quickly than many of his rivals.

Before long, Friedman had acquired a second strategic advantage. When the bankers from Credit Suisse First Boston went to work for Chubais, organising Russia's first voucher auction, they did some research for themselves on the side, preparing lists of companies which would be worthwhile investment targets. These lists proved invaluable, almost instantly boosting CSFB to the top of the Russian capital markets. But they also served as a precious blueprint for the Alfa group, thanks to Mikhail Alexandrov, a young Russian who had worked with the initial CSFB shock-troopers and then defected to Friedman's company.

'You have a bunch of multinationals coming to them [CSFB] letting them know what their plans are in Russian acquisitions,' explained Charlie Ryan, the young American who set up his own investment bank in Moscow. 'This is not a fact lost on little Michael Alexandrov. So Michael very cleverly takes the whole list of Western companies interested in making acquisitions in Russia, quits CSFB and goes and joins an unknown group called Alfa-Bank.'

With his list in hand, Alexandrov persuaded Friedman to become one of the first indigenous Russian financial investors – buying large stakes in the Russian firms he knew the big Western multinationals were interested in acquiring, and then selling them on for a large profit. The small but growing band of Western bankers in Moscow, even the CSFB team whose research Alfa was using, was impressed by how quickly the Russian group had grasped the essential logic of the first stage of privatisation.

Theoretically, aggressive investors like Alfa were supposed to be the work-horses of Russia's market transition, the force which would change the way the economy actually functioned – restructuring companies at the shop-floor level, bringing in experienced strategic investors with the money and the know-how to turn the country around, factory by factory. But in practice, Alfa had a hard time putting its classic idea to work. Most Russian plants were in such terrible shape, and the Russian economy overall was doing so badly, that it was often impossible to lure in the investment and the know-how required to turn factories around.

In the end, Alfa made a little money from its early foray into corporate restructuring and gained valuable experience. But they did it the hard way. Ironically, Alfa would have reaped greater profits – and needed to do a lot less work – had it simply invested its capital in Russia's grossly undervalued natural resources.

'It turned out that the way to make money was to be incredibly speculative and not to worry about restructuring,' Stephen Jennings, then the co-head of CSFB's Russia team, told me. 'If they had put that money into Lukoil or Gazprom they would have earned a lot more money.'

Before long most Russian businessmen, including the oligarchs, would realise that the surest way to build fortunes was not to waste time and energy on the back-breakingly difficult job of changing the way factories were run. The real money-spinner was to grab a piece of

Russia's vast mineral wealth – an economic epiphany that would guide the way in which Russia's greatest private fortunes were amassed. But for the country itself, it was a most unfortunate reality: with huge and relatively easy money to be made in acquiring Russia's natural resources, the best and most adventurous business talents were diverted from the crucial job of making the productive branches of the economy actually work.

The Apparatchik – Mikhail Khodorkovsky

Most 5-year-olds have crazy, impractical ambitions; they dream of becoming astronauts, rock singers or ballerinas. Not Mikhail Khodorkovsky. As far back as he can remember, he always wanted to do just one thing – become the manager of a Soviet factory. He was so focused, so young, on that one goal that even in kindergarten the other children nicknamed him 'director', the Soviet equivalent of referring to a kid as 'CEO'.

Most of the oligarchs are flamboyant, larger-than-life alpha males. They dominate every conversation, become the focus of every room. You can imagine all of them chafing at the constraints of the regimented Soviet system, rebelling in big and in small ways until finally the system collapsed and they were free to flex their will-power on a brave new world.

Khodorkovsky is different. Although he's in his mid-thirties now, and one of the most powerful oligarchs, when meeting him you can still see the traces of the obedient little teachers' pet whose wildest childhood dream was to become a Soviet red director. Khodorkovsky has mouse-brown hair, wide naïve-looking mud-coloured eyes, a large face and geeky, over-sized glasses. He has a surprisingly soft speaking voice, a slight stutter and a smile which is so gentle it is almost wimpish. While most of the oligarchs flaunt their private jets and bejewelled mistresses, Khodorkovsky is determinedly, even boringly, bourgeois. He makes a point of dressing down, regularly wearing jeans to work and putting on a tie only under duress. His favourite restaurant is Maharaja, a Moscow curry house which even Western graduate students can afford, and he scolds his wife when she spends too much money on clothes. He is unashamedly uninterested in high culture, preferring Abba and the Soviet crooners of his parents' generation to the Russian classical composers and Western pop stars his wife occasionally forces him to endure. In public with his wife, Khodorkovsky likes to act slightly kitten-whipped, complaining about the starvation diets she imposes on him and the cunning tricks she employs to manipulate him.

Khodorkovsky's emphatically ordinary persona is too consistent to be a façade, but it is deceiving nonetheless. This seemingly unprepossessing man is one of Russia's smartest and most ruthless businessmen. In one company he took over, he installed video-cameras in every office to monitor his new employees – and fired more than a third of them when he decided they weren't working hard enough. In one Siberian oil town, some of his workers are too scared to criticise him on the record.

Born in 1963, the year before Friedman, Khodorkovsky comes from a very different background. Khodorkovsky is one of the insiders, a savvy young operator who flourished in the Soviet system and was smart enough to use his *ancien régime* connections to do even better under the new order. Like Friedman, Khodorkovsky is Jewish and his first effort to fulfil his childhood dream was thwarted by his ancestry. After receiving a degree in engineering from the Mendeleev Institute in Moscow, he had hoped to be assigned to work at a leading defence plant. It was not the most prestigious post on offer to students graduating in his year, but it was the one he wanted because it would bring him closer to his goal. As the top student in his class, the young Khodorkovsky thought he would be a shoo-in for the position. Yet his choice was refused: although no formal explanation was ever offered, he assumes that, as a Jew, he was deemed unsuitable for the high-security military plant.

Ironically, as in Friedman's case, anti-Semitism turned out to be a blessing in disguise. It locked Khodorkovsky out of the behemoths of the Soviet system – which were dying – and forced him into the quasi-private sector. He set up a 'centre for the scientific-technical creativity of young people', a characteristically ponderous Soviet moniker for one of the first officially permitted forms of business actitivity. Like all the businessmen who survived the natural selection of that era, Khodorkovsky was a chameleon. His centre, whose lumpy name was soon abbreviated to Menatep, became first a *kooperativ*, then a bank as the laws governing private business developed.

Its business activities were equally protean. Khodorkovsky and his group imported computers, a sector which yielded a sixfold profit for every invested rouble; they dabbled in currency exchange; they sold specialised computer programmes; they experimented with the construction business. Like Friedman, some of their fattest early profits came from a less obvious business – acting as intermediaries for state enterprises which wanted to convert their useless non-cash roubles into cash or a necessary service.

It was a typical pattern for a business started in the mid-1980s. But Khodorkovsky's entrepreneurial evolution was stimulated by one very important competitive advantage: from the outset he enjoyed the patronage and protection of senior Communist Party and government officials. The young Khodorkovsky was the Soviet equivalent of a corporate high-flier. While studying for his chemistry degree, he had diligently pursued a parallel career in the Komsomol, the communist youth league and training ground for future nomenklatura bosses. By the time he graduated, he was the deputy head of his institute's powerful Komsomol committee. Had Khodorkovsky been an ethnic Russian, the next logical step would probably have been to begin climbing the ladder of the most powerful institution in the USSR, the Communist Party. But even though, as a Jew, that path was effectively closed to him, his prospects under the old regime were excellent. The Soviet party bosses 'respected him, some of them even loved him', according to Leonid Nevzlin, one of Khodorkovsky's earliest business partners.

Even after the USSR collapsed, Khodorkovsky remained adept at winning the trust of older Soviet-era government officials. While the other oligarchs soon started to swagger, bragging that they ruled Russia, Khodorkovsky was careful to act humble. When Yevgeny Primakov, a 68-year-old veteran KGB agent, became prime minister in 1998, Khodorkovsky was one of the few oligarchs to establish a working relationship with him. The two men, Khodorkovsky told me, represented alien epochs and outlooks – 'we were like a cat and a dinosaur' – but the young oligarch smoothed over their differences with his tactful behaviour. 'With people of his age I always act respectful and for that reason they always treat me well,' he explained.

In the late 1980s, when Khodorkovsky began his experimental ventures in the fledgling market economy, he did so with the blessing of the communist regime. 'To a certain extent, Khodorkovsky was sent by the Komsomol and the party [into the private sector],' Nevzlin said. Having dispatched their hard-working protégé to build a capitalist beachhead, the party establishment protected and supported him. The Menatep bank's links with the government were so close that in 1990, Khodorkovsky and Nevzlin were appointed economic advisers to Ivan Silaev, prime minister of the Russian Federation, while continuing to work in their own company. It was a tremendous honour: in those days businessmen were marginal figures, barely a cut above muggers, and the party still ruled supreme. It was also an immensely valuable experience, allowing Khodorkovsky and Nevzlin to acquire that most valuable of currencies: government contacts. A year later, when Gaidar launched his market revolution, Khodorkovsky was perfectly placed.

One of the unintended consequences of Gaidar's reforms was to rip up the old financial arteries which under communism had connected businesses with one another, and with the government. The ex-Komsomolites at Menatep soon discovered that creating their own network – in effect, privatising the flow of government money – was one of the most lucrative businesses in Russia's market economy.

Their business started with factories that were having a hard time extracting credits or payment from the collapsing Russian state. Like a cheque-cashing company, Menatep gave the enterprises their money up-front and then collected the payment they were owed from the central government, taking a hefty cut in the process. Before long, Menatep began to perform the same service for regional governments waiting for roubles from Moscow. From there it was a short step to the real Klondike – handling the federal government's own finances, through a plethora of schemes ranging from servicing the fat bank accounts of government departments to becoming a conduit for money which needed to travel from one branch of the federal government to another.

The links between private business and the government which were struck up almost from the first day of market reforms would seem to be the antithesis of the young reformers' goals: cronyist, murky and dangerously fertile ground for corruption. But at the time, things did not look quite that way. The reformers found themselves surrounded by a hostile, inefficient and endemically corrupt apparat. What could be more natural than to hand over some of the apparat's former functions to the nation's plucky new band of capitalists, young men who belonged to the reformers' generation and shared their mindset.

For Khodorkovsky, one benefit of these schemes was that they strengthened Menatep's already robust personal network. In each transaction, Menatep won the gratitude of another provincial factory director, the trust of another powerful regional government head, and improved its relationship with the Moscow ministries. The schemes were also hugely profitable. With double-digit monthly inflation, the men at the centre of financial transactions could make huge windfalls just by holding up the transfer of money out of a government department's bank account for a few extra days, or delaying repayment of a debt for a few weeks. As one of Khodorkovsky's partners told me, 'It was hard not to make money.'

Inevitably, that money soon began to colour the relationship between the future oligarchs and the state. The businessmen were already millionaires; their peers in government were scraping by on $100 a month. Before long, entire ministries would be supplementing their miserly state salaries with pay-offs from Russia's private businessmen. But the new relationships were about much more than stuffed envelopes, and that was what made them so strong. They were about a whole new network of alliances based on new friendships, clever arguments and even ideology. A brand new system of *blat* – the Soviet-era word for political influence and connections – was being created. Like communism, it was held together not just by greed but also by its own system of beliefs, only this time the article of faith was the market economy.

'The young reformers' team was not corrupt,' Nevzlin said. 'And, because of its intellectual strength, it was a serious barrier in the apparat's effort to make money. But even then, without any corruption at all, people learned how to push the decisions which were convenient for them through the Gaidar government. Since they loved the market so much, all you had to do was explain to them how your project was so important for the development of a market economy.'

The financial schemes which Khodorkovsky and his team developed during the first few months of the Gaidar government exponentially increased their capital. Now they had to decide what to do with it, and Chubais' voucher privatisation gave them the answer. Some of Russia's biggest factories were on the auction block. For Khodorkovsky, it was a precious 'chance to achieve my childhood ambition', with some bells and whistles attached: instead of becoming merely the director, now he could be the owner.

Menatep's drive to acquire a chunky industrial portfolio was boosted by cleverly taking advantage of one of the weaker rivets in Chubais' streamlined privatisation machine. After the first stage of voucher auctions, the remaining state stakes in enterprises were sold off through a variety of means, including investment tenders. In theory, the tenders were designed to help remedy one of the shortcomings in the process – the failure of the first stage of privatisation to bring much-needed capital into the companies which were sold off. Investment tenders were supposed to fix that, by requiring that potential buyers pledge to make an investment in the company as well as pay the government cash up-front. But, in Russia's volatile market economy, handing over assets on the strength of a future promise was to invite sharp dealings. Rivals allege that Menatep was one of the most systematic, and the smartest, manipulators of the scheme.

'Menatep was very involved in the investment auctions,' Friedman claimed. 'They used to make very high investment pledges. Then they would back them with Menatep bank guarantees, which would then run out [before the investment had been made]. They had a whole system. They are, to this day, still fighting court cases over this. Gradually, they are losing some of the stakes they acquired [in this manner]. This is how property was grabbed up in our country.' (In court, Menatep argued that it had failed to make some of its promised investments only because they no longer made economic sense.)

While Menatep's system for acquiring companies may have been carefully worked out, at least initially, its choice of assets was more haphazard. By the company executives' own admission, Menatep's mass privatisation shopping spree was an eclectic scatter-shot exercise – they bought everything from a titanium-magnesium plant near Moscow to textile factories, glass factories and food processing companies. They chose companies because they had a good relationship with their directors, because their undergraduate training as chemists gave them some expertise in the sector, or because the factories had played an important role in the Soviet economy and they believed they would continue to be significant. But mostly they bought, as shoppers in any sale do, because prices were at bargain-basement levels and they knew a deal this good couldn't last for long.

Some of their purchases, such as the food processing companies, turned out to be complete duds. But, with high inflation washing away the group's mistakes like the forgiving tide sweeping clean a beach, bad buys weren't a serious problem. There was so much easy money in Russia, and the companies were so cheap, that Khodorkovsky and his comrades felt the only way to learn whether a business worked for them was to buy it.

Gradually though, through trial and error, Menatep began to pull together what was starting to be called a financial-industrial group, a conglomerate of related industrial holdings and a bank able to provide the factories with financial services. Financial-industrial groups, known as FIGs, soon became the object of desire for every ambitious Russian entrepreneur. Although Western economists were almost immediately sceptical of the logic behind them, they had one obvious advantage: by closing financial operations behind the wall of a single owner, they became more opaque. That brought barter deals, strong-arm treatment of minority shareholders and avoidance of taxes within the reach of relative newcomers like Khodorkovsky.

Better still, the FIGs, both in theory and in practice, soon acquired their own powerful political patron in the cabinet – Oleg Soskovets, the deputy prime minister and leader of the party of war, the hard-line Kremlin faction which advocated a more authoritarian style of governance including the ruthless suppression of breakaway Chechnya. With their emphasis on giganticism and their attempt to bring all the enterprises in a particular sector under the control of a group of cooperating owners, the FIGs reminded some observers unfavourably of the monopolism of the Soviet economy. For conservatives like Soskovets, that was precisely their appeal. Ironically enough, by 1995, just three years after Russia's market revolution started in earnest, the country's capitalist pioneers and its nostalgic political hard-liners began to make common cause.

But while the FIGs found favour with the Kremlin conservatives, the old guard on the factory floor found it difficult to adjust to the reign of the future oligarchs. For all his Komsomol connections, as far as the red directors were concerned Khodorkovsky was an outsider who had not climbed his way up the Soviet industrial apparat. He began to clash with the old management: 'We tried to reach agreements with the [old] directors, but eventually we had to fire them. We did not manage to keep a single one. They could not understand that they no longer worked for themselves.'

The problem, Khodorkovsky said, was that like Dugelny of the Novosibirsk Tin Factory, the red directors were used to running their plants as their own property. Any extra revenues they could squeeze out, preferably out of sight of the taxman and their own infrequently paid workers, would trot along a well trodden trail to their own off-shore bank accounts. They did not take kindly to the idea that the money should go instead to Menatep: 'We told them right away: "Guys, let's make a deal. We are your partners, we pay your salaries, you will get a share – But you must work honestly." No one did.'

The Blue Blood – Vladimir Potanin

In 1997, when Vladimir Potanin was at the height of his power – fresh from a job as deputy prime minister, about to announce a joint venture with British Petroleum, and with an empire controlling a purported 10 per cent of Russia's GDP – *Euromoney* magazine described him as his country's J. P. Morgan, the Russian equivalent of Wall Street's aristo-cratic investment banker. The phrase did not quite capture the man Potanin was, but it definitely captured the man he desperately wanted to be.

All the other oligarchs, even Khodorkovsky, still had a bit of the hustler in them, a bit of the guy who's sweet-talked his way up from the streets to the corner office and still can't quite believe his luck. Most of them could be a little ironic about their success; they flaunted their money with the ferocious gaucheness of men who never stopped wor-rying that they might lose it.

Potanin was different. He was a Soviet blue-blood, and he was con-vinced he would become a capitalist one as well. He never had to barter theatre tickets or drink vodka with airport customs officials; he went straight from a promising Soviet career to a $300m bank. While the other oligarchs were still decorating their offices with leopard-skins and mirrors, Potanin was buying graciously battered English antiques. He spoke the best English, hired Westerners first and most aggres-sively, started doing deals with major Western players the earliest. Potanin aspired to become more than an oligarch; he wanted to lunch in the best board-rooms on Wall Street as an equal, not just as some exotic specimen from the Russian taiga.

Potanin looks like a quintessential Russian, only healthier and in better shape. He has pink skin, a pug-nose, blue eyes and sandy hair. He is trim and moves with the coiled grace of an athlete. Give him an extra six inches (Potanin is 5'6", on a good day) and he could walk into one of the worker-hero groupings of statuary so favoured by Soviet socialist-realist artists and not look out of place.

The son of a senior Soviet foreign-trade official, Potanin – who was born in 1961 – spent his childhood following his father to foreign postings including New Zealand and Turkey, an almost unheard-of privilege in the cloistered USSR. When he returned to Moscow it was to attend the prestigious Institute of International Relations, the training ground of the Soviet diplomatic corps. He was born to rule and, with the unselfconscious arrogance of his caste, he knew it.

'I was usually chosen as the captain of the team when we played sports,' Potanin told me. There was no embarrassed chuckle, no hint of self-deprecation, no body language which explained: My PR told me to say this, but I realise I sound like an egotistical jerk. 'In youth organisations, like the Komsomol, I was always in a leadership position as well. I was good at organising people.'

After graduating in 1983, Potanin began his inevitable climb through the bureaucratic power structure, following his father to work at the Ministry of Foreign Trade where he shone, winning prizes and promotions. By 1989, he was offered one of the ministry's plum jobs: a foreign posting, probably in either Belgium or Canada.

The opportunity to go abroad was one more sign of privilege. Yet, ironically, as the Soviet Union's collapse accelerated so the advantages which had ensured Potanin's advancement suddenly threatened to become golden handcuffs. While the other future oligarchs – many of them outsiders – had been laying the foundations of their market empires, he was building a civil service career in a country which soon would no longer exist.

Just in the nick of time, Potanin grasped the enormity of the changes going on around him. He refused the coveted job abroad and decided to set up his own business instead. At first, he hoped to make up for his late start by leveraging his nomenklatura connections into ownership. In 1990, he approached his former bosses and colleagues urging them to convert the state-owned trading firm where they worked into a private company, which would be owned by its own workers and managers.

Potanin's old comrades agreed with his idea in theory, but they couldn't quite summon the nerve to put it into practice. After months of nagging and cajoling and persuading, a frustrated Potanin finally gave up. Instead, he decided to concentrate on his own small venture: Interros, a foreign trading company whose starting capital was just $10,000 and which had only a handful of employees.

Interros used Potanin's experience and connections in the foreign trade sector to help steer imported consumer goods through the labyrinth of Russian officialdom, but at first its only clients were the minnows of the *kooperativ* economy. Potanin helped Microdean, one of Russia's first home-grown private retailers, to stock its expanding chain of Moscow shops with computers and other imported consumer goods. He also worked closely with Oleg Boiko, one of the most prominent private entrepreneurs of the time. But Potanin knew the business could not last long. Microdean and Olbi, Boiko's group, were learning how to negotiate the import maze for themselves. Soon, Potanin and his address book would be superfluous.

More importantly, like so many of the future oligarchs, Potanin swiftly realised that the real money was to be made in banking. Just as he was beginning to plan this strategic move, he met the man who would make it possible: Mikhail Prokherev, the talented young professional banker who would become his business partner. For Potanin, the encounter was a godsend and years later he still remembered it with a recall of detail so rich and so tender that it sounded almost like the memory of a lover.

'It was 31 March 1991, in this very building where my office is now, that we were first introduced to each other,' Potanin told me, sitting on the third floor of a dirty white skyscraper which was part of a row of cold, virtually indistinguishable towers known as the Russian Wall Street. 'When I met Prokherev, everything fell into place. The right man had appeared. When you have an idea, you need to add the man and then everything is wonderful. That is what happened.'

Potanin now started working furiously to open up his own bank, wooing young, ambitious sons of the nomenklatura like himself from the established state-owned banks and beginning to court clients. By the spring of 1992, a few weeks into Gaidar's market revolution, Potanin and his partners had a banking license.

But Potanin was still lagging behind Russia's capitalist pioneers. When Chubais launched the voucher privatisation programme, Potanin reluctantly judged his business too poor and too immature to participate. His company, which eventually became known as the Oneximbank group, missed out on both the profits of mass privatisation and the valuable experience of working with vouchers.

At the end of the year, however, his establishment connections came through with another and even more golden opportunity. The International Bank of Economic Cooperation, the state-owned bank where Prokherev had worked and the alma mater of many of Potanin's new employees, was crumbling under the weight of the Soviet Union's collapse. On the verge of bankruptcy, the IBEC was barred from working with Russian clients lest they, all still state-owned companies, be drawn into its crisis. Someone had to take over IBEC's accounts. What could be more natural than turning them over to those bright young men, most former colleagues, at Oneximbank? They worked in the same building as IBEC, they used the same computer network and – most important of all – were part of the same nomenklatura.

Those accounts were worth $300m, a huge sum in these early days of Russia's market transition. All of a sudden, Potanin had his big break. Even in a country where most fortunes were built on the back of government connections, he earned an enduring reputation as the nomenklatura's favourite capitalist, the tycoon who had been appointed by the old elites rather than making his own way. Years later, he was still a little touchy about it.

'Basically, they gave us $300m,' he conceded. 'Although I admit that for us it was quite a big boost, at the same time it was not a golden spoon with which we were fed.'

Potanin was at least partly right: he and his colleagues did much more than simply swallow what they had been given. They used their powerful starting position to expand aggressively, focusing on the two areas which Khodorkovsky had already discovered were the most lucrative. The first was to start moving from the purely financial sphere into industry. Potanin began to build beachheads in attractive Russian enterprises by offering them loans, persuading them to hold their accounts in his bank and starting to make plans to buy some of them outright.

At the same time, he was pushing into a second lucrative business: handling the government's money. Before long he had been awarded two of the juiciest accounts: the State Customs Agency, which maintained a regular balance of about $1bn, and yielded an annual profit of about $20m; and Rosvoruzheniye, the state arms trading company which kept 'a few tens of millions of dollars' on Potanin's books.

What made the state accounts, especially the Customs Account, particularly valuable for Oneximbank was that holding them allowed the group to create and control a closed circuit of some of the biggest flows of money in the country. Many of Russia's biggest exporters were Oneximbank's clients and often its shareholders. Tariff and customs charges were among the biggest expenditures these companies faced. But as money moved from the companies to the Customs Service, it always stayed on the balances of Oneximbank. Potanin says these 'long payment chains' brought the bank revenues of tens of millions of dollars a year.

The state accounts swiftly built Oneximbank, already swelled by the clients it inherited from MBS, into one of Russia's mightiest economic forces. By 1997, after a spree of industrial acquisitions, *Business Week* estimated that Potanin controlled nearly 10 per cent of Russia's GDP, a relative share double that of the Rockefellers at their peak and more than forty times Bill Gates' proportionate stake of the US economy.

Yet Potanin was adamant that it was cutting-edge market professionalism rather than good old fashioned Soviet *blat* which won the business for his group: 'We gave [the state] a high quality product, which allowed the state to receive its payments promptly and smoothly. But our country is such that people now act as if we stole something. We don't deny that it was profitable for us to do this. But it's absurd to think people should work for the state and not make any money doing so.'

Potanin's emphatic justification notwithstanding, the billions of dollars of government money which flowed through Oneximbank began to raise eyebrows. Eventually even Yeltsin, whose style of governance was marked by a Reaganesque disdain for detail, came to discover that somehow this ambitious banker in his early thirties had become the custodian of a huge piece of the Russian state's assets. In October 1997, at one of his Kremlin meetings with all the oligarchs, Yeltsin challenged Potanin about the accounts with a joky comment that had an iron undertone:

'So, I hear you're living well,' Yeltsin told the banker.

'How do you mean, living well, Boris Nikolaevich?' Potanin replied.

'I mean that it's good to have Rosvoruzheniye's money!' Yeltsin shot back.

Irritated and defensive, Potanin raised the stakes: 'Yes, and it's good to have the customs money, too. If I had my way, I would keep it all too, because your *chinovniks* don't know how to handle it.'

In retrospect, Potanin was enormously pleased with his quick retort: 'I think that Yeltsin expected me to be embarrassed that he knew [about the accounts]. I suspect that he had been briefed and told this was a very shameful thing, that people had said, "As soon as you accuse Potanin of holding the state accounts he will lower his eyes and say, 'Yes, Boris Nikolaevich, I'm ashamed to admit it but it's true. We will immediately give it all back.'"'

Instead, Potanin triumphantly told me, his own robust reaction brought a smile to the president's lips. But that Mona Lisa grin, one of Yeltsin's trademark political expressions, proved to be a pyrrhic victory. As time went on, resentment about Oneximbank's extraordinary success at winning government business grew, particularly among the other oligarchs who were fighting for a piece of the same pie. Eventually, it would provoke a devastating conflict known as the bankers' war.

For now, however, Potanin was riding high. And in dealings with the Russian government, he enjoyed an important advantage: of all the major oligarchs, only Potanin was a full-blooded ethnic Russian.

'Many people [in government] were starting to be troubled by the high number of Jewish entrepreneurs in the country,' Nevzlin, one of the founders of Menatep who is himself Jewish, told me. 'Vladimir Potanin played on that quite intensively. But the thing was that sometimes Vladimir Olegovich was speaking to people who had hidden loyalties. A mother who was not quite Russian, for example. And so on several occasions we learned what was going on.'

For the oligarchs, ethnicity never became the big issue but it never stopped being a small one either. Potanin's ethnic Russian roots were not the only thing that made him slightly different from the other oligarchs – sometimes the first among equals, other times the odd man out – but they were always part of the equation.

7

THE NOMAD AND THE IMPRESARIO

The Nomad – Boris Berezovsky

IT WAS A cold winter morning but Aleksandr Korzhakov, Yeltsin's body-guard and best friend, was in high spirits. He had just won a game of tennis, the favourite sport of the president's entourage, and was luxuriating in the strong, hot jets of water spraying down on him in the lavishly outfitted shower-room of the President's Club – Moscow's most exclusive club for sports and socialising, founded by Boris Nikolaevich himself.

But as Korzhakov lathered up, a familiar face popped up in the adjacent shower. Boris Berezovsky had inveigled his way into the President's Club and he was not about to let an opportunity to network with the man the Russian newspapers were calling the power behind the throne go to waste.

'There I am, washing in the shower, but does that stop him? No, all the same he comes in and joins me,' Korzhakov recalled.

The din of water pounding against the ceramic tiles might have deterred lesser men from launching into conversation, but not Berezovsky.

'I don't hear half of what he's saying, but he keeps on shouting,' Korzhakov told me, still torn between awe and disgust at Berezovsky's chutzpah. 'Berezovsky never did sports. He came to the club to prevent other people from doing sports. To approach the necessary people with his questions, his affairs, his issues. He uses every person to the maximum. That is his principle of life.'

By the time he made it to the elite shower-rooms of the President's Club, Berezovsky, who was born in 1946, had already made a fortune with his talent for using people to the maximum. Slight and balding, with lovingly manicured hands and a fondness for larding his conversation with Latin phrases, he began his unlikely climb to power as a mathematician.

Like most of the future oligarchs, by the late 1980s he had begun to dabble in the private sector. Like all of them, he built his capitalist fortune using bricks – indeed often entire walls and buildings – torn away from the decaying edifice of the Soviet state. But while most of Berezovsky's colleagues and competitors were empire-builders, hoping to found business dynasties which would endure for generations, he was a corporate nomad who danced from one venture to another, amassing money and influence along the way but always eventually pulling up his tent and moving on.

Most of the time, the man who, in 1997, *Forbes* magazine named the ninth most powerful entrepreneur in the world, denied outright ownership of any of the companies with which he was associated. He had friends in the management, he offered advice, but he rarely admitted to being a direct shareholder. The set-up was perfectly legal and, at least in principle, there was nothing untoward about it; yet somehow, Berezovsky grew richer and richer. Next to the oil and gas barons, he was probably Russia's most effective rent-seeker – and all thanks to a genius for getting close to the right people at the right time and using them to the maximum.

Berezovsky's ladder of personal connections began in the late 1980s with Vladimir Kadannikov, the director of Avtovaz, the central Russian plant which once manufactured more cars than any other factory in the world. Berezovsky's entrée to the Avtovaz empire was through his first career: his mathematical work designing complex industrial systems. But with perestroika swirling around him, when Berezovsky travelled to the city of Togliatti and saw the army of shiny saleable Ladas rolling off the assembly line in the thick coniferous forests on the banks of the

Volga, inspiration struck. He saw a consumer brand which he could ride to prosperity in the new Russia and he persuaded Kadannikov to share his vision. The two schemes they developed – the Logovaz car dealership and the AVVA investment pyramid – would become the prototypes for the financial and political shell games which Berezovsky would eventually parlay into one of the most powerful roles in the country.

The economic sleight of hand which created Logovaz was the same technique which red directors and nouveaux riches owners across the country – working with everything from aluminium smelters to paper-mills to oilfields – were using to enrich themselves and beggar the state. The basic idea was to separate the profit-centre – the sale of the actual cars – from the cost-centre: the production of cars. Logovaz, presided over by Berezovsky and Kadannikov, took over selling the cars and collecting the cash, while Avtovaz, like some ancient dowager lumbered with the debts and crumbling estate while her spendthrift son takes his personal income off to the gaming holes of Europe, was left to pay the workers and at least in theory, the suppliers and pay the state its taxes. In principle, of course, there was nothing untoward about the set-up: Logovaz and the thousands of analogous sales companies attached to Russian factories paid for the product. But untransparent accounting made it easy for the daughter firm to prosper while the mother factory languished beneath a growing mountain of unpaid debt.

What made schemes of this kind particularly ingenious was that the government often acted as creditor of last resort, especially when a mammoth factory like Avtovaz was concerned. Even when Avtovaz was unable to pay its taxes or its workers, it never quite went broke. Time and again, the government forgave its tax debts or issued it cheap loans.

Berezovsky's second wheeze with Kadannikov was AVVA, another controversial but perfectly legal venture. In theory, an investment fund set up to build a new model Avtovaz car, probably across the border in high-tech Finland. In practice, AVVA's chief purpose appeared to be using Avtovaz's brand-name recognition to tap into the Russian public's weakness for get-rich-quick schemes.

Every society has its moments of money madness, when a natural discovery or a sudden social fetish throws the entire citizenry into a frenzied pursuit of instant fortunes. In seventeenth-century Holland it was the tulip craze, when a single Viceroy bulb sold for two *lasts* of wheat and four of rye, eight pigs, a dozen sheep, two oxheads of wine, four tons of butter, a thousand pounds of cheese, a bed, some clothing and a silver beaker. A century later, the English were avid subscribers to the South Sea Bubble, a scheme which consisted of supposed trading opportunities in South America. Alan Greenspan has hinted that similar animal spirits could be behind the late twentieth-century American appetite for Internet stocks.

But in the first years of market reforms in Russia, the money madness was probably more fevered than it had been anywhere else, ever before, since it was not just about tulips, South Sea bonds or Internet stocks but about the entire economy. After decades of communist subsistence, suddenly it was okay to get rich – but only a very visible minority seemed to know how to do so. Following a few months of mute shock, the rest of Russia threw itself into a panicked search for the secrets of its lucky compatriots' success, which made Russians an easy mark for pyramid schemes. Terrific fortunes magically seemed to be within the grasp of anyone with the courage to make a simple investment.

AVVA was one of the first schemes to cash in on this naïve desperation, attracting millions from the Russian masses. For its bond-holders AVVA proved to be a bad investment but, along with Logovaz, it produced Berezovsky's first fortune. By the early 1990s Berezovsky – who in the Soviet era had had to scrimp to buy winter tights and school notebooks for his children and enjoyed the use of just half a car, sharing it with a friend – was wealthy enough to send his two eldest daughters as fee-paying students to Cambridge University in England and acquire a glamorous young second wife.

But that was just the beginning and in 1993 Berezovsky decided to raise his game. He would try to apply the technique he had pioneered with Kadannikov in Togliatti to Boris Yeltsin in the Kremlin.

'Borya saw how Korzhakov had managed to become the éminence grise of the Kremlin,' another of the future oligarchs told me. 'And he thought, "Am I worse, am I stupider than that barely literate *muzhik*? No, I'm not." So Berezovsky decided he would do what Korzhakov had done.'

To displace Korzhakov, Berezovsky needed a way into the Kremlin and the Yeltsin family circle. By the end of 1993, he had found one. Yeltsin, fresh from the bloody battle with parliament in October, had written his second book of memoirs, *Zapiski prezidenta* (*Notes of a*

President). Berezovsky, who had formed a useful friendship with Valentin Yumashev – the former journalist and trusted Yeltsin family friend who had ghosted the president's first book of memoirs – offered to publish the work.

For Berezovsky, Yumashev offered the ideal entrée to the Kremlin. To produce Yeltsin's first autobiography, Yumashev – a cheerful round-faced 36-year-old who had worked as a reporter at *Komsomolskaya Pravda*, a middle-brow Moscow daily – had been thrown into instant intimacy with the president. At one point, the two men secluded themselves with Yeltsin's in-laws in a village in the Kirov region in north-eastern Russia and spent two weeks there wandering through meadows and reclining on haystacks as the president poured out his life story to his amanuensis. When Yumashev recommended Berezovsky as publisher of the second volume of memoirs, the first family trusted his recommendation implicitly.

There was something almost endearing about the amateurish, jerry-rigged nature of the project. Here was Yeltsin, president of an erstwhile superpower, nearly two years after the launch of market reforms, looking for a publisher of his memoirs with all the sophistication of some doddering uncle searching for a vanity press.

But remarkably, the Kremlin's fumbling approach was typical of the Russia of that time. By the mid-1990s, red directors and *kooperators* were already salting away tens of millions of dollars in Swiss bank accounts; yet, like the rest of the Russian establishment, they had only the foggiest notion of how advanced capitalism worked. The idea that most things – say, the autobiography of a president – were products which could be sold for money to someone who could use them to make a profit – a publishing house, for instance – was still alien. The old regime had operated on connections, not cash, and so – as much by inertia as anything else – the new regime continued to do so too.

Kadannikov, the key to so much of Berezovsky's success so far, again played a crucial role. For the denizens of the Kremlin, Berezovsky was a strange and slightly exotic creature, separated from the beefy bosses of the nomenklatura as much by his Jewish intellectual background as by his nouveau riche success. But Kadannikov was 'one of us' – a good-looking man of Yeltsin's age and caste, and an old acquaintance from the days when they had both been mid-ranking apparatchiks. For Yeltsin, his participation gave the project a seal of legitimacy, just as membership of a Princeton eating club or a Harvard MBA might reassure a 60-something member of the East Coast WASP establishment.

'Everyone respected Kadannikov, both Boris Nikolaevich himself and those who were with him,' Korzhakov told me. 'Kadannikov was very wise and Berezovsky was at his side.'

The memoirs were duly published and Berezovsky's Finnish 'friendly companies' did the Kremlin proud. The book was rolling off the presses within a few weeks and the colour was brighter and the pages thicker than the washed-out onion-skin text that Russian publishers produced. Berezovsky had his foot in the Kremlin door.

Because the publication of the book had not been a business transaction but a nomenklatura-style personal favour, the act of a loyal retainer, Yeltsin wanted to thank his lieges for their faithful service. The best reward, he decided, would be to admit them to the President's Club.

For Berezovsky, whose metier was working his personal connections, this membership was a priceless gift. The President's Club was a place for the friends of Yeltsin's heart, not his head. It was where the old gang from Sverdlovsk, the Urals region where he had been party boss, and newer friends like Shamil Tarpishchev – Yeltsin's tennis coach and beneficiary of one of the great Loophole Economy farragoes, the National Sports Fund – took their ease. More recent allies, men like Chubais or Gaidar with whom Yeltsin had joined forces for reasons of political conviction or expediency rather than personal affection, were not invited. Neither, of course, were any of the other future oligarchs for whom, as Friedman put it, the Kremlin was as far away as Mars. Berezovsky was the only one admitted and he immediately took advantage of his exclusive access to get even closer.

'The [Yeltsin] family would often come to the club to play sports, or to swim in the swimming pool, or to use the cosmetic beauty treatments,' Korzhakov explained to me. 'So Berezovsky now had direct access to them. If Tanya Dyachenko [the president's younger and favourite daughter] gave him her direct telephone number, what could anyone do to stop him?'

In forging an ever closer relationship with the Yeltsin family, the Kremlin leader's memoirs continued to serve Berezovsky well. Even in Russia, offering a naked bribe to the president was beyond the pale. However, as Yeltsin's publisher, Berezovsky had a legitimate reason to deliver a steady flow of royalty cheques to the Kremlin.

'"This is from the German sales, Boris Nikolaevich," he would say one month,' according to one presidential aide. 'The next month it would be another cheque, maybe from the sales in Japan.'

Only Berezovsky could say whether the royalties were real or padded, and in a way it didn't really matter. All that counted was that he had found a legitimate, unembarrassing way of supplementing the Yeltsin family income. Like everyone else confined to a state salary amidst the voracious consumerism of the new Russia, the Yeltsins could use the extra money.

Traditional nomenklatura perks – cars, bodyguards, country retreats, servants – meant that Yeltsin and his clan, like the general secretaries of yore, could live in comfort in Russia without spending a single kopek. But in the new Russia, that kind of Soviet-style extravagance was no longer enough. Western luxuries – like sending Boris Yeltsin junior, Tatyana's son, to Millfield, an English boarding-school – were becoming de rigueur for the Russian élite, and the president's publishing ventures provided the means for the first family to pay for them.

Thanks to this mutually satisfactory financial relationship, together with Berezovsky's immense personal charm, the entrepreneur's intimacy with the Yeltsin family, if not with the president himself, grew. His allies began popping up in key Kremlin positions, including Yumashev, who by 1997 had been elevated from ghostwriter to Kremlin chief of staff, a job at least as powerful as the prime minister's.

Cleverly, Berezovsky made a special point of cultivating Tatyana, whose tremendous influence on her father would play a pivotal role in the 1996 elections. In his 1997 memoirs, Korzhakov – by then a poisonous enemy of Berezovsky – claimed he won the heart of the president's daughter with generous gifts.

'He figured her out quickly,' Korzhakov wrote. 'Tanya worships gifts. So first Berezovsky gave her a Niva [a Soviet version of Jeep], then he gave her a Chevrolet.'

Before long Tanya was a frequent visitor to the Logovaz Clubhouse, the former Smirnoff mansion in central Moscow which Berezovsky had lovingly restored as a sort of personal salon. Businessmen and politicians summoned to her office in the Kremlin – disconcertingly done up like a snow princess boudoir, with white marble walls and flouncy ivory curtains – often found their conversation interrupted by calls from Berezovsky on Tatyana's private mobile telephone. One summer

Tatyana was spotted holidaying with Berezovsky and Roman Abramovich, his business partner who would eventually emerge as a Kremlin power-broker in his own right, on Berezovsky's yacht in the Mediterranean.

'As for my relations with Tatyana,' Berezovsky coyly told me, 'I know her very well, although I meet with her quite rarely. I very much hope that my advice to her is helpful.'

Soon, Berezovsky began to use his new personal network to expand his business interests. He first took aim at ORT, the state-owned national television company. By then, television had become a lucrative business in Russia. Starved of consumer goods under communism, Russians were shopping with a vengeance and television was the best way to reach them.

More importantly, in Russia, with its huge swathes of steppe and tundra, feeble civil society and tabloidish regional press, national television was the key to political power. Berezovsky realised early on that the airwaves would make the next president and, if he controlled them, they could transform him from a jumped-up car salesman into a king-maker.

So Berezovsky set about convincing his new friends in the Kremlin that it was in the president's interests for him to control ORT. Korzhakov – who, in a Russian illustration of the Peter principle, had climbed to a position of political power which far outstripped his intellectual resources – was a particularly soft target.

The problem, Berezovsky explained to Korzhakov and other paranoid Kremlin apparatchiks, was that the emancipated Russian media had taken Gorbachev's glasnost and Yeltsin's democracy too far. The president was under attack from all sides and particularly from NTV, the private television company established by Vladimir Gusinsky, another future oligarch. The only solution was to create a well financed, robustly pro-Yeltsin television station, and Berezovsky promised to do just that if he were given control over ORT. He pushed his plan with characteristic relentlessness.

'They [Berezovsky and Yumashev] began to break me,' Korzhakov recalled. 'Me and Ilyushin, the [president's] senior aide. Gradually, we said to them, all right, prepare the documents, we will study them and think how it can be done. It was a state-owned channel and to suddenly make it private seemed somehow . . . unethical. We had to think how to make it look nice. That was one thing. The other thing that was frightening was the financing of that channel.'

Berezovsky assuaged these concerns with his usual indirect approach. He would not seek outright ownership; 51 per cent of ORT would remain in the hands of the state. Instead, he and a group of other 'well-off people' would take over the remaining 49 per cent, finance the station and ensure it took a pro-Yeltsin line. By cleverly placing his own people in key positions in the company, before long Berezovsky controlled the station as surely as a majority owner, but without the full burden of financial responsibility.

A year later, the full genuis of Berezovsky's conquest of ORT would be apparent. Claiming he needed more money to properly fund the television station, he persuaded the Kremlin to hand him control of another state-owned company at a knock-down price – this time an oil company.

But in 1994, Berezovsky had not yet become that voracious. Instead, he hit on another idea. Around him, other future oligarchs were perfecting ways of enriching their companies by diverting government monies through their own accounts: Potanin had the customs accounts, Menatep had dozens of smaller deals. Berezovsky decided he would make a play for Aeroflot.

The national airline was a clever choice. Thanks to its international routes, it had a steady flow of hard-currency income, some of it paid in cash. And Aeroflot was also a good way to bet on Russian market reforms; if the country grew more prosperous, airline traffic would take off. In fact, taking over Aeroflot (or at least its accounts), was such a good idea that Berezovsky was not the only one who came up with it. Gusinsky, a former theatre director turned banker and media mogul, wanted the accounts too.

The two entrepreneurs had already begun to clash on the airwaves, with Berezovsky bad-mouthing the political line taken by Gusinsky's NTV in order to score points for himself in the Kremlin. With the rivalry over Aeroflot, the struggle intensified.

'Berezovsky at that moment entered into a very fierce conflict with us,' Sergei Zverev, one of Gusinsky's senior executives, told me. 'Eventually, either one or the other had to triumph.'

Gusinsky having decided he'd try to cut a deal, the two men held several meetings at which he offered to compromise and described to

Berezovsky the plan he had worked out for restructuring Aeroflot. Berezovsky heard him out attentively, then shook his head. The wheels of the apparat had already been set in motion, he explained, and it was now too late to stop them: 'Whoever wins, wins.'

Initially, Gusinsky thought he was winning – a government resolution was even passed formally appointing him Aeroflot's banker. But he didn't hang on to the juicy accounts for long. Just as the conflict reached its peak, Sasha Bekker's story about the Novosibirsk Tin Factory was published. The article had tremendous repercussions in Moscow thanks to one of the more creative manoeuvres of Dugelny, the plant's director: to make sure state officials backed his privatisation scheme, he gave everyone who mattered in government, from local KGB agents to central bank economists, free Tin Factory shares. The recipients of his largesse included one very powerful Moscow minister – Soskovets, the leader of the party of war.

When Bekker revealed this fact on the pages of *Segodnya*, a newspaper owned by Gusinsky, Soskovets was outraged. The article did so much damage to Gusinsky's links with the government that Bekker was nicknamed 'the $100 million journalist', because that is what his articles cost his employer in lost business. The first casualty was the Aeroflot deal. An infuriated Soskovets sent an aide to tell the Aeroflot board that the Russian cabinet had considered the matter and recommended that Avtovazbank, a company linked to Avtovaz and Logovaz and closely connected to Berezovsky, should handle the Aeroflot accounts.

The board members of what was then still a state-controlled company knew better than to disagree. The Aeroflot accounts went to Avtovazbank and Berezovsky became the airline's not-so-hidden éminence grise. Before long a number of Berezovsky allies were installed in key posts, including Valery Okulov, the husband of Yeltsin's elder daughter. Berezovsky had perfected his technique: 'As for Aeroflot, I have no financial interest in it,' he told me. 'I have no Aeroflot shares. I have, at times, taken an interest in what happens at that company and I have a lot of people who used to work with me who now work with Aeroflot, which I think is very good.'

Swiss authorities would later allege that Aeroflot's hard-currency receipts had been systematically misappropriated to the tune of at least $200m, through Andava and Forus, two Swiss-based companies which ostensibly provided the airline with financial services. But thanks to the

Kremlin connection – after all, Aeroflot had become the Yeltsin family firm – inside Russia the airline had political teflon: no matter what machinations investigators uncovered, they could never make them stick. Berezovsky has dismissed the investigation as a political campaign to discredit him.

With his victories at ORT and Aeroflot, by the middle of 1994 Berezovsky had clawed his way out of the provinces; he was in the big leagues now. But his new prominence came at a price. In the summer of 1994, his Mercedes was blown apart by a bomb; he survived, but his chauffeur was killed.

The violence shocked the future oligarchs. All of them admitted to sharp practices, but the one line they prided themselves on drawing was not resorting to physical violence against one another. That was the purview of the petty hustlers of the hinterland, the ex-con *mafiosi* or a few fiercely competitive sectors like the metals trade. The attack on Berezovsky suggested that the one rule of big business in Russia was starting to get blurred.

Russia's future oligarchs were scared. Most of them already had their own bodyguards, but now they began to hire musclemen to shadow their wives and children. More and more of them started to send their families to live permanently abroad. In their anxiety, old rivalries seemed to melt away and even Gusinsky rallied round. The day after the explosion, he and Zverev went to visit Berezovsky in a show of solidarity. A few days after that, Gusinsky lent him an armoured Mercedes, to use while he waited for a replacement for his old, shattered car.

The rapprochement did not last long, however. By the end of the year the two men would be locked in their bitterest conflict yet, and this time it would be a battle which would go beyond their personal business interests to threaten Russia's fragile post-communist democracy.

The Impresario – Vladimir Gusinsky

Going to see Vladimir Gusinsky always made me nervous. Not because he was mean (although he could be) and not because he hated me (although occasionally he did), but because he was so damned unpredictable. One moment he would be all jokes and bonhomie and bear-hugs, deciding to be interviewed over lunch in a trendy restaurant and bringing along his vivacious wife Lena. But the next minute, or the next time, he would be in a rage, furious and Olympian. Once he began an interview with a full-fledged Russian tirade – yelling, purple-faced, arms pounding the air for emphasis – accusing me of misrepresenting him in particular and Russian businessmen in general. Then, in a flash, he subsided. 'It's okay, Chrystia', he said with a wink, 'I know it's not your fault, I know there is a wider conspiracy against me in your company and I know you can do nothing about it.' When I tried to contradict him, he looked at me pityingly, but kindly: I was obviously too young and unimportant to have been let in on the corporate plot.

Gusinsky acted in the same way with everyone. His employees always breathed a sigh of relief when he went on holiday: they would have a respite from the tears and screams and generally living life in fast-forward. Even on vacation, Lena told me, he couldn't let up. For Gusinsky the stress, the high drama and the constant conflict were an addiction, and after 72 hours away from it all he would go into withdrawal, usually quite literally getting sick.

The best word for his temperament – with all his volatility, his passion and his mania for control – is operatic – a description which is especially apt because in his past Soviet life Gusinsky was a theatre director. Even after he left the stage to become a *kooperator* and later an oligarch, he never stopped being a larger-than-life theatrical figure, always convinced that, God-like, he could control the action from his director's chair.

Gusinsky even looks like a theatre director, of a particular kind. He's not one of those European auteurs, all angles, irony and shabby-chic clothes. Instead, he looks more like a Las Vegas impresario, the old-fashioned type. He's a little flashy – he used to wear a huge diamond pinkie ring until his PR chief told him not to – and his wife, whose tongue is as sharp as her manicure, favours leopard-print and leather. Gusinsky is neither tall nor heavy, but he seems big. He has an outsized square face, a colour so high it is almost aubergine and dark chocolate hair and eyes. He wears large, ugly rectangular glasses, but his expression is so mobile that you don't really notice them.

Like every Russian of his generation, Gusinsky belongs to a family which was battered on the Bolshevik anvil: in the 1937 purges, his

GOOD NIGHT AND SWEET DREAMS....

A thought to sleep on:

"The future belongs to those who believe in the beauty of their dreams."

Eleanor Roosevelt

SUNRISE · SUNSET

Sunrise tomorrow will be at <u>7'35</u>

Sunset tomorrow will be at <u>7'36</u>

TOMORROW'S WEATHER

low <u>58</u>° high <u>77</u>°

⦿ sunny ○ partly sunny ○ cloudy ○ chance of rain ○ rainy

maternal grandfather was executed and his grandmother was imprisoned in a labour camp. Gusinsky was born just as the terror was abating, in 1953, the year of Stalin's death. As a boy, Gusinsky wanted to be a physicist, but like so many of the oligarchs he was rejected from his chosen university because of his Jewish background. Instead, he studied engineering at a more humble institute. But by the time he graduated, his plans had changed: he got a degree from a Moscow drama school and began to stage plays in a few provincial theatres.

Then, one cold, grey February day in 1987, Gusinsky decided to change his life again. Suddenly he was fed up with the obsequiousness, the compromises, the petty politicking of life on the Soviet stage: 'I suddenly thought to myself, God damnit, I am so sick and tired of it all.' He decided to try his hand at business.

The dramatic decision, the willingness to turn his life upside-down based on a moment's ennui, was trademark Gusinsky. We tend to think of Russians as fearful stoics, which is what both communism and tsarism taught most of them to be. But Russia has also always had its wild men: the *skoptsy*, Orthodox religious fanatics who castrated themselves in the name of God; the escaped serfs who fled to the freezing freedom of the Siberian forests; the dissolute aristocratic gamblers who gave us Russian roulette. Like most of the New Russians, Gusinsky was a throwback to this free-wheeling tradition.

'I've always had a healthy streak of adventurism in my character and a certain feeling of being bullet-proof. All idiots and madmen probably feel the same way,' Gusinsky once told me. 'I always risk everything. A man must regularly, every five to seven years, change his life. If he doesn't do that, he becomes internally boring. Girls stop loving him, and his own children stop respecting him. Even dogs no longer come up and sniff him. Don't laugh, it is true – a man must be loved by women, children and dogs. Those three categories are the essentials of life.'

As a struggling entrepreneur, Gusinsky had plenty of scope to indulge his love of risk. He tried everything: driving a gypsy cab, hawking blue jeans on the black market, trading Western cigarettes. His first success was copper bracelets, the 1980s Soviet equivalent of New Age crystals. Vaguely connected with the ill-digested Eastern philosophies which were in vogue at the time, copper bracelets were popular as a putative defence against high blood pressure and general ill-health.

Gusinsky figured out a cheap way to make them, using the copper wire from broken-down trams. In exchange for a few bottles of vodka he could get spools of it, enough to make hundreds of bracelets. Now he was rich enough now to move into the bigger leagues of construction and real estate.

It was in these early days of eclectic business activity that Gusinsky struck up his first important political friendship in meeting Yuri Luzhkov, a mid-ranking Moscow city bureaucrat who would later become mayor and one of Russia's most powerful politicians. As Luzhkov – a small muscular man with a bald, bullet-shaped head and boundless energy – grew more powerful, Gusinsky prospered with him: his construction company got city jobs, his real estate firm had an easier time than most obtaining city land and permits, and Luzhkov even let Gusinsky, who had been working from a basement in a suburban factory, set up his headquarters in Moscow city hall.

Gusinsky's real breakthrough came when he realised that the city of Moscow's most valuable resource was its operating capital. He persuaded Luzhkov to transfer the money from Soviet-era banks to a consortium of commercial banks led by Gusinsky himself. Until then, Gusinsky's bank had been a sideline, which was little more than the accounting department of his wider operation. Now, suddenly, he was transformed into a banker of real substance. Many of the oligarchs made their first big fortunes in the same way: Potanin with the Customs accounts, Berezovsky with the Aeroflot accounts – but Gusinsky had the dubious distinction of coming up with the idea first.

No matter how big his empire became, Gusinsky would always be slightly tainted by these early years. He would always be Luzhkov's oligarch, the street-smart hustler who figured out how to parlay a political friendship into a fortune and cut every corner he had to along the way. What I liked about him, however, was that he admitted it. Once they became rich enough to buy their suits in Italy and their investment bankers on Wall Street, some of the other oligarchs started trying to forget they had been spawned by a sordid system; Gusinsky at least had the decency to remember.

'I cannot say I am an absolutely honest man, an example for everyone,' he told me. 'Nor can any person who survived in this country before 1985, or who built great things after 1985. We all have things which we would not like to tell our children. As we say in Russia, the lucky child suckles on two mothers. There are people with whom you can establish relations and receive a lot.'

Like so many of the oligarchs, in the beginning Gusinsky was a corporate omnivore. In early 1992, when Mikhail Leontiev walked into his office, the latest enticement became the newspaper business. Not even Gusinsky, with his fondness for bold self-flattering predictions, could have predicted then that by the end of the decade the humble proposal would grow into Russia's dominant private media empire and the healthiest part of his conglomerate, known as the Most group.

Short, dark-haired, bright-eyed and given to iconoclastic opinions, Leontiev was one of the new Russia's most influential journalists. Born in 1958, he was part of the Soviet baby-boomer generation which grew up without ever truly believing in communism. He studied economics at one of Moscow's most prestigious institutes, but soon fell out of mainstream Soviet professional life because of what he calls 'light dissent activities', the sort of political unorthodoxies which were enough to spoil an official career but too mild to provoke real repression.

As a consequence, Leontiev spent his working days in the 1980s scraping a living on the fringes of the official Soviet economy – for a while he survived by tutoring university students for their exams, later he became a night-watchman. But, in his off-hours, he moved in the intellectual circles which were plotting what would become, in less than a decade, the economic and political transformation of Russia. Before long, Leontiev began to contribute articles to the Soviet Union's increasingly daring newspapers and magazines, and by 1989 he had a full-time job in Moscow's first private daily newspaper, *Kommersant*.

As a reporter, Leontiev took a special interest in the brash, slightly shady *kooperators* who were starting to emerge on the Moscow scene. By the time the Soviet Union collapsed, Leontiev had met, interviewed and befriended most of the future oligarchs. He became closest to Gusinsky; soon Leontiev and Gusinsky were going out together with their wives and children, spending long Sunday afternoons in each other's homes eating and scheming.

In those days, Gusinsky was still a lot closer to peddling copper bracelets and driving a gypsy cab than to advising the Kremlin and jetting around in his private jet. It was he, as much as Leontiev, who stood to benefit professionally from the new friendship. Leontiev introduced Gusinsky into his intellectual circles and began to put his name forward when, for instance, a visiting World Bank official was in town and wanted to meet some of Russia's budding capitalists.

In the middle of 1992, it was Leontiev's turn to ask Gusinsky for a favour. By then Leontiev was working for *Nezavisimaya Gazeta*, an independent newspaper founded in 1991 in the heat of the pro-democracy movement. Frustrated with their mercurial editor and their starvation wages, *Nezavisimaya Gazeta*'s top journalists decided to try to set up a publication of their own. They began to canvas Moscow's moneymen to see if they could find a backer; but no one was interested.

Finally, Leontiev was deputised to approach Gusinsky, who after long consideration decided to back the project. One reason was his friendship; another was Gusinsky's theatrical personality and love of the public stage. Most important of all, Gusinsky was the first of the future oligarchs to grasp how central a role the media would play in the advancement of business interests. All of them, of course, had already discovered that politics and commerce were intimately intertwined. Yet Gusinsky was the first to fully appreciate to what extent, in Russia's nascent democracy, the political process was not confined to the corridors and saunas of the Kremlin but extended to its newspapers and television programmes.

The first issue of Gusinsky's new paper, christened *Segodnya* (or *Today*) rolled off the printing presses on 23 February 1993. It was an instant success. Gusinsky had the subtlety, and his journalists had the professional integrity, to save *Segodnya* from becoming the kind of blatant mouthpiece for its proprietor's commercial and political interests which many of the newspapers later established by other oligarchs would become. Instead, *Segodnya* was allowed to become one of Russia's freest, most honest liberal daily newspapers, rivalled only by *Izvestia*, the slightly fustier but occasionally more authoritative Soviet-era dowager.

Even so, Gusinsky's vested interests did not go unserved. For one thing, although most of *Segodnya*'s journalists were too proud to write *zakaznye* or 'ordered' articles, they submitted to a milder form of censorship. Gusinsky's own businesses were definitely off-bounds. As he put it: 'My own publications don't write negatively about me. I am the publisher and there must be some limits.' Sometimes, the limits would go further than that. Periodically, Most executives would ask *Segodnya* not to criticise some politician or businessman with whom crucial deals, like the bid for the Aeroflot accounts, were being transacted. (As in the case of Aeroflot, the journalists sometimes ignored their requests.)

For Gusinsky, these measures were defensive and he was careful not to use the newspaper as his puppet. It's not that he was a champion of the free press, although he sometimes posed as such, but he had a keen interest in preserving *Segodnya*'s reputation. If his paper was credible and influential, Gusinsky thought, then maybe some of its lustre would rub off on him.

Even by 1993, as Gusinsky began to become seriously rich, he was finding it hard to shake off his image as a slighty shady small-timer. Founding and owning a highbrow newspaper, committed to the democratic and capitalist values supported by Moscow's liberal intelligentsia, magically transformed Gusinsky into a player, a man whose views counted. At the price of a few million dollars a year – *Segodnya*'s annual losses – it was a bargain.

Later on, as Gusinsky's commercial appetites became more focused, his media interests would become a source not only of image and influence but also of profit. But in the early, heady years of Russia's capitalist transformation, there was so much of what Leontiev called 'stupid money' in Moscow, and so many easy ways to make a killing, that running a newspaper as a profitable business simply didn't make sense. When the *Segodnya* team asked Gusinsky to send in some number-crunchers to help make their newspaper more economical, he told them it would be a waste of resources.

'Think about it,' Gusinsky exhorted. 'Managing a newspaper is just as complicated as managing a bank, and requires a whole new language. Imagine I take a man, who is currently either making a profit for me or making savings for me of $100m a year. I send him to work at the newspaper, which is currently costing me losses of $8m a year. As a result of his work, the losses are cut from $8m to $2m. So, what did it cost me – $94m! What do I need that for? You should all just do what you like. I know you don't steal.'

Gusinsky's calculated decision to let *Segodnya* lose money was characteristic of the forces and the logic which shaped the earliest years of

Russian capitalism. Western advisers and aid-donors unrelentingly counselled Russians to restructure their rust-belt factories and run their new businesses in accordance with the best Western corporate practices. They were frustrated when the Russians failed to heed their advice.

But the problem was not a lack of entrepreneurial drive or an insufficient passion for money. It was simply that Russia's narrow layer of talented businessmen and managers directed their efforts where they would yield the highest reward. In the early years of Russian capitalism – and to a worrying extent in the later ones too – that tended to lie in exploiting the arbitrage opportunities between lingering Soviet prices and the world market, in buying up cheap state assets, in profiting from the Central Bank's negative real interest rates and in securing juicy government contracts.

Even after much of the 'stupid money' had dried up, Segodnya failed to become a major money-spinner for the Most group. But establishing the newspaper was Gusinsky's defining business move. As Segodnya swiftly gathered public kudos, frustrated journalists in other media began to see him as a potential benefactor. Among them were two leading television figures: Yevgeny Kisiliev, Russia's most popular anchorman, and Oleg Dobrodeev, a top producer.

Both worked for ORT, the state-owned television channel. As 1993 wore on, and the conflict between the hard-line parliament and the president began to escalate, the two men found their journalistic freedoms at ORT increasingly curtailed and decided to look for a moneyman to help them to go private: Gusinsky was the obvious choice.

Their first point of contact with the Most group was Zverev, an old friend and one-time fellow pro-democracy activist. At the end of May, Zverev invited Kisiliev and Dobrodeev to his 21st-floor office in the Moscow city hall skyscraper overlooking the Moskva river. As the two men laid out their proposal to set up an independent production company, Zverev grew more and more excited. Segodnya had been up and running for just over three months and, recently, he and Gusinsky had begun mulling over the idea of making a bolder foray into the media business by setting up their own television network. Now, he had two of Russia's top television executives sitting before him.

Abruptly, Zverev called for a break in the meeting. He liked their idea, he told Kisiliev and Dobrodeev, but maybe they should set their sights higher. Why not create not just a production company but a whole television station? As the two visitors tried to absorb this escalation in their plan, Zverev rushed out of his office to Gusinsky's far grander suite just around the corner. His eyes sparkling with excitement, he burst into Gusinsky's private room and exclaimed: 'You know how we were talking about creating our own television station? Well, I have two people in my office who can do it for us. There are no two better men for the job in all of Russia.'

Zverev fetched Kisiliev and Dobrodeev, introduced them to Gusinsky, and the four men sat down to a two-hour discussion. By the end of it, what would become Russia's first privately owned television station was born.

'To be honest, when we walked into the building we had no idea about forming an entire television station,' Kisiliev, a fair-haired, handsome man with a Walter Cronkite growl, told me. 'But we left it with the thought – why not?'

For the new station to work, Gusinsky knew that it needed more than creative talent. It needed a progressive manager, someone hardheaded, politically savvy and able to swim in the violent currents of Russian capitalism. For Dobrodeev and Kisiliev, the right candidate immediately sprang to mind: Igor Malashenko, the 38-year-old Soviet army brat, Dante scholar and former Central Committee ideologue who had worked with them at ORT before being sacked as part of the new, repressive climate at the station. Desperate for revenge against the apparatchiks who had kicked him out, Malashenko jumped at the offer.

Just a few days after that first May meeting, the group went to work. In contrast with *Segodnya*, creating a brand-new television station required serious investment. According to Malashenko, in its first fifteen months of existence the new television company – which was dubbed NTV, the Russian acronym for Independent Television – ate up more than $30m. Almost all the money came from Gusinsky; he had invited two other bankers to join him in the project, but they dropped out almost immediately.

The biggest challenge was to find a way to get on the Russian airwaves. Initially, NTV struck a deal with a regional St Petersburg channel and in October began to broadcast a few of its news programmes there. But Gusinsky's ambitions were much higher than that; he wanted to create Russia's first national private television station. To do so, he needed to be granted broadcasting rights to one of Russia's main national terrestrial channels, at that time a state monopoly.

In most Western countries, the divvying up of precious terrestrial television channels is a formal, carefully regulated competitive process. But in Russia, with its legacy of state ownership and central planning, there was no established system. One thing was clear, though. Only one man had the power to take a decision of such tremendous political, and potentially commercial, significance: Boris Yeltsin. To win the Kremlin's approval, Most set its formidable lobbying and PR machine in motion, drawing on everything from intelligence gathered by the ex-KGB agents in its private security force to friends in parliament and good ties with Moscow journalists.

First, they needed to find a soft target. Dobrodeev suggested Most should focus its sights on taking over channel 4, a mongrel jointly controlled by the two state-owned national television companies which each had channels of their own. By day, the underfunded channel showed amateurish programmes prepared by Russian universities, and by night it broadcast cheap shows rejected by the two main state channels.

Next, they needed to refine their arguments. For Most, the battle between the Kremlin and the parliament – which erupted into open street fighting in October, just as the first NTV shows began to appear in St Petersburg – provided a helpful backdrop. The Most group strongly supported the president throughout the conflict. State-owned television, never completely certain who would triumph and instinctively somewhat sympathetic to the communist-dominated parliament, was more ambivalent. The contrast helped Gusinsky and Zverev to make a powerful case that the Kremlin would benefit from giving Most a channel of its own.

But neither the weakness of channel 4's programming nor Most's firm support of Yeltsin played a decisive role. What was really crucial, as with all Russian government decisions, was steering the draft presidential decree through the corridors of power until it landed on Yeltsin's desk with all the signatures of his subordinates reassuringly saluting at the bottom of the page. As usual, Zverev – who served as a kind of foreign minister for the Most group, orchestrating its relations with all levels of government and with other private financial empires – led the campaign.

Zverev began his offensive by nudging the public debate in NTV's favour. 'We unveiled a whole campaign in the mass media on the theme that Russia needed independent commercial television,' he told me. 'There were many articles written and published on that theme, various people spoke out about it, leading television personalities and so forth.'

Once the public was softened up to the idea, Zverev began the laborious process of *vizirovat*, or getting signatures on the draft presidential decree. For two months he walked the corridors of the Kremlin, drank tea in waiting rooms, lobbied old friends and persuaded the heads of the two state-owned television channels which controlled channel 4 to back the plan.

Yet, for all Zverev's contacts and cunning, somewhere the decree was being blocked. Worse still, he had no idea who was blocking it. His breakthrough was serendipitous. One autumn afternoon, Zverev and Kisiliev were sitting in one of the white-walled mansions in the Kremlin complex waiting for a meeting with a presidential adviser. After they had been kept waiting for the obligatory twenty minutes, the adviser's office door swung open and they were invited in. They both recognised the man he had been ensconced with – Shamil Tarpishchev, the tall, lean Tatar athlete who had become Yeltsin's tennis coach and a member of his inner circle.

Nudging Kisiliev, Zverev asked if the television anchorman knew Tarpishchev. He did.

'I see that his office is just across the hallway,' Zverev told his colleague. 'When we're finished here, let's drop by and talk to Tarpishchev about channel 4.'

They did so, and in the course of the conversation Zverev realised it was none other than the powerful tennis coach who was blocking their deal. He couldn't believe his luck! Now that he knew what the problem was, he could try to solve it. Tarpishchev's objection, it turned out, was that he had a plan of his own for channel 4: he wanted to turn it into Russia's first all-sports network. It was easy to convince him to drop that plan – where would he find the funding? Zverev asked – and even easier to win him over to Most's rival proposal by promising to devote a certain amount of airtime to sports. As ever, Zverev was relying on one important piece of ignorance: like everyone else in Russia apart from the Most group, Tarpishchev hadn't yet figured out that television could actually make money.

With Tarpishchev neutralised, the signature-gathering process picked up speed. By the middle of January 1994, the decree had been signed and NTV was born, with airtime on channel 4 every night from 6 p.m. to midnight. Like Tarpishchev, the Kremlin hadn't yet twigged the commercial value of television: Most got the channel almost for free.

'The licence, in practice, never cost us anything at all,' Malashenko admitted. 'The cost was just a few kopeks. It was such a small sum that it wasn't even worth remembering. It was a purely political decision.'

As usual – the same was true of government bank accounts, export licences and natural resources – the Russian state seemed unable to appreciate that its assets had a market value. And as usual, the smartest and best-connected businessmen were the beneficiaries of the government's ignorance.

With NTV on air every day and *Segodnya* on the desk of every Russian opinion-maker, Gusinsky had transformed himself into Russia's first media baron. Now he began steadily to acquire new titles and expand into other media: before long his empire would include a news magazine, a trashy Russian version of *Hello!*, a radio station and satellite TV. His real estate and banking deals with Moscow city hall had given him money; his media interests gave him influence. Gusinsky had become what no private Russian businessman had been since 1917 – a significant, independent, political force.

As his power grew, so Gusinsky began to change. Always a volatile, frenetic workaholic, now he started to become somewhat grand. He might not yet be opening doors in the Kremlin with his foot, but among Russian businessmen he carried himself as the first among equals. He had always had a weakness for personal ostentation; now he began to seriously indulge it, buying a private jet and a fleet of ever showier new cars.

Gusinsky now began to make public political pronouncements. In private, he sometimes allowed himself to hint that he had more real power than the faltering state itself. When Tatarstan, an autonomous republic in central Russia, began to clamour for greater independence, forcing the Kremlin into political contortions to retain its loyalty and prompting murmurs of civil war, Gusinsky half-jokingly said to his partners: 'What's all this about Tatarstan? If it's necessary to take care of Tatarstan, I'll send fifty men from my security force and they'll take care of it and that will be that.'

For Russia, and especially for its government, this kind of behaviour was astonishing. The Soviet Union had been a culture of *uravnilovka*, literally levelling out, a term for the party's policy of making sure no individual light shone too brightly against the backdrop of the collective. Imperial Russia had practised something of the same philosophy, with peasants expected to give way to views of the *obshchina*, or rural community, where even wealthy nobles were expected to assume positions of grovelling subservience before the absolute power of the autocrat.

Even in the new order, cautious up-and-comers took care to strike a loyal pose, at least in public. On one of my first meetings with Khodorkovsky, at the time probably a far richer man than Gusinsky, the future oligarch was careful to insist on his absolute deference to the will of the state. If the prime minister were to ask him to step down as head of his bank, Khodorkovsky said he would do so at once: 'That is how Russia is organised. The state is always the dominant force in the economy.'

If that was still the rule, as 1994 rolled on Gusinsky seemed to have forgotten it. Inevitably, it was not long before the Kremlin decided to remind him.

The moment of reckoning came one dreary December afternoon, as Yeltsin and his retainers were finishing off a late lunch. Over the dregs of the meal, the president leaned across the littered table and addressed himself to Korzhakov, his friend and chief bodyguard, and Barsukov, the chief of the revamped KGB.

'Why can't the two of you deal with what's-his-name, with Gusinsky?' Yeltsin thundered. 'What's he up to? Why does he trample around everywhere? Everyone is complaining about him, including my own family. I can't count the number of times that Tanya [the president's younger daughter] or Naina [his wife] have been driving somewhere and the road has been blocked to make way for Gusinsky. His NTV has got too big for its boots, it behaves insolently. I order you: deal with him.'

Coquettishly, Korzhakov put up a few half-hearted objections: Gusinsky did not seem to have broken any serious laws, so how could he, an ordinary, honest law-enforcement official, take action against him? According to Korzhakov's own scurrilous memoirs, at least, an irritated Yeltsin quickly made it clear that he had no patience for such pedantry.

'It's not important!' the president roared. 'Grab on to something, persecute him everywhere, give him no quarter. Create such an atmosphere that the ground burns beneath his feet.'

This was exactly the command Korzhakov had been waiting to hear. A year earlier, he had helped Gusinsky get a licence for NTV; but over the past few months, his attitude towards the businessman had soured and privately he had begun to employ all manner of covert stratagems to curb Gusinsky's growing power. Now, the president had openly instructed him to get rid of this turbulent priest. Korzhakov was only too delighted to comply.

In the Kremlin, hostility towards Gusinsky had been building for months. One source of friction was the inevitable antipathy between a liberal media and an increasingly authoritarian government. In late 1993, when NTV got its licence, the great political divide in Russia was still between the communists and the democrats and the businessman and the president were still on the same side.

But Yeltsin had always been a problematic champion for Russian liberals and this moment of harmony, like so many others, quickly slipped into discord. As 1994 rolled on, Yeltsin increasingly began to turn to the party of war and the hard-line measures they recommended. Economic reforms again seemed to stall as the red directors lobbied for various special protections and most of the young reformers, including Gaidar himself, were pushed out of office. On political matters, the party of war was even more influential. Moscow began to take a tougher line with Chechnya and started to arm its own backers in the region.

The ascendancy of the party of war began to provoke friction between the Kremlin and the Most group. Like much of the Moscow intelligentsia, Most journalists were liberally inclined. Worse yet from the Kremlin's point of view, they had a disconcerting tendency to discover and publish embarrassing facts such as the story about Soskovets and the Novosibirsk Tin Factory. The Most group's coverage of

Chechnya, especially NTV's even-handed effort to present the Chechens' side of the story as well as Moscow's, infuriated the Kremlin even more.

'NTV was very dangerous,' Gusinsky told me. 'Just imagine – for the first time ever a television channel had appeared which you could not control. To which, if you said – "Hey there, stop covering Chechnya!" – they would just keep on covering it.'

Kremlin officials were incredulous. They had given Gusinsky his channel and now he was using that gift to attack them!

A further and even more significant count against Gusinsky was his alliance with Luzhkov. With presidential elections less than two years away, Yeltsin was becoming nervous about his own political longevity. The Moscow mayor, with his robust Russian nationalism and canny combination of Soviet nostalgia with an 'enrich yourself' spirit, was wildly popular among Muscovite voters. To the Kremlin, he started to look like a potential challenger.

'Luzhkov was changing,' Korzhakov told me. 'He was beginning to think about the presidency and Gusinsky's support was making him feel stronger.'

As they watched their televisions or heard fresh gossip about the chumminess between Luzhkov and Gusinsky, Yeltsin and his Kremlin entourage began gradually to accumulate a powder-keg of resentments. All that was missing was someone to light the match . . . Berezovsky was delighted to oblige.

'Berezovsky would regularly report to us where and what Gusinsky had said about the president, how he had insulted him, how he wanted to deceive him,' Korzhakov wrote in his memoirs. 'And Berezovsky achieved his goal – in the president's entourage, Gusinsky began to be viewed as a dangerous enemy.'

In a conversation with me and in several interviews in the Russian media, Korzhakov even claimed that Berezovsky had tried to persuade him to arrange Gusinsky's assassination. However, many, including Berezovsky himself, dismiss the allegation as unfounded.

For Berezovsky, portraying Gusinsky as a menace helped to enhance his own power. The more the Kremlin feared Gusinsky, the more it was prepared to build up Berezovsky as a counterweight. In the opinion of Leontiev and many others, Berezovsky's strategy made him a 'professional traitor'. Rather remarkably, Gusinsky took a more philosophical view. From his perspective, Berezovsky was just playing the game of Russian capitalism according to its own particularly savage rule-book. It wasn't personal, it was business, and when this round was over there would be no hard feelings.

'Berezovsky just took advantage of the situation,' Gusinsky told me. 'If he hadn't done it, some other John Doe would have. I don't think it was wrong. Berezovsky is just like me – no better and no worse. We are all the same. Good people are kind and generous but they rarely succeed in life. It is bad people who succeed, and they are rarely kind and generous.'

Whether Berezovsky's behaviour was good or bad, one thing was certain – it was successful. By late 1994, in Kremlin circles Luzhkov and Gusinsky had been established as public enemies number 1 and 2 and the pressure was on. Korzhakov and Barsukov, who generally preferred to hunt in a pack, began to urge Luzhkov to sever his ties with Gusinsky. Twice, Korzhakov told me, they cornered him in the exclusive President's Club and warned him to part ways from his old friend and ally.

In the last days of November, the screw turned tighter and Gusinsky's powerful security service, run by Felix Bobkov, the former deputy head of the KGB, reported worrying rumours. One version was that a *kiler*, a private assassin, had been commissioned to murder Gusinsky. Another was that, in some unknown way, Korzhakov was preparing to attack.

Then, on the first day of December, the president gave Korzhakov the fateful command to deal with the turbulent priest – at least according to the latter's memoirs. That day, Gusinsky received an unexpected call from Georgi Rogozin, Korzhakov's deputy, inviting him to the Kremlin for a meeting.

When Gusinsky arrived, Rogozin's agenda was immediately apparent. The Kremlin was unhappy both with Gusinsky's friendship with Luzhkov and with the coverage of the Kremlin and the war in Chechnya on NTV. To appease the president, Rogozin suggested, Gusinsky should produce some *kompromat* – the Russian term, inherited from the suspicious Soviet-era, for compromising materials – about the Moscow mayor.

'It was suggested to me that I betray Luzhkov,' Gusinsky recalled. 'He said, "We need Luzhkov's bank accounts." I said I didn't know about them, but even if I did, how could you think I would give them to anyone? What do you think my children would say about me after that?'

It was, Gusinsky said, a 'very long and complex conversation'. But by the end of it, he thought he and Rogozin had agreed a truce. It was not until the next morning, on Friday 2 December, that Gusinsky realised he had disastrously misjudged the situation.

Like most New Russians, Gusinsky had moved from Moscow's crowded and polluted city centre to a country dacha where he lived with his wife Lena, his two-year-old son, his mother and the family's nanny. Like all of the Most empire, the home was heavily guarded by Gusinsky's private security force. At about 9.15 a.m., the usual time he set off for the 40-minute drive to his office, Gusinsky stepped outside into the lightly falling snow and his two-car cortege prepared to head down Rublovskoe Shosse, a four-lane highway known as the President's Road because it was the route Yeltsin took from his own dacha into the Kremlin.

But as Gusinsky was climbing into his armoured car Zhenya, the head of his personal guard, warned him that there had been some problems. A group of armed men had driven up to the house and tried to provoke Gusinsky's guards into a fight; some of the men were masked and most carried automatic weapons. Worst of all, Zhenya was sure they were not what the Russians called *bandity* – they had the look and bearing of professional soldiers, perhaps KGB or the Ministry of the Interior.

When Gusinsky's motorcade set off for the city, the armed men – driving three cars, one of which was the personal vehicle of Barsukov, the KGB chief – followed. They wanted to be noticed, waving their machine guns outside their car windows, openly videotaping Gusinsky and his entourage and trying to force the Most vehicles into the ditch.

'We decided to demonstratively tail Gusinsky,' Korzhakov recalled in his memoirs 'The banker's bodyguards were nervous and Gusinsky himself was frightened to death.'

Once he arrived at his 21st-floor office, a shaken Gusinsky summoned his closest advisers – Zverev, his PR and information chief, Malashenko, the head of NTV, and Bobkov, the ex-KGB agent who ran his security service – and frantically began trying to figure out what was going on and how to respond. Gusinsky's first move was to call two senior Moscow police chiefs and ask them to help him identify the armed group which had pursued him into the city and was now surrounding the office building. Soon, the policemen came back with an answer: the armed pursuers worked for the infamous Presidential Security Service, headed by Korzhakov.

Gusinsky blanched. To his mind, the Presidential Security Service was the modern equivalent of the *oprichniki*, Ivan the Terrible's notorious squads.

'Absolutely everything was permitted to them,' Gusinsky later told me. 'They drove around the streets of the city drunk, they did anything they wanted. There was no more terrifying and powerful person in Russian than their chief, Korzhakov. It was the most terrifying service in Russia. It was like a regiment of death.'

Worse still, the Most executives realised immediately that even Korzhakov would never put on such an overt show of force without the explicit approval of the president himself. Gusinsky had become a pawn in a larger Kremlin game, and he was on the wrong side.

Yet, despite his strong suspicion that Yeltsin had personally authorised the siege of his office, Gusinsky (ever the impresario) decided to try to stir things up. He had an influential friend in the security forces: Yevgeny Sevastyanov, a bearded, soft-spoken academic who had joined the pro-democracy movement in the late 1980s and been rewarded with the post of head of the Moscow municipal branch of the FSK, the revamped KGB. Gusinsky telephoned Sevastyanov and told him about the armed men outside his building, urging that he should send someone out to investigate immediately – after all, the gunmen were just 100m from the White House, which by then served as the seat of the Russian cabinet.

Of course Gusinsky, who knew perfectly well who the men were, was setting his friend up: 'I was being a bit of a provocateur,' he later admitted to me. 'It was interesting for me to see how the federal government structures would react to the actions of the Presidential Security Service.'

Sevastyanov took the bait. Korzhakov, who fancied himself a sort of James Bond-style secret service agent, had neglected standard police procedure and failed to inform other police agencies of his operation. Since Sevastyanov had no idea that the armed men were actually working for the Kremlin, he sent out an anti-terrorist team to investigate.

Korzhakov's men were astonished. They were the crème-de-la-crème of Russia's law-enforcement organisations, the untouchables, and here were five ordinary Moscow KGB agents brandishing their guns and demanding to see their documents. Before long, a fight broke out. A Moscow agent fired a shot into a tyre of one of the three cars driven by the president's men. Another bullet grazed the shoulder of a presidential guard, leaving him unharmed but, to his fury, spoiling his new leather jacket. Another one of the president's men was knocked to the ground by a powerful right-hand hook from a young woman who was part of the Moscow KGB team.

Just as the two forces were on the verge of a pointless and bloody shoot-out, one of the Moscow KGB agents recognised one of the presidential guards: they had once worked together. The hostility dissolved into stiff smiles, guns were holstered, hands were roughly shaken and the KGB agents drove away.

But the violence had raised the stakes. All morning, Gusinsky and his team had been watching events unfold in the icy, concrete parking area 21 storeys below. From the start, Malashenko had insisted that the Most group's only defence was the weapon which had helped to get it into trouble in the first place: the media. Bobkov demurred. Perhaps a back-room political solution could be found, he argued. After all, going public was an extreme move, and one which would put the Most group openly and inexorably into conflict with the president.

As Sevastyanov's team drove away, Gusinsky realised that taking to the airwaves was now his only option. Malashenko and Zverev hit the telephones, personally calling all the journalists they knew (particularly Western ones) and inviting them to come to the Most offices immediately.

Their SOS signal did not go out a moment too soon. Infuriated by the behaviour of Sevastyanov's team, Korzhakov sent an additional group of men to the Most building; they wore black balaclavas and camouflage fatigues and were heavily armed. The men began roughly to search Gusinsky's cars and ordered the three bodyguards who had been sitting inside to get out. Then they forced them to lie face-down on the snow-covered concrete and beat them with their heavily booted feet and the butts of their guns.

That scene – the three bruised and bloody bodyguards lying face-down on the snow, encircled by a group of masked men raining blows down on them – became the defining image of the conflict. Dubbed as the faces-on-the-snow incident, the confrontation was almost immediately seen as a turning point in Russia's political and economic development . . . but as yet no one could tell what kind of a turn it signalled.

The battle took on such iconic significance because the arrival of Korzhakov's bruisers coincided with the appearance of the press. As the president's men bore down on the hapless security guards, more than thirty television cameras, belonging to everyone from CNN to Japanese TV to NTV itself, were there to record every blow of icy boot to broken rib, each rivulet of blood seeping on to the snow below. Korzhakov's men might still behave with the lawless brutality of the *oprichniki*, but they were *oprichniki* operating in the television age.

'Our [journalistic] colleagues really supported us,' Gusinsky recalled. 'I think what stopped those butchers was the presence of hundreds of journalists here, who understood that what was happening was lawlessness.'

Eventually, on the personal order of Viktor Yerin, the minister of the interior who had been petitioned by his friend Korzhakov, a police team arrived at the Most building and arrested the beaten bodyguards. By 1 a.m., however, they had been released. The Moscow police were disgusted by the flimsy charges, which had been conjured up in a transparent effort to get at Gusinsky. In fact, a local government prosecutor was so incensed by the incident that he tried to bring criminal charges against the presidential guard for exceeding its authority. A delighted Gusinsky declared the pugnacious lawyer a civil society hero.

But Korzhakov, against whom the investigation was of course swiftly dropped, had already taken one scalp that day. Sevastyanov, the head of the Moscow KGB, was fired by presidential decree even as the president's men were beating Gusinsky's bodyguards. As Sevastyanov later wryly told me: 'We have a saying in Russia – don't fight with the strong, or take the rich to court. As soon as my boys called me up and said, "These are Korzhakov's men but, while we were figuring that out, we got into a fight with them", I told them, "Well done. You can congratulate yourselves on having got the chief of the Moscow KGB fired today."'

When Gusinsky finally reached home at 2 a.m. next day, his wife was so nervous that she greeted him at the door with a Winchester in her hand. When he saw the gun and Lena's fierce stare, Gusinsky smiled, probably for the first time that day.

'I can tell you, she was ready to defend herself,' Gusinsky recalled with a proud grin. 'She's a Kuban Cossack.'

Over the next few days, things became even more tense. Korzhakov publicly declared that he was going hunting for 'geese', a reference to one of Gusinsky's nicknames. The pressure on Luzhkov, on Most bank and on the Most media interests intensified. All of this occurred against the background of an escalating conflict between the Kremlin and the separatist fighters in Chechnya. The fighting was going badly wrong and this was making the Kremlin even more defensive and trigger-happy than usual.

Three days later on Monday 5 December, Gusinsky decided to send Lena, their son and their nanny to London. Normally, they would have flown on the private jet which was one of his favourite executive toys, but the businessman worried that a still-wrathful Korzhakov might not allow his private plane to leave Russian airspace. So, instead, the family bought tickets for British Airways' scheduled daily 5.30 p.m. flight to Heathrow.

As Lena and her small entourage wove their way through the dirty winter slush and the evening traffic towards Sheremetyevo airport, Gusinsky headed for the Kremlin where Rogozin had called him in for another meeting. To Gusinsky's first request that his wife and son be allowed to leave the country, Korzhakov's deputy responded with a coy non-answer: maybe they would be, maybe they wouldn't be, it all depended on Gusinsky's conduct. With that Gusinsky, never the most tranquil of men, exploded.

'I started cursing him, his relatives, his mother, his father, his grand-fathers and his grandmothers,' Gusinsky said. 'Then I told him what would happen to him personally [if my wife was not allowed to leave]. I said that I wouldn't need my security guards or anything, I would strangle him with my own bare hands. I said that I would kill him. It was all very clear. Because you know what we say – there is no fiercer fighter than a scared Jew.'

Years later, Gusinsky was still proud of his outburst, and certain that it had helped to ensure the safe passage of his wife and son out of Russia. But, of course, Rogozin and Korzhakov were far from van-quished and over the next few days, as the pressure continued,

Gusinsky realised he was a sitting duck. The only option, he decided, was to leave Russia – temporarily, he hoped. On 18 December 1994, four days after the Kremlin sent its army to Chechnya and three days after my brother Adik left Russia for ever, Gusinsky followed his wife to London.

Two months later, I joined Gusinsky in the genteel salon of London's Park Lane Hotel. He was chairing one of his weekly meetings with his top executives – during those days, the entire Most team shuttled back and forth so often that 'going to London became like catching the Metro for us', one of them told me. The group of gesticulating leather-jacketed Russians surrounded by a haze of cigarette smoke, the proud ringing of mobile phones and the bright, hard smiles of young wives looked profoundly out of place in that sedate English sitting room.

But Gusinsky was deeply indifferent to both the snooty looks of the waiters and the elegance of his surroundings. He was talking about Russia and wondering if it would ever be safe for him to go back: 'It is very simple to find a reason to arrest a man in Russia. I could wake up tomorrow and be told that I drink the blood of young babies, or have been molesting teenage girls. Anything, any trumped-up charge at all, is possible.'

While Gusinsky watched and waited, his businesses began to die. Although NTV continued its brave coverage of the Chechen war, on other issues Gusinsky's journalists were muzzled as he sought a truce with the Kremlin.

'He imposed a very strict censorship on us,' Leontiev recalled. 'It was a request from him which we could not refuse. We used to say to him: "Vov, you know that you are destroying the newspaper. We are now more boring than everyone else." And he would reply: "Guys, I understand you, but be patient. Wait another month and a half and then, well, if we have to die, let's die with music."'

The banking arm of Gusinsky's group was in even greater jeopardy. Of all businesses in Russia, banking was the one most deeply dependent on the favour of the state. Now that Gusinsky had been officially declared the Kremlin's *bête noire*, other banks and retail clients began to fear that Most was no longer credit-worthy. After all, any day now, it seemed, Korzhakov might close down the bank altogether.

The attack on Gusinsky also sparked a crisis for Moscow city hall. To a large extent, Gusinsky had been hounded as a proxy for Luzhkov, whose initial reaction was exactly as the Kremlin had hoped; he quietly cooled his alliance with Gusinsky – on the day when Korzhakov's men swooped down on the Most group, the mayor was unavailable to speak with his erstwhile friend – and he took care to publicly pledge his fealty to Yeltsin.

But, even as he bowed his head to the tsar and distanced himself from the tsar's enemies, Luzhkov privately vowed never again to be so dependent on the whims of the central government. The faces-on-the-snow incident had underscored his vulnerability. When faced with a choice between city hall and the Kremlin, many of Luzhkov's closest financial and political allies had deserted him. In the aftermath of the attack, the Moscow mayor withdrew from public life and considered how to protect himself against future betrayals.

Luzhkov's solution was to become an economic tycoon in his own right. Now convinced that he could trust no one but himself, he used Moscow's tremendous political clout to build up a vast financial and industrial empire directly run by himself and his first lieutenant. This new conglomerate, an unwieldy hybrid of business and politics, was called Sistema. Controlled by a branch of government but operating in the private sector, Sistema soon became the most muscular practitioner of what Russians eventually began to call state capitalism – a new and increasingly popular genre of economic life which was not quite central planning, but not a free market either.

'The ideology of Sistema was born out of the conflict with Yeltsin,' Gusinsky explained. 'He [Luzhkov] understood that he had to do something so that no one would betray him again. To ensure that no one betrayed his business, he had to have control. To have control he had to own a share. That's all. It was very simple.'

With Gusinsky trapped in London and Luzhkov focused on building up his own financial and political machine, Korzhakov and the party of war seemed to grow more influential every day. No longer content merely to advise the president on matters of war and peace, the body-guard began to dabble in the economy. Ten days after the faces-on-the-snow incident, Korzhakov took it upon himself to write to Prime Minister Chernomyrdin, instructing him on how to conduct negotiations with the World Bank for a multi-million-dollar loan.

The letter, which was leaked, horrified the Moscow intelligentsia. *Izvestia* was prompted to ask its readers, 'Who rules Russia – Yeltsin,

Chernomyrdin, or General Korzhakov?' Some pundits drew parallels with Rasputin and the chaotic final days of the Romanov dynasty. Others compared Korzhakov and his crackdown on Most with the attacks on Soviet businessmen which had marked the beginning of the end of the New Economic Policy – the brief respite in the 1920s when the Bolsheviks allowed small and medium-sized business to flourish. Just as that was cut short by the Great Terror and Stalinism, many Russians had worried all along that Russia's young capitalism would come to a bitter end. The brazen attack on Gusinsky seemed to signal that the nay-sayers might be right.

'It wasn't a conflict between Korzhakov and Gusinsky,' Sevastyanov argued. 'It was a conflict between the nascent, free society and a new-fangled totalitarianism. Korzhakov was the carrier of the idea of a new totalitarianism. It seemed to him that the emerging system of government, and the situation in the country as a whole, was spinning out of control. It would only be possible to reassert control using coercive methods.'

Even the darkest prophets did not predict a return to Soviet-style dictatorship, but the freedoms and promises of 1991 did appear to be at an end. Instead, Russia seemed to be settling for a newer, lazier version of totalitarianism in which some political liberties, some economic opportunities would be allowed, but the ageing and ill-tempered bear of the state would have the power to interfere wherever and whenever it liked. After three tumultuous years of market and political reforms, the party of war seemed to be ruling Russia.

8

THE FAUSTIAN BARGAIN

IT DOESN'T HAPPEN very often, but every once in a while a really Big Idea – a premise so timely or so powerful that it changes the shape of our lives – comes along. A disaffected Russian intellectual reads Marx, is inspired to marry his theories to the indigenous terrorist tradition and bang!, the world's first communist dictatorship is born. A group of paranoid US military engineers decide to use their fancy new computers to create an electronic communications network so decentralised that it will be safe from the Soviet threat and yahoo!, forty years later that network has become the Internet and is transforming the global economy. In post-communist Russia, the Big Idea was an intricate privatisation scheme known as loans-for-shares and its ultimate result was the deformed capitalism which has impoverished and embittered the country.

Loans-for-shares was not the obvious kind of Big Idea: it was not a grand political theory nor a brilliant invention. It wasn't idealistic, like Gandhi's non-violent resistance movement, or particularly smart. It didn't even have the distinction of being soul-numbingly evil, like Nazism or apartheid. Instead, loans-for-shares was a Big Idea very much in the cheesy, sleazy, look-out-for-number-one spirit of the New Russia.

Its strengths were audacity and cunning, so much so that it was months before anyone outside a small circle of Moscow insiders realised what was really going on.

At heart, the loans-for-shares deal was a crude trade of property for political support. In exchange for some of Russia's most valuable companies, a group of businessmen – the oligarchs – threw their political muscle behind the Kremlin. What made that bargain a Big Idea and not just run-of-the-mill corruption was its scale. Over the course of four months, the government privatised the behemoths of the Russian economy – a half-dozen huge enterprises, including the world's dominant producer of nickel and several reserve-rich oil companies – selling them for a fraction of their potential market value. It was the sale of the century.

Loans-for-shares was also politically radical. Thousands of red directors had already been enormously enriched by privatisation. For example, the Soviet-era managers of Gazprom, Russia's natural gas monopoly, and of Lukoil and Surgutneftegaz, two of the largest oil companies, were savvy enough to use mass privatisation to become the owners of huge chunks of Russia's mineral wealth. But that was essentially a process of redefinition rather than of redistribution, with the Kremlin just formalising the red directors' ownership of assets they had already effectively controlled in the Soviet era.

Loans-for-shares was revolutionary because it did the opposite: it took companies away from their red directors and gave them to a handful of thrusting entrepreneurs. These men became oligarchs – and it was the convoluted loans-for-shares scheme which created them – a scheme so brazen and so bizarre that five years later it's still hard to understand why the Russian government actually did it. Consider: it couldn't be purely out of weakness – it would have been easier simply to give the enterprises to their red directors. It couldn't be sheer corruption either – if it had been, why not give them to the real political insiders like Yeltsin's daughters or Chubais' wife?

So what was the motivation? Of course, in the messiness of real life – and Russia is nothing if not messy – there were many. The state *was* weak; many of its apparatchiks *were* corrupt; the future oligarchs *were* brilliant lobbyists, adept at playing on all the divisions in Yeltsin's schizophrenic government. But, in the end, loans-for-shares was implemented for one central reason – because the government in general and the young reformers (who still controlled the privatisation process) in particular took the calculated gamble that this was the Big Idea which could save Russia's capitalist revolution. Loans-for-shares bought Yeltsin the political, financial and strategic support of the future oligarchs in the upcoming presidential elections. It meant pawning Russia's crown jewels, but if that was the price of keeping the communists out of the Kremlin, the young reformers were willing to pay up.

'I understood the loans-for-shares programme perfectly well,' Gaidar told me on a rainy afternoon in his office three years later. 'The loans-for-shares created a political pact. They helped to ensure that Zyuganov [the communist leader] did not come to the Kremlin. It was a necessary pact.'

That 'necessary pact' turned out to be a Faustian bargain. The young reformers defeated the communists, but they lost their souls in the process. They had come to power as democrats; to stay there, they created a shadowy, unelected cabal. They had come to power to create a fair, equitable law-abiding market economy; to keep it, they sponsored one of the world's sleaziest insider deals. Ultimately, loans-for-shares destroyed the young reformers: it cost them their ideals, their reputations and eventually their jobs. Worse yet, ultimately it scotched any remaining short-term hopes for the emergence of healthy, prosperous Russian capitalism. Instead, Russia's market economy is now corrupt, distorted and inefficient and loans-for-shares is both cause and symbol of its malaise.

It took us a while to abandon the image of Boris Yeltsin on the tank as the defining icon of the New Russia. The collapse of the evil empire, the velvet revolution and the end of history were such hopeful stories, and we in the West had such a stake in them, they were hard to stop believing. But now that so many of us have given up on the dream of a resurrected Russia, we have been seduced by a titillating new set of images: gangsters, shootouts, drugs, prostitutes, money-laundering and kick-backs. Blaming Russia's woes on these lurid forms of crime and corruption is easy, and exciting – but it's not really true. Russia has been looted certainly, but the biggest crimes have not been clandestine or violent or even, in the strict legal sense, crimes at all. Russia was robbed in broad daylight by businessmen who broke no laws, assisted by the West's best friends in the Kremlin – the young reformers.

The loans-for-shares programme began to creep into life in the dying days of 1994. It was a dark time for Russia and for the lurching effort to create democracy and capitalism, when Yeltsin was becoming authoritarian and bellicose, curtailing press freedom and threatening war against Chechnya. Economic reforms seemed stalled. Voucher privatisation was almost complete, but it was not at all clear what would happen to the companies still in state hands. The macro-economic outlook was bleak: the annual inflation rate was 215 per cent, the rouble grew weaker every month.

But for at least one man – Vladimir Potanin, the Soviet blue blood – this harsh political and economic environment looked like an opportunity. He had been the slowest to join the capitalist race, but once he decided to become a capitalist he thought big. Managing the government's money or buying up the rust-belt factories the state was selling for a song was a nice enough racket to start with, but soon Potanin wanted much more. He sensed that it was now, in the embryonic years of Russia's capitalist revolution, that the great fortunes – those which would make names and endure for generations – would be built. To create his own, to establish the house of Potanin, he wanted a piece of the only assets which the demented system of central planning had been unable to destroy: Russia's natural resources. By the autumn of 1994, Potanin had already decided which nugget he wanted: Norilsk Nickel, the gargantuan producer of nickel, cobalt and other precious metals in the far north.

It was a daring choice. Norilsk Nickel, eked out of the frozen tundra through almost immeasurable collective sacrifice in the 1930s, was not just a metals mine. It was 'the pearl of the north', a national legend and for millions of Russians a potent symbol of both the pain and the achievements of the agonising Stalinist industrialisation drive. With annual sales estimated at more than $25bn, it was also one of the few truly valuable enterprises in an economy dominated by unprofitable Soviet albatrosses.

Potanin already had a significant link with Norilsk Nickel. It was one of the clients which Oneximbank, his company, had inherited after the collapse of the Soviet banking system. Now he wanted to elevate himself from Norilsk Nickel's banker to being its owner. To make this brazen proposal more palatable, Potanin hit on the idea of disguising it with weasel words. He wouldn't actually suggest 'buying' Norilsk Nickel at a knock-down 'price'; instead, he would offer to 'manage' the company in exchange for a 'loan'. He had come up with the cunning rhetorical device which would soon mature into the loans-for-shares scheme.

Potanin's idea made fantastic progress. By October 1994, Yeltsin had signed a decree authorising Interros, Potanin's holding company, to manage the state's stake in Norilsk Nickel and other major enterprises with which he already had a relationship. But, as Potanin soon discovered, getting a decree signed was one thing but implementing it was something altogether more difficult.

Now he needed allies. To get them, he decided to make his plan more ambitious. He wouldn't just try to capture Norilsk Nickel for himself; he would set his sights on an entire herd of valuable Russian companies and bring together a pack of up-and-coming private businessmen to join him in the hunt . . . and in feasting on the eventual kill.

The men Potanin invited into the deal were a veritable who's who of Russian business. He remembers consulting with Khodorkovsky, the apparatchik oligarch; Aleksandr Smolensky, another future oligarch who had begun as a small-scale Soviet entrepreneur and gone on to found the Stolichny banking group; Vladimir Vinogradov, head of Inkombank, and later a sort of junior oligarch; Petr Rodniov of Imperial, a bank established by the oil and gas barons; and Vitaly Malkin of the Rossisky Kredit bank, and eventually a junior oligarch. Friedman, the outsider oligarch, was also in on the preliminary talks.

The series of meetings which this group held, generally either at Potanin's or Khodorkovsky's headquarters, was epochal. The first time when the small, disparate band of adventurers who had made fortunes in the wild early days of Russia's capitalist transformation gathered and sought to advance their private interests collectively, it was the beginning of the oligarchy.

The reaction to Potanin's plan was mixed. According to Nevzlin, one of Khodorkovsky's partners, their group was immediately enthusiastic. Smolensky was more reserved, saying he wouldn't participate directly but would be happy to help finance deals fronted by other future oligarchs. A few were totally dismissive: the plan seemed too grasping, even by Russian standards, ever to work.

'The scheme proposed selling property which was worth billions of dollars for mere kopeks. It seemed unrealistic and I reacted coldly,' Friedman told me ruefully. 'But, as you see, it turned out to be very realistic.'

A core group committed to the plan quickly emerged. Perhaps surprisingly, that group quickly agreed on a rough and ready division of Russia's most valuable companies. 'We reached an agreement on who would take what. We agreed not to get in each others' way,' Nevzlin admitted. 'In this respect there was an element of insider dealing.' Potanin would get the best company, Norilsk Nickel, because he had come up with the plan in the first place. Khodorkovsky would get Yukos, a huge Siberian oil company. Other, smaller enterprises were earmarked for the more junior players.

The next hurdle for Potanin was to win government support for his new, expanded scheme. At the time, the Russian political establishment was split; in early 1995, the conflict was particularly intense. The party of war had just persuaded Yeltsin to launch the disastrous attack on Chechnya. In response, for the first time, Russia's horrified liberals began to attack the Kremlin. Gaidar publicly announced his opposition to the president and many of the young reformers thought that Chubais, who was still clinging to a seat in cabinet, should resign. To implement loans-for-shares, Potanin needed to get the support of both factions, and of their warring leaders: Chubais and Soskovets.

Soskovets, the deputy prime minister, was the easier to win over. He was, as Potanin put it, one of the 'ideologists' of FIGs, the huge financial-industrial conglomerates which the loans-for-shares programme would eventually create, and he had backed Potanin in his initial efforts to take over Norilsk Nickel. Just as importantly, he and the future oligarch spoke a common language and belonged to a common tribe. Potanin was a nomenklatura baby and he had no problem in charming a middle-aged red baron like Soskovets.

Chubais, also a deputy prime minister, was more difficult to convince. He was reluctant to compromise his principles – and to tarnish his golden Western reputation – by condoning insider privatisation. But if anyone could persuade him, it was Potanin. The two men were not yet close friends, but they too already had a lot in common. Both were young, English-speaking and so aggressive as to sometimes be called arrogant. Moreover Potanin, with his well-cut suits and mastery of Western business jargon, was exactly the sort of home-bred tycoon Chubais had hoped his market revolution would create. Potanin began to meet with Chubais to sell him on the scheme.

For Chubais, one of Potanin's most powerful arguments was that loans-for-shares would raise money for the cash-strapped Russian treasury. By the beginning of 1995, the young reformers had succeeded beyond their wildest expectations in their pledge to transfer property to private owners, but they had failed miserably in their promise to stabilise the economy. Chubais vowed that 1995 would be the year when the government finally brought down inflation and rescued the rouble. To do that, he needed to find non-inflationary sources of state revenue: precisely what Potanin and his consortium so temptingly offered. Chubais also liked the idea of using the future oligarchs to break the back of the red directors and – he hoped – bring better management to Russia's moribund industry.

But still, Chubais had reservations. So far, the young reformers had tried to make privatisation as fair and as open as they could. The loans-for-shares scheme, by contrast, was a naked insider give-away. 'There is no competition, no openness,' Chubais complained to Potanin. 'It is not in our tradition.' So Potanin promised to make the process at the very least look less egregiously corrupt, and the future oligarchs won their second vital government supporter.

Finally, the business consortium was invited to present its scheme to the full Russian cabinet at a meeting on 30 March 1995. Potanin was chosen as spokesman; Khodorkovsky and Smolensky went with him to offer moral support.

The plan which Potanin outlined was an early version of loans-for-shares. Speaking in the name of the business consortium, he said the group was prepared to offer the government a loan of up to Rbs 9.1 trillion [£1.12bn sterling]. In exchange, the consortium collectively would be entrusted with the management of the state stake in a number of leading companies, including Norilsk Nickel and Yukos (which ultimately were sold off through the scheme), UES, the national power company, and Rostelekom, the national telecommunications operator (which were eventually excluded from the programme).

Potanin's historic offer would transform Russian politics and the Russian economy; it was also a measure of how dramatically Russia had already changed. Three men, two of them barely in their thirties and all unknown ten years earlier, had become so powerful that they could presume to make a bargain with what was left of the once omnipotent Soviet state. For men born and bred in the belly of the Soviet system, I thought, it must have been somewhat intimidating to enter the vast chandeliered cabinet meeting room and address the assembled ministers on equal terms.

Apparently not.

'Me worried? What did I have to worry about?' Potanin replied in answer to my question. 'We, in our banks, had comfortable material circumstances. It was the government which had a hole in its budget. They were the ones who were worried. I just wanted to calm them down, say to them, there is a concrete idea. We'll collect a billion or two dollars.'

As it turned out, his sangfroid was perfectly justified. After Potanin had finished speaking, Prime Minister Chernomyrdin said he liked the sound of his scheme. Then he asked the two most powerful figures in his cabinet – Chubais and Soskovets – what they thought. This was the crucial moment: the two men disagreed over almost everything, and either one was probably strong enough to stymie the programme. But Potanin's skilful lobbying paid off.

'Soskovets said that he, in principle, at a preliminary stage, thought it was interesting,' Potanin remembered. 'Chubais just silently nodded his head, meaning, we'll work on it. And that was it.'

Loans-for-shares had passed its first and most important political test. History was being made.

But apart from the future oligarchs and a few cabinet ministers, hardly anyone realised what was going on. The scheme was so brazen, and so downright weird, that many of the smartest observers of the Russian economic scene, especially the Western ones, refused to take it seriously.

My notebook from April 1995, a few days after the fateful cabinet meeting, records the views of one such doubter – Anders Aslund, a Swedish economist. 'It's absolutely outrageous,' Aslund spluttered. 'The implication is, we should get richer at the expense of the state.' But Aslund, an intelligent Western analyst and generally one of the best informed, assured me that I need not fear the plan would ever be implemented. And why not? 'Because it's so stupid!' Aslund went on to insist that Chubais, a personal friend, would never allow the programme to go ahead: it was 'impossible' that he could ever sanction such a rip-off. I and my editors at the *FT* were almost equally dubious.

A few of my Russian friends were much smarter. The day after the cabinet meeting, Kakha Bendukidze, the owner of the gas exploration company in Arctic Gaz-Sala, warned me that loans-for-shares was an effort 'to set up an oligarchy in the Russian economy'. That afternoon, Mikhail Zadornov, a leading liberal MP who would later become minister of finance, voiced the same fear in exactly the same terms, telling me that the proposal could be 'the beginning of an economic oligarchy'. Unfortunately, they were right.

Throughout the spring of 1995, the businessmen continued to push their radical plan. Two tasks remained. The first was patiently to nudge the scheme through the sclerotic Russian bureaucracy, the more complicated job was to finalise the list of companies which would be sold off. Doing that was more difficult than it might seem. Loans-for-shares was not implemented by a Western government, with full control over its own bureaucracy and property. It was the act of a desperately enfeebled state, so anaemic it was unable to perform basic functions such as collecting taxes or maintaining its monopoly over coercive force. Although this shadow state formally 'owned' the companies which were ultimately sold off, the Kremlin had little real political or economic control over them.

This meant that loans-for-shares was not quite a straightforward give-away. Instead, the Kremlin basically gave the future oligarchs a federal mandate to try to wrest control of some choice assets away from the red directors who were their effective owners. A good parallel is with the Crown mandates which the British monarch granted to 'companies of adventurers' like the Hudson's Bay Company, to exploit the Canadian wilderness. The Crown granted them a monopoly to try to squeeze profits out of vast expanses of forest, but their success depended on their ability to persuade or coerce the indigenous people to do business with them.

'These were companies which the government was simply unable to sell,' Khodorkovsky told me. 'They were run by very powerful directors, men who could raise up eighteen governors, eighteen regions. That was why they were not included in the first stage of privatisation. So it wasn't a question of just making a list of what the government would sell and choosing what you would buy. It was a question of whether you were able to reach an agreement with the [red] directors. That was the basic condition.'

So the businessmen set about wooing the Soviet-era directors of the companies they wished to acquire: Khodorkovsky spent weeks befriending the managers of Yukos, the oil company he had set his sights on; Potanin won over the directors of Sidanco, the oil company he would eventually obtain, but met a more prickly response at Norilsk Nickel, the prize he most ardently desired.

Some of the red directors were strong enough to fend off the oligarchs altogether. Vagit Alekperov, the head of the oil company Lukoil, and Vladimir Bogdanov, the chief of Surgutneftegaz, another leading oil group, did that by forcing the Moscow businessmen to admit them to their group and effectively becoming oligarchs themselves. Other Soviet-era directors were not sufficiently strong or smart to buy out their own companies, but they did have the muscle to force the government to withdraw their enterprises from the loans-for-shares list.

Through these tussles in the echoing corridors of Moscow ministries, on the floor of the Duma, the lower house of the Russian parliament, and in dozens of provincial cities, the final list was reduced and reduced until in the end just twelve companies remained. All that was left now was to get final approval for the process from the Kremlin and to kick-start the sale of the century.

The key man in this last stage was Alfred Kokh, a round-cheeked young reformer from St Petersburg with an unruly mop of dark hair, an exuberantly dirty mouth and a biting sense of humour. By the summer of 1995, he had replaced Chubais as acting head of the GKI. Potanin, who would eventually become Kokh's personal friend, was dispatched to sell him on the loans-for-shares scheme.

Kokh was almost instantly sympathetic to what he described in his memoirs as 'Potanin's brilliant idea'. Like the rest of the young reformers, he immediately grasped the essential political logic of the proposed pact. 'We had to survive all the political strife of the next one and a half years,' he later told me. 'In this fashion, we ensured the support of the banks for the president in the presidential elections.' He also liked the thought of outwitting the communists by disguising privatisation as a loan programme. But it was the fiscal argument that the scheme would almost instantly provide revenue for the cash-strapped Russian treasury which, according to Kokh, finally swung the political balance in the future oligarchs' favour.

The crunch came in the middle of August when Kokh had just returned from his summer holiday and was starting his new job at the GKI. But his first cabinet meeting was a disaster: 'I was very forcefully beaten over the head.' The problem was money. The year was nearly over and the GKI had only raised a fraction of the Rbs 8 trillion it was budgeted to bring in through privatisations.

Anxious not to be attacked a second time, Kokh was ready with a sheaf of specific proposals when the cabinet held its next weekly meeting. He presented his list: one plan was still in its infancy, another was 20 per cent developed, a third was just over half complete, a fourth was almost ready to be implemented. Desperate for cash, it was this technically advanced proposal which piqued the interest of Kokh's fellow ministers. What idea, they asked, was so nearly ripe for the picking?

'"Oh you remember, it's the one that Potanin was talking about with the loans,"' Kokh replied. '"The technical work is done, there is even a draft presidential decree."'

And that, Kokh recalled, was all it took to persuade the Russian cabinet to go ahead. 'Right, that's it,' his cabinet seniors decreed. 'We have no alternative. There's nothing else we will have time to prepare between now and the end of the year.'

Months of intense bureaucratic lobbying had finally paid off and the plan was ready to roll: all the decrees were drafted, the laws were written, the apparatchiks were appeased. The government, by contrast, had been too disorganised and aimless to come up with a privatisation scheme of its own. As they would so often do over the next few years, the future oligarchs had beaten the state at its own game. On 31 August, just a few days later, Boris Yeltsin signed decree number 889, the document that would make a handful of lucky Russians billionaires.

The programme signed into law by the president was not too different from the plan proposed by Potanin five months earlier. The government would still allow private businesses to manage the state stake in a group of key companies in exchange for loans. But, instead of doing the deal directly with a single consortium, the government would auction off the right to manage the state's shares in a process which would ostensibly be 'open and competitive' but in reality was dominated by insider deals. Thanks to the fierce lobbying of the future oligarchs, foreigners were barred from directly participating in the competitions for seven of the companies on offer, including Norilsk Nickel, Sidanco, Yukos and Lukoil.

The government also elaborated on the terms on which the loans would be offered. For the first three months, the state would pay its creditors a low rate of interest. The loans would run out in September, 1996, after which, the government would have two options. One would be to repay the loan and take back its shares. The second would be to sell off the shares which had been used as collateral. If the state opted for the second choice, the lender would be paid 30 per cent of the difference between the privatisation sale price and the initial sum he had lent the state. More importantly, the lender would act as the government's sales agent, organising the second auction himself. (In theory, this second round of auctions would also be open to all comers, although when the time came the initial lenders all succeeded in buying the stakes they had held in trust.)

It was a fiendishly complicated scheme, but few of its twists had much practical significance. Loans-for-shares was designed as a vehicle to deliver valuable state companies to the future oligarchs, which is exactly what it did. But there was method in the seeming madness of cloaking so straightforward a transfer of ownership in convoluted loan schemes and multi-stage auctions.

One advantage of the complexity was that it shielded the plan from many of its potential critics. The communists could be appeased with assurances that Russia's crown jewels were not actually being sold, merely pawned to help the treasury through a momentary tight spot.

And Western observers, always lecturing Moscow about the virtues of competition and the dangers of cronyism, were reassured by the government's promise that both the first and second stage of the loans-for-shares process would be managed through open competitive auctions. In September 1995, even that staunch defender of free markets, the *Economist*, gave the final version of the plan its grudging approval. The whole process would be above board, the magazine confidently pronounced: 'they [the Russian businesses] will not be allowed to sell shares to themselves on the sly'.

Perhaps most important of all, the complicated two-step plan implicitly bound the economic fortunes of the future oligarchs to the political fortunes of the Yeltsin administration. In the autumn of 1995, the businessmen received stakes in Russia's most valuable companies only in trust. The final, formal transfer of ownership would not take place until the autumn of 1996 and in 1997 – after the presidential elections. A communist Kremlin would probably cancel the second, crucial stage of the loans-for-shares process, but Yeltsin was more or less guaranteed to finish the programme he began. When he signed the decree, the Kremlin chief bought himself the constituency which a year later would guarantee his re-election.

As Ulyukaev, one of the young reformers, put it: 'We gave them just one of two keys [to the property]. They would receive the second key only after the elections.'

The stage was now set for a final, ferocious struggle for the loot. A few red directors made a last-minute bid to hang on to their Soviet inheritance. The clubby alliance of Moscow businessmen, formed so readily in the spring, began to fray, and conflicts both public and private started to break out. Enterpreneurs excluded from the deal, including future oligarchs temporarily out of favour with the Kremlin, like Gusinsky, began to protest.

But, in the autumn of 1995, the loans-for-shares scheme rolled invincibly forward. The smoothest auctions were for a 5 per cent stake in Lukoil and a 40.12 per cent share in Surgutneftegaz. Strong enough to fend off the future oligarchs and rich enough to contribute some money to the treasury, the Soviet barons of these companies – acting in part through closely affiliated firms – bought the companies they already managed. They were not shy about using every inch of their local control to ensure that they won: on the day of the Surgutneftegaz auction, the nearest airport was mysteriously shut down and road-blocks manned by armed guards materialised on the main land routes into the remote Siberian city of Surgut, where the sale was held, thus physically preventing one outside bidder from competing.

Things grew even more heated when it came to Norilsk Nickel, the inspiration of the entire process. The most serious clash was between Potanin and Anatoly Filatov, the mine's red director. Taking on a figure of Filatov's national stature took a lot of chutzpah; Potanin later admitted that he felt he was attempting the impossible, 'like something out of a fantasy novel'. More audacious still was Potanin's aggressive strategy. Instead of trying to make a deal with Filatov, he risked a head-on conflict. Even when Norilsk Nickel's management suggested a compromise – Potanin would get lucrative contracts to export their metal to the West, but not the company itself – he turned them down.

Potanin's rejection meant war. Filatov deployed the whole weight of his three decades as a Soviet industrial boss to fight off the 34-year-old upstart. He fired off a threatening letter to Kokh, he lobbied the Kremlin, he got the local governor to protest against the sale. But somehow, perhaps thanks to his alliance with Soskovets, an even more powerful red baron, Potanin fended him off.

Prevailing over Filatov was the crucial victory. But back home in Moscow, with the auction set to go ahead, Potanin encountered a final rival. Rossisky Kredit, a bank which had been on the fringes of the springtime consortium, broke away from the pack and – in defiance of the tacit agreement that Norilsk Nickel 'belonged' to Potanin – mounted a rival bid.

This was doomed from the start. Potanin's bank, Oneximbank, was an official organiser of the loans-for-shares privatisations, even though it was also a participant. Would-be bidders had to register their intention to take part with Oneximbank and place a cash deposit in the private bank as a guarantee of their seriousness.

Did Potanin's role at the heart of the process mean the auction itself was skewed in his favour? He claims it was not; his rivals insist it was. At any rate, on the fateful afternoon of 17 November 1995, when the bids for Norilsk Nickel were opened, Potanin's friend Kokh suddenly discovered an irregularity in Rossisky Kredit's submission. As Kokh, full of shocked propriety, put it in his book: 'I smelled a rat.'

In the view of this most impartial of judges, the $170m guarantee which Rossisky Kredit had issued to Kont, the company through which it was making its bid, exceeded the bank's total capital. Rossisky Kredit tried to make some new last-minute provisions, but Kokh insisted that the rules did not allow it and the bank was disqualified.

That left just three bidders, all stalking-horses for Potanin. The starting price for the 38 per cent stake was $170m. Two of Potanin's companies bid $170m exactly; the third bid $170.1m, and, just like that, Potanin owned a controlling interest in the world's leading producer of nickel and platinum. A few weeks later, Potanin acquired a majority interest in the second asset on his shopping list – the Siberian oil company, Sidanco – obtaining control of 51 per cent for only pennies more than the state's floor price of $130m. Two years later, British Petroleum would pay more than four times that price for a 10 per cent stake in the oil company.

Meanwhile, Khodorkovsky was preparing to claim 'his' enterprise: Yukos, another vast Siberian oil company. In contrast with Potanin, Khodorkovsky sought – and achieved – a velvet take-over, winning the cooperation of the company's top management. But, like Potanin, he feared rival buyers might step in. His non-aggression pact with Potanin meant that Khodorkovsky was fairly confident he could fend off Russian rivals, but he was still vulnerable to a wealthy indirect foreign bidder.

Yukos had been classed as a 'strategic company' which foreigners were officially banned from buying, but Khodorkovsky worried that might not be enough. Outsiders might try to find loopholes in the law, perhaps by acting in concert with a Russian company. To neutralise this threat, Khodorkovsky first tried to find his own foreign partner to beef up his bid. But, he told me, his tentative feelers to a few Western banks were frigidly rejected: 'they looked at us as if we were crazy.' The loans-for-shares scheme was so byzantine and Russia, on the eve of elections which might bring the communists back to power, was considered such a poor bet, that Western banks were not willing to risk their money.

But Khodorkovsky was still worried that some other outside investor might not be so cautious. To keep foreign rivals away, Menatep (his group), launched an intense legal and political campaign spearheaded by Konstantin Kagalovsky, a whip-smart Muscovite with a pink face and floppy caramel-coloured hair. Kagalovsky was perfect for the job: before joining Menatep, he had been one of the young reformers and had gained an insider's knowledge of both the Russian government and the West, having served as Russia's representative to the International Monetary Fund.

A few years later, Kagalovsky agreed to explain to me his technique for keeping the foreigners out. The key, he said, was to ensure that the law banning foreign participation was intentionally vague and thus open to multiple interpretations. If the foreign firms did decide to try to find a legal loophole and make a bid for Yukos through Russian partners, Kagalovsky would warn them that Menatep would take them to court. With a law so open to interpretation, and the home court advantage, Menatep would stand a strong chance of winning.

The whole point, he said, was to transform the decision for foreign firms from a purely legal question – Could they find a legal technicality that would permit them to participate in loans-for-shares? – into a political one – Did they have the domestic connections and savvy to outfox a powerful Russian company in a battle waged in the murky swamp of Russian legislation?

'When the laws are unclear, then you can't simply hire lawyers [and have them decide the issue],' Kagalovsky explained. 'You have to decide yourself whether you are willing to run the risk. It was possible to explain this to our competitors.'

This was an impressively devious scheme and it worked. But, how, I wondered, had Kagalovsky ensured that the laws were written in so precisely vague a fashion as to make it legally too risky for foreigners to participate? I assumed, as a matter of course, that Kagalovsky wouldn't tell me; but out of a kind of journalistic duty, I asked anyway.

To my surprise, Kagalovsky gave me a frank and rather proud answer: 'Well, of course, I wrote the law myself, and I took special care with it.'

It was a sort of epiphany for me. In the nearly four years I had spent in Russia by then, I had heard dozens and dozens of foreign businessmen complain about the country's obscure and fuzzy laws and explain how they were a barrier to investment. It was a really serious problem, everyone agreed, but, with more than a touch of condescension, we

Westerners assured ourselves that it was part of the terrible legacy which Russia had inherited from the Soviet Union. After all, we sagely concluded, surely a new market-based legal system could not be created overnight?

The one explanation which I don't think occurred to any of us foreigners was that maybe the Russians were just as smart as we were, and quite aware of the obscurity of their laws. Blinkered in equal measure by our patronising attitude and our innocence, I don't think we imagined that Russia's laws were vague on purpose; that their obscurity was not an accidental barrier to investment, which would be removed as soon as the ignorant Russians understood the problem, but that it was quite intentional and its explicit goal was to keep us out.

Having thus discouraged foreign competitors, Khodorkovsky still faced a domestic challenge. A troika of Russian banks – Rossisky Kredit, which had made the attempt to claim Norilsk Nickel, Inkombank, and Alfa, Friedman's company – decided to make a bid for Yukos. Frustrated by their failure to make inroads against their more established rivals during the first wave of loans-for-shares auctions, the group decided to make their campaign a public and political issue. At least two members of the troika had been part of the Russian business group which first plotted the loans-for-shares scheme in the spring, but now they decided to blow the whistle on their colleagues.

The three banks issued a public statement calling on the government to halt the 'ill-prepared and questionably organised' programme and accusing Khodorkovsky of being unfairly favoured by the Kremlin. Their angry complaint fell on fertile ground. The 17 December parliamentary elections were just a few weeks away and both the left and the right were looking for ammunition to use against the government. The communists happily seized on the conflict as further evidence that the entire privatisation programme had been a corrupt and nefarious plot, and the liberal opposition was almost equally vociferous. Boris Fyodorov, a former minister of finance and future deputy prime minister, warned that unless the government swiftly called a halt to its 'shameful' scheme, complicit ministers were likely to 'wind up behind bars'.

The game, it would seem, was up. The businessmen's clique had fallen apart; December parliamentary elections were looming; politicians of all stripes were attacking loans-for-shares. Surely the government would lose its nerve and, at the very least, postpone the controversial privatisations until after the ballot? Absolutely not. As usual, the criticism served only to harden the young reformers' determination. By questioning the auction process itself, the troika of banks was questioning the integrity of the government and of the young reformers, and that was the one thing Chubais would never countenance.

'The government told us, "We are going to punish you for kicking up such a fuss,"' said Friedman, head of the Alfa group, claiming the authorities dispatched inspectors from the tax service and the central bank to harass his company. 'Chubais told me: "You are putting the auctions themselves in jeopardy, and that is not permissible. It is better for me to have a bad auction than no auction at all."'

To no one's very great surprise, when the auction for Yukos took place on 8 December, the outsider troika of banks found themselves excluded for technical reasons, just as Rossisky Kredit had been. That left the field open to Khodorkovsky who, acting through Laguna, a front company, won 45 per cent of Yukos for $159m, just $9m above the starting price. (In a simultaneous 'investment auction', Khodorkovsky's team won an additional 33 per cent stake in exchange for a pledge to invest $150.125m.)

There was only one major loans-for-shares auction to go, and this was the most byzantine of all. Its protaganist was Berezovsky. Busy networking, he was slow to wake up to the huge financial potential of the loans-for-shares process. But as 1995 rolled on and he watched the scheme transform younger and less well-connected entrepreneurs into world-class tycoons, Berezovsky decided that he wanted a piece of the action.

Getting this would not be easy. Unlike Khodorkovsky and Potanin, who had already spent a few years building up a corporate team and industrial base, Berezovsky was still a nomad. He was brilliant at making the right friends at the right time, but how in the world could he singlehandedly take over a huge company and then run it? He needed an ally with experience at the coal-face of Russian business, and in 1995 he found one in the person of Roman Abramovich and his team of young turks at Runicom, an oil trading group. The two decided to try to take over an oil company.

But by then it was already late in the game and all the big enterprises were spoken for. With the creativity which marked his ascent in

Russian business and politics, Berezovsky found an iconoclastic solution: he decided to create a new company, Sibneft, by combining the Omsk refinery, one of Russia's best equipped, with a Siberian oil production enterprise, Noyabrskneftegaz. As Eugene Shvidler, a Runicom trader who later became president of the newly formed Sibneft, told me later, it was a logical combination because the refinery, the oil production company and the oil trading firm already had close links.

Creating Sibneft may have been an elegant idea, but time was running out since Yeltsin's decree stipulated that the loans-for-shares process must be completed by the end of the year. After that, with presidential elections just a few months away and the appetites of Potanin and Khodorkovsky already satisfied, who knew if the Kremlin would ever again authorise such a give-away? Desperate to secure his prize before the stroke of midnight, Berezovsky turned to the man who, in that enchanted autumn, was the fairy godmother for all the future oligarchs: Alfred Kokh.

Late in November, Berezovsky visited Kokh's office and asked him what he needed to do to get Sibneft included in the loans-for-shares process. Kokh sketched out a complicated bureaucratic and political process, concluding with the biggest obstacle of all: there was a requisite 30-day public notification period before the auction could take place. To get his sale in before the end of the year, Berezovsky needed to complete the paperwork by the last day of November – in just three days' time.

As soon as his afternoon meeting with Kokh was finished, Berezovsky worked out a rough timetable. Every minute counted. Suddenly he realised he needed to begin lobbying the Kremlin first thing the very next morning. But to do that, he needed the right draft decrees. So, even though it was already late, he summoned his armoured car and ordered his chauffeur to drive him to Kokh's apartment on Tverskaya, Moscow's glitzy central thoroughfare. Russia's privatisation chief was already undressed and in bed watching television, but he didn't resent the intrusion.

'I got up, drove to work, sat at my computer and wrote the draft presidential decree,' Kokh told me. 'It was in my interests. I wanted to earn $100m for the [state] budget.'

Now the ball was in Berezovsky's court, and all his manipulative talents and political connections would be put to the test. He faced one formidable adversary – the prime minister who, according to Kokh, was fiercely opposed to the creation of Sibneft and its inclusion in the loans-for-shares process. But Berezovsky had no time left for diplomacy and so, risking a rift with Chernomyrdin, he went to work directly on the Kremlin. There, he argued that he needed to be given Sibneft in order to finance ORT, the television network he already controlled thanks to Yeltsin's largesse. Hopeful that under Berezovsky's influence ORT would act as a sycophantic counterweight to Gusinsky's critical NTV, the presidential clique (including Korzhakov) was readily persuaded.

With Korzhakov's support, Berezovsky somehow managed to electrify the stiff cogs of the Kremlin machine. On 27 November, just three days before the final closing date, a special presidential decree creating Sibneft and authorising its sale through the loans-for-shares process was signed. With that stroke of the pen, Yeltsin made his publisher an oil baron. The sale itself, on 28 December, provoked the by now routine controversy. Unbowed by their previous defeats, the troika of dissident banks decided to make one last stand, this time led by Inkombank. Yet again, the outside contender was disqualified and the group backed by Berezovsky won, with a bid of $100.3m, just a shade more than the starting price of $100m.

Loans-for-shares was such a naked scam, such a cynical manipulation of a weakened state, that – especially now, as Russia continues to fall apart – it is tempting to dismiss the rapacious oligarchs who instigated it as just plain evil. Yet as I watched them plot and profit, I couldn't help asking myself how different the Russians really were from our own hero-entrepreneurs, the gizmo-makers and Internet tycoons and financial wizards our society so fawningly lauds for producing an era of unprecedented prosperity. Every businessman seeks the most profitable opportunity. Russia's tragedy is that the best opportunity was ripping off the decaying state. Expecting the future oligarchs to forgo that Klondike – to piously retool an ancient Soviet factory or energetically hawk copper bracelets when they could be taking over vast oil companies – would be like asking the cat to stop hunting mice, or Bill Gates voluntarily to cease decimating his weaker rivals. The future oligarchs did what any red-blooded businessman would do. The real problem was that the state allowed them to get away with it.

Most of the time, the Russian government let the oligarchs get away with murder because it was too weak to stop them. But with loans-for-shares, there was a further twist. The young reformers created the oligarchs, thinking they could harness their avarice and cunning to the reformers' own ends – first by employing them as a wrecking ball against the red directors and then by using them as a tool in the 1996 presidential campaign. But eventually, and maybe inevitably, it went wrong. As Aleksei Ulyukaev explained, 'We were like Doctor Frankenstein and they were the monster.'

9

THE DAVOS PACT AND THE
FIGHT FOR THE KREMLIN

FEBRUARY IS ALWAYS a gruesome month in Moscow. The early charms of
winter snow wear off in December, the consolation of New Year holidays is long past and there are still three months of grimy slush to slog
through before the relief of spring. In 1996, February was even more
dismal than usual. The communists had dominated the parliamentary
elections two months earlier and looked set to storm into power in the
June presidential ballot, bringing an exhausted country another round
of political turmoil.

It was thus with some relief that a few dozen prominent Russians set
off for the pristine and exclusive ski slopes of Davos, Switerland, where
they would participate in the World Economic Forum, an invitation-
only annual gathering of presidents, CEOs and media luminaries. For
the Russian delegation the shmoozing began early, on the tarmac at
Sheremetyevo airport, as the humblest and most punctual of the Davos
guests – a half-dozen journalists – stepped into the Russian government
jet chartered for them by the Swiss organisers.

To their delight, the Tupolev 134 was still empty, which offered the
hacks a rare chance to pile into the spacious front seating area normally
reserved for senior government officials. By the time Russia's rulers

made their tardy entrance, the best seats had been taken. It was a per-version of the natural order of things and Russia's masters were not amused.

Angriest of all was Gennady Zyuganov, the leader of the Communist Party. With his burgundy complexion, moon face and mud-coloured hair, Zyuganov looked forgettable, and until a few months ago this son of village schoolteachers had been so. But now people were beginning to say that he would be Russia's next president, and that is how he was starting to expect to be treated. As he walked past the journalists into the back of the plane, he shot them a look of pure fury. They loved it.

'It was so pleasant to look into the cramped back seats and see the blood pound into Zyuganov's face as he stared at us with hatred. It's a moment we all think back to often,' said Mikhail Berger, a leading eco-nomic columnist and one of the travellers that day.

But the liberal journalists' delight at Zyuganov's airborne discomfi-ture was shortlived. A few hours later, their airplane landed in Zurich and the Russians were ushered into a large, comfortable bus to make the 165km trip to Davos. As they eased into their seats, the Russian ambassador to Switzerland pulled up in a limousine. Before him were a group of men who could make or break his career – two cabinet min-isters, three governors of powerful Russian regions. Only one could be singled out for the honour of riding in the official car. The situation was every diplomat's nightmare, and Stepanov handled it by drawing on the skill which centuries of autocracy have bred into the Russian civil ser-vice: an acutely sensitive nose for power. The ambassador decided the best bet was Zyuganov and whisked him away in his chauffeured limo, leaving Yeltsin's ministers to take the bus.

'The mid-ranking *chinovniks* sensed that Zyuganov was the-president-but-for-five-minutes,' Berger recalled. 'He was the hero of Davos.'

Stepanov was not the only one eager to curry favour with the Kremlin's heir-apparent. Western businessmen and politicians flocked to Zyuganov's side, and many pronounced him an acceptable substitute for Yeltsin. Even that stern arbiter of capitalist correctness, the *Wall Street Journal*, admiringly described Zyuganov's Davos performance as a combination of 'a bulldozer's power and a prize-fighter's balance' and said he had 'bedazzled the West'.

Russia's home-grown businessmen were less impressed. Many of them had been worried about the dangers of a communist victory for some time, but it wasn't until they got to Davos that that fear crystallised into action. For Khodorkovsky the turning point came as he sipped coffee in a hotel café, eavesdropping on a conversation between Berezovsky and George Soros, the American financier and philanthropist who took a close interest in Russian affairs.

'I heard Soros saying – "Boys, your time is over. You've had a few good years but now your time is up,"' Khodorkovsky told me. 'His argument was that the communists were definitely going to win. We Russian businessmen, he said, should be careful that we managed to get to our jets in time and not lose our lives.'

Khodorkovsky felt as if he had been slapped in the face. A communist victory wasn't just a possibility, he suddenly realised, it was almost a certainty – and the West wouldn't do anything to stop it. If the oligarchs wanted to safeguard their empires, they would have to do it themselves.

But how? Back in Moscow, Yeltsin's erstwhile supporters were angry and divided. They had no taste for a return to orthodox communism, but they were by no means certain that the ailing Kremlin chief represented a better alternative. So great was the disenchantment that in early January Gaidar called for the president to make way for another, stronger democratic candidate. Some leading reformers went even further – like Boris Nemtsov, the governor of Nizhny Novgorod, who cautiously suggested that maybe Zyuganov could be won over to market principles.

But one man was neither convinced that Zyuganov could be converted to social democracy, nor resigned to the inevitability of a communist victory – Chubais, who had doggedly clung to his post in the Yeltsin administration even as other liberals abandoned him. The president repaid his loyalty in characteristically Machiavellian fashion – in January he fired Chubais and, adding insult to injury, accused him of making 'grave mistakes in privatisation'. Chubais interpreted the sacking as a necessary pre-election appeasement of Russia's angry people; but, all the same, the dismissal was a bitter personal blow and it was an uncharacteristically subdued Chubais who flitted on the fringes of the Russian delegation at Davos a few weeks later.

'Chubais arrived as just an ordinary citizen, it wasn't even clear who he was representing,' Berger recalled. 'He kept to himself the whole time, speaking to almost no one.'

But on 5 February, the fifth day of the conference and normally a time when the proceedings began to wind down, Chubais snapped. The Western establishment had all but crowned Zyuganov as the next Kremlin chief and none of the other Russians seemed to have the wit or the spine to explain how dangerous the communist leader really was. Chubais called Moscow and instructed Arkady Evstafiev, his trusted PR and general dogsbody, to prepare a dossier of Communist Party documents for him and fax it to Switzerland. That compilation of turgid party resolutions and half-baked economic plans provided the ammunition for a press conference which turned out to be the first shot in the Russian elite's united attack against Zyuganov. With all the fury of a modern-day Luther, Chubais lambasted foreign business leaders for defecting from the true capitalist faith and for being taken in by Zyuganov's 'traditional, classic Communist lie'.

'There are two Zyuganovs, one for foreign and one for domestic consumption,' Chubais thundered. 'If Zyuganov wins the Russian presidency in June, he will undo several years of privatisation and this will lead to bloodshed and all-out civil war.'

Chubais' inflammatory rhetoric did little to dim Zyuganov's appeal for the West; one contemporary press account said it would do no more than raise an eyebrow or two on Wall Street. But it struck home with a much more important constituency: the future oligarchs. Sitting next to Gusinsky, Berger watched Chubais' press conference inspire a political epiphany: 'Gusinsky is listening to Chubais, who says, "The Communists are planning to nationalise private property and reimpose state control. Here is their declaration. Here is their economic doctrine." Gusinsky listens and says, "Hell, if they are really planning to do all that, then there's no point in going back to Russia." A few minutes pass, and Gusinsky says, "Hell, I don't like Chubais, but he's a real fighter. He inspires respect. I'll offer him a job." Then a few more minutes pass, and Gusinsky, now very excited, concludes, "You know, I think he's the only person who can fight with the Communists."'

Chubais' performance made an equally strong impression on Berezovsky. A few hours after the press conference, Berezovsky ran into Zverev, Gusinsky's right-hand man, on the stairs of the Fluela Hotel, a six-storey, cream-coloured chalet in the heart of Davos. Over the past two years, Berezovsky and Gusinsky had been bitter rivals, but now he told Zverev he wanted to meet him. Despite the bad blood, Gusinsky accepted the invitation and the two went for lunch at the hotel bar.

According to Zverev, who joined them for the first part of the meeting, Berezovsky started the conversation by proposing that they bury their differences in order to collectively combat the communist threat. Remarkably, Gusinsky agreed and the bitterest feud in Russian business was suddenly over. Their rapprochement had terrific political significance. In agreeing to join forces with Berezovsky, Gusinsky was effectively signing up to join the oligarchy from which he had been excluded because of his long-running conflict with the party of war. Bringing Gusinsky into the tent gave the oligarchs – and their Kremlin allies – a virtual monopoly over Russia's airwaves: together Gusinsky's NTV and Berezovsky's ORT accounted for most of the national viewing audience.

Having declared a truce, the two media moguls next began to discuss practical measures to fight the communists. Almost immediately, they agreed that Chubais was the man to manage their campaign. But before going further, it was necessary to bring Russia's other oligarchs into what later became known as the Davos Pact. As the Swiss conference drew to a close, Berezovsky and Gusinsky widened the alliance by summoning their colleagues to a private supper; the other diners included Khodorkovsky and Vinogradov, founder of Inkombank and a kind of candidate member of the oligarchy.

Their meeting, and the political compact they forged, were unprecedented. As they had scrambled to build personal fortunes out of the wreckage of the Soviet Union, Russia's leading businessmen had had little time for public politics. Although some of them had united to orchestrate loans-for-shares, they had never before taken collective political action. But on that crisp Swiss night, they formed a powerful political alliance.

'It was the first time that all of us had decided to work for a single political goal,' Khodorkovsky told me. 'We agreed with the boys together that we would not try to live with the Communists. Instead, we said we would work to re-elect Yeltsin.'

Not all of Russia's future oligarchs were at Davos that year. So, as soon as they returned to Moscow, Berezovsky, Gusinsky and Khodorkovsky called another, wider meeting. Potanin, as the initiator of the loans-for-shares deal, was at the top of their list; as was Aleksandr

Smolensky, the banker who had been on the fringes of that sweetheart privatisation programme. They also invited two of the most vocal opponents of loans-for-shares, Friedman and his partner, Pyotr Aven. Like everyone else, the Alfa group was afraid of the communists. More importantly, as they and Gusinsky had so painfully learned the year before, in Russia dissenters never won. The only way to prosper was to bend your will to that of the collective.

Loans-for-shares had given most of these men their fortunes. The Davos Pact made them political players. Together, the two events made them into oligarchs. Russian pundits even coined a new word to describe the seven and their power – the *semibankirshchina*, or the reign of the seven bankers, a reference to the *semiboyarshchina*, the era in medieval Russian history when seven boyars presided over the country. On that freezing day in February, within the ornate walls of Berezovsky's Logovaz Clubhouse, the *semibankirshchina* held its first full meeting.

The group swiftly agreed that Zyuganov must be stopped and that Chubais was the best man to help them do it. Few of the future oligarchs considered Chubais to be a personal friend and some of them had recently viewed him as a bitter enemy. But they all admired his managerial talents and respected his rather Spartan ability to rise above personal feelings and support the president who just a few weeks earlier had humiliatingly sacked him. The oligarchs invited Chubais to meet them, and he agreed to run their campaign.

A marathon of political labour lay ahead. But first Chubais needed to tell his team, the St Petersburg branch of the young reformers, about the unusual new alliance he had joined. Appropriately enough, they met in their home-town, whose melancholy canals and elegantly crumbling Imperial architecture reminded them of their innocent academic apprenticeship. Officially, the purpose of their late February meeting was to hold an economic seminar. But theoretical arcana were soon forgotten as Chubais used the occasion to announce his new political project.

His supporters were less than thrilled. Evstafiev worried that, by agreeing to back the unpopular president and form a pact with the notorious oligarchs, yet again his beloved boss was accepting a job which would make him the most hated man in Russia. 'For Chubais, it meant pushing your head into the noose and waiting for it to be tightened,' he explained. Other young reformers were equally dubious. 'I thought it was a very bad idea both because I thought Yeltsin was not electable and the alliance with the businessmen was politically dangerous,' recalled Sergei Vasiliev.

Never one to brook dissent, Chubais paid little heed to his friends' objections. And on the big issue of the day, he was right. By uniting with the oligarchs, he was able to keep the communists out of the Kremlin and restore himself to Yeltsin's favour. But the Davos Pact also sowed the seeds of a humbling defeat. Before long, the oligarchs would be at war with one another, and with Chubais. That battle not only forced Chubais out of office; ultimately, it threatened the entire economic order which the Davos Pact had been formed to preserve.

Like the gun – which will be employed to deadly effect in the final scene – innocently hanging on the wall in the first act of a melodrama, the poisonous conflict between Chubais and the oligarchs was set in motion at their very first meeting. The future bone of contention was the precise terms, both financial and political, according to which Chubais accepted the oligarchs' proposal that he manage Yeltsin's re-election campaign on their behalf.

In the spring of 1996, the Davos Pact itself was a closely held secret. Even two years later, when the Russian establishment was already preoccupied with the year 2000 presidential battle, most of the participants remained reluctant to discuss the financial aspects of the deal. But, inevitably, details began to leak out. I first discovered that there might have been a financial side to the alliance in my own living room, less than four months after Yeltsin's triumph at the polls. The deputy editor of the *Financial Times* was visiting Moscow and I held a dinner party in his honour. One of my guests was Mikhail Zadornov, then chairman of the parliament's budget committee, and one of the liberal opposition MPs I most respected.

When we began to speak about the then barely suspected role the oligarchs had played in Yeltsin's campaign, Zadornov stunned us all by saying that their contribution had been much more central than any of us had imagined. 'They hired Chubais,' he insisted. We were incredulous. To persuade us, Zadornov offered another, astonishing detail: 'They paid him $3m, I know, I saw the documents.'

A few days later I interviewed Berezovsky and, as we sat around a dainty white table in the Logovaz Clubhouse, for the first time he described the pact which had been forged in that very room. He confirmed that the oligarchs had paid $3m to finance Chubais and his team, but was reluctant to say much more.

Over the next few months, dribbles of information leaked out in the Russian press which broadly confirmed that Zadornov and Berezovsky had been right. The payment turned out to have been an interest-free loan paid by Stolichny Bank, Smolensky's company, to a private foundation, the Fund for the Defence of Private Property, which had been established by Chubais and the young reformers. The money was invested in astronomically high-yielding government treasury bills. Better still, the young reformers would not have to repay the principal until 2001, by which time the rapid devaluation of the rouble was likely to have geometrically diminished the dollar-value of their debt.

Off the record, two of the oligarchs who were part of the Davos Pact told me that all six companies had contributed equally to the $3m kitty. Half of the money, the two said, was to go to Chubais as a salary; the rest was to go to his fund to allow him to maintain a staff, rent office space and so on. None of this seemed at all questionable or unethical. At the time, Chubais was not a government employee. The fee he received was in line with the wages being paid to Russia's most talented managers; it was unexceptional by the standards of political spending in the West. And yet, years later, all the oligarchs remained hugely uncomfortable about openly discussing the details of the deal.

Khodorkovsky refused to discuss the issue at all: 'I've never spoken about the financial side of our arrangement and, with God's help, I'll go to my grave without ever speaking about it.' Potanin talked, but with terrific caution, insisting that, 'Chubais did not get any wage at all from us.' There was, however, 'a scheme of contributions which did not violate the election law'. Friedman was a bit more forthcoming, admitting, 'We paid Chubais an official salary, which he declared [to the tax authorities] and everything.' But when it came to the size of the fee, one of Russia's sharpest businessmen suddenly lost his head for figures: 'I don't remember exactly how much it was.'

Chubais' supporters were equally queasy. In the autumn of 1998, I sat with Evstafiev in a small, windowless room in the offices of the Fund for the Defence of Private Property. After some uncomfortable probing, Evstafiev conceded that the oligarchs had paid the fund a significant sum in exchange for Chubais' election work. But he was brimming with justifications and qualifications. Yes, the loan was interest-free and, yes, it would only become due in 2001. But . . . it was a credit, it was in roubles, it was only so that 'some sort of structure could exist'. And, anyway, Chubais and his allies could have made much more money – tens of millions of dollars – had they gone ahead with their plans to set up a private consulting and investment firm rather than work on Yeltsin's campaign. At that moment, Kokh, the former GKI chief who occupied the adjacent office, strolled in and offered a more pithy explanation. 'Oh come on, Arkasha,' he said. 'Those bankers were just saving their own asses.'

True enough, so why all the equivocation? The heart of the matter seemed to be a kind of Victorian squeamishness about money and earning a salary which was as much a part of post-communist Russia as the wild consumerist indulgences of its nouveaux riches. After 70 years of communism, Russians – especially politically prominent ones – seemed to feel there was something somehow sordid about being paid a wage. The transaction was not a straightforward exchange of services for money, but a more demeaning procedure in which the wage-earner was purchased heart, soul and conscience by his employer.

This lingering Marxist morality tainted the deal between Chubais and the oligarchs even as it was being struck. At least some of them, in some half-conscious way, felt they were buying Chubais for more than five months of campaign management. And, on the same inchoate level, Chubais resented being bought, even for a few months. As in a doomed Tolstoyan love affair, even as they sealed their political marriage their bitter separation was already inevitable.

'This agreement was why, later, he fought so hard against the oligarchs,' Nevzlin, the Menatep executive, told me. 'Chubais couldn't accept that he had once been hired by them. It was an uncomfortable situation for him.'

By late February, the Davos Pact had been sealed and Chubais had been recruited. Now all the oligarchs needed to do was sell their services to the president, which would not be easy. Nearly five years after he came to power, Yeltsin-the-democrat had become Tsar Boris. His wild energy had degenerated into an Oblomovian paralysis: Yeltsin seemed to spend most of his time either in a sanatorium recovering from what spokesmen then said were 'colds' but aides later admitted were heart attacks, or drinking vodka and sweating in the *banya*, Russia's steamy version of the sauna, with his cronies. On the international stage, too, the fearsome Siberian bear had become a circus clown, raising global titters with stunts like his impromptu attempt to conduct a military orchestra in Germany.

In this diminished condition, Yeltsin had become a virtual hostage of the party of war, entrusting his election campaign to its chief, Oleg Soskovets. The oligarchs knew Soskovets would not welcome their interference. Luckily, thanks to Berezovsky's Kremlin connections, they had a direct route to the president. In early March, the members of the Davos Pact assembled in a chandeliered Kremlin hall to offer their services. But Yeltsin, as stony-faced as a sphinx, was a hard sell.

'It is very hard to influence him,' Potanin later told me. 'You never know whether he shares your views or not. He is closed and gives nothing away.'

On this occasion, the president was especially hard to sway, refusing to be budged from his comfortable faith in Soskovets. Everything was going perfectly well, he insisted, so there was no need for a radical shift in campaign strategy. The oligarchs were frustrated and worried: their meeting with Yeltsin was a precious opportunity; somehow, someone had to figure out a way to get through to him. Finally, summoning the iron nerve which had made him a Russian political legend, Chubais interrupted Yeltsin's complacent monologue with one sharp sentence: 'It is not so, Boris Nikolaevich!'

Not very many men dared to contradict Russia's modern tsar and the room fell into an uneasy hush. The uncomfortable silence dragged on for a full two or three minutes as Yeltsin considered what to do with his impertinent knight. At last, he seemed to decide to believe him and the oligarchs heaved a collective sigh of relief. The campaign had not yet begun, but already one of their strategic choices – the decision to enlist Chubais – was proving to have been the right one.

The ice broken, the oligarchs made the president a brazen offer. They would help him to turn around his campaign, volunteering their money and their know-how, but only if he ditched Soskovets as manager and replaced him with Chubais. The oligarchs left the Kremlin on good terms with the president, but without a clear commitment to their deal. Yeltsin had been too close to the party of war, for too long, to abandon it on the strength of a single conversation with a group of jumped-up hustlers.

But the oligarchs had a powerful political supporter and one who was privately advancing their cause with the president: Yuri Luzhkov. Since the faces-on-the-snow incident, the Moscow mayor had made his peace with the Kremlin. Now, as the communist threat mounted, he became one of the most powerful defenders of Yeltsin and the status quo he represented. However, Luzhkov was an unlikely ally for the Davos Pact; he hated Berezovsky, the guiding spirit of the alliance, with a passion only exceeded by his visceral disgust with Chubais.

Yet just as the red peril had been enough to end the bitter animosity between many of the oligarchs, it pushed Luzhkov on to the same side as his old enemies. Back in January, Shakhnovsky, Luzhkov's erudite and cunning chief of staff, had arranged a secret meeting with Yeltsin's daughter Tatyana to warn the Kremlin that the party of war was botching the campaign. A month after that, Luzhkov himself spoke directly to the president.

'I saw that the people to whom the president had entrusted his campaign were doing a bad job,' Luzhkov told me. 'I turned to the president and said, "Boris Nikolaevich, if you do not find other people [to run your campaign] you will lose."'

Luzhkov told the president that he should appoint Chubais to run his campaign. Coming from the Moscow mayor, it was an amazing suggestion. With his faintly authoritarian, defiantly nationalist and openly dirigiste policies, Luzhkov was one of the young reformers' most bitter and most effective antagonists. In our conversation, he repeated his routine attacks against Chubais' 'criminal' privatisation drive and described the young reformers' as 'Bolsheviks'. 'Our dispute was so intense,' he recalled, 'that Chubais tried to bring criminal charges against me.'

With the communists at the Kremlin door, Luzhkov was prepared to set aside his old grievance. He knew Chubais was a talented organiser, a man who could get results. 'He conducted privatisation in an iron way,' the mayor explained. 'I thought he would be a good campaign manager, and, as it turned out, I was not mistaken.'

Luzhkov's quiet intervention was a telling moment. For one thing, like the Davos truce between Berezovsky and Gusinsky it was a sign that, for all the passion of Russia's political wars, few of them were so deep and enduring as to rule out an equally intense friendship just a few months later. I called it 'Snowflake Politics' because Russian political alliances and animosities seemed to melt away almost as soon as they had crystallised. That was an important characteristic of a still-adolescent democracy, which depended more on the personalities and interests of the particular moment than it did on political institutions and clearly articulated, long-held ideologies.

Some people hoped that the powerful and disparate coalition which united behind Yeltsin in 1996 signified the emergence of a more mature and enduring system. Those who came together to counter the communist threat were a diverse group: the oligarchs, the young reformers, the authoritarian mayor of Moscow, the liberal intelligentsia, the nascent middle class. But they had one important thing in common: they were all winners in Yeltsin's radical experiment and they were ready to fight to hang on to their gains. For all the sins against democracy of the campaign – and there would be many – this was a truly cheering sign. It inspired optimists to predict that, after Yeltsin's victory, it would be possible to build a strong and lasting political constituency to press for the further reforms required to bring Russia's half-finished revolution to a successful conclusion.

Maybe it was possible – but that pro-reform constituency was never built. One reason can be divined in the strange and fleeting alliance between Luzhkov and Chubais. Most of the pro-Yeltsin coalition was based on the same Snowflake Politics which linked these two giants. The Yeltsin campaign gave the new Russia the brief and delightful illusion that it was a politically unified whole. But without someone to do the grinding work of building political institutions and a political ideology to keep together at least part of the pro-Yeltsin coalition, in the longer term it was doomed to collapse. The snow melted and Russia's winners set about fighting amongst themselves for the spoils they had protected from the communist usurpers.

In the spring of 1996, however, the grand coalition was just forming. By early March, the businessmen and their allies had managed to put their case to the president and won a partial victory. Yeltsin agreed to the oligarchs' offer to set up a campaign team, known as the 'analytical group', under Chubais' leadership and on the businessmen's bank roll. The team began to meet regularly in Chubais' temporary office on the

24th floor of the blue and grey skyscraper which also housed Gusinsky's Most group and much of city hall.

But Yeltsin gave the oligarchs the go-ahead with the Darwinian caveat which was his political signature – the Soskovets-led campaign structure would also remain in place. The two rival machines were left to fight it out as a complacent Yeltsin watched their battles from above. Meanwhile, the clock was steadily ticking away the time of less than four months which now remained before the presidential ballot.

Much of Russia's future would depend on these court intrigues. But to most of us in Moscow, they were invisible. What was on view, and almost painfully so, was the increasing political impotence of the Yeltsin regime and of the ageing titan himself. The Kremlin was losing – both in its war in Chechnya and in the battle to pull the Russian economy out of its dizzying depression. Most Russians still wanted democracy and a market economy; they just weren't sure they liked Yeltsin's violent and impoverished version very much.

Yeltsin began his battle to turn the tide of public opinion in Yekaterinburg, the gritty capital of Russia's industrial rust-belt where the president had lived for more than three decades as he scrambled up the Communist Party ladder. On 15 February, barely a week after the oligarchs formed the Davos Pact, Yeltsin journeyed to his home-town to officially announce his decision to run for a second term. A plane-load of reporters, including me, went with him.

Unlike the damp grey winters of Moscow, the climate in the Urals and southern Siberia is almost exactly like that of the Canadian prairies: bright sun, baby-blue skies and temperatures regularly plunging below −20 degrees Celsius. For a grimy workshop of a city like Yekaterinburg, it is the most forgiving season, with a pristine blanket of white temporarily expiating the sins of central planning and the bobbing tide of dark fur hats giving the city a merry, almost yuletide air. Going indoors was another matter. I stayed at the stolid Intourist Hotel – a poorly lit, draughty monstrosity with erratic plumbing and brown viscous water spewing from the taps, when they worked at all. The service revolution, which had brought to Moscow a half-dozen glittering hotels complete with marble foyers, chandeliers and $500-a-night rooms, had not yet reached the heartland.

Yet, as I ventured on to the streets, what struck me most were not the persistent and vile relics of the Soviet era but the bizarre new ways of life which were pushing up through the cracks of the old system. My first glimpse of the weird new Russia came, appropriately enough, at a cemetery. Yeltsin was due to visit that afternoon to privately pay his respects to the graves of his parents, so I went early to see what the president would see.

As I searched for the burial spots of Yeltsin *père et mère*, I was immediately distracted by another, far more flamboyant tombstone. Towering over a small private garden in one corner was a 9-foot marble statue of a man who was a caricature of the New Russians: bull-necked, a muscular chest revealed by the open buttons of a carefully sculpted shirt, feet aggressively planted apart in a marksman's stance. A sea of fresh flowers lapped at his feet and he gazed out over a jade-inlaid picnic table, obviously built so that his loved ones could follow the tradition of sitting with the dead on major anniversaries in style and comfort. Thoughtful friends had even allowed Mikhail Kuchin, as the inscription below identified him, to carry in death what appeared to have been his most treasured possession in life – the keys to a Mercedes, the coveted trademark carefully on view.

Those keys, the cemetery keeper told me, had helped to kill him. Mikhail, along with a driver and two bodyguards who were buried under humbler tombstones nearby, had died when his chaffeur inserted them into the ignition, igniting a car bomb. It was a sad way to go for one so young – Mikhail was only 25 – and so rich, the keeper told me, but what could you expect? He was co-owner of the local casino, and it was a dangerous business. Since his death Misha had become a sort of cult figure for the local youth who often came to pay their respects to Yekaterinburg's patron saint of living fast and dying young.

This surreal city was part of the new Russia which Yeltsin would have to conquer to be re-elected. As the presidential convoy swept into town that afternoon, his chances looked lukewarm at best. The whole spirit of his visit seemed more Brezhnevite than democratic. His procession through the city – an Afghan war memorial, a factory, a school – had the remote, disinfected air of an inspection by some high-ranking apparatchik, not the more approachable feel of a flesh-pressing politician shilling for votes. Everywhere Yeltsin went he was either hidden behind the darkened windows of his limousine or surrounded by a human wall of dark-coated bodyguards.

Yekaterinburgers wondered where their vigorous local leader had gone. 'We need the young Yeltsin, not this frail ageing man,' Nikolai Popov, a 52-year-old welder, told me. After his heavy-handed debut on the streets, Yeltsin retreated to Yekaterinburg's main auditorium to deliver the speech which would officially launch his bid for a second term. It was such a strange, rambling performance that it seemed to justify the name-calling of one of the crusty old communists picketing outside, who cursed 'our democratically elected alcoholic' as I walked past into the hall.

Yeltsin started out strongly enough, reminding people of the historic achievements of his regime – 'for the first time in many centuries, there are no political prisoners in Russia' – and warning them not to fall prey to a lazy 'nostalgia' for the Soviet past which had actually been a time of 'long queues, shortages and ration cards'. But, soon enough, the president's speech degenerated into the string of odd, off-the-cuff remarks and strange musings which had come to characterise Yeltsin whenever he was let loose by his handlers.

The most bizarre moment came towards the end. Apropos of nothing at all, Yeltsin suddenly decided to try his hand at match-making, and on a suitably presidential scale. While visiting Konfi, a confectionary factory, that afternoon, he said he had been impressed by the beauty of the girls on the assembly line. Most of them, alas, were single. Not to fear, the Kremlin chief had a solution: Konfi should do a deal with a military college just up the road – and here Yeltsin treated the national television audience to his knowledge of the city's geography, spending a few minutes describing its exact location – and pair off its girl workers with the college's cadets en masse. 'And soon, they will all get married,' a beaming Yeltsin concluded.

I returned to Moscow deeply depressed. A communist comeback would be horrible, but I was starting to wonder whether a Yeltsin victory would be very much better. When I went to see Gaidar a few days later, I discovered he was being haunted by the same doubts. 'The problem is that, while it's quite clear what Zyuganov would do if he wins, it's not clear what Yeltsin would do,' he admitted, flashing the broad, placid smile he always managed to muster no matter how grim the situation. 'I think Yeltsin's realistic control over the country is limited. The real people who control the country are those who control the information Yeltsin gets.'

Inside the Kremlin, things looked even worse. Yeltsin and his party of war cronies seemed determined to live up to the aphorism that history repeats itself – the first time as tragedy, the second time as farce. They veered wildly between menacing efforts to recapture the authoritarian might of the Soviet Union and episodes of incompetence so absolute as to be comical. The Soskovets team was so disorganised that it almost failed to collect the public signatures required to register the president as a candidate. The campaign was only bailed out thanks to the last-minute intervention of Luzhkov and his efficient city hall. Vyacheslav Nikonov, a suave political consultant who was the grandson of Vyacheslav Molotov, the Stalinist foreign minister, described the world behind the red Kremlin walls as 'a bordello'.

But it was a whorehouse with absolutist aspirations. Soskovets routinely harangued the Russian cabinet to get the vote out for Yeltsin – any way they could. Then the party of war had an inspiration: why bother strong-arming the population into supporting Yeltsin when they could just cancel the elections altogether?

'I thought we should not have elections,' Korzhakov told me bluntly two years later. 'I spoke about it to various people and they all said, "You're right, let's not have elections."'

Korzhakov and his allies had good reason for wanting to cancel – or more coyly, postpone – the ballot. For one thing, their secret service analysts were warning them that Yeltsin stood a serious chance of defeat. They also feared the effects of a closely fought campaign on the president's health. A bout of intense political activity could, as Korzhakov put it, 'put the president in the grave'. Most compelling of all, though, was the dawning realisation that even if Yeltsin did win, his conservative cronies might lose.

Now that the analytical group was on the scene, the party of war risked being eclipsed. In the words of Emil Pain, a senior Kremlin aide, the two rival campaign teams were 'two bears – and only one of them could survive'. The obvious way to determine the winner would be to see who was best able to lead Yeltsin to victory at the polls. But the party of war was starting to worry that Chubais and the oligarchs might be the better campaigners. As the elections drew closer, the hard-liners realised there was only one sure way for them to triumph – cancel the vote.

In mid-March, the communist-dominated parliament gave them the perfect pretext. On Friday 15 March the Duma passed a bill condemning the Belovezh Accords as illegal. The Accords were the three-way deal between the leaders of Ukraine, Russia and Belarus in December 1991 which had dissolved the Soviet Union. Millions of Ukrainians and Belarusans saw the agreement as a historic liberation, but many Russians would never forgive Yeltsin for his 'crime'. Less than four months before the elections, it was a brilliant political card for the communist parliamentarians to play.

The party of war chose to interpret the vote differently. By challenging the legality of the Belovezh Accords, the parliament was effectively declaring that the Soviet Union still existed, the hard-liners argued. That amounted to a challenge to the very existence of the Russian Federation: in fact, it was treason. The president, who had so bravely used force to dissolve a rebellious parliament in 1993, must be equally tough in dealing with this new threat.

Yeltsin agreed. On Saturday morning, he rushed back into the Kremlin from his country dacha and conferred with his team. On the order of the president and with the agreement of his key ministers and advisers, Korzhakov and his aides set about the happy task of preparing the paperwork for an anti-parliamentary coup. Like all defeated plans, this one subsequently became an orphan – apart from the loquacious Korzhakov, no one was very eager to claim credit for it. But other Kremlin insiders confirmed that as the laws were being drafted on that crucial Saturday they had the president's full support.

'I can tell you one thing – Korzhakov took no steps without a direct order from the president,' Shakhnovsky, the Moscow city chief of staff, told me.

Friedman – who, like all of the oligarchs, was drawn in to the weekend intrigue – concurred: 'They all signed that piece of paper, the one about dissolving the Duma and postponing the elections.'

On Sunday morning the security forces started to act. They had dissolved the parliament once before, in 1993, and they were determined to learn from their mistakes. Then, the Kremlin had announced its intention to shut down the Duma while it was in session and the rebellious

MPs had refused to submit, blockading themselves inside the White House and setting off a prolonged, embarrassing and ultimately bloody stand-off. This time, the security forces knew better. They moved in over the weekend and fabricated a bomb scare so as to evacuate the already practically deserted parliament buildings near the Kremlin, where the Duma had been relocated after the 1993 battle. Then they sealed off the legislature with crack interior ministry troops, parked two military vehicles on the busy thoroughfare in front of the Duma and searched the offices of high-ranking communist deputies.

As his soldiers moved into position, Yeltsin held a series of last-minute meetings. The oligarchs and their allies were, of course, fiercely opposed; they were betting on winning an at least nominally democratic poll, not on installing Yeltsin as an ageing dictator at the mercy of his military. Worse still, the dissolution of parliament would be an automatic victory for the party of war.

So, the Davos Pact dispatched Chubais to work his magic on the president. As soon as the tense encounter was over, Chubais went back to his office and told the rest of the analytical group what had happened, that he had urged the president to think of his historical legacy. Zverev, a Most executive and member of the analytical group recalled: 'He said to Boris Nikolaevich "You must be the man who builds democracy in Russia."' Yeltsin was silent for a moment, then he reminded his former minister that he too might not go down in history with a perfect record: 'And you, Anatoly Borisovich, made a lot of mistakes during privatisation.'

The conversation was part of a drip-drop of discussions which eventually wore away the president's resolve to postpone the elections. According to Korzhakov, the turning point came when Yeltsin received Anatoly Kulikov – his minister of the interior and the man who would bear direct responsibility for a presidential order to dissolve the parliament. Kulikov told Yeltsin that the draft decree was illegal and that he would refuse to implement it. Chernomyrdin, who spoke to the president next, took the same line.

These two voices – of Yeltsin's strongman and of his prime minister – had a powerful impact on the president. But the young reformers worried that the domestic interventions might not be enough and they decided to play what had always been their trump card – their close contacts with the West. As Chubais presented his arguments to the

Kremlin leader, Gaidar took his case to another president: Bill Clinton. He went to US Ambassador Thomas Pickering, told him of the drastic decision Yeltsin was about to take and asked him to bring Clinton in on the effort to change Yeltsin's mind.

Gaidar was taking a huge risk. The American connection had always been the Russian liberals' best asset but, in the increasingly nationalist domestic climate, it was also their greatest liability. Gaidar – and by association Chubais – would risk calls of treason or worse if it were widely known that Gaidar had invited the US to intervene in an internal crisis. His meeting with the ambassador was thus a closely held secret. When I asked Gaidar about it more than two years later he was still reluctant to give any details, allowing only that, 'Yes, that meeting did take place.'

Remarkably, not only was Gaidar's meeting with the US Ambassador concealed from the wider public; the cancelled coup itself remained generally unknown until after the presidential vote. Yeltsin's flirtation with dictatorship flared up and then fizzled out on that March weekend; but within the Kremlin the episode was crucial. As information about the cancelled coup gradually leaked out after the election, some observers were tempted to see those 48 hours as a seminal ideological moment for the president when he had faced a choice between dictatorship and democracy – and he had picked democracy. Yeltsin's own campaign team took a less romantic view.

'If Yeltsin had been threatened by certain defeat in the elections, he would not have permitted them,' Nikonov, who worked with the analytical group, told me. 'He would not have given up power.'

But even if 17 March was not an ideological crossroads, it was certainly a practical and political one which pushed Yeltsin further away from the party of war and slightly closer to the analytical group. A week later, Yeltsin boosted the authority of the group with a bureaucratic decision which was meaningless outside the Kremlin's walls but hugely important within them. Since mid-January, Soskovets had been officially in charge of the campaign. On 22 March, Yeltsin gracefully sidestepped Soskovets' power, creating an entirely new structure to run the campaign – the Election Council – chaired by the president himself. It was a subtle gesture, but the hard-liners immediately understood that it was the beginning of the end.

The definitive victory of the analytical group came a month later, immediately after Yeltsin made a campaign trip to Krasnodar, a farming city in the centre of the communist-dominated Red Belt. Although Yeltsin had rejected the political strategy of the party of war, he still enjoyed their company. When the Kremlin chief travelled south, as always Korzhakov was at his side. The result was a disaster. Yeltsin stalked through Krasnodar like a party boss of old, surrounded by a praetorian guard of minders wearing gangster sunglasses and frowns. The only locals who got within 100 metres of the president were the sycophantic regional officials who clung as close to Yeltsin as they could, their faces distorted by what Malashenko – the NTV boss and member of the analytical group – described as 'nightmarish, hypocritical, unnatural smiles'.

It was all horribly reminiscent of Yeltsin's strange and stilted performance in Yekaterinburg. At this rate, he would be trounced by the communists. The analytical group had to convince the president to take an entirely new approach, and Malashenko and Chubais were nominated for the job.

They started by showing Yeltsin photographs of his visit to Krasnodar, then pictures of his 1991 campaign. The contrast was stark: in 1991 he had been Russia's most successful populist, a flesh-pressing, barn-storming people's hero. Still possessed of some of the finest political antennae in the country, Yeltsin got the point immediately. At a meeting of the Election Council that afternoon, he publicly lashed out at the party of war, accusing Korzhakov of 'making me a second Brezhnev' and vowing to campaign his own way from then on. On his next campaign trip, a visit to Khabarovsk in the far east, Yeltsin did just that. Ordering his cavalcade to make an impromptu stop, he dived into the crowd. The onlookers were thrilled, pushing their way up to him to make a complaint, offer a compliment or just to squeeze his hand. The analytical group was even more delighted. Not only had Yeltsin rediscovered his old knack for campaigning, but by embracing their approach the president had finally sidelined the party of war.

'Korzhakov understood, from that moment, that his role was over,' Malashenko recalled, smiling with remembered glee. 'I, Chubais and our allies were now the victors.'

With the party of war vanquished, a close-knit nine-person core campaign team swiftly emerged, drawing together members of the analytical group with a few liberal Kremlin aides. This inner circle took over day-to-day management of the campaign, meeting daily and briefing Yeltsin at least once a week.

Two of the group's key members were Zverev and Malashenko, both from the Most group, who represented the oligarchs in general and Gusinsky in particular. The two were talented in the occasionally black arts of public relations, as practised in post-communist Russia, and through the Most media empire they had an automatic channel for building up the president's image. Shakhnovsky, the Moscow mayor's right-hand man, was another member and served as the group's link with the capital city's influential and well organised political machine. He was also a formidable player in his own right, described to me by one admirer as 'Russia's most intelligent and most cunning apparatchik'. There was also a splattering of Kremlin advisers, politicians and academic analysts.

There was only one woman in the group, but her role was crucial. Tatyana Dyachenko, the president's daughter, was the team's not-so-secret weapon. With her on their side, they could finally trump what had always been the party of war's strongest suit: its natural psychological affinity with the president and daily access through Korzhakov. A lifelong Daddy's girl who, at 36, still lived with her parents, Tatyana was uniquely able to convey the realities of the New Russia to her father in a form he could understand. As Potanin put it, she was the group's 'emotional translator'.

The official leader of the team was Viktor Ilyushin, a senior Kremlin aide and a close Yeltsin confederate since the 1970s when the two men had worked together in Yekaterinburg. Little known outside the political establishment, Ilyushin was what Russians call the group's political *krysha* or roof, the powerful patron who was able to deflect attacks within the bureaucracy.

Then there was Chubais. Just as the iron general had distinguished himself within the reform team by his administrative brilliance, so his greatest contribution to the election drive was as a superbly skilled manager. His other vital function was to mind the money. As the oligarchs had told Yeltsin at their first meeting, Chubais was the only apparatchik they trusted not to steal their campaign contributions.

In his role as financial controller, Chubais served as a link between the election team and its bank-rollers – the oligarchs. The most important contribution of the members of the Davos Pact had been, as

Shakhnovsky put it, to 'wake up' the president. Now that Yeltsin had been roused, their direct participation in the campaign diminished – although Berezovsky sometimes couldn't resist dropping in on the daily meetings of the core campaign team.

The oligarchs continued to play an important, if still somewhat murky, financial role. To make sure that the campaign bills were paid promptly and the division was equitable, they met once a week, generally either at Berezovsky's mansion or Chubais' office. A healthy mutual suspicion was the order of the day: the gathered oligarchs named and shamed those of their number who had not paid up. 'He who hadn't paid would be attacked and we would say, "You haven't paid! Pay up!"' Friedman recalled. He also admitted that, thanks to Russia's convoluted laws and sympathetic bureaucrats, in the end none of the oligarchs was left seriously out of pocket: 'There were various schemes, no one lost too much money on that affair.'

With the election team formed and the president finally committed to its overall strategy, the group at last began to roll out the most effective political campaign Russia had ever seen. Rather unsettlingly, the young English-speaking technocrats actually turned out to be much better at propaganda than the neo-Soviet hard-liners they usurped.

The genius (and also the perversion) of the campaign was that it combined all the new, hip democratic skills Russia had learned since the collapse of Communism with the old repressive, authoritarian techniques it had not yet forgotten. It was MTV meets Big Brother and, in a country itself confused about which universe it belonged in, it was unbeatable. In February, the president had looked like a doddering Politburo chief. Now he was suddenly transformed into a protean politician with a sure ability to strike just the right chord with every constituitiency – a kind of Russian Bill Clinton. One minute wrapped in the Red Flag and bowing before the flame of the Unknown Soldier, the next minute a newly agile Yeltsin was appealing to the young in their own, pop argot. One of the entertainment impresarios the media barons had brought into the campaign, Sergei Lisovsky, even created a pro-Yeltsin rock music video.

Yeltsin's clever advertisements and focus-group-driven personality changes would not have been out of place in a Western election campaign. But what guaranteed his success was that his campaign team broadcast its slick message with a steely disregard for democratic nicety which would have done the Politburo proud. The Russian media, which had so bravely reported on the Kremlin's failures in Chechnya, abruptly went back to its old propagandistic ways. Not only did the three national television channels and the main national newspapers all openly support Yeltsin, but – subtly and not so subtly – they launched a concerted campaign to whip up a broader, anti-communist mood in the country.

This control over the airwaves and printing presses was matched by a reanimation of the regional network of governors and factory directors which had been such an important element in the Communist Party's control over the country. When he first took power as a democratic rebel, Yeltsin told the governors to 'take as much power as you can'. Now he and his team reminded them of their political debt to the Kremlin. Opposition candidates found themselves blocked from the local media, their speaking engagements at state institutions like universities abruptly cancelled and their hotel reservations prone to vanish at the last minute.

In command of the airwaves and of the government, the campaign team mounted a sophisticated dirty war against the communists. Russia's most popular psychics – clairvoyants, crystal-ball readers, astrologists – were put on the Kremlin payroll to convince the highly superstitious Russian masses that a Yeltsin victory was in the stars. When Zyuganov hit the campaign trail, the team sometimes managed to ensure abysmal coverage by sending fake programmes to journalists, who consequently arrived either several hours late or several hours early at every communist event. They even produced a series of false, and worryingly extremist, 'secret' communist economic programmes which the oligarchs publicised in their newspapers.

'We've produced so many versions that the communists themselves can't remember which is the real thing any more,' Zverev proudly told me at one point in the campaign.

After Yeltsin's victory, most observers, especially those who worked for Western governments or Western investment banks, were happy to forget what it had taken to win. But the violence which some of Russia's smartest and most liberal technocrats had done to democracy – on democracy's behalf – continued to trouble me. To discover how the team justified what it had done, I invited the NTV boss Malashenko to supper.

We started off on a warm enough note. A sternly handsome man with silver hair and a martial physique, Malashenko seemed to be by far the most interesting person in the Tsars' Hunt, a gloriously kitsch combination of monarchist fantasy and nouveau riche extravagance that included waiters dressed as Russian peasants, the hides of every beast native to Russia's forests and a small gurgling brook. With a gently ironic smile, Malashenko said he had chosen the restaurant, a favourite with the new Russian establishment, 'so you can get a taste of Russian exotica'.

We began to talk about his political beliefs and motivations. Malashenko, who had been recruited by Gorbachev to join the Central Committee in the 1980s, sounded like a characteristic product of that hopeful era – one of the young men who, while not a dissident and certainly motivated by careerist considerations, had contributed mightily to the collapse of communism.

'I have a reputation of being a very, to put it mildly, pragmatic man and so you may not believe me, but when I went into the Central Committee I was motivated, in large part, by idealistic convictions,' Malashenko explained, managing to look dignified even though he was flanked by two child-sized, brightly painted wooden tsarist soldiers. 'It may seem naïve, but I remember that I truly could not understand the events in Vilnius [in January 1991, when Soviet policemen killed thirteen democracy activists in the Lithuanian capital]. To this day I remember my state of total intellectual shock.'

Malashenko's horror was shared by all of democratic Russia, and in large measure it was this revulsion which cost Gorbachev his domestic constituency and cleared the way for Yeltsin. But, as they began to build a new Russia alongside their new president, men like Malashenko gradually lost the moral sensitivity they had learned in the Gorbachev era. A measure of this transformation was the indifferent public reaction to the fighting in Chechnya, a bloodbath in which tens of thousands of people died. Malashenko, deeply repelled by the Soviet use of force in Lithuania, described the 1995–6 Chechen war merely as 'a serious mistake, what you call in English a "miscalculation".'

When I demurred, suggesting stronger language might be called for, Malashenko held his ground: 'I was referring to Talleyrand, who once uttered the famous phrase, "That is worse than a crime, it is a mistake." For me, also, there is nothing worse than a mistake. From time to time, every government kills people.'

Malashenko brought the same cold morality to bear on the presidential election campaign. I wanted to know how he justified the nakedly partisan approach taken by his television station and the Russian media as a whole; but after two hours of verbal sparring, the mood seemed too tense for me to risk introducing yet another inflammatory subject.

Just as I prepared to slide into some innocuous post-prandial chit-chat, the day was saved by Eddie Opp, a Moscow-based American photographer who had come with me to the interview. Eddie had struck up an instant rapport with Malashenko, himself an avid amateur shutter-bug. In the midst of some friendly techno-chatter, Eddie casually slipped in the most important question of the evening.

The day before the final ballot, Eddie had been watching television with a Russian friend and had come across *Burnt by the Sun*, an Oscar-award-winning indictment of Stalinism. Eddie had commented on the 'interesting coincidence' that an anti-communist television film festival should coincide with the presidential elections. Soon put right by his Russian friend, who was stunned by his American pal's naïveté, the penny dropped and Eddie realised the airwaves were being manipulated to secure a pro-Yeltsin vote. 'I thought it was very wrong,' Eddie recalled, his voice rising in remembered outrage.

Now he turned to his new-found photographer-comrade and asked, with piercing innocence: 'Is something like that possible on your channel? I think it was very wrong and manipulative.'

For a moment Malashenko, who coordinated the entire Kremlin media campaign and probably personally selected the anti-communist movies that were shown on election eve, seemed to wonder whether the question was some sort of strange Western joke. But, looking into Eddie's expectant face, he realised it was not and responded with a world-weary sigh: 'You are probably right. The problem is that during the elections nothing depended on you, on Eddie and Chrystia . . . but it depended directly on me whether the next president would be Zyuganov or Yeltsin. I think, and I thought, that Zyuganov would be a catastrophe. I had to . . . how shall I put it? . . . sell my soul to the devil.'

'Do you really think that's what you did?' I asked, amazed by his frankness.

'Of course I don't,' Malashenko replied with not a little scorn. 'But from the point of view of a middling Western intelligence, perhaps that is what I did.'

'By that you mean my intelligence?'

'Yes, yours. You are absolutely right. I live in my own system of coordinates, that is the pure truth.' And with that Malashenko and his bodyguards swept out of the restaurant.

At that moment, I hated Malashenko – but I also felt a flicker of respect. He and the other steely lieutenants of the Yeltsin campaign were far less admirable figures than the heroes of the Gorbachev era, the brave dissidents who believed that truth could bring down the Soviet dictatorship and saw their faith vindicated. The Malashenkos were more ambivalent creatures who openly played the political game for personal benefit and had no qualms about using almost any means to achieve their ends. But they took a kind of hangman's pride in their work, and sometimes I understood why. Men like Malashenko thought that the new Russia was too fragile for Western morals and manners. It needed hard-hearted pragmatists like them, men willing to dirty their hands and stain their souls, just to survive. I'm still not sure whether they're right.

Democracy and its discontents was an issue which also preoccupied the most quixotic candidate of the 1996 campaign: Mikhail Gorbachev. Undeterred by an opinion poll rating of just 1–2 per cent – less than the support for Vladimir Brintsalo, a flashy New Russian whose chief campaign asset was a shapely wife who flashed her sculpted bum in her husband's television ads – the former Soviet general secretary decided to try to return to the Kremlin, this time through the ballot box. For most Russians, his campaign was an absurd footnote to a fraught period dominated by the scheming of the oligarchs and the prospect of a communist revanche. But it captured the imagination of Western newspaper editors who still remembered Gorbymania. And so, less than two months ahead of the June presidential ballot, I reluctantly set off to join the former Soviet chief on the campaign trail.

Submitting to the routine discomforts of domestic Aeroflot flights with a Nobel-prize-winning, former superpower leader just a few rows ahead (there was, of course, no business class) was a surreal experience, like catching a Greyhound with Ronald Reagan. It seemed to underscore Gorbachev's reduced status in the New Russia he had helped to create, and the absurdity of his political quest. But Mikhail Sergeyevich, and his wife Raisa – campaign-ready in designer sunglasses and a buttercup-yellow suit – were unperturbed by the humiliations of ordinary Russian life. Gorbachev grinned with a lottery-winner's delight when a few intrigued passengers approached him for an autograph. When we landed in the springtime sunshine in Rostov, a city in the southern Russian steppes that were Gorbachev's homeland, he bounded off the plane and on to the campaign trail like a track star enthusiastic for the race to begin.

Gorbachev was lucky to enjoy the rituals of campaigning for their own sake, because the scenes which greeted him over the next few days would have deterred all but the most inveterate pol. For me, the greatest shock was to discover how thoroughly the Kremlin juggernaut acted to block rival candidates, even one like Gorbachev who posed no real political threat. At the last minute, a planned meeting between Gorbachev and the professors of Rostov University was cancelled – a Kremlin decree banned presidential candidates from 'politicising' the universities, though it did not seem to apply to Yeltsin himself. Unofficially, the blackout seemed to apply to the media as well. In the end, only one small, privately owned radio station dared to interview Gorbachev, who found himself in the ludicrous position of being trailed by international camera crews but ignored by the obscure local newspapers and television channels in the small towns he visited.

Regional government leaders were equally stand-offish. The head of Rostov *oblast* was – by absolute coincidence, of course – called off to a meeting in Moscow on the day Gorbachev arrived. In Stavropol, the province Gorbachev had run as all-powerful first secretary for 8 years, the story was the same: the governor and his deputies were all away on urgent business trips. Other opposition candidates had to negotiate an identical Kremlin-erected obstacle course; but for Gorbachev, being snubbed by the nomenklatura of the Russian steppes must have been particularly galling. The rural functionaries and journalists of Rostov and Stavropol who refused to meet him in May 1996 would have fallen over themselves for the privilege of hosting him as general secretary just five years earlier. Many of them owed their jobs to the local boy who had risen to the very top of the Soviet system.

Gorbachev was frustrated, but understanding. 'Of course, I know why the local officials are so afraid,' he told me at one campaign stop. 'At this moment, disloyalty could be very costly for them. I have been through the whole drama of Russian leadership, from becoming divine when you are in power to being cursed as soon as you lose it.'

What was more disturbing for Gorbachev, and shocking for me, was that when he did manage to find an audience he was usually reviled, attacked for precisely those democratic achievements which still made him a hero to the West. When he addressed a packed hall of sunburnt farmers in Krasnogvardeysk, a small town where he had attended primary school, he was heckled by an audience openly yearning for a return to the communist system he had helped to dismantle.

Gorbachev's rhetorical question: 'Should we give power back to the communists?' was greeted by enthusiastic clapping and shouts of, 'Yes, the Communists! It was better then', 'You sold out the country' and 'Russia needs a strong hand.' Gorbachev, the only ruler in Russian history to give way to a democratically elected rival, was aghast. 'Do you think some sort of Tsar can save you?' he scolded. 'I think we need not a strong hand but a wise head.'

But as Gorbachev's humble campaign cortège traversed the legendary black-earth plains of southern Russia, his praise for democracy ran up against a wall of popular yearning for despotism. A typical question was handed to the podium on a paper slip at an open-air rally in leafy Gorky Park in Rostov-on-Don: 'Mikhail Sergeyevich, why did you allow Yeltsin to become president?'

'Who is to blame for this? It is you who voted for Yeltsin,' Gorbachev – a fierce critic of Yeltsin during his rise to power in the early 1990s – quite sensibly retorted. 'But you should have annulled the vote,' a voice called from the audience.

Blamed for being insufficiently tyrannical towards his own people and for not suppressing wayward eastern Europe with Soviet tanks, Gorbachev was sometimes tempted to strike a martyr's pose. Faced with the pro-communist hecklers in Krasnogvardeysk, finally he responded with anger: 'Whoever doesn't want me, let him go to the party he chooses, that is his right. But this is what I am calling for, I will stand to the end. Crucify me if you will. This is how I see your excitement. I remember Jesus Christ when he went to Calvary. They spit on him, they spit and shouted, "Crucify him." Is that not a lesson for us? Are we humans or are we not? Will we ever stop being serfs? Will we ever become citizens?'

The peculiar combination of self-pity and self-aggrandisement which inspired Gorbachev to compare himself with the Messiah was one of the former Kremlin's chief's least attractive personal qualities. But the question he asked at the end of his tirade – 'Will we ever become citizens?' – was one that haunted me as we travelled from one shabby auditorium to another. Transforming the oppressed Soviet collective into a country of independent citizens was the essence of the democratic revolution which Gorbachev began and Yeltsin had pledged to continue.

By the time we arrived in Privolnoye, the sleepy village of 4,000 people where Gorbachev was born, it was apparent that, at least in the provinces, that revolution was only half complete. Gorbachev's *zemliaky*, literally 'people of the same land', were clearly no longer in the grip of a totalitarian state and expressed their grievances with the current government freely and enthusiastically. Yet they had not become citizens either. An economic collapse which would only accelerate over the next few years restricted their life choices as painfully as the political straitjacket of the USSR, and they were cynically certain that their votes could not make a difference.

'Our great-great-grandparents were the tsar's serfs, our grandparents and parents were the Politburo's serfs and we are Yeltsin's bums,' Valery, a tattooed 23-year-old village youth who described himself as a 'businessman', told me. 'We are too poor to leave, and there's nothing to do for us here if we stay. We just drink, go wild, and steal our neighbour's chickens. What is the point of working – every day life just gets worse and worse.'

By the final lap of the campaign, Zyuganov, the communist contender, seemed decidedly deflated. The bravado with which he had strutted the swank hotel corridors of Davos a few months earlier was gone; in less time than it had taken to melt the Russian snows, the oligarchs' juggernaut had transformed him from president-in-waiting to a designated loser, dejectedly waiting for the polls to confirm the inevitability of his defeat.

When I joined Zyuganov on his last major campaign trip before the first round of the elections – a swing through three of Siberia's major cities – the change in tone was striking. He no longer seemed able to summon the energy to describe the future economic policies of a government he had little chance of heading. Instead, all but admitting he was doomed to fail, he made a half-hearted effort to rally his supporters for a heroic eleventh-hour communist conversion drive. What galled them all was that this should not have been impossible. The assembled crowds of party faithful were the losers in Russia's market transition: army officers, research scientists, pensioners. All of them were barely getting by, squeezed by the state's diminishing support for the elderly, the military and education. A great many of their countrymen were in the same boat. According to official statistics, the economy had shrunk to half its size in 1991; wages were on average lower than they had been before reforms began and often paid months late; odd medieval epidemics, including the bubonic plague, had reappeared; people were even dying younger.

So why weren't voters flocking to the communists? Elections across eastern Europe – where the shift to a market economy had been swifter, more successful and uncomplicated by civil wars and the loss of historic territories – had already demonstrated that impoverished voters were inclined to punish reformist governments for the pain of the market transition by bringing the communists back into office. When the campaign kicked off in the spring, Zyuganov and his allies had had every reason to believe that Russians would be guided by the same instinct to 'kick the bastards out'. But, as he trudged through the Siberian taiga, it was painfully apparent to most of his supporters that this 'logical' outcome would not come to pass. One reason was that, in the words of one Moscow banker, Zyuganov and his supporters were 'the nation's losers'.

In countries such as Poland and Hungary, the old communist establishment had been forced from power by a ragged crew of dissident intellectuals as the Soviet bloc collapsed in 1989. A few years later, when the revamped communists of eastern Europe ran for office they campaigned as their countries' natural parties of power, the technocratic elite of the *ancien régime* which had the skills needed for governance. In Russia, by contrast, most of the old elite had remained firmly and prosperously in place. Consequently, the Russian communists represented a very different slice of the population from their eastern European comrades. They were the hard-line holdovers from the old Soviet Communist Party, the only apparatchiks who were too stupid or too obstinate to make it in Boris Yeltsin's Russia and too stolid to dream up a new version of socialism, like the communist-lite programme which their Polish cousins had devised. In the end, all that was left to them was nationalism.

'Yeltsin's reforms have ended with the total collapse of the state,' Zyuganov complained to an audience in Akademgorodok, a scientists' ghetto in central Siberia. 'It is humiliating to admit, but our country is weaker and smaller than it has been since before the days of Peter the Great.'

The communist attack on Yeltsin's patriotic failings reached a sentimental peak the next day in Krasnoyarsk, a robust frontier city. There, as usual, a motley crew of local activists preceded Zyuganov to the microphone, one of them a moustachioed actor. Voice dripping with emotion and arms sweeping out in histrionic gestures, he recited a melodramatic verse about the sorry fate of a Second World War veteran fallen on hard times and forced to beg: 'Recently he traded his Red Star medal for two bottles of vodka and a loaf of bread, this is what fate – and Yeltsin – have done to one of the liberators of Berlin.'

It was a stylised and sentimental performance, but it struck precisely the right chord with the 800 mostly grey-haired loyalists packed into the hall. Tears in their eyes, they jumped to their feet and banged out their approval on their wrinkled palms. This was the generation which had made huge personal sacrifices to build the Soviet Union. Now, in its twilight years, it was suffering the double indignity of a decline in an already modest standard of living and a loss of the spiritual compensation of living in a great power.

As Anatoly Lukyanov, a former member of the communist Politburo, explained to me a few days before I joined Zyuganov on the campaign trail: 'We communists always understood perfectly well that the Soviet man, the citizen of Russia, had fewer political rights than a European. But that shortfall was compensated for by the sense of belonging to a great nation, a great state.'

'What did Mr Yeltsin do? He took away that sense of world importance,' argued Lukyanov, who spent a year in prison for his role in the failed 1991 putsch. 'Any party which takes advantage of this will be on top. That is why the communists have so many patriotic slogans, slogans of statehood, of nationhood.'

The communists' nationalist rhetoric worked, up to a point. Zyuganov met a warm reception in Siberia, but his supporters were almost entirely middle-aged. Younger people simply weren't interested in his nostalgic message of a lost empire. To them Zyuganov was irrelevant, as meaningless to their new lives as the music, fashions and bizarre Soviet rituals of their parents' generation. The few people under thirty who came to listen to Zyuganov in Krasnoyarsk didn't love communism, or hate it; they were merely mildly intrigued by it in the same way that they might be interested in some dying species in a zoo.

'We've just come to see Zyuganov, to see what a communist leader actually looks like,' Marina Mezhnyeva – a brunette economics student in a fashionable fluffy black sweater and jeans, who had been twelve when the Soviet Union collapsed – told me in Krasnoyarsk. Her friend Andrei, a gangly 18-year-old in a T-shirt emblazoned with the Chicago Bulls logo, agreed: 'When our moms and dads were young, they used to say the sorts of things Zyuganov is saying now.'

In the end, the youngest contingent of voters in Krasnoyarsk came to the conclusion that the Kremlin spin-doctors were so aggressively trying to sell to the whole country. 'We will probably end up voting for Yeltsin not because we like him, but because we like reforms,' Marina told me. 'He is the lesser evil.'

10

DIVIDING THE SPOILS

As HE STROLLED through the corridors of the White House, by then the seat of the Russian cabinet, on the afternoon of Wednesday 19 June, Arkady Evstafiev felt tired but happy. It was nearly four and a half months since the fateful afternoon when his boss, Chubais, had called from Davos and asked him to fax over some Communist Party documents, and every day since then had been gruelling. But now Evstafiev, a former journalist with the faintly Asiatic look of so many Russians – olive skin, slanted eyes and cheekbones as broad and flat as a dinner-plate – was starting to think he could relax. The first round of Russia's two-stage election process had taken place three days earlier, and Yeltsin had been comfortably in the lead. He seemed certain to win in the final run-off against Zyuganov in three weeks' time. Like all the other members of the Davos team, Evstafiev was feeling triumphant and a little light-hearted as he stopped for small talk with acquaintances in the hallway and popped into the offices of several friends for a chat.

Just before 4 o'clock, as he inched towards the exit, Evstafiev bumped into Sergei Lisovsky – the wolf-faced, long-haired, bejewelled impresario who was the Puff Daddy of the Davos team. Intensely hip (at least by Russian standards), Lisovsky was the man behind Yeltsin's political rock videos. The two chatted briefly, then Evstafiev moved on to gossip with yet another friend, while Lisovsky walked to the door and made his way towards his chauffeur-driven car in the parking area outside.

A few moments later, Evstafiev followed him – and stepped towards a political trap which would reshape the new Russia. Evstafiev and his colleagues were not the only ones who had realised that a Yeltsin victory was inevitable. The party of war sensed it too, and they were terrified. The way things were going, Yeltsin would win and their enemies, the Davos team, would get the credit for keeping him in power. Somehow, some way, the party of war had to trip them up and restore themselves in the president's favour. And they had to act fast, before the second round of voting and the beginning of the new political era.

To leave the White House compound visitors had to pass a final checkpoint, a small hut manned by armed guards and a metal detector, like a mini-border crossing. As Evstafiev approached the hut, he heard shouting. Entering, he saw a group of uniformed men questioning Lisovsky. Thinking it was some sort of routine bureaucratic snafu, Evstafiev stepped in, brandishing his potent talisman of nomenklatura power – his pass to the White House, personally signed by Prime Minister Chernomyrdin. To Evstafiev's surprise, the pass had no effect. Instead, the guards who were questioning Lisovsky turned their attention to him too.

"'Hey, this one's with him, too,'" one of them said.

With that, three uniformed men with automatic weapons grabbed Lisovsky and Evstafiev and began herding them back towards the White House. A senior officer ordered the guards to beat the two prisoners with their rifle butts if they spoke to each other or tried to break away. Then they were taken into separate interrogation rooms, with guards posted at the doors, and their captors – who they soon discovered were Korzhakov's infamous *oprichniki* – began to question them about a mysterious cardboard Xerox box containing $500,000 in cash. Snap! The trap had slammed shut.

For a long time, there was a debate about how exactly the trap had been set. Where did the $500,000 box come from? Were Evstafiev and Lisovsky the innocent victims of a crude set-up by the party of war? At first, that's what the Davos team claimed; but, Russia being Russia, it wasn't quite so simple. By 1998, several members of the Davos team were ready to admit to me that, as a matter of course, the Yeltsin machine paid many of its political expenses in 'black money' – cash, usually US dollars, which could not be traced by the taxman or the monitors of campaign finance laws. The campaign team needed some place to store the black money and – as Zverev, the Most executive and member of the analytical group, explained – what vault could be safer, more secure, and further from the prying gaze of the communists than the strong-boxes of the White House itself? 'Everyone knew perfectly well that is where we kept it.'

So Korzhakov was probably telling the truth when he insisted to me that he didn't plant the Xerox box: according to several members of the campaign team, either Lisovsky or Evstafiev or both were carrying it when they tried to walk out. But Korzhakov was being disingenuous when he claimed that he ordered his men to stop them because 'money was simply being stolen, in cash, from the campaign'. The fact is that black money was ferried in and out of the White House all the time, and Korzhakov knew that better than anyone else because it was his job to provide security for the people carrying it. The Xerox box filled with half a million dollars in cash – so irresistibly symbolic of the New Russia – was actually the MacGuffin of the 1996 campaign. In and of itself, it meant nothing at all. It was just a plot device, a cue for the final showdown between the party of war and the Davos team, a battle which was as inevitable as it would be ruthless.

In the White House interrogation rooms, the fight soon started to get nasty. Separated and denied access to lawyers or telephones, Evstafiev and Lisovsky faced a barrage of questions from interrogators trained in the unforgiving school of the KGB. At about 1 a.m. Anatoly Trofimov, head of the Moscow branch of the revamped KGB and a key figure in the Korzhakov faction, swept into the room where Evstafiev was being held. 'A cell is ready for you at Lefortovo,' he said, tauntingly referring to the infamous KGB prison in downtown Moscow. 'A special team is coming now to take you there.'

For Lisovsky, sitting in a room next door, the situation was particularly disturbing because it echoed a brutal attack on a friend of his just the day before. Boris Fyodorov, the former head of the National Sports Fund and one of the piranhas of the Loophole Economy, had been sitting in a parked car outside Moscow State University with a woman friend. At midnight, a man leaned through the window and shot him in the stomach; then he pulled out a knife and stabbed him repeatedly in the chest. The assailant was never found, but Lisovsky feared the same fate would befall him.

Evstafiev was less worked up. The situation was so 'absurd' and Korzhakov's strategy seemed so 'insane' that he couldn't take it too seriously. He also had a further source of solace in that although the presidential security service had taken away his mobile telephone, wallet and all-powerful White House pass, they had overlooked his pager. With covert glances at its small digital screen, Evstafiev could follow the drama beginning to unfold outside the small, shabby room where he was trapped. Chubais and the oligarchs had realised that he and Lisovsky had been detained, and they were preparing to ride in to the rescue.

By chance, as Korzhakov's special operation at the White House unfolded, his adversaries were holding a meeting of their own. That evening, the key figures in the Davos team – Berezovsky, Gusinsky, Chubais, Malashenko, Zverev and Boris Nemtsov, the reformist governor of Nizhny Novgorod – had all agreed to meet for supper at the Logovaz Clubhouse. They had gathered to talk about how they would run the country after Yeltsin won, but instead they found themselves in the midst of the biggest political crisis of the campaign. The first warning that something was amiss was a bleep on Malashenko's pager at about 10 p.m. – apparently, Lisovsky had been arrested. Then Chubais' mobile telephone rang: Evstafiev had vanished too, no one had had word from him for several hours.

As the mobile phone calls and pager messages flowed in and the group began to piece together what was happening, they realised that they were under observation. A cameraman appeared on the fourth-floor balcony of a peeling yellow apartment block opposite the club, openly filming the arrivals and departures, activity in the courtyard and movement behind the wide picture windows of the main rooms. Then a shiny black Mercedes with blue-flashing lights on its roof, like the cars in the official Kremlin fleet, pulled up and parked obtrusively outside the front door. Korzhakov was watching his enemies and he wanted them to know it. 'They were trying to scare us,' Malashenko told me. 'At one point, it even seemed as if they were trying to provoke Berezovsky's security guards into a fight.'

The oligarchs and the politicians realised the final battle had begun. 'We knew absolutely that if Korzhakov and Barsukov won, there would be no elections,' Gusinsky recalled. 'They would try to keep Yeltsin in power with force and blood. We would have been, probably, arrested or destroyed. Certainly arrested. Why have the hassle of gathering us from all around Moscow? Here we all were together in one place, just to give them joy.'

To survive, they had to start fighting back immediately. Their first duel was with Mikhail Barsukov, the head of the revamped KGB and a leading member of the party of war. At around midnight, Chubais – an ordinary citizen with no official status – picked up his mobile phone and dialled the private home telephone number of the man who occupied what had once been one of the most feared posts in the world. Barking obscenities with a creative flair which left a lasting impression on the listening oligarchs, Chubais let Barsukov have it: 'If so much as a single hair on Evstafiev's head is damaged, you will pay for it. You have until the morning: either all my people are released, or I will destroy you. One or the other, Misha, you must decide. You no longer have a middle way.'

As usual, the affair would ultimately be adjudicated by one man alone – Boris Yeltsin – and the oligarchs began a mad scramble to reach him. It was already long after midnight and Yeltsin, worn down from two months of boisterous campaigning, was asleep in his dacha at Davidovo, a pretty village outside Moscow. As they had done throughout the campaign, they turned to Tatyana. Malashenko, who had worked most closely with her, telephoned her and asked her to intervene. Alarmed, Tatyana and Yumashev, Yeltsin's ghostwriter, drove over to the Logovaz Clubhouse and joined the group there.

Tatyana started off by calling Korzhakov and ordering him to release Evstafiev and Lisovsky immediately. But the president's bodyguard was unimpressed: 'She spoke to me in a nervous voice, almost as if she were my boss. I can't stand that sort of tone, particularly when god knows who is using it. She had no authority to give me orders.' Tatyana then had no choice but to go directly to her father. She drove out to his dacha, woke him and told him what was going on.

By the time Korzhakov himself arrived home, the officer at the entry-way had received an urgent phone call from the president, who wanted to speak to his chief bodyguard immediately. 'Aleksandr Vasilievich, what is going on?' Yeltsin asked in a voice still soft with sleep.

Korzhakov urged him to go back to bed: 'Boris Nikolaevich, don't be concerned. Everything is under control. Nothing will be made public, until you decide what to do. So, please, sleep, and tomorrow we will report to you.' That answer seemed to appease the president, who put down the phone and tried fitfully to resume his rest. Korzhakov went to bed as well, and 'slept beautifully'.

But while their adversary and their judge sank into the arms of Morpheus, the oligarchs battled on. They had spoken with all the decision-makers; now their second step was to take the battle to the airwaves. With its web of wire-taps, network of police informers and libraries of compromising personal secrets, the party of war was Russia's most powerful player of the Soviet-style political game of clandestine intrigue. Fighting on those terms, the oligarchs and their political allies didn't stand a chance.

But what they could do was dominate Russia's new political arena – the world of public politics. In the middle of the night, working from the doll-house interior of the Logovaz Clubhouse, the oligarchs launched a media blitz. Malashenko called his team at NTV. Berezovsky called his television station, ORT. They all called CNN, the BBC and any Western journalist whose home number they happened to have on hand. I got my call at about 2 a.m. from Dima Volkov, a friend who had risen to become one of the top journalists at Gusinsky's *Segodnya*. Turn on NTV, he instructed. Sleepily, I obeyed.

When the screen flickered on I discovered that Gusinsky's television channel was screaming out the story of the confrontation with the sort of urgent, martial music and swirling graphics usually reserved for emergency war reports. Every fifteen minutes or so, Kisiliev, the anchorman and NTV founder, would flash on to the screen looking suitably grave and worried: 'We again interrupt our night-time programming for an emergency report,' he would intone, and then offer a new titbit from the nocturnal battle.

The television coverage was crucial because it forced the conflict into the open. Now that Kisiliev had christened it an 'emergency', neither Korzhakov nor the president would be able to sweep the incident under the carpet of public opinion. Even more significantly, the media offensive allowed the oligarchs and their political allies to define the terms of the battle. Korzhakov had picked the fight in the hopes of finding some dirt – what the Russians call *kompromat* – on the oligarchs and using the incriminating information to improve his own position in the Yeltsin court. But the oligarchs had dramatically raised the stakes. Through the prism of television, they magnified the detention of Evstafiev and Lisovsky into an attempted coup. Korzhakov was no longer just a courtier jockeying for power, he was a power-mad tyrant seeking to overthrow Russian democracy. But to get the Russian public on their side, the Davos team needed a powerful messenger. Neither Chubais – the most hated man in Russia – nor the oligarchs – who came in a close second through eighth – fitted the bill. Luckily, they knew someone who did: Aleksandr Lebed.

A broad-shouldered, gravel-voiced former general, Lebed was the sleeper hit of the 1996 campaign. With his dry wit, commanding manner and a-pox-on-all-their-houses outsiders' message, Lebed had drawn a remarkable 15 per cent of the vote in the first round of the elections, coming in third after Yeltsin and Zyuganov. The Davos team, which had quietly supported his campaign, accurately calculating that he would draw votes away from the communists, had urged the president to bring him into the Kremlin fold. Yeltsin took their advice. Two days after the first ballot and just a day before Evstafiev and Lisovsky's fateful trip to the White House, he had appointed Lebed head of the National Security Council, giving him wide authority over all of the country's 'power' ministries: the security forces, the army, the ministry of the interior.

As the crisis escalated, Chubais telephoned Lebed from the Logovaz Clubhouse and briefed him. Lebed immediately drove back to his offices on Staraya Ploshchad, the hulking granite block of buildings a stone's throw from the Kremlin. There he went to work on the *vertushkas*, the elite closed telephone system which gave the top members of the government access to one another. He reached Barsukov, who shouted at him and told him to mind his own business. Korzhakov would not even deign to take his call.

They would regret their rudeness. Rebuffed by the 'power' officials and indebted to the oligarchs for their prior political support, at 4 a.m. Lebed stepped into the Moscow darkness and, with the moon gleaming redly in the background, made an electrifying statement to the waiting NTV and ORT camera crews.

'Maybe the only thing we achieved in these past five years was that the first round of the elections was held democratically. But now they are trying to stop the second round,' he growled. 'I will get to the bottom of this – this is my first impression. I will find out the details. Any rebellion will be crushed, and crushed ruthlessly. He who wants to return the country to a time of bloody upheavals will not get any mercy.'

Lebed's intervention helped, but the Davos team still had an anxious few hours ahead of them as they paced the parquet floors of the Logovaz club and waited for the dawn and the political resolution it would bring. The tension affected everyone differently. Chubais, ever the workaholic warrior, methodically kept on hitting the phones. Berezovsky was even cooler. As cigarettes were tensely smoked, fingernails nervously gnawed and *zakuski* (Russian snacks) anxiously wolfed down all around him, Russia's arch-intriguer announced that the battle was already over: 'We've won!' he declared. 'Tomorrow there will be no Soskovets, no Barsukov, no Korzhakov. Yeltsin will chase them all out.' With that, Berezovsky decided to celebrate. He ordered a bottle of cognac from one of the tuxedoed waiters and attacked it in the Russian fashion, drinking shots in quick succession. By morning, the bottle was almost empty and Berezovsky's comrades were mightily impressed. 'He is a man who internally is absolutely without fear,' Gusinsky recalled admiringly.

Meanwhile, Evstafiev and Lisovsky were still sweating it out in the White House. But, as the television offensive began to put pressure on the party of war, the balance of power started to shift. Evstafiev's mood began to lighten at about 2 a.m. when, as the guards led him to a different room to face a new interrogator, he caught a glimpse of Kisiliev on television denouncing Korzhakov's 'attempted coup'. From that moment on, Evstafiev grew ever more confident and the guards around him became increasingly anxious. As the operation began to go wrong, the senior officers fell into an increasingly frantic round of buck-passing. Gradually, the guards' threats melted into soft, conciliatory phrases and even apologies. 'We don't want you to be left with any hard feelings,' they told Evstafiev. 'After all, we're not really to blame and we didn't beat you.' Eventually they grew so pathetic that Evstafiev started to feel sorry for them.

By about 3 a.m., the frenzy of fear and mutual recriminations had become so absorbing that Korzhakov's men seemed to forget about Evstafiev and Lisovsky altogether. They were left alone in their rooms as their captors made frantic telephone calls to try to find out what was going on. 'It was a total panic, all their plans had gone awry. They began to be afraid of what they had done,' Evstafiev told me later. Finally, Evstafiev decided he had to take the initiative. 'Shall I leave now?' he asked.

The guards told him to go – but that wasn't good enough for Evstafiev who insisted that someone accompany him to the final outdoor checkpoint where he had been stopped 12 hours earlier. Reluctantly, one of the guards saw him out. As they walked the 100 metres of pavement into the clean summer dawn, the young officer continued to grovel.

'I really hope that we will not be enemies,' he offered hopefully as he shepherded Evstafiev through the last metal detector and, finally, into freedom. A few moments later, Lisovsky was released too.

Chubais and the oligarchs had achieved their first goal: their colleagues had been liberated. Now they would try to move in for the kill. After going home to shower and change, the group reconvened in Chubais' office just across the street from the White House.

Meanwhile, Korzhakov was just beginning his daily routine. He woke up just after 6 a.m., and by 7 a.m. he was on his way to his regular morning game of tennis when his plans were interrupted by the ringing of his car-phone. It was the Kremlin, summoning him to the president's office for an 8 a.m. meeting. The end game had begun: Yeltsin was awake and preparing to sit in judgement on his feuding courtiers.

Korzhakov and Barsukov went first, and the chief bodyguard, generally so much in tune with the moods of his master, thought the 40-minute meeting went well. Yeltsin, he felt, approved of everything he had done. The only thing he was angry about was the 'media fuss'. Korzhakov thought that was just fine. After all, as he pointed out to the president, it had been the Davos team and not the party of war which had electrified the airwaves. Relieved that things were going his way, a placid Korzhakov returned to his office to await the president's final verdict.

The inquisition continued. As the morning wore on, Yeltsin met with his prime minister, then with Lebed. Expressionless as always, he gave nothing away. The country, and the warring factions, watched and waited. Inside the Kremlin, Yeltsin told his staff that he was preparing to declare a compromise – Korzhakov would be punished for provoking the embarrassing affair by being withdrawn from the campaign team, but he would keep his job as chief of the president's security service, and would remain a close personal friend.

'The president decided slowly. It was a very difficult decision for him, a personal one,' Sergei Medvedev, Yeltsin's press secretary at the time, told me. 'He had worked with Korzhakov for a very long time and trusted him.'

But Chubais was not the sort of man to settle for a compromise. As he prepared for his own meeting with the president, scheduled for around noon, he sought a way to force Yeltsin to take a decision which he knew would be personally devastating but which he believed was politically crucial. He chose the same tactic which had served him and the oligarchs so well during the night: maximum publicity. When Yeltsin rang Chubais to summon him to the Kremlin, the young reformer warned the president that, whatever the outcome of their discussion, he and Malashenko had already called a press conference for early that afternoon. The announcement was a tacit threat: if Yeltsin chose to back the party of war, the well-oiled media machine which had produced his first-round election victory might turn against him.

When Chubais' turn to see Yeltsin finally came, he walked in with a heavy sense of his own importance: 'The fate of the country, without exaggeration, was hanging on a very, very thin thread.' While Chubais and Yeltsin talked, two of Chubais' key allies – Malashenko and Lebed – huddled in the corridor outside. Inside the president's vast office, Chubais was deploying all his formidable analytical and rhetorical talents to convince Yeltsin to make a final break with the party of war. Korzhakov believed that Chubais delivered an ultimatum: 'Either you choose us and you win the election, or the financiers and I will withdraw our money and you will lose.' Zverev told me that what swung the balance was one final, specific example of Korzhakov's malicious KGB-style political manipulation. Korzhakov had written Kisiliev a threatening letter. In a classic example of *kompromat*, he accused the NTV anchor of serving as an undercover KGB agent – code-named Alekseev – and warned that he would reveal his secret unless Kisiliev toned down his criticism. When Chubais showed him the letter, Yeltsin, who despised *kompromat* and had a soft spot for television stars, was revolted, exclaiming: 'What bastards!'

Ultimately, Chubais' strongest argument was an appeal to the one cause always dearest to the president's heart – his own self-interest. 'Chubais succeeded in convincing Yeltsin that Korzhakov, for the sake of his battle with Chubais, was willing to jeopardise the elections and provoke an unpredictable conflict in the country on the eve of the elections,' Leonid Nevzlin, the Menatep executive, told me. 'He did what it is necessary to do with Yeltsin. He convinced him it [Korzhakov's action] was against Yeltsin's best interests.'

Finally persuaded, Yeltsin acted swiftly and ruthlessly. With Chubais still at his side, he called Korzhakov's office, where the party of war leaders had gathered, and asked to speak to Barsukov first. After less than a minute, Barsukov mutely handed the telephone over to Korzhakov. Yeltsin – his hero, his friend, his adopted father – tersely instructed him to write a letter of resignation immediately.

Korzhakov was crushed: 'Those were his last words to me. That was all. He didn't even bother to address me politely as Aleskandr Vasilievich, or dear Sasha, or respected friend. It shows what kind of man he is. You can spend eleven years side-by-side with him, you can protect him with your own chest, you can save him from God knows what, and he can part with you as peacefully as if he is taking off a holey sock and throwing it away.'

Korzhakov's defeat was so obviously a personal tragedy that some Russian liberals couldn't help feeling rather sorry for their old nemesis. Not Chubais. For the first few moments, Yeltsin's decision had overwhelmed him. When Chubais stepped out of the president's office, his face was so pale and his expression so bleak that Malashenko and Lebed were certain that all was lost. But, within a few moments, Chubais had recovered and was planning the next move. Yeltsin was famously mercurial – the Davos Pact had to make it impossible for him to change his mind. As Kokh explained: 'We had to formalise the success we had achieved. Otherwise we could not rule out that over the next few hours they [the party of war] would win back the initiative.'

To do that, Chubais and Malashenko raced over to the Radisson-Slavyanskaya, an American-managed hotel, for their press conference, to tell the world what the president had decreed. When they reached the podium, the mood was electric and Chubais, so often caricatured as a bloodless bureaucrat, was as openly exultant as a gladiator fresh from the kill. The power struggle within the Kremlin was over; the party of war had been defeated; the reformers would control the new political order after Yeltsin's inevitable victory in the second round of voting. Democracy had triumphed over the forces of darkness.

'Today, in the night and the day, Boris Nikolaevich took the decision to fire Soskovets, Barsukov and Korzhakov,' Chubais declared. 'He thus hammered the final nail into the coffin which contained the illusion of a military coup against the Russian state. The game we were playing was far more serious than poker and its price was blood.'

As I stood among the jostling crowd of journalists at Chubais' feet, it was impossible not to be moved. For all the compromises and corruption, the Chechen war and the give-aways of state property, Russia again seemed to be on the right track. We gave Chubais a standing ovation when he arrived in the room, and another one when he left.

But victory did not come for free. The greatest price Russia paid for the defeat of the party of war may have been the abrupt deterioration of the president's health. When Yeltsin met with the core campaign team assembled by Chubais and the oligarchs two days after the sacking, the agony of the decision was written on his pale and puffy face. 'He looked quite bad,' Zverev told me. 'He told us then that the events had been very difficult for him.' Naina, Yeltsin's wife, compared sacking Korzhakov with the pain of losing a beloved member of the family. Some members of the Davos Pact thought that firing Korzhakov had been so hard on Yeltsin that it provoked the heart attack he suffered a few days later.

Yeltsin's illness would not stop him from winning in the second round, however. As Vasily Shakhnovsky, the Moscow city chief of staff, put it, 'If we had to, we would have got a mummy elected.' But a disabled president – as Yeltsin would become for the first eight months of his second term – did cast a serious shadow over the brave new order which Chubais and the oligarchs had been hoping to usher in.

Nor was the president's heart the only casualty of Korzhakov's downfall. Chubais, Gusinsky, Berezovsky and Malashenko viewed the defeat of the party of war as a black-and-white triumph, a victory which would ensure that the righteous dominated Yeltsin's new administration. But some of the members of the Davos Pact took a less Manichean view. For all his faults, they argued that Korzhakov had played a vital role in maintaining Russia's political equilibrium. Worse yet, they feared that the tribalistic 'them-vs-us' attack on Korzhakov and his allies could herald a whole new era of political blood-letting.

'It is such an American attitude, to divide the world into good and bad,' Friedman told me. 'But in our inchoate world everything is much more relative.' For all his faults, the oligarch insisted, Korzhakov had fulfilled one very important function: 'He was the enforcer. People feared him and that fear, which is part of the Russian political tradition, in many ways anchored the vertical power structure of the state. Korzhakov collected dirt; he knew who every governor was sleeping with, who was paying him bribes and so forth. Maybe this was a stupid, pig-headed way of influencing the regional authorities, but it worked. If some governor tried to do something against the Kremlin, Korzhakov would just say, "Look, I'm just going to throw you in jail and only then will we start worrying about whether it was legal or not."'

Without Korzhakov, the Kremlin's own Dirty Harry, the ad hoc political order which Yeltsin had improvised with bubble-gum and shoe-string after the collapse of the Soviet Union threatened to fall apart. In dispensing with Korzhakov, and hoping to thus forever purge Russia of the party of war, Friedman argued that the Davos Pact was guilty of the same idealistic naïveté which led them to believe that communism could be buried in a few months of shock therapy: 'It is the same situation as with socialism. "We'll just ban socialism," we thought, "introduce some new laws, and all will be well." Bullshit. It was the same with Korzhakov. "Korzhakov will go," we thought, "and immediately we will have a democratic society and all will be wonderful." It hasn't turned out that way.'

On 3 July, two weeks after firing Korzhakov, an ailing Yeltsin was elected to a second term. He won 53 per cent of the vote, a 13 per cent lead over the younger, more vigorous Zyuganov who had enjoyed more than thrice the president's popularity at the beginning of the campaign. The plot hatched in the mountains of Davos five months earlier had worked brilliantly.

The oligarchs were euphoric. On election day, I visited Berezovsky in the Logovaz Clubhouse where the earliest results of the ballot would not be available for another six hours, but he was already absolutely certain that Yeltsin would win and was thrilled about the victory he had done so much to achieve. Big capital, as Berezovsky termed it in his rough but articulate English, had defeated the communist threat. Yeltsin's historic redistribution of property, and its beneficiaries, were no longer at risk.

'It is very simple,' Berezovsky explained, grinning broadly and toying with a bejewelled pen. 'Big capital is not altruistic – we needed to protect our business. We realised that communism was again a reality in Russia and we realised that civil war was also a reality.'

By voting for Yeltsin, Berezovsky believed, the Russian people had endorsed the first stage of the Yeltsin revolution: the destruction of communism. Now, having won, Yeltsin would turn his energy to the second stage: building a new, resurrected Russia. His goal now would be to 'build a palace named Yeltsin'. It sounded to me as if the oligarch expected there to be a pretty big guest-house named 'Berezovsky' right next door.

Two days after I spoke with Berezovsky, Chubais made an even more ambitious claim on his president's behalf. In a nakedly triumphant press conference Chubais described Yeltsin as the most important Russian leader since Peter the Great. The president, he said, was greater than Witte and Stolypin, two major Imperial reformers; more visionary than Alexander II, the tsar who liberated the serfs. Some of the Russian reporters I was standing next to had an instant, cynical interpretation: Looks like Tolya wants to get back into government, they muttered, and we're being asked to deliver his letter of application. The truth was even more disturbing – Chubais really meant it.

Now he was telling us about the Russian people. They were all heroes, Chubais insisted, because every time they had been asked to choose between communism or democracy they had unswervingly opted for the latter. In fact the Russian people, and their political leaders, had made such a correct and noble choice that they had demonstrated their superiority to their former eastern European vassals who, for all their complacent talk of Westernisation, had re-elected excommunists. 'It is absolutely clear that Russia is wiser than its neighbours,' Chubais declared.

At that point, most of the reporters in the room gulped or gasped or started to shift awkwardly in their seats. Chubais had gone so far over the top that we were all starting to feel embarrassed, the same squirming, pit-of-the-stomach sensation you get when your grandmother starts puffing your accomplishments to the neighbours, starting with kindergarten.

The defeat of the communists was certainly a historic moment, but surely it was somewhat premature to beatify Yeltsin? As for the countries of eastern Europe, with economies enjoying robust growth, candidate membership of the EU and more Western investment than Russia, despite a fraction of the population, surely they saw little to envy in Moscow? 'Chubais is wonderful when he is the underdog, but he just doesn't know how to handle victory,' one of my friends whispered.

But the iron general was unstoppable. He went on to lecture the defeated Zyuganov about the concessions he would be required to make to re-emerge as an acceptable figure in Russian public life (give up the title 'communist' and champion private property, for starters). Then he started to wax poetic about the delights which awaited Russians now that they had made the right choice. There would be a sharp increase in foreign investment, flight capital would flow back into the country, and by 2000 the economy would be booming with an annual growth rate of 10 per cent.

It was a stunning instance of hubris, but it accurately reflected the confidence – the ecstatic sense that Russia had won a new and hopeful beginning – felt by the Davos team at that moment. When the frail president met with the core campaign group on 4 July, the day after his re-election, it was clear that he too shared their belief that now everything was again possible. It was the first audience which the president – still too weak to offer the Russian public anything more than a brief, carefully edited television appearance – granted that day. The team filed into his office.

As they raised their champagne flutes for a victory toast, an official photographer clicking away to record the moment, Yeltsin turned oracle: 'Now I am certain that in 2000 Russia will be a rich, democratic country.'

His supporters were taken aback. 'We were all exhausted from that many-month-long race, from the sleepless nights,' Malashenko recalled. 'The last thing we were expecting to hear, God help us, was about what would happen in 2000. But at that moment he really had that desire: he wanted to change so much about himself and his country.'

Yeltsin's political backers wanted to change things, too. Once the champagne had been drunk, the Davos Pact settled down to divide the spoils.

'This is how it has always happened in Russia,' Friedman explained, with a self-mocking smile which seemed to say that he knew he and his colleagues were sleazy bastards but that there wasn't really anything they could do about it. 'Various clans would come closer to the throne and begin to divide [the loot]. Then they would be chased out and others would come in. A constant change of favourites. In Russia this is traditional.'

Now that Yeltsin had been re-elected, the clan closest to the throne was the oligarchs. Individually, they had all been men of considerable wealth and influence before the campaign began, and occasionally they had pooled their power. But their united drive to re-elect Yeltsin marked a dramatic shift. Their ad hoc and shifting alliances had, at least temporarily, been transformed into a single club with regular meet-ings and clearly defined members. Berezovsky, Gusinsky, Potanin, Khodorkovsky, Friedman, Aven and Smolensky were the core of the group. Vladimir Vinogradov, of Inkombank, and Vitaly Malkin of Rossisky Kredit sometimes attended their meetings: they had the same half-way-house status, Friedman joked to me, as 'candidate members' of the old Soviet Politburo. They had became a feared force in the land, and Russia's richest businessmen lobbied to be admitted to the charmed circle, complaining to their friends when they were not allowed in.

Early on, all the oligarchs had learned that the way to make fortunes in the new Russia was by manipulating the state. In 1996, they took that one step further and began to run the political process itself – an experience which marked each of them as individuals and bonded them as a group. Even after the final vote their weekly meetings con-tinued, usually in the Logovaz Clubhouse but sometimes at Gusinsky's office, or Khodorkovsky's, or at Potanin's dacha. Whenever an unex-pected crisis erupted, the oligarchs made sure that each member of the group was informed. Naturally, their relationships remained shot through with rivalry and mutual suspicion and the alliance was never formalised. But in the fire of the election campaign they had been forged into what the Russians call a *kollektiv*, a working team.

'We're a country of collectives,' Friedman told me with a sigh. 'Even our oligarchs feel more secure when they are acting collectively. Of course, each one tries to reach some private agreement with someone else. But our psychology is such that, when we've all come together, it's another, more serious, matter.'

Yeltsin's victory at the polls had given that *kollektiv* tremendous power. They had taken the key strategic decisions and had paid a lot of the bills. The Boris Yeltsin who was re-elected on 3 July 1996 had been created by the oligarchs – or so, at least, they believed. Now they expected to reap their reward.

Some of the oligarchs began to profit even before Yeltsin's re-election. A week before the first ballot, Gusinsky was rewarded when Gazprom, in which the government owned a controlling share, acquired a 30 per cent stake in NTV. Gazprom also provided NTV with a $40m loan, on favourable terms. Later that year, NTV, which had only been broadcasting in peak hours on its national channel, was given the slot for 24 hours a day for a nominal fee.

'I won't conceal the fact that, if not for our participation in the election campaign, NTV would have been unlikely to obtain the entire channel,' admitted Malashenko, the NTV chief. 'It was never a prior condition. But we understood that if Yeltsin won the elections, then we would get that channel. And that is what happened.'

Other oligarchs also began to bask in the Kremlin's favour. A day after the run-off, Boris Jordan, the RussianAmerican investment banker who had become Potanin's business partner, was allowed to return to Russia. His visa had been revoked in May, as part of a struggle over a steel mill which enjoyed the protection of the party of war. Now Jordan was free to come back.

These perks were relatively trivial. Far more important for the oligarchs was to ensure that the second stage of the loans-for-shares scheme – in which full ownership of the companies would be transferred to them – went ahead as planned. They also sought continued, or even expanded, access to lucrative government bank accounts, like those of the State Customs Agency. And they wanted to control the privatisation of the state's remaining valuable assets, companies such as the national telecoms provider and a few second-tier oil firms. To do all of that – to in fact institutionalise their influence over the new administration – the oligarchs believed that their men should join the government. Potanin became a deputy prime minister and Chubais was appointed Yeltsin's chief of staff.

For most of the oligarchs, Potanin was the obvious man to put forward for the cabinet post. One reason was his growing friendship with Chubais; the other was that Potanin, unlike all the other oligarchs, was not Jewish. The oligarchs rarely made a big deal about their Jewishness or about Russian anti-Semitism; but they knew enough Russian history not to want to push their luck too far. As Khodorkovsky put it: 'We [Jewish capitalists] irritate the public enough as it is. Why irritate them even more?'

There was just one powerful dissenting voice. Gusinsky thought that sending Potanin into the government and leaving all the rest on the outside was just asking for trouble. At a meeting of the oligarchs in his office to discuss the issue, Gusinsky argued that once he became a minister, Potanin would feather his own nest and neglect everyone else's. When the oligarchs held an informal vote on the issue, Gusinsky was overruled and Potanin joined the government as planned. But the objection turned out to be prescient, foreshadowing a wider conflict which would erupt just a year later during what Russian observers dubbed 'the bankers' war'. One of the chief *casus belli* would be his colleagues' allegations that Potanin had used his government post to enrich himself at the other oligarchs' expense.

Chubais' re-entry into the government would eventually become equally contentious. But in the summer of 1996 it was a uniformly popular initiative, at least among the oligarchs. It was the president who took some convincing. Yeltsin's first choice for the powerful position of his chief of staff was Malashenko; but when he offered him the job on 9 July, Malashenko turned him down flat.

'As a man, I do not have a bad attitude to Yeltsin,' Malashenko told me. 'He is an interesting personality – dangerous, but interesting. He is like a bear: he seems always to have such a good-natured smile, but it is known that the bear is the most dangerous beast for its trainers. But although I believe that I had and continue to have good relations with him, I could not accept his invitation because it would have made me his political hostage. I had no independent political base of my own.'

It was only after Malashenko's refusal that the president turned to Chubais. Offended at being the president's second choice and still hoping to start his own investment business, he was reluctant. Eventually though, at the urging of the oligarchs, the young reformers – who saw an opportunity to launch a new wave of change from the beachhead of the Kremlin – and the president himself, Chubais accepted.

Having agreed to take the Kremlin job, Chubais met with the oligarchs to discuss what his relationship with them would be now that he was back in office. It was a tricky issue. For six months, he had worked closely with the seven businessmen, at their behest and on their payroll. Now he would be in a position to have tremendous influence over government decisions which would affect their financial empires.

For Chubais, and for the entire young reformers' team which he now de facto led, it was a crucial moment. Would he become a creature of the oligarchs whom he had, in large measure, created through the loans-for-shares scheme? Or would he try to revive the market reform drive which had petered out in 1995 – a course which would inevitably hurt the oligarchs by cutting their access to cheap state credits and property? Chubais decided to try to break free.

'I will take the job,' he told them, 'but I will treat all of you equally and I will not be able to support anyone's special interests.'

In the eyes of the young reformers, Chubais' declaration marked the end of what Gaidar had dubbed their 'deal with the devil', the alliance they had formed with the oligarchs to keep out the communists. They realised that breaking the connection would be difficult – but doing so, they believed, was vital to the next stage of economic and political reforms.

The oligarchs, however, saw the situation quite differently. When Chubais made his announcement to them on a hot July day, just a few weeks after their glorious joint election victory, he thought he was filing for a divorce. Yet to his listeners, it sounded as if he was just mouthing the dry formalities required of a government official and, more importantly, promising not to do any special favours for individual oligarchs. But they assumed that, with the *kollektiv* as a whole, it would be business as usual. 'We thought it was a normal, formal position, but that the consultations would continue,' Khodorkovsky told me.

This misunderstanding between Chubais and the oligarchs would have devastating consequences. He and the young reformers intended to pursue reforms independently; the oligarchs expected him to represent their interests in the Kremlin. Within a year their conflicting expectations would collide violently, sparking a crisis which helped to tip Russia into the financial collapse of 1998. But in the happy summer of 1996 both groups were confident that now they would reap their deserved rewards.

A few months after Chubais went to work in the Kremlin, the oligarchs received further confirmation that they were the new government's favoured sons. In October, Berezovsky was named deputy head of the Kremlin's Security Council. The oligarchs had become so powerful that Gusinsky joked that his wife would have to start addressing him very formally by name and patronymic and use the respectful 'Vy', the second-person plural, like the French 'vous'. Even their children began to feel like royalty. At his British boarding-school, one of Berezovsky's young sons snapped at a teacher who dared to admonish him: 'Don't tell me to do anything, I am the king of Russia.' Russian democrats started to worry that Berezovsky junior was right.

'This new nomenklatura is insolent and is not subject to any rules,' Sergei Kovalyev, the former dissident, told me. 'They are getting new privileges, and eating increases the appetite.'

Yet even as Russian democrats began to fear that an omnipotent financial oligarchy had taken over the country, fissures had begun to appear within the alliance. The rifts were still invisible to many of the oligarchs themselves, but over the next year they would grow deeper. Soon the oligarchs and the young reformers would again be at the barricades. Only this time, instead of the communists they would be fighting each other and the new government they had done so much to install.

11

CHAMPAGNE TOO SOON: STORIES FROM THE NEW RUSSIA

RUSSIA HAS ALWAYS been a country of bust and boom. The eastern Slavic tribes eking out a living in the cold forests of Muscovy were rarely more than one meal away from starvation. Every good harvest or successful hunt was an occasion for euphoria; each failure meant hunger and often death. These rhythms of famine and feast were assimilated into the Orthodox calendar. Maslenitsa – a raucous, ribald Slavic version of Mardi Gras – was followed by the strict 40-day Lenten fast, a regimen so austere that it sometimes killed young children and the elderly. Then came the groaning tables of the Easter banquet and the cycle began again. Communism followed the same pattern of deprivation and indulgence, purge and thaw – though, as in old Russia, the hard times always lasted longer than the good ones.

For most Russians, the hard times became even harder after the capitalist revolution. But by 1997, after seven lean years, it looked as though the ancient wheel of Russian life was turning and the fat years were about to begin. Suddenly Russia was hip, hot, happening, the global economy's next big thing. Foreign fund managers came charging in, pushing the stock market to a 130 per cent increase, one of the best returns anywhere in the world that year. Western bankers started stuffing money down Russia's throat, floating bonds for obscure regions which had not known what a fax machine was five years earlier. The mania for anything and everything Russian reached such a fever pitch that some investors started buying up companies they couldn't even pronounce or locate on a map, just to be part of the 'great Russia play'. Moscow, for most of its history a global synonym for 'hell-hole', became a desirable place to live. In a loving, atmosphere-drenched cover story, *Newsweek* dubbed it Europe's coolest city. Even some of those cynical Russians who had managed to flee their miserable birthplace began moving back.

Russian politics was beginning to look sunny, too. The old Yeltsin was back, his heart patched up by cardiac surgeons and his sense of purpose restored by the 1996 election battle. With him came the young reformers. Anatoly Chubais and Boris Nemtsov, the Nizhny Novgorod governor, both became first deputy prime ministers and Yegor Gaidar headed an economic reform committee which became the new government's brain-trust. A delighted US Treasury dubbed the new cabinet line-up 'the dream team'. You could understand why: the young reformers were back in the saddle, the president was actively and openly behind them, and it looked as if Russia's half-finished market revolution would finally be completed.

The good times were starting to roll. These are some stories from Russia's capitalist feast – and the voices of one or two Cassandras who warned that, as always in Russia, famine might not be too far away.

When the young reformers had first stormed into government in 1992, their objectives had been heart-stoppingly ambitious but they had also been fairly crude: tear down communism, stop inflation, sell everything you can. The second stage of their revolution was more delicate and more complicated: they needed to impose the rule of law, clean up the budget and the budget process, create a rational tax system and an effective tax service, and on and on. They even began trying to make Russian apparatchiks less corrupt – a Sisyphean task if ever there was one – by requiring all government officials to fill out an annual income declaration. One of their biggest missions was reining in the natural monopolies, the huge, partially state-owned behemoths Russia had inherited from the Soviet Union which choked up the economy by encouraging payment arrears and strangled it by blocking competition.

For investors, the young reformers' attack on the natural monopolies was one of the most significant signs that the second wave of their market revolution really had begun. I watched the battle at Unified Energy Systems, the national electricity company, and like most people I was mightily encouraged by what I saw. The man in charge of that front was Boris Brevnov, a former commercial banker from Nizhny Novgorod who had been swept to Moscow on Nemtsov's coat-tails. Young, slim, brown-eyed, Brevnov was part of a new generation of Russians who gave hope to visiting Westerners but mystified most ordinary Russians. Like Nemtsov, he was born and raised in Russia's traditionally backward provinces, but Brevnov, who was just 16 years old when Gorbachev came to power, had come of age late enough to be almost unscarred by the Soviet experience.

What struck me most when I first met him, back in the days when he was still a hustling enterpreneur in Nizhny Novgorod, was his ability to instantly accept a woman of his own age – me – as an equal. With most Russian men I was accustomed to going through a frustrating initial few months of acquaintance during which I would be alternately patronised, dismissed and softened up with a barrage of sexual innuendo. There was none of that with Brevnov, who took me seriously from our first meeting. His modernity showed in other ways as well; he was perfectly at ease with Westerners and had recently married Gretchen Wilson, an exuberant Kentucky girl, who was also an investment banker.

Most striking of all, Brevnov exuded an almost American can-do spirit and sense of unlimited possibilities. It was a world away from the rather beguiling cosmopolitan cynicism of the Moscow intelligentsia, with its cigarettes and sage predictions that, in the end, nothing would ever really change. Nor was Brevnov's approach quite the same as that of the driven, crusading young reformers. His world-view was sunnier, perhaps even slightly naïve: somehow, after a decade of turbulent reforms, the Russian provinces were producing the kind of enthusiastic, jogging-in-the-morning-working-until-late-at-night, clean-cut young men who grow up in the Mid-West confident of earning their first million by the time they are 30 years old.

Brevnov's appointment in early April as first vice-president of UES astonished the Moscow establishment, which instantly wrote off the fresh-faced young man from Nizhny Novgorod as a one-day wonder. By capacity UES was the world's biggest power company, and as the supplier of all of Russia's electricity through its regional daughter firms it was the nervous system of the Russian economy. But UES's management had allowed the company to drift into total chaos. Blackouts had become commonplace in Russia, affecting even vital services like hospitals and military bases. The situation had become so dire that no one was particularly surprised when, in the winter of 1996, a frantic officer in Murmansk took matters into his own hands and sent a platoon of armed sailors to the local power station to force its director to restore electricity to the dock where his nuclear submarine was moored. Foreign investors, who owned some 27 per cent of UES shares, were scathing about it too – dubbing it, in the words of one investor, 'easily the world's worst managed electricity utility'.

When Brevnov first tried to wade into these Augean stables on a sunny spring morning in April 1997, two worlds collided: that of the young Westernised commercial banker and that of the elderly UES managers, veterans of a lifetime of five-year plans who still proudly kept portraits of Lenin and posters of their industry's favourite Bolshevik *bon mot* – Electrification plus Soviet power equals communism – on their walls. The culture clash between Brevnov and the UES old guard led by Anatoly Dyakov – the company's 60-year-old president and a former Soviet deputy minister – was joined absolute. The UES veterans served their visitors cognac; Brevnov offered them only bottled water. The UES veterans loved their grandiose offices with the thick double doors that had signalled status in the Soviet era; Brevnov wanted to replace his with a Western-style glass door as a symbol of openness. The two camps even fought over the dull question of accountants: Brevnov favoured using PriceWaterhouseCoopers; Dyakov objected, claiming the big international firm was in the pocket of the CIA.

More serious issues were at stake, too. It took Brevnov weeks to be given access to the company's financial records, and crucial papers seemed to be constantly disappearing. But gradually, with the backing of the government, the majority shareholder in UES and of the foreign investors, Brevnov began to take charge. On 1 June, at the annual general meeting, he was elected chief executive while Dyakov was relegated to the largely ceremonial post of 'honorary president' and appointed chairman of the board of directors.

As Brevnov and his team, largely drawn from Nizhny Novgorod and including a few foreigners seconded from the World Bank, took over they made some disquieting discoveries. Dyakov had lacked the foresight and political power of the smartest red directors, who had used the privatisation process to transfer a lucrative stake in the company into their own hands. But Brevnev's investigations showed that the UES chief had set up a web of offshore companies into which he was channelling a considerable chunk of the electricity company's revenues. This was not, however, illegal, and Dyakov has never been prosecuted.

Politically and practically, it was too late to recover the money, but Brevnov started to put a stop to the financial leakage. Gradually, his restructuring drive made progress on other fronts as well. He began to chip away at the system of cross-subsidisation, which had forced Russia's struggling industry to pay for the power in peoples' homes. He created an experimental wholesale market in electricity which he hoped would extend eventually to the entire country. Corrupt regional power station managers, some of them among the most powerful figures in their provinces, were sacked. Brevnov also made inroads into the massive problem of arrears by pressing for payments to be made in cash: 12 months after he had started his job, cash collection was up by 15 per cent.

Brevnov wasn't perfect. Like so many of the young reformers, his head was slightly turned by the speed with which his career and his crusade seemed to be progressing. On one occasion he used the UES corporate jet to fly to the United States to pick up his wife and newborn son. This might not have raised eyebrows in the West, but Russians, already irritated by the youth and self-righteousness of the young reformers, cried foul and the scandal was on the front pages for days. But at UES itself, his shake-up seemed to be working. The company was one of the engines of Russia's remarkable stock market boom, with UES shares more than doubling in value in the first eight months of 1997. At the same time, Brevnov began pulling down the industrial electricity tariff, cutting it by more than 10 per cent in 1997, a measure which the young reformers hoped would help revive the flagging Russian manufacturing sector.

Taken together, the quiet revolution at UES, a more dramatic power struggle which Nemtsov had initiated at Gazprom, the tightening of fiscal discipline and a raft of measures designed to make the government (and the use of government funds) less corrupt, all began to reshape the Russian economy. After a worrying nine-month hiatus, it looked as if the promise of Yeltsin's re-election was going to be fulfilled.

As Brevnov told me, with the arrogance which came so naturally and so earnestly to the young reformers: 'We are doomed to success. Since all the good managers are on our side, how can we fail?'

On 15 November 1996, Dmitry Zimin stood on the floor of the New York Stock Exchange and watched a new combination of letters – his letters! – flash up on the big board for the first time. Company founders always say that it's a euphoric moment: I've heard one compare it with the thrill of losing his virginity, another say it was as momentous as giving birth. But there can't be too many people who have felt quite the same 'pinch-me-am-I-really-here' swirl of conflicting emotions which almost overwhelmed Zimin. At an age when most Russian men were already dead, the small, jumpy gold-toothed 63-year-old engineer had embarked on a new life in a world so alien it could just as well have been on another planet. He had journeyed from the heart of the Soviet military machine – working on anti-missile defence systems in a top-secret Moscow factory – to the control room of the greatest wealth-producing engine the world has ever known.

As Zimin stood there, watching the electronic stream of stock quotes through his thick mad-scientist glasses, he suddenly felt horribly disoriented – a kind of existential motion sickness at the huge social, cultural and economic distance he had travelled. The share price of his company, one of the Russian capital's leading mobile phone providers, was rocketing higher and higher. That was supposed to be a good thing: all successful IPOs spike sharply upwards from their offering price on the first day of trading. It helps to give the new stock some momentum and offers the early investors a reward for their faith. Zimin knew all of that – his American investment bankers had explained it several times – but at that particular instant the small part of his brain which was still Soviet rebelled. 'Someone is making money out of us!' he thought, and he was outraged. Lazy investors were getting rich on the back of his hard work: it was horrible, it was what his teachers of Marxist-Leninism had called 'capitalist exploitation'.

But then Zimin took a deep breath and forced his Soviet instincts back into his subconscious. In the new world he now inhabited, he told himself, helping other people make money was good, it was what capitalism was all about. Repeating the sentence over and over in his mind like a mantra, he affirmed: 'Actually it's wonderful that our investors – ours, not anyone else's – are making money from us.' It worked. All at once, Zimin felt good again: 'It's a great feeling. I was proud and scared.'

Zimin's capitalist epiphany was an important moment not just for him but for the whole country. Beeline, his company, had become one of the most powerful symbols of what everyone hoped was the coming market boom. Part of it was timing: it was the first Russian company to be listed on the NYSE since the Bolshevik revolution. Beeline also represented 'good' capitalism, the kind of productive, greenfield business activity which Russia needed if it was ever to rise out of its economic doldrums. Most important of all, as a company run by middle-aged engineers from the ultra-conservative defence sector, it seemed to show that the market revolution was for everyone and not just the young, slick New Russians.

Skinny, constantly in motion and rarely without the cigarette he held in the old-fashioned four-fingered Russian-style, even after his IPO had made him a millionaire Zimin still looked more like the Soviet radio engineer he had been than the Russian capitalist poster-boy he had become. When I first met him in late 1996 he was more than a little stunned by the changes which had transformed his country, his company and himself.

'For 35 years I have worked in the same building right here, in the suburbs of Moscow,' he told me. 'But while I was still here, the very country I was living in changed completely. The country changed, the economy changed and the company changed. Somehow, you don't expect a revolution to happen like this.'

For Zimin and his colleagues, the slow, dwindling collapse of the Soviet Union had gradually killed off their old way of life. But they saw the end of the old era as an opportunity, not a disaster. As their factory fell into disuse and their salaries began to be paid more and more erratically, Zimin and his friends used the spare time to experiment with wacky inventions and new business ideas. It took them a while to settle on mobile telephones and even longer to figure out how to turn a profit.

What helped was the early partnership Zimin and his friends struck up with a family of US businessmen. By the late 1990s, joint-venture had become a swear word for many foreign investors: all too often, the pioneering outsiders who had had the guts to put money into Russia found themselves squeezed out by the locals as soon as their business began to turn a profit. Beeline was a cheering counter-example.

Augie Fabela, the American entrepreneur who co-founded Beeline with his father, first met Zimin in early 1991. The Fabelas now live in Florida, but they used to be based in the Mid-West and they still have the look and mindset of successful, hard-working, ever so slightly provincial, corn-belt Chamber of Commerce stalwarts. Augie has a big, wide face, earnest-looking even through the Tampa tan. He wears formal suits, fully buttoned-up, to the 7 a.m. breakfast meetings he favours. The only hint of roguishness is the glitter of his pinky ring.

When Augie and his father, a slightly more wrinkled and compact version of the son, made their first trip to what was then the Soviet Union, they were terrified. This was, after all, still the evil empire and who knew what might happen? Before leaving for the airport, father and son both signed their wills.

Once they arrived in Russia, the Fabelas, who had owned a factory which manufactured mobile phones in Mississippi, set off on a tour of Soviet plants, looking for potential partners who might help them to expand some branch of their business to the USSR. As soon as they spotted Zimin, it was business love at first sight. The Fabelas, who spoke no Russian, had been having a hard time making a connection with their hosts: everyone seemed stilted, formal. Then suddenly they came across this older engineer who was so animated that his passion swept right through the linguistic and cultural barriers.

'Here was this little man,' Augie told me, 'pounding his hands up and down, waving and talking, talking, talking. It really stuck in our minds.'

That one visual image was the beginning of Beeline. The Fabelas insisted that Zimin be included on a list of engineers they were sponsoring on a visit to the US. In the States, Zimin had the usual 'Soviet-man-encounters-Western-consumer-culture' experiences. Supermarkets, instant cash machines, rented cars – everything was a revelation. The most significant discovery, though, was that he and the Fabelas were on the same commercial wavelength.

They started working together and quickly dropped the idea of manufacturing mobile phones – which Zimin and his fellow engineers had been very keen on – for the sexier project of setting up a mobile telephone service in Moscow. Here, Zimin's long experience working in the Soviet defence industry came in handy. Through his old contacts, he was able to obtain the radio frequency licence which the fledgling company needed to set up a mobile telephone network. Better still, Beeline paid almost nothing for the privilege, thanks to the same state ignorance of what things were worth in the new market economy which had allowed Gusinsky to get his first television channel effectively for free.

The partnership had its ups-and-downs. The cultural gap between the American service-oriented Fabelas and the Soviet engineers was a divide not too different from the mutual incomprehension that separates geeky computer programmers from the flashy sales side of their industry. Augie was always coming up with new tricks – like the cute little Beeline name and logo which infuriated the engineers until it became an almost universally recognised brand name in Russia.

The engineers could drive Augie crazy, too. What frustrated him most was the way one tiny malfunction would prompt them to shut down the entire Beeline phone system in the middle of a workday afternoon to do a careful diagnostic examination. When Fabela told them to just slap on a band-aid solution and work out the deeper bugs at 2 a.m., while their customers slept, the Soviet engineers were shocked. 'Don't worry, Augie,' they told him, 'in Russia it's normal for our phones not to work.'

The biggest crisis came in 1994, when it seemed as if the Fabelas would share the fate of so many Western joint-venture partners and be forced out of the business they had created. Sistema, the voracious conglomerate which Luzhkov had sponsored to ensure his own financial and political independence, had acquired a share in Beeline and wanted to drive the Americans out. The Fabelas, however, dug their heels in. This was an astonishing reaction. Not only was Luzhkov no slouch at getting his own way but Vladimir Yevtushenkov, the mayor's shadowy *consigliere* and the chief of Sistema, was a truly intimidating figure. When this pair of innocent, slightly oafish Americans refused to give in, Yevtushenkov couldn't believe it.

'He [Yevtushenkov] definitely is a control person,' Augie Fabela told me, smiling slightly at his own understatement. 'He likes control and I think he was personally very surprised with our level of persistence, that we didn't just go away.'

But, like so many Russian strong-men, Yevtushenkov eventually developed a grudging respect for foreigners who had the chutzpah to stand up to him. He told them they could keep their roughly 45 per cent share of the business – but only on certain terms. The Fabelas, he told them, had taken advantage of Russia's naïveté when they had founded the firm with Zimin. Their stake in the company was worth much more than the $2m they had already paid for it. 'You've taken advantage of Russia and we're not here to be taken advantage of,' he warned. So, even though the joint-venture deal had already been negotiated, and the increased value of the company could be said to be due to the Fabelas' work in building it up, Yevtushenkov told them they would have to pay up to stay in . . . to the tune of $12m.

Most foreign investors would have gone to court or to the American embassy. But the Fabelas, quite pragmatically, decided that 'this is Russia' and that if they tried to start a legal battle 'we would lose'. They gritted their teeth, 'adjusted emotionally', tried to secure new 'bullet-proof' guarantees that they would not be pushed out a second time – and raised an additional $12m for the venture. After that traumatic episode, it was more or less clear sailing. The entanglement with Yevtushenkov even turned out to be an advantage. Now that Sistema was a partner in the business, Beeline found itself protected by the powerful *krysha*, or roof, of the Moscow city machine. Russian business partners became warily respectful, Moscow bureaucrats openly fawning. (Sistema, which by then owned a competing Moscow mobile phone company, was bought out by the Beeline founders on the eve of the IPO.)

Two years later, everyone's patience paid off. On Wall Street, Beeline did even better than Russia's most optimistic cheerleaders had predicted. The IPO raised $127.5m, valuing the company at $700m (suggesting, perhaps, that the intimidating Yevtushenkov had had something of a point?). Initially priced at 20.5 cents each, the shares swiftly climbed as high as 33 cents in the first few weeks.

Better yet, Beeline wasn't being bought by the hard-core, high-risk hot money which had decided to specialise in the post-communist market; instead, mainstream fund managers were getting in on the act. When

Zimin, Fabela and Alan Apter, their investment banker, went on a road-show to pitch Beeline to prospective buyers, 'they spent very little time asking us questions about politics,' Apter told me. To Apter's delight, these new buyers were starting to treat Russia like a normal country.

In fact, Russia's prospects had begun to seem so bright that the highly educated young professionals who had fled the country at the end of the Cold War were starting to trickle back. On the late November day when I met Zimin, he had just finished interviewing a 28-year-old Russian woman who had emigrated to Australia three years earlier. She spoke fluent English and had a good job there as a computer programmer. But now that the Russian economy was picking up, she felt her prospects were even better back home. Zimin had just offered her a job and he was sure she was only the beginning of what he called the 'brain tide' home.

Suddenly, Beeline wasn't just a mobile phone company; it was the first real piece of evidence that Russia's market revolution was starting to work. Apter said it was the beginning of 'a clear trend in the market'. Gaidar, who travelled to New York to personally witness the IPO, put it more emotionally: 'It was a triumphal moment, a very, very happy time.'

For the first six months of 1997, the happy time just got better and better. Investing in Russia no longer seemed to be strictly for connoisseurs – it had gone mass market. Sold on a high-concept story-line – Yeltsin had vanquished the communist threat and inflation had been conquered, therefore an economic boom was inevitable – many of the new buyers had startlingly little specific knowledge about Russia, and they were in no hurry to acquire it. One loquacious Texan fund manager I met was typical of the new breed. He loved Russia, he told me, and was investing heavily in regional telecoms and utility stocks, two of the hottest sectors of the moment. But when I asked which ones, he hesitated.

'Honey, I don't have to pronounce 'em, I just have to buy 'em,' he finally told me with a big grin.

The feeding frenzy extended to the debt market. In June 1996, the Russian government had had to offer annualised returns of as much as 200 per cent in order to lure buyers to its domestic debt. Now, just over a year later, private Russian companies – whose credit rating by defini-tion had to be lower than that of the sovereign borrower – were being lent hundreds of millions of dollars at rates typically just 4 percentage points higher than US Treasury bills. The implication was truly breath-taking: lenders believed – and were betting – that the risk of default by major Russian companies was so low as to command just a 3 per cent premium over the risk of default by the US Federal Reserve.

More importantly, the virtuous circle which many of the young reformers had hoped for appeared to be working. As outside capital began to flood into Russia, Russian companies seemed to be responding by doing their best to make sure that part of that wave flowed in their direction. Western accounting standards, transparent corporate governance and respect for minority shareholders became the country's new catch-phrases. In a few high-profile cases, big companies actually pulled back from measures to restrict shareholder rights in the face of investor protest.

In April 1997, Mosenergo, the Moscow municipal power company, dropped a plan to restrict the voting rights of its shareholders. In February 1998, Sidanco, Potanin's oil company, bowed to investor pressure and cancelled a convertible bond issue which would have diluted the holdings of minority shareholders. As an apologetic Potanin admitted to me afterwards, Russia's business rules were changing, and abusing shareholder rights was no longer quite as acceptable as it had been.

At both Sidanco and Mosenergo, the desire to attract outside investment over the long haul triumphed over a short-term effort to increase the power or assets of the management. What one Western investor called 'the lolly-grab' seemed to be over. Russia's *comprador* capitalists may have made their money in a time of chaos, but now they wanted to settle down and enjoy it in a more stable, predictable environment. They were growing up. At least, that was the optimistic theory of the young reformers. As Nemtsov explained when I interviewed him in May 1997: 'You could say, broadly, that the period of the initial accumulation of capital, which always, even in America, was accompanied by banditry, corruption, lobbyism, and so forth – that period is ending in Russia.'

Russia's robber barons were also starting to think that the era of bandit capitalism was drawing to a close. In late 1997 I had lunch with Vladimir Yevtushenkov who, after his own fashion, warmly endorsed Nemtsov's view.

The Moscow city *consigliere* was not one of the oligarchs, but he had come to rival them in wealth and power. Unlike them, however, he kept an insistently low profile. I was anxious to discover who this shadowy figure – whom everyone in Moscow had started to talk about – really was, and had begun to bombard his office with almost daily faxes and telephone calls. After a few weeks, he – or more likely his secretaries – gave in and I was summoned to tea. Of medium height, with olive skin, dark brown hair and blue-grey eyes, Yevtushenkov had the kind of Slavic look you find from Kaliningrad to the Kamchatka. His flashy gold watch and well-cut suit gave him a sheen of money. On one of his office walls a prominently displayed portrait of Yevtushenkov, wearing a cloth cap and standing in Red Square, suggested the provenance of that wealth; Luzhkov's office was decorated with an almost identical painting of the mayor himself, by the same artist and captured in exactly the same pose, down to the cloth cap which was Luzhkov's sartorial trademark.

The glimpse of the man and his sanctum was fascinating, but my actual conversation with Yevtushenkov was brief and repeatedly punctuated by the insistent peal of his mobile telephone and visits from the petitioners who crowded the sofas of his office in an elegantly restored old mansion. It was a frustrating reward for days of telephone calls, and I said so. Yevtushenkov promised we would meet again soon for lunch and, arm encircling my waist, marched me out. To my surprise, a few days later my telephone rang and one of his bevy of secretaries put me through. I was to come to his office at once, he said, and we would have our lunch. Intrigued, I obeyed.

When we left his office, Yevtushenkov got behind the wheel of his Audi Quattro himself and, windshield wipers flying to clear away the falling curtain of wet snowflakes, we raced through Moscow's crowded streets followed by a Jeep and a Mercedes full of bodyguards. When we arrived at White Sun of the Desert, a posh Central Asian restaurant, Arkady, the owner, rushed out to greet Yevtushenkov personally and ushered us to the best table in the house, an arrangement of low Uzbek-style couches grouped near an indoor brook. Before long, it seemed that most of the other diners were hovering around us, smiles that were half-way between servility and bonhomie plastered across their faces.

'I don't know who half of these people are, but they all know me, so I just smile,' Yevtushenkov murmured.

The sycophantic treatment continued as a parade of slippered wait-resses brought out a huge array of dishes – literally, the restaurant's entire menu – and were interrogated by Arkady as to the freshness of each one. It was a life not only of wealth but of power and, as the fawning continued, I could see why the New Russians might be loath to disrupt the new order for a more equitable version of capitalism. Yet, to my surprise, Yevtushenkov launched into a kind of nouveau riche riff on Nemtsov's predictions of an end to the robber-baron era.

Russia, he told me, was changing. Before, Russians had withdrawn their assets to the security of Swiss bank accounts as swiftly as they could. But now a new era was beginning. Why, these days, many of his friends kept a mere $15–$20m abroad, instead of $50–100m. Even rel-atively poor men like Arkady, he was certain, were not storing all of their money in foreign bank accounts. Turning to the restaurateur for confirmation, Yevtushenkov inquired: 'Why, I bet you only keep $3–5m in your Swiss bank account! And the rest goes right back into your business, aren't I right?'

Draining their Swiss bank accounts to a lean $20m may not have seemed the most overwhelming vote of confidence in the Russian econ-omy, but for the country's new capitalist princes it amounted to a major reassessment. Many of Russia's robber barons were starting to say that the slash and burn era of the country's capitalist revolution had ended – although I could not quite believe they were acting on their new-found convictions just yet.

Even more strikingly, it was not just the Moscow nouveaux riches who were starting to plan for the long-term. Even in Russia's rust-belt, people seemed to be coming to terms with the country's latest economic revolution. Russia's huge elderly factories, especially those on the vast Siberian plain which were safely remote from potential invaders, were structurally ill-suited to the new economic order. Gigantic, labour-intensive, technologically antediluvian and thousands of miles from the markets of both western Europe and eastern Asia, they had been designed to serve a self-contained, centrally planned economy interested chiefly in churning out tonnes of steel and armies of tanks. As Russia struggled to adapt to a post-industrial age more dependent on micro-chips and consumer services, the future of these dinosaurs was uncertain at best.

The Zlatoust Metallurgical Factory, a steel mill 1,320 kilometres south-east of Moscow straddling the continental divide between Europe and Asia, was one of the thousands of dilapidated plants battling for survival in the new system. Founded at the turn of the century by a tsarist merchant, the steel mill had been one of the solid Shire horses of the centrally planned economy. By the 1980s it had spawned a city of 200,000; but with the collapse of communism, the mill's and indeed the entire town's whole reason for existence had vanished.

'What happened to us was savagery,' exclaimed Sergei Kliukvin, a small, energetic white-haired man with meaty, machine-chewed hands who was the manager of one of the mill's best-equipped workshops. Pointing to idle vacuum-arc furnaces once used to make high-grade steels for spacecraft and nuclear missiles, Kliukvin lamented: 'One minute we were being whipped up to fulfil the plan and then suddenly work stopped.'

Orders from the defence industry, once the mill's biggest customer, dried up, pushing production down from 1.2m tonnes of steel a year a decade earlier to just over 380,000 tonnes in 1996. Trapped in a web of inter-enterprise debt, the mill was increasingly forced to do its business through awkward barter transactions, receiving payment in goods ranging from butter to cars and paying its own bills in kind.

Even privatisation had backfired. Like so many of the *compradors* who had triumphed in the first frenetic stage of privatisation, the plant's new owners turned out to be more interested in asset-stripping than in investment. According to court documents and to Vyacheslav Skvortsov, the factory's current director, the owners not only failed to make a pledged $180m investment but they also diverted tens of millions of dollars from the mill by exporting steel at artificially low prices to foreign partners and pocketing the profits – one of the most popular techniques for smuggling flight capital out of the country. The looting only stopped when Skvortsov was appointed director of the plant and, to their astonishment, blew the whistle on its owners. His six-month crusade ended in November 1996, when a court stripped the privatisers of their stake and gave it back to the state.

To the outsider, it looked like a hollow victory. Zlatoust, literally 'Golden-lipped', was set in an environment of tremendous natural beauty: a deep, natural gorge, surrounded by hundreds of miles of untouched fir forest and the blood-coloured earth which is characteristic of the mineral-rich Urals. But the vista was spoiled by the steel mill, a sprawling eyesore of discoloured smokestacks, long, poorly maintained workshops and acres of discarded machinery and coils of metal. Thanks to the perverse talents of Soviet planners, the surrounding town was just as bad, managing to combine cabin-fever remoteness from civilisation with lung-choking pollution. It was a bleak place. But, to my astonishment, the people of Zlatoust seemed to be bearing up to their current trials with stoic dignity and even with hope.

'We have no economic reserves, but we have an unbelievably patient people,' Skvortsov told me. 'They know that any reform requires sacrifice and victims. They are willing to earn almost nothing.'

I heard much the same story on the factory floor from Viktor Cherepakhin, the weather-beaten 50-year-old manager of workshop number one. He and the rest of the plant's work-force received only 20 per cent of their wages in cash, on average about $30 a month. The rest was paid in factory cheques which bought a sad array of shoddy consumer goods and unappetising foodstuffs – whatever the mill could barter for metal – at the company stores. Nonetheless, Cherepakhin, who told me 'the steel is in my blood', was a market man.

'It is much better now,' he insisted, saying he relished the liberties and responsibilities the transition to capitalism had brought. 'Earlier there was a plan, constant pressure from above. Now it is freer, we take our own decisions. Everything depends on us. I will never be rich, but now I know that my grandchildren could be.'

Hearing this from Cherepakhin – a man who had come of age in the Soviet era and would never fully adapt to the new order; who worked in a rust-belt industry which would never again achieve the prestige it had enjoyed under the weapons-focused communist regime; and who lived in the Russian provinces whose deprivation relative to the big cities, particularly Moscow, seemed to grow every day – it was easy to believe that Russia's tortured market reforms really were starting to work. As one of the reformers put it in July 1997: 'Now, at last, we are reaping the rewards for all our hard work. 1998 will be the year of the harvest.'

Yet even as the first capitalist crop seemed to be maturing in the rocky fields of the Russian economy, a few wispy clouds began to appear on the horizon. One of the biggest dangers was the disintegration of the state and the stubborn failure of civil society to emerge from the wreckage of communism. Ordinary people were finding ways to muddle through in their private lives, but the state and social institutions were dangerously slow to be rebuilt. In the excitement of Russia's second burst of market reforms, the fragility of the social and political infrastructure was easy to overlook. But, occasionally, I would glimpse some disturbing back-room political drama or episode of social collapse.

One of the most striking examples of the haphazard way in which the once-great ship of Russian state was being steered was the government's slapstick approach to setting and meeting two of its big targets for 1997: paying off pension arrears by 1 July 1997 and wage arrears by 1 January 1998. Even the budget-hawks at the IMF encouraged the government to keep these two promises, which were seen as central to preserving the tattered social contract between the citizen and the state.

In the end, both deadlines were met. But on the way there, the government betrayed an almost comical amateurism. One problem was Yeltsin, whose occasional descents from Olympus sowed panic among his underlings. A characteristic episode came in late January 1997 as Yeltsin, fresh from his hospital bed, was preparing to bring Chubais and Nemtsov into the cabinet. Towards the end of the month the president attended a meeting of the VChK, a top-level emergency commission created to sort out Russia's financial crisis, including paying off the pension arrears.

The government's tentative plan being to pay off the Rbs 15,000bn pension backlog by 1 July, at the meeting the relevant officials presented and explained the plan. Yeltsin, flanked by Prime Minister Chernomyrdin and Chubais, then still the Kremlin chief of staff, was there along with most of the cabinet. The group included Potanin, who had been appointed deputy prime minister after Yeltsin's re-election. In his six months in government, Potanin had been stunned by the slap-dash way in which national policy was made. It was like a 'circus', he told me, and he never quite managed to get used to it. This particular meeting was even more disturbing than usual. Out of the blue, Yeltsin interrupted the speaker to offer his own opinion as to when the pension arrears should be paid off.

'I think we should pay off the arrears not by 1 July, but by 1 April,' the Kremlin chief rumbled.

The assembled ministers were thunderstruck. Meeting the initial 1 July deadline would be hard enough. The government's monthly cash revenue was a slender Rbs 12,000–13,000bn; in order to avoid building up fresh pension arrears, they had to spend Rbs 2,000bn of that on monthly pension payments. This meant that if it was to pay off the Rbs 15,000 pension backlog over the next five months, by 1 July the government would have to devote Rbs 5,000bn a month – more than a third of its total revenues – to pensions. To pay them off by the 1 April deadline proposed by Yeltsin would mean spending Rbs 9,500bn a month – an astronomical three-quarters of total revenue – on pensions.

That was plainly impossible; but, as Potanin looked around he saw that none of the senior officials seated at the conference table was prepared to contradict the president: Chernomyrdin and Chubais, not to mention the frightened minister of finance, were all keeping their mouths firmly shut and their expressions carefully blank. Potanin started to get very, very scared. 'I thought to myself, Yeltsin will wait for five more seconds of silence and then he'll say, "The decision is taken!" It will be an impossible situation.' He decided that someone had to stop the president before it was too late.

'Boris Nikolaevich, we won't be able to do it by 1 April,' he said.

Yeltsin, surprised at being publicly challenged, shot back: 'And why is that?'

Potanin looked around the room for support, but his colleagues assiduously avoided his eyes. He had started the conversation and he would have to finish it. 'Everyone began to look down at the floor,' Potanin recalled. 'So I said to the president, "We won't be able to devote Rbs 9,500bn a month to pensions."'

Yeltsin usually reserved his presidential firepower for the big picture, but on this occasion he turned out to have a clear grasp of the numbers involved. 'What do you mean Rbs 9,500bn? It would only be Rbs 7,500bn,' the president insisted.

'No, it wouldn't be,' Potanin explained. 'Paying off Rbs 15,000bn in two months is Rbs 7,500bn a month. But we also spend Rbs 2,000bn a month from the budget on pensions, so that's Rbs 9,500bn altogether. Even if we pay off the arrears by 1 July, that will be Rbs 5,000bn a month.'

'You're right, it would be five,' Yeltsin agreed, nodding his head gravely. 'So, should we pay them off by 1 July?'

'Yes, by 1 July,' Potanin agreed.

'That's it, the decision is taken,' Yeltsin roared, and the matter was closed.

Inwardly, the entire cabinet sighed with relief. But the episode illustrated how easily Yeltsin's mercurial will could dictate and distort major government policies.

The same seat-of-your-pants style was applied to trying to pay off all wage arrears by 1 January 1998. On Christmas Day 1997 – six days before the clock ran out – I glimpsed just how jerry-rigged the government's approach to that second deadline was. Brevnov, the young chief executive of UES, and his American wife Gretchen had come to my apartment for Christmas dinner. Thanks to the atheist habits of the communist era, Christmas is a relatively minor holiday for Russians, whose chief midwinter festival is New Year. Those Russians who do celebrate it do so according to the old Gregorian calendar, on 7 January. The 25 December is a regular working day – which meant Brevnov arrived late and, even after he did turn up, was constantly pulled away from the table by calls on his mobile telephone. At about 9 p.m. his phone rang again, and he hurried into the hallway for a twenty-minute conversation.

When he returned to the table, torn between frustration and amusement, Brevnov told us who the caller had been: the chairman of Sberbank, the state-owned bank which held the lion's share of the nation's private savings. He had been calling to commiserate with Brevnov about their shared plight. As the deadline to pay off the wage arrears approached, both men were being pressured by Chubais and Chernomyrdin to give the government some money.

I was surprised, having been under the impression that, under Brevnov's stewardship, UES had been promptly and regularly paying all its tax bills. Silently kicking myself for my credulity, I asked Brevnov how large UES's tax arrears were and how much he planned to pay off before the end of the year. Laughing, he explained that UES and Sberbank did not owe the government anything. But Sberbank controlled the huge cash pool of the savings of millions of ordinary Russians and, thanks to Brevnov's emphasis on increasing cash payments, UES was relatively cash-rich as well. That made both these partially privatised but still state controlled companies obvious targets for Chubais and Chernomyrdin's eleventh-hour money collection drive. The banker and Brevnov had been discussing just how much money they would be forced into lending the state and trying to figure out how bailing out the Russian treasury squared with their commitments to their own customers and shareholders.

Before long, it became apparent that the Christmas Day cash drive had not been a one-off event. Gradually, stories began leaking out about clandestine private loans which the Russian government had been arranging with Western creditors to fill the holes which kept appearing in the country's strained public finances. In late November and early December 1997, Western bankers said they had discreetly lent Russia $950m. Privately, the IMF confirmed the deal had taken place, although the Russian treasury refused to comment. Even George Soros, the American financier and philanthropist, had been personally called on to help bail out the Kremlin. As he admitted to a group of us Moscow journalists a few months later, in June 1997 he had received an urgent call: the Russian cabinet was struggling to pay off its pension arrears by 1 July and, despite the ministers' best efforts, the numbers didn't quite add up.

In a few weeks, the financial crunch would ease: Russia had issued a $2bn eurobond and would receive the money from the international loan in early July. But the eurobond revenues would not solve the government's immediate problem. The cabinet needed the money now.

'They were stuck,' Soros said. 'The payment [from the eurobond] was on a Thursday and the government needed the money on a previous Thursday. It would have been embarrassing for them to go to the banks and say, "Please pay us a week before".'

In desperation, Moscow turned to one of the few men in the world with pockets sufficiently deep to come up almost instantly with several hundred million dollars. Soros was happy to oblige. He had already spent tens of millions of dollars supporting Russian reforms through his charitable foundation and was eager to back the young reformers in their second burst of change. He was also involved in Russia as a private investor, and bailing out the government in its hour of need might serve him in good stead in the future.

'There was one loan, one period of a few days when we did make a sort of a bridge loan to enable the government to pay the pension arrears,' Soros said. 'It was a bridge loan really just to bridge a one-week period between the receipt of the eurobond issue and the payment. So, it was a very well secured loan, a very favourable interest rate.'

A few months later, when the Kremlin was struggling to meet its second deadline and pay off the wage arrears, the Russians came knocking at Soros' door again. This time the legendary financier refused their request. 'I did not want to make a habit of it,' he recalled with a small smile. When the story came out, the Russian government was acutely embarrassed by the revelations and even Soros himself seemed later to regret that he had been so candid. But his indiscretion, and the frantic telephone calls I had witnessed on Christmas Day, were a useful counterbalance to the generally euphoric mood of 1997. The young reformers may have been in charge again and may have been trying to move the country in the right direction, but they presided over a fragile shell of a state.

Another source of weakness was the federal government's increasingly tenuous grip over the provinces. Traditionally, Russia had been a highly centralised state, in both the tsarist and communist eras. But, as he struggled to wrest political power from Gorbachev and the Soviet authorities, Yeltsin had enlisted the Russian regions in his cause, urging them to seize as much autonomy as they could handle. Over the next few years, the power of the regions grew. In theory, the emergence of strong, locally rooted governors could help stabilise Russia's notorious volatile politics. But some forceful governors, emboldened by direct elections which made them politically independent of Moscow, began to preside over their provinces like feudal lords, with little regard for the supposed suzerainty of the Kremlin.

Popularly elected regional leaders also had the might – and the political incentive – to oppose the belt-tightening social welfare measures which the young reformers were championing in an effort to improve Russia's feeble fiscal position. In the long run, the proposed package of reforms was likely to benefit the regional governments, but it threatened to alienate their voters in the short term. If provincial governors decided that was too high a price to pay, there was little the Kremlin could do to coerce them.

The young reformers didn't need to look too far afield for examples of regional leaders thwarting their plans. The capital was Russia's strongest, and most bristlingly independent, region of all. Luzhkov had fought with the reformers from the very outset, successfully excluding Moscow from the mass privatisation programme. The reformers had hardly been back in office for a week before Moscow city hall was warning them that one place where many of their plans would never be implemented was in their own neighbourhoods. In mid-March 1997 Valery Shantsev, the deputy mayor, told me that the city government had already decided that housing reform, an integral part of the young reformers' effort to balance the budget, was a bad idea because the populace was too poor to pay higher prices. The city, therefore, intended to boycott the federal programme and appeared quite fearless about the consequences.

'Chubais could be sacked tomorrow, but Yuri Mikhailovych [Luzhkov] will be here until the year 2000,' Shantsev told me with a tight, smug smile. 'In any battle, in any fight, it is Yuri Mikhailovych's position which will prove to be superior.'

If the state was weak, civil society was even more degraded. A major part of the problem was corruption, starting with the government bureaucracy and spreading outward. Russia, always a country of deceit and evasion, had become a place of vanishing professional and ethical standards where anything, it seemed, could be bought and sold. The traffic was in everything, from university degrees to licences to practise lucrative professions; from the all-clear from the tax inspector to flattering articles in newspapers. Sergei, a 22-year-old fourth-year law student at Moscow State University [MGU], Russia's Harvard, told me he had to pay a $5000 bribe to be admitted to the course and $500 every year to ensure he passed his exams.

Even for foreigners, it became impossible to live without some degree of corruption. Traffic police routinely stopped even the most law-abiding driver and would reel off a litany of supposed offences, including driving a dirty car – which, in Luzhkov's Moscow, was actually against the law. It was almost impossible not to be guilty of something and the official punishment was to be forced into the labyrinth of Russia's bureaucracy: paying the fine meant hour-long queues at Sberbank and then more queues to retrieve one's seized driver's licence. The easier solution was 'to pay on the spot', a euphemism for a modest cash bribe, generally of $5 or $10. The practice was so routine that when one officer flagged me down on a highway outside Moscow, he informed me – before even bothering with my imaginary traffic violation – that he had three young children – which I took to be a hint that he thought he deserved an extra-generous bribe.

Almost every other professional could be bought and sold as well and, by the late 1990s, corruption had become so open and ordinary that many Russians assumed the rest of the world operated in the same way. One autumn afternoon a young PR man from Tatarstan, an autonomous republic on the Volga in central Russia, called my office to ask if I was interested in writing about the region's telecoms sector in the *FT*. I wasn't, so he proposed paying me a fee. Surprised to be offered a bribe so blatantly and by a complete stranger, I asked him to fax over his terms. He did: $5,000 to write 'an advertisement which will look exactly like a regular article'.

With my Western salary and passport, I had the luxury of declining kick-backs, but for most locals the choice was not so easy. For the ordinary Russian, to be engaged in any sort of business meant plunging into a world of cash in unmarked envelopes and deals with bent bureaucrats. The practice had become so widespread that many government officials no longer had the heart to deny it. When I asked the deputy governor of Kemerevo, a rough mining and heavy industrial region on the edge of Siberia, what the conditions were for small business start-ups in his *oblast*, he replied with disarming honesty: 'It's very difficult for our small businessmen. To establish a company you probably have to bribe forty bureaucrats.'

The everything-is-for-sale mentality extended to more primal desires as well. Sex had become one of the boom industries of a society delighted to slip the censorious constraints of the Soviet era. By night, Tverskaya, Moscow's main shopping area, was lined with an army of young call-girls (wearing mini-skirts even in the snow) five or six deep and stretching for blocks. Nor were the sexpots restricted to the capital city. Even the dingiest provincial hotels, where clean sheets or fresh food might be hard to come by, had installed a strip-tease platform – complete with mirrors, shiny pole and beefy local girls – in their cramped restaurants.

In their exuberant embrace of the money culture, Russians seemed to have quite matter-of-factly accepted sex as just one more commodity. A survey of female students at MGU in the early 1990s found the top career choice to be hard-currency prostitute. Once the New Russians became richer than the foreigners, being a tycoon's concubine became an equally desirable profession. One of the oligarchs was notorious for the high turn-over of his young mistresses and respected for his generous treatment of them: he preferred beauty pageant winners in their late teens and would set up his choice in a modest Moscow apartment with her own car, pager and mobile phone. When the affair ended, usually after six months, the young woman kept the car and apartment and her patron would pay for her remaining years in university. When I shared this piece of gossip with a Russian friend whose own daughter was about to enter MGU, her reaction stunned me: 'I wonder,' she asked me, 'if we can introduce your oligarch to Katya, she's very pretty and mature for her age.'

Disturbingly, life and death also began to be traded with something approaching insouciance. Under-employed young men took to advertising their eagerness to become assassins in the classified ads, using the blunt code phrase 'willing to take on any dangerous work for a high fee'. Petty criminals began to murder for pathetically small trophies: real-estate shysters killed gullible pensioners in order to inherit their apartments; one crime ring, posing as a car-repair shop, killed and dismembered car owners just to steal their vehicles. Some of Russia's roughest criminals organised themselves into gangs and developed sophisticated businesses whose reach extended far beyond Russia's borders. In the West, this international *mafia* was often caricatured as the root of Russia's problems. But within Russia, it seemed less significant. The entire country was so criminalised – from the small-town racketeers who terrorised the traders in one market-place I visited in western Siberia to bribe-taking Kremlin officials – that the *mafia* was almost unexceptional, just one more *matrioshka*, the Russian nesting doll, in the interlocking layers of lawlessness. For ordinary Russians, local hoodlums posed a more immediate physical danger; for the country as a whole, the red directors, oligarchs and crooked apparatchiks caused far greater economic damage.

Optimists dismissed the sex, violence and corruption as the regrettable but temporary side-effects of rapid social and economic change. Sometimes, I could see their point. There was even something invigorating about a society so fully and exuberantly prepared to live on the wild side. As in the pioneer West or Chicago in the Prohibition era, rules in the New Russia were made to be broken. That created a world which was often dangerous and sometimes plain evil, but also seemed to be fiercely alive.

It was the kind of world which Ayn Rand, herself a Russian *emigrée*, might have liked, where the state was too weak to demand much in the way of taxes and social rules had deteriorated to the point where the supermen could do pretty much as they liked. If only the young reformers' second burst of change could rein in these animal spirits and prod the economy into growth, it seemed that Russia's innate anarchic vigour might make it one of the booming economies of the twenty-first century.

Amid the general optimism of 1997, just occasionally a cautious voice would put the counter-argument. One of the most cogent cases I heard was made by Kyoji Komachi, the deputy chief of mission at the Japanese embassy. With the silvery hair of middle age, Komachi was an old Russia hand. Japan, with its formality, respect for tradition and constricted spaces, was almost the perfect antithesis of boisterous, revolutionary, expansive Russia. But Komachi, who spoke Russian fluently, had a deep knowledge of and affection for Russia and was optimistic about its long-term prospects. In the shorter term, however, he was worried. Russians, he said, 'have begun to drink champagne too soon'. Although there were only the barest signs of an economic revival, Russia's financial and political elite had begun to behave as if victory were already assured. Moscow's leading businessmen spoke of rivalling huge multinational firms within 5 years, and lived a lavish lifestyle to match. Politicians confidently described Russia as the newest tiger economy and predicted that next year it would put Asia in the shade.

The problem with the premature euphoria, Komachi argued, was that Russia hadn't yet earned the right to begin feasting. The nation as a whole still needed to spend a couple of decades tightening its belt and laying the foundations for future prosperity. But the Russian establishment, Komachi felt, was too cocksure and self-indulgent to do that. Few of them had a sense of collective responsibility sufficiently powerful to inspire personal sacrifices for the common good.

To illustrate his point, Komachi told me a story from his childhood. Humiliated by its military loss and economically devastated, Japan in the 1940s and 1950s was (he thought) in a similar predicament to Russia following the collapse of communism. In those days, it was impossible to survive without trading in the black market. But one Japanese judge felt that, as an arbiter of the law, he ought not to resort to black-market deals. As a result, he was unable to buy enough food to sustain himself and eventually starved to death. The principled judge became a Japanese folk-hero, proof that even in its dejected state the country still had citizens and state officials who put the law and their personal honour above life itself.

In the New Russia, Komachi feared, there were no equivalents. And without men like the judge, he wondered how Russia would muster the extraordinary strength required to pull itself out of its crisis.

12

No Honour Among Thieves –
The Bankers' War

On 25 July 1997, Moscow seemed to be settling into its usual summer languor. It was a hot, sunny Friday and soon Russians would be fleeing the cities for leafy country dachas or the seaside. But the headquarters of the Federal Property Commission, in a sullen, elephant-grey highrise near the centre of the capital city, was buzzing with activity.

A hive of shiny luxury cars – black Mercedes, a few Jeeps – swarmed around the front door, parked two abreast on the road and occupying every inch of concrete kerb. Inside, *le tout* Moscow seemed to have assembled: ambassadors rubbed shoulders with cabinet ministers and the oligarchs chatted to ladies in revealing evening dresses. They were all waiting for the auction of the year – the privatisation of Sviazinvest, the giant state-owned telecommunications holding company. At precisely 5 o'clock that afternoon, officials from the Federal Property Commission and the Ministry of Telecommunications would open two sealed envelopes and announce the new owner of 25 per cent plus one share in the coveted telecomms firm.

Everyone present felt sure the sale would mark the high point in what had already been Russia's best year since the collapse of communism. With a starting price of $1.2bn, the privatisation would be a significant boost for the government's depleted coffers. Moreover, after the compromises and controversy of the loans-for-shares scheme, the Sviazinvest sale was being billed as the beginning of a new, cleaner era in Russia's capitalist evolution.

When the winning bid was revealed at about 10 minutes past five a shudder went through the crowded auction room. One of the members of the losing consortium moaned, and the government privatisation officials broke into huge grins: the company had been sold for 1 billion, 875 million and 40 thousand dollars, 59 per cent higher than the reserve price and easily the highest sum ever raised in Russia's 5-year privatisation drive. Vladimir Bulgak, the telecomms minister, was exultant.

But the government's triumph was short-lived and within a few days, the Sviazinvest sale began to sour. What was supposed to be the last chapter in bandit capitalism became the prelude to a war among thieves. Sviazinvest raised nearly $2bn for the Russian treasury, but at the cost of tearing apart the already fraying coalition which had secured Yeltsin's re-election in 1996. The rupture plunged the country into a divisive political battle, a conflict known as the bankers' war. Two years later, Russia was still counting the costs.

Although the war erupted in late 1997, it really began on 4 July 1996, the day after Yeltsin's re-election. At first, it seemed that the oligarchs and the reformers might happily coexist. Soon, however, their alliance began to come under serious strain. Compared with the communists, the young reformers had judged the oligarchs to be a relatively progressive force – part of the new order, rather than the old. But by 1997, the young reformers' vantage point had changed. Their goal now was not to defeat communism but to rein in bandit capitalism, and the oligarchs were Russia's bandits-in-chief.

The young reformers expected the oligarchs to put up a fight for their privileges, but they didn't think it would be very fierce or protracted. Paradoxically, the reformers believed that the bandits themselves would be among the chief beneficiaries of their proposed reforms. The creation of a liberal, open, law-abiding market economy would deprive the oligarchs of the opportunities to acquire state property on the cheap or to profitably administer government programmes.

But it would also help to attract foreign investment into the Russian economy, promote a boom in Russian share prices and spur the country into economic growth. As the owners of Russia's biggest businesses, the oligarchs would ultimately be the chief beneficiaries of such liberalising measures.

'Frankly speaking, I did not foresee how swiftly and how fiercely the conflict would develop,' Gaidar told me. 'We did not foresee how short-sighted the strategy of the so-called oligarchs would be, to what degree they would prove unable to understand their own self-interest. They were the very richest and so they stood to suffer the most if the Russian market fell. We did not expect them to be more moral than they are, but we did expect them to be wiser than they showed themselves to be.' But privileged groups rarely voluntarily surrender their special status – and the oligarchs proved to be no exception.

The battle which set off the bankers' war started for the same eternal reason that Cain killed Abel and Hitler marched on the Sudetenland: one of the oligarchs felt he was not getting his fair share of the loot. The aggrieved party in this case was Gusinsky, whose gripe just about made sense in the weird moral world of the oligarchs. Gusinsky had been shut out from the great bonanza of loans-for-shares. Yet, thanks to his television and newspaper empire, he had played a crucial role in the Davos Pact. When Yeltsin was re-elected, he felt he deserved to be rewarded on the same scale as the others. Sviazinvest dovetailed neatly with his media interests and would thus, Gusinsky felt, make the most appropriate prize.

Convinced that Sviazinvest had been implicitly earmarked for him, in the same wink-and-a-nudge way that the loans-for-shares companies had been divvied up, Gusinsky began his campaign to take it over. As with loans-for-shares, the government was too weak and disorganised to privatise Sviazinvest under its own steam: in fact, by 1996, the state had twice tried and failed to sell it off. Instead, the job of getting Sviazinvest ready for the auction block fell to Gusinsky.

It was a delicate task. The telecommunications giant was not really a company itself, but rather a collection of stakes in other companies: 88 regional telecomms firms and Rostelekom, the dominant long-distance and international carrier. Sviazinvest held a 38 per cent stake (and 51 per cent of the voting shares) in each of its subsidiaries, theoretically giving it control over what analysts predicted would soon become one of the fastest growing sectors in the Russian economy. But for all its immense potential, at its inception Sviazinvest was, as one Western investment banker put it, little more than 'a virtual company' because its value depended entirely on its owners' ability to control its feisty regional subsidiaries, particularly the mighty Rostelekom. A further complication was the Russian military, which shared the country's antiquated telephone network with the civilian population and was intensely suspicious of private investors, particularly foreigners. To give Sviazinvest any real value, and to prevent the telecomms bosses and military generals from sabotaging the government's third effort to privatise Sviazinvest as they had done the first two attempts, the red directors and the top brass had to be won over. Gusinsky spent nearly a year doing just that.

By the spring of 1997, Gusinsky's diplomatic campaign was completed: the red directors and generals had been appeased, and the government was finally free to decide under what terms it would sell off the company. Gusinsky, the prime mover in the process so far, went to see Chubais, now in the cabinet, to explain how he thought the privatisation should be structured. By then Gusinsky was already pulling together a consortium of foreign investors, including Telefonica, the Spanish telecommunications company, and Credit Suisse First Boston, the international investment bank. He wanted the sale to be open to Western bidders, but asked that his fellow oligarchs be barred from participating.

But Chubais, eager to distance himself from the taint of the loans-for-shares scheme, had a different agenda. He wanted the Sviazinvest sale to inaugurate a new, open and unimpeachably competitive era. When a 28 April presidential decree announced the sell-off of 25 per cent plus one share of Sviazinvest, the auction was declared open to all comers.

That decision disappointed Gusinsky, but it pleased Potanin. With his blue blood nomenklatura background, Potanin had always been slightly different from all the other oligarchs and the gap grew when he was appointed a deputy prime minister. He had gone into the cabinet with the consent of the other oligarchs (although Gusinsky had voiced a minority dissenting opinion) and as their unofficial representative. But before long, the others began to complain that Potanin was reneging on their deal; he was not helping them and, to make matters worse, he was aggressively assisting his own group. Potanin was unhappy with the situation too. The other oligarchs, he told me, constantly demanded that he help them to set up sweetheart deals with the government. When he refused, they turned round and accused *him* of dipping into the state trough.

The biggest bone of contention was the other oligarchs' suspicion that Potanin was establishing a personal political alliance with Chubais and the young reformers, who had declared war against the oligarchs and their bandit capitalism but somehow had designated Potanin as a white oligarch. As Mikhail Berger, the Russian journalist, explained: 'Chubais became the victim of his own pragmatism. He thought, there are seven or eight bankers, and I have debts to each of them. That is very costly. Maybe it would be better to select one of them, the richest and the strongest, and to treat the others as I treat the rest of the world, strictly according to the rules. To take one and depend on him is cheaper. He chose Potanin.'

For Gusinsky, convinced that he had an unimpeachable right to Sviazinvest, Potanin's service in the government and close relationship with the young reformers made him the most intolerable of possible rivals. For one thing, Gusinsky complained that Potanin had managed to secure the richest government account of all: the state customs account, into which exporters had to pre-pay their customs duties and which generally ran a balance of more than $1bn. Equally galling, from Gusinsky's point of view, was the international respectability which Potanin had acquired through his service in the cabinet.

Potanin's driving sense of manifest destiny, Gusinsky's sense of entitlement to Sviazinvest and the latent antagonism between Potanin and the other oligarchs all added up to an accident waiting to happen. But at first it seemed as if a conflict could be quite painlessly averted, since Potanin was still a cabinet minister. At Chubais' request and to Gusinsky's considerable relief, Potanin agreed that, to prevent a conflict of interest, his group would not bid for the telecomms giant.

But then, in March, Yeltsin shuffled his cabinet and suddenly Potanin was no longer a government minister. Potanin immediately announced that, on principle and for the sake of 'the development of capitalism in the country' he would not respect any 'prearranged deals' and would 'compete with everyone, everywhere'. In other words, he intended to make a play for Sviazinvest. At the begining of April, he told Chubais of his intentions and was assured that the new first deputy prime minister 'supported his position and that it was right'. Next, he informed Gusinsky, Friedman – who had joined the consortium Gusinsky was putting together to bid for Sviazinvest – and Berezovsky, who had no direct interest in the deal but was beginning to see himself as a sort of oligarch-in-chief and liked to have a hand in all the country's major business and political affairs.

Potanin's bombshell announcement set off frantic rounds of negotiations. While the back-room political debate raged, Potanin's investment bankers at the Moscow-based Renaissance Capital, in which he owned a stake, went to work. Two Renaissance founding partners were instrumental in structuring the deal: Boris Jordan, the brash third-generation Russian–American who was starting to be nicknamed 'the tsar' of Russia's fledgling capital markets, and Leonid Rozhetskin, a 30-year-old lawyer and investment banker. Like Jordan, Rozhetskin had a family connection with Russia, but of more recent vintage. In 1979, he and his mother had fled to New York from what was then still Leningrad when Rozhetskin's father, a senior apparatchik, was caught up in a political purge and sent to jail. Almost twenty years later Rozhetskin, a muscular man of medium height and slightly greying hair, still had something of the Soviet immigrant about him: his metal glasses, gave him the air of a Russian professor, his precise use of words and proud vocabulary hinted that he was not quite a native English speaker, and he had the exile's insatiable appetite for work.

Sviazinvest would be expensive, with the government expected to set a starting price of around $1.2bn and the market clearing price predicted to be above $1.5bn, so the Renaissance team began to line up foreign partners. It wasn't easy. According to Rozhetskin, Gusinsky and Friedman were so widely believed to have the deal sewn up that foreign investors had little interest in discussions with Potanin's group. But eventually two powerful players were won over. One was Soros, who had been one of the biggest and earliest investors in Jordan's Sputnik investment fund and whom Jordan saw as 'a mentor, a sort of father figure', proudly displaying his photograph alongside family snapshots in the cabinet in his office. Deutsche Morgan Grenfell (DMG), the international investment bank whose Moscow office was run by Boris Jordan's older brother Nick, also agreed to try to raise additional capital for the deal.

By May, the Renaissance team had made good progress. Even so, Rozhetskin's heart sank when he opened *Kommersant*, Russia's business daily, one sunny morning and discovered that the GKI the state privatisation agency, had already set the complex auction process in motion. It was all happening so fast; Potanin had begun seriously working on the deal only after being fired from the government in March. His team had to court the same bureaucrats Gusinsky had been wooing for more than a year, they needed to meticulously prepare the legal documents for a bid and, most important of all, they still had to raise about $500m.

Renaissance's financial and legal preparations for the auction took place against a background of intense negotiations between Potanin, Gusinsky and Friedman, periodically dragging in the government or one of the other oligarchs as an arbiter. Their discussions were frequent, often angry and always devious. Myriad financial and political permutations were mooted, at one point even including a possible merger between Potanin and Gusinsky's banking operations.

The one interpretation of the negotiations which seemed the most convincing was that Potanin, known as one of Russia's most cunning bargainers, used the talks mostly as a feint to convince Gusinsky that he wasn't really serious about mounting his own competitive bid for Sviazinvest. That is what Potanin's American partners thought he was up to, and they admired his guile. Potanin's ploy, if that's what it was, was abetted when one of his consortium's key investors – Ken Dart, the plastic containers millionaire who was one of the major foreign investors in Russia – pulled out at the last minute. His withdrawal helped to convince Gusinsky that Potanin would be unable to mount a threatening bid.

It was only on Monday 21 July, just five days before the auction, that Gusinsky finally realised Potanin was a serious challenger when Soros' involvement – which the Potanin group had tried to keep a secret – leaked. Gusinsky also learned that Jordan, with his brother at DMG and his excellent network of Western investors, was the person putting together the financial side of the deal.

Suddenly, Gusinsky got very mad and very scared. He redoubled his pressure on the government and his threats against Potanin. Alfred Kokh, the GKI chief, felt the strain most acutely. He sensed Russia was at a crossroads, and he was not sure he was the man to choose its direction. Instead, he advised the warring oligarchs to turn to Chubais – on holiday at a friend's villa on the Côte d'Azur – for a final decision. The oligarchs liked the idea. Chubais, now firmly reinstated in the president's favour, was the *de facto* head of the Russian government.

On Tuesday, the oligarchs telephoned Chubais and told him they would fly out to see him the next day. Chubais was unenthusiastic. Like most Russians, he took his vacation time seriously and felt he could tell the oligarchs everything they needed to know over his mobile telephone. Undeterred, on Wednesday morning Gusinsky and Potanin held a meeting with some of their partners at the Most headquarters, then set off for Vnukovo airport where Gusinsky's Gulfstream was waiting.

At the last minute, Kokh dropped out of the trip. He had wanted to join them but Prime Minister Chernomyrdin, fearing the whole matter was spiralling out of control, would not give him permission to leave. 'There's nothing for you to do there,' he grumbled, and Kokh remained in Moscow. By contrast, Berezovsky, who loved to be at the centre of the action, had no such compunctions. As Gusinsky put it, 'He always has to be the master of ceremonies at every wedding and the chief toast-maker at every wake.' Berezovsky saw Potanin's initiative as a threat not only to Gusinsky but to the entire, previously cosy collusion between the oligarchs and the Kremlin. He too boarded Gusinsky's plane, hoping to help him make his case with Chubais.

For men on the brink of corporate war, they were a relatively jovial party. One of the oligarchs even brought along two movie videos to watch as they flew across Europe. The private jet landed in Nice, then the troika boarded a helicopter – this time Potanin paid for the rental, since the jet was Gusinsky's – and flew to the villa where Chubais was staying.

Red-haired and fair-skinned as he was, even the Mediterranean high-summer sun was not enough to give Chubais much of a tan. But, after a tense autumn with the president on the edge of death and a hectic spring spent spearheading a new wave of reforms, he was enjoying his first real holiday in nearly a year. Normally tense and highly strung, his mouth habitually pursed and his forehead a mass of determined wrinkles, Chubais looked relaxed and almost carefree. He had been reluctant to be disturbed, but now that the oligarchs had come he wanted to settle the issue once and for all.

The three oligarchs asked Chubais to explain the government's position. They wanted to know whether, as Gusinsky insisted, Sviazinvest had been implicitly reserved for the Most group as a reward for its election services, or if (as Potanin hoped) the contest really would be open to all comers. Chubais' answer was unequivocal: 'No one has a special right to Sviazinvest. Both the president and the prime minister agree with me about this.' Whoever bid more at the auction 48 hours later would win.

Potanin was thrilled. 'That was the answer I flew there for,' he told me later. But Gusinsky was incandescent with rage. In 1995 and 1996, when the loans-for-shares sales took place, Chubais had tolerated and indeed sponsored sweetheart deals for the other oligarchs. How dare the government now, when his own turn had finally come, suddenly become insistent on fair and open auctions? 'Chubais decided to end the unfair games and begin fair ones, but he did it unfairly,' Gusinsky insisted. As Friedman, his partner in the Sviazinvest bid, put it: 'Why did they have to become fair at this particular moment?' Worse yet, Gusinsky felt he had been doubled-crossed by Chubais and Kokh. When, in the autumn of 1996, they had given him their consent to try to prepare Sviazinvest for privatisation, he had assumed their approval implicitly meant the company would be reserved for him.

Anxious to somehow appease Gusinsky – but unwilling to give up his own bid for Sviazinvest – Potanin tried to persuade Chubais to sponsor some sort of grand compromise in which all of the oligarchs would get an additional piece of what was left of the state pie. 'Potanin decided to try a trade – to get some big pieces without auctions. There was an idea that there would be a second and third round [of loans-for-shares] and big blocks of privatisation,' Gusinsky recalled. But Chubais would not even entertain Potanin's vague proposal. Sviazinvest, as he had told the oligarchs over the telephone, would be sold to the highest bidder – as would all the other state companies remaining to be privatised.

'I was crazy with anger,' Gusinsky admitted. 'I said, "Tolya, this will all end with a huge purge of everyone. I will not simply let it go. I will fight as hard as I can. There will be a big conflict, it will all end very badly. My only weapon is publicity. I do not know how to use anything else. So you had better be very sure that your deal is fair, that you have never directly or indirectly taken money from Oneximbank. If so, you won't have problems. It will all pass. But if not, then you will have problems." He [Chubais] said, "We won't have problems."'

The eating, drinking, shouting, threatening and cajoling lasted for six hours. But after midnight, at the end of the marathon session, the oligarchs left Chubais' villa with the same answer he had given them the day before: the auction would be won by the highest bidder.

This time the oligarchs took a speedboat to Gusinsky's jet and then flew back to Moscow, arriving between 6 and 7 a.m. on Thursday, the day before the auction. The Renaissance team met Potanin on the runway. As they had logged frantic 20-hour days in the final preparations for the auction, they had been haunted by niggling doubts about Potanin's commitment. Would he really risk the wrath of the other oligarchs? To their relief, Potanin returned from France determined to go ahead. Over the ensuing, tense 36 hours, he occasionally flirted with second thoughts, but Jordan and the Renaissance team told him it was simply too late to pull out and that even if he tried to do so the Renaissance group and the Western investors they had assembled would go ahead without him anyway.

Meanwhile, the other oligarchs stepped up the pressure against Potanin. At 10 a.m., less than four hours after the troika touched down at Vnukovo airport, the warring parties gathered again, this time in central Moscow at Berezovsky's Logovaz Clubhouse. Berezovsky, his enthusiasm for intrigue for once exhausted, struggled against sleep and kept dozing off in his chair.

The meeting itself was even more aggressive than the long lunch in France. For two hours, the oligarchs and their aides shouted and banged their fists on the table. 'Potanin sat back and basically took the hits from the others,' Jordan recalled. 'We almost felt that we had to go through this, that we had to go through this punishment over the next two days.' The clans adjourned for lunch, then reconvened for more of the same that afternoon in Gusinsky's office. Berezovsky, finally convinced there could be no resolution, boarded a plane and left for his own holiday that night. But for Potanin and Gusinsky, there was no exit. Friday morning, the day of the auction, dawned and their tense negotiations continued. A few hours before the bids were due to be opened, Potanin came to Gusinsky's office for one last time. For weeks, he had been ambiguous about whether or not he would participate at all and had tried to conceal the strength of his consortium. Now he gave Gusinsky a clear signal of his intentions.

'Two hours before the contest Potanin sat right here in my office,' Gusinsky told me, pointing to the tan leather armchair to his right. 'From that conversation I finally understood the limits to which they would probably bid.'

A little while later, Potanin telephoned Gusinsky to reinforce the message. 'Maybe he had been hoping that we would bid a low price, because we had publicly stated that we would pay $1.5bn,' Potanin recalled. But now the time for subterfuge had ended. 'I said to Gusinsky, "Volodya, be ready for a fight. My investors are serious, so make an effort. There will be a battle. Don't expect an easy victory."'

Potanin's last-minute warning sent Gusinsky into a panic. A group from Telefonica – one of his partners – and his own team of executives were waiting in a neighbouring room as Gusinsky rushed in and suggested they raise their bid from a planned $1.7bn to $1.9bn. At first, both Telefonica and Credit Suisse agreed to go along with Gusinsky's proposal, but then the Most consortium ran up against a technical obstacle. As a large public company, Telefonica could not take such a significant decision without the approval of its board. In the two hours remaining, it was physically impossible to secure that consent.

Meanwhile, Potanin and his team had also been making their final preparations for the 5 p.m. auction. Thousands of technical details needed to be checked and double-checked – all in the knowledge that a single trivial mistake might be enough to thwart their entire effort. Rozhetskin became an expert in the obscure Russian rules governing the notarisation of documents. The group was put further on edge by their fear that Gusinsky and his team might be bugging their telephone conversations or even their offices. They spoke only on mobile telephones which used the GSM frequency, the most difficult type of line for Russians to tap. Starting on Thursday morning, the day before the auction, they had stopped mentioning possible bid prices aloud, instead jotting down the figures on scraps of paper.

The Renaissance team worried that even their own secretaries might be spying on behalf of the Most group. So, instead of preparing a single letter with the bid price, on Thursday Rozhetskin had his secretary print out dozens, naming a range of possible bids between $1.2bn and

$2.5bn. The group's anxiety was further stoked on Friday morning, when the bankers met in Jordan's 5th-floor office, where huge windows overlooked the Moskva river. Suddenly, a window-cleaner appeared outside and lingered there all morning. 'We still don't know whether he was a plant or not, but he definitely looked that way,' Rozhetskin told me.

With blinds drawn and communicating through scribbled notes, Rozhetskin and Jordan agreed they would bid high, somewhere between $1.8bn and $1.9bn. Then Rozhetskin spoke to Soros and confirmed the range with him. That afternoon, after Potanin's last meeting with Gusinsky, the two bankers drove over to the Oneximbank offices to decide on a final price. When Jordan and Rozhetskin arrived, Potanin, accompanied by his partner Prokherev, led them to a windowless room deep inside the building on one of the highest floors. This room, which Rozhetskin had never seen before, was specially insulated and equipped with anti-bugging equipment to prevent electronic surveillance. Whispering, the four men determined a final price.

By now, it was getting late; it was just after 3.30 p.m. when the group left the soundproofed room. As they stepped out, Potanin proposed one last mental ploy in his battle against Gusinsky. Turning to Rozhetskin, he suggested that the young lawyer arrive at the auction alone and without fanfare, creating the impression that the Oneximbank consortium expected to lose. Accompanied only by his assistant, Vladimir Smolianov, Rozhetskin got into a company car and told the driver to head for the Federal Property Commission on Leninsky Prospekt. Speeded along by Potanin's elite 'killer' licence plates, it was a drive which normally took about twenty minutes. Even so, as the driver fought his way through Friday afternoon rush-hour traffic, Rozhetskin was anxious. After all that effort, to lose the bid because of a traffic jam would be tragic.

To his relief, they pulled up to the dirty grey Soviet office building in plenty of time, at about twenty minutes to five. Rozhetskin, recognising Gusinsky's Jeep, saw that the rival consortium had already arrived. Feeling like 'zombies' after two weeks of working around the clock, Rozhetskin and Smolianov got into a musty elevator and rode up to the 7th floor. When they stepped out, an excited whisper went through the crowded room. At a quarter to five, Rozhetskin and Smolianov walked into the bidding room itself; the government officials running the auction were already there, sitting in a row behind a long table. At exactly 5 o'clock, Friedman and a Telefonica executive, representing the Most consortium, stepped into the room. The auction could now begin.

The commission asked for the bids to be submitted. Friedman unfastened his soft leather briefcase and brought out an impressive-looking, huge smooth envelope. Inside was a *matrioshka* of ever smaller, prettier envelopes. Opening the final one, Friedman produced a thick professional wad of papers. Rozhetskin, slightly intimidated, tore open his own ordinary, slightly battered envelope and fished out a small folded sheet of paper. The two men walked up to the commission table and handed over their bids.

The chairman of the auction commission took Rozhetskin's bid first and began to read it aloud. When he came to the price – $1.875bn and $40,000 – the Telefonica representative emitted a high-pitched moan. Friedman kept quiet but turned very, very pale. A few endless minutes later, the official read through the Most consortium's bid and announced their offer: $1.71bn. Struggling to be gentlemanly in defeat, Friedman rose from his seat and walked over to Rozhetskin to congratulate him. But, for several painful moments, he was physically unable to raise his hand. Eventually he managed, then he and the Telefonica executive hurried out of the room. Rozhetskin stayed behind to fill out a few forms confirming Mustcom – the investment vehicle Potanin had created for his consortium – as the winner, then stepped over to an empty corner of the room to call Jordan with the good news.

Jordan was jubilant. He and his wife were at home getting ready to join the entire Renaissance team for a long weekend in the south of France; when his mobile phone rang, he was packing his holiday suitcase. He was tired and pretty sure his consortium would lose the auction: 'Those guys wanted it so bad that we thought they were going to pay anything for it.' His first reaction to Rozhetskin's news was total disbelief.

'Stop bullshitting me,' Jordan snapped.

'No, no, no, we really won,' Rozhetskin insisted.

Thrilled, Jordan phoned an equally incredulous Potanin. Then they all gathered at Potanin's office for a celebratory toast before finally heading off to France where, with a group of Soros executives, the partying continued.

For Renaissance the deal brought an immediate financial fillip. Part of the investment, about $500m worth, was syndicated out to investors after the auction. Renaissance and Deutsche Morgan Grenfell were responsible for raising the money and they charged a 10 per cent premium over the auction price, earning a healthy $50m profit on the transaction according to Rozhetskin.

For the young reformers, the auction also seemed to be a triumph. Chubais had kept his promise. The government had steadfastly rejected efforts to rig the deal and the auction had been won by the highest bidder. Nearly $1.88bn had been raised – the highest revenue of any privatisation – of which 71 per cent would go straight to the federal budget. Western analysts generally agreed that the $1.88bn price was consistent with the underlying value of the company's assets. Western investors, already excited about Russia, became even more confident, pushing the stock market up 2.3 per cent on the day of the Sviazinvest auction alone.

Soros expressed the general hopeful consensus: 'I felt that by participating in the Sviazinvest auction I could move things forward from what I call robber capitalism to legitimate capitalism. The auction was a watershed. I don't think it will be possible to go back.'

But almost immediately some people began to worry that, instead of inaugurating a bright new era, the Sviazinvest sale might set off a dark and destructive bankers' war. The first sign came even as the Oneximbank group were drinking their victory glasses of champagne in Potanin's office. As they were celebrating, the telephone rang. It was Nemtsov, the first deputy prime minister, who congratulated Potanin but delivered a warning. 'Nemtsov said, watch out, the shit is really going to hit the fan now,' Rozhetskin recalled.

Realising that the losers' revenge could be very costly, Potanin had already tried to negotiate a truce and been rebuffed. As soon as he learned the result of the auction he telephoned Gusinsky, offering to begin talks immediately about cooperating over Sviazinvest. Gusinsky agreed, and told Potanin to come over right away. But five minutes later his secretary called Potanin's office and said the meeting had been cancelled. On Saturday morning, less than 24 hours later, as Potanin put it, 'the war began.'

Gusinsky's and Berezovsky's television stations, which had been generally supportive of the young reformers, launched a scathing attack against the government. They focused on Sviazinvest, alleging that Chubais and Kokh had unfairly favoured Potanin, but also abruptly assumed a more generally critical tone about the young reformers and everything connected to them. As the media campaign escalated, and as the aggrieved oligarchs began to make their case with the prime minister and in the Kremlin, Chubais started to grow nervous. Urged on by Berezovsky, Chubais convened a series of meetings of all the oligarchs, including those who had not been involved in the Sviazinvest contest, to try to broker a truce. 'We were invited to serve as arbiters,' Khodorkovsky, the apparatchik oligarch, told me.

The marathon sessions, which began within a week of the auction and continued every three or four days, took place in Chubais' private office on the 24th floor of the Moscow city hall building, the gloomy Soviet skyscraper which also housed the Most group. Many of the gathered oligarchs suspected that Chubais had assembled the group in the hope that the pressure of his peers would rein in Gusinsky's rage, rather than because he was genuinely prepared to annul the Sviazinvest sale. But if that was his purpose, he was sorely disappointed by the consensus which emerged. The assembled oligarchs were unanimous: Potanin was in the wrong and he should give Sviazinvest to Gusinsky to prevent all-out war.

Buoyed by the support of their fellow oligarchs, Gusinsky and Friedman proposed a solution. Their consortium, they said, was ready to match Potanin's $1.88bn bid for Sviazinvest. The government should annul Potanin's bid on some technical pretext and allow the Most group to buy the 25 per cent stake for the higher price. Peace would then be restored among the oligarchs and the treasury's revenues would be unchanged.

As it became apparent that the oligarchs were united behind Gusinsky and that he and Berezovsky were determined to carry through with their threat to start a bankers' war, even some of the young reformers began to think that discretion might be the better part of valour. 'They should give Sviazinvest to Gusinsky and they will have Gusinsky on their side for ever,' urged Sergei Vasiliev, part of the St Petersburg gang.

Chubais, however, stuck to his guns. 'No, the auction has taken place,' he insisted. 'It was all fair. I can't behave otherwise.' Potanin, facing the united opposition of his colleagues, also refused to back down, earning him the grudging admiration even of his detractors. At the end of it all, nothing had changed. Gusinsky still believed he had been deceived by Chubais and by Potanin and deprived of his rightful winnings. Potanin and Chubais continued to think the Oneximbank group had won fair and square. Potanin had Sviazinvest. But Gusinsky, his sense of injury deepened by the supportive consensus of the other oligarchs, decided he would have his revenge.

For the young reformers, the bankers' war was a particularly bitter blow because they had created the men who were now destroying them. Now the oligarchs were turning on their Dr Frankenstein, using many of the skills and resources with which their creator had endowed them.

As in the 1996 election campaign, Gusinsky and Berezovsky used their domination of the airwaves to mould the public debate. Again they used verifiable facts, presented in the worst possible light, to demonise their opponents. Again they used their relationship with Tatyana Dyachenko, Yeltsin's daughter, to help sway the president. And again, where they were confident they would leave no footprints, they used dirty tricks to learn their targets' secrets and knock them off balance.

Potanin and Jordan, already 'paranoid' about surveillance during the run-up to the Sviazinvest bid, began to complain of even more relentless espionage. 'Everywhere I went, I got filmed,' Jordan told me. 'I don't think Gusinsky would even deny it. This was serious stuff. Millions of dollars were spent on it. We had guys break into the grounds of Luzhki [the Oneximbank group's dacha complex] trying to take pictures.' The vengeful oligarchs even managed to obtain video footage of Alfred Kokh joining the Oneximbank group, including Potanin, on holiday at the Côte d'Azur less than a month after the Sviazinvest sale. The video, with the slightly shaky focus of a hand-held camera and the awkward angles of a covert investigator, showed Kokh and Potanin relaxing poolside at the FF18,000-a-night Hotel du Cap with their wives and children. More embarrassingly, it also showed the men riding a speedboat out to a Mediterranean island where they were joined by the mistresses they had flown over separately from Moscow.

The clandestine home video never reached Russian television screens. 'We do have one rule among us,' a Most executive explained to me self-righteously. 'We would never go into each other's private lives, mistresses, and so on.' But within the Moscow establishment it was widely screened – even I got a look – and was used both as a form of psychological pressure and to make it impossible for Kokh to deny his close personal relationship with Potanin.

The centrepiece of Gusinsky's and Berezovsky's campaign, and the main battlefield in the bankers' war, was a flood of compromising revelations about the hitherto seemingly squeaky-clean young reformers. The dirt started with Kokh, the privatisation chief whose friendship with Potanin and relatively relaxed personal ethics made him the easiest target. On 18 August, Aleksandr Minkin, one of Russia's premier muck-raking journalists and Gusinsky's personal friend, published an article in his weekly newspaper, *Novaya Gazeta*, breaking the story that Kokh had been paid a $100,000 fee by an obscure Swiss book-keeping company to write a book about Russian privatisation. As I learned when I looked into the matter, Servina, the Swiss firm, had several close connections to Oneximbank. That connection to Potanin and the huge sum of money for a book of questionable commercial value started to raise questions about whether the young reformers were in the pocket of one of the oligarchs.

It turned out to be an incredibly damaging allegation. Many Russians already hated the reformers, but even their most bitter enemies had believed they were morally unimpeachable, driven by ideology rather than venal self-interest. Now, with the $100,000 pay-off to Kokh, it looked as if the young reformers might not be so pure after all.

By 1997, within the Russian establishment book honoraria had become the almost openly accepted way for politicians to receive financial support from loyal businessmen. But, in the opinion of the Russian public, what might be tolerable behaviour from President Yeltsin – a 60-something veteran of the Soviet Politburo – was less acceptable coming from the young reformers. For them, age and personal history offered less of an excuse.

More importantly, the young reformers stood for something quite different from politics as usual. Both in 1991 and in 1997, they had swept into office as agents of radical, cleansing change. An essential part of their self-proclaimed mission was to root out the corruption which pervaded the Russian bureaucracy and to sever the incestuous money-lubricated links between business and government. That, after all, had been the whole point of the Sviazinvest stand-off. As Russia's self-appointed corruption-busters, the sheriffs who had volunteered to lead the fight against bandit-capitalism, the reformers had to be purer than Russia's run-of-the-mill politicians. Like Caesar's wife, they had to be above the merest whisper of suspicion. With Kokh's $100,000 book, the whispers began.

As the public criticism of Kokh's book deal mounted, the government began to turn against the young reformers. Government prosecutors, possibly egged on behind the scenes by Gusinsky and Berezovsky, opened an investigation into Oneximbank's links to the payment and began to call in Kokh for regular and unpleasant interrogations. Yeltsin started to grow more hostile towards them as well. He was angered by the disclosures in the press and probably fed further poisonous revelations by Berezovsky's influential contacts in the Kremlin – including Yumashev, the presidential ghostwriter who had become the Kremlin chief of staff when Chubais moved back to the cabinet. In late August, the president implicitly endorsed the aggrieved oligarchs' charge that Kokh had favoured his friend Potanin throughout the privatisation process.

'The scandal around Sviazinvest and Norilsk Nickel [the nickel mining concern Potanin had acquired through the loans-for-shares privatisations] is connected to the fact that a number of banks are closer to Kokh's soul,' the president said in remarks broadcast on national television. 'That is not the way it is done. Everything must be honest, open and built on legal principles.'

Yet while the disclosures about Kokh may have taken some of the shine from the young reformers' reputations, they were far from mortally wounded. Kokh had never been one of the leading intellectual or political figures among the wider circle of young reformers and, anyhow, almost before the scandal began, he was gone. He left the GKI on 13 August, ostensibly in order to pursue a business career but probably because of the bankers' war, and was replaced by another Chubais loyalist, Maxim Boiko.

So the young reformers started to fight back, and indeed took a coveted scalp of their own. On 5 November, Yeltsin fired Berezovsky, the most powerful oligarch of all, from his post as deputy head of the Security Council. The president's surprise decision followed a lengthy evening meeting at his dacha the day before with Chubais and Nemtsov.

Thanks in large part to Nemtsov's strengthening personal relationship with Yeltsin, the Kremlin chief had helped the reformers to deliver a powerful blow in their now open battle against the oligarchs. 'This is an important step in Russia's effort to move away as far as possible from oligarchical capitalism,' a triumphant Nemtsov declared.

Chubais, always fiercely loyal to this team, became ever more aggressive in his defence of Kokh. The so-called scandal, he insisted, had been a trumped-up politically motivated attack instigated by the oligarchs. The young reformers, including Kokh, had nothing to apologise for. Indeed, the whole country should be grateful to them for undertaking the thankless and exhausting task of reshaping Russia into a market economy. It looked as if the bankers' war might backfire against the oligarchs who had begun it, leaving the young reformers even more powerful. As one Chubais aide gleefully put it on the day Berezovsky was sacked, 'This is our Stalingrad.'

Then the bankers struck again. Kokh, it turned out, was not the only reformer who had supplemented his income with hefty book fees paid by companies connected to Oneximbank. On 12 November, an unseasonably cold, overcast Wednesday, the muck-raking journalist Minkin appeared on Gusinsky's radio station to reveal a second book scandal. Five young reformers, including Chubais himself, Kokh and Boiko had been commissioned to write chapters in a second book, yet another history of Russian economic reforms, and each had been paid $90,000, bringing the total bill to a hefty $450,000. Worse still, whereas the links between Servina (the buyer of Kokh's first book) and Oneximbank had been tenuous, the second book was directly tied to Potanin. The book's publisher, Segodnya Press, was 51 per cent owned by Oneximbank. Chubais' initial justification that the fees had been largely donated to charity did little to appease public hostility. The charity to which he said he and his co-authors planned to contribute their advances was the Fund for the Defence of Private Property, the organisation created and controlled by the young reformers which they had used to receive election funds from the oligarchs in 1996. Chubais had used it in 1996 to receive the $3m election fee from the oligarchs.

In breaking the story, Minkin had been categorical about its implications. The book fees were, he insisted, 'a veiled bribe'. For the first 24 hours after Minkin's radio broadcast, Chubais fought back with equally robust counter-charges. He threatened to sue Minkin for slander (he eventually did and lost), dismissed the accusations as *kompromat* and described the public outcry over the book as 'an atom bomb' detonated by the vengeful oligarchs. But even as Chubais, with typical bravado, was defending himself in public, his fate and that of the young reformers was being decided in the privacy of Yeltsin's Kremlin office.

On Thursday morning, the day after Minkin's broadcast, Chubais had (at the president's instruction) presented Yeltsin with a written explanation of the $450,000 book deal. Yeltsin was infuriated by what he read. Normally the most persuasive of courtiers, at this crucial moment Chubais' eloquence failed him. Some insiders said he was insufficiently repentant; others claimed that he had angered the president by seeking to distance himself from his four protégés who were also implicated. Whatever the reason, Chubais' fate was sealed in that instant. Yeltsin immediately ordered the preparation of a decree sacking one of Chubais' co-authors, Aleksandr Kazakov, deputy head of the presidential administration and Chubais' closest ally in the Kremlin.

Chubais' enemies – sensing that, for the first time since the president's re-election, Russia's Bismarck might be vulnerable – were jubilant. Yevtushenkov told me that when Luzhkov first heard of the second book he reacted with just six fiercely happy words: *'Yvolit' yego! Yvolit' yego! Yvolit' yego!* Fire him! Fire him! Fire him!' Even Chernomyrdin, who since the triumphant return of the young reformers to the cabinet in the spring had been forced to play second fiddle in his own administration, began cautiously to take a few pot-shots. 'Above all, I am troubled by the ethical side of things,' he said. 'No one is forbidden from writing and publishing books, even members of the government, but everything must be in reasonable bounds.'

Most significantly of all, Chubais began to change his tune. On Friday, when Kazakov's sacking was announced, Chubais shifted to a tone of unaccustomed humility: the book fees, he admitted, were 'perhaps too high'. But his newly contrite pose did not appease the Kremlin. On Saturday, two more of Chubais' co-authors were sacked: Boiko and Pyotr Mostovoy, head of the federal bankruptcy agency. Unusually, the Kremlin gave a specific reason for the dismissals – the book deal – and, in a written statement, disclosed that Chubais had been dressed down by the president who had told him in a weekend telephone conversation that his conduct had been 'impermissible'. Chernomyrdin was even more severe: 'No one has a right to compromise the president, the government and the very cause of reform itself. I am ashamed of my government colleagues.'

Of the five co-authors, only Chubais was left and Moscow political pundits began to lay odds on how long he would survive. They didn't have to wait too long. On Wednesday 19 November, exactly a week after Minkin's revelations, Chubais was stripped of his job as minister of finance. He retained the title of first deputy prime minister, but – in an uncharacteristically delicate display of salami tactics by a president who usually felled his opponents in a single bear-like blow – he had been terribly weakened. Chubais had been humiliated, his allies were gone and now he had lost his only remaining practical source of power: hands-on control over a ministry. 'Chubais is a political corpse,' Lilya Shevtsova, an analyst at the Carnegie Centre in Moscow, told me. 'He has lost his air of professionalism and he has lost his image as an honest guy.'

Nemtsov, the young reformers' poster-boy and the only electable politician among them, also began to take a few hits. Like Kokh, Nemtsov had struck up a personal friendship with the Oneximbank leadership and had taken to spending weekends at Luzhki, the group's luxurious dacha complex outside Moscow. Like most of Russia's nouveaux riches, the bankers' personal habits were salacious and high-rolling. Before long, Russian television viewers were treated to video footage of Nemtsov and a group of Oneximbank bankers lounging in warm water as teenage strippers performed on a concrete island in the complex's swimming pool. It wasn't illegal, unethical or even, by the standards of the New Russians, particularly unusual behaviour, but it did chip away a little of Nemtsov's precious man-of-the-people image. Yeltsin, who had seemed to be grooming him as a successor, started to grow less supportive and began to strip him of some of his powers.

By the supremely relaxed standards of the Russian political elite, the young reformers' punishment seemed out of all proportion to their crimes. Chernomyrdin himself was rumoured, although the allegations were later withdrawn, to have made at least a billion through the privatisation of Gazprom. But as advocates of a better, cleaner kind of capitalism, the young reformers had to be better and cleaner themselves. 'This bit of unethical behaviour is nothing compared to what senior ministers have got away with,' one Western investment banker in Moscow explained. 'But if you set yourself up as the champion of reform, you can't do what others can.'

And now, after five years of loyally supporting the capitalist revolutionaries, Russia's liberal media – much of it owned by Gusinsky – turned its sights on the young reformers as well.

'Our editors-in-chief and our journalists learned a very important thing,' Gusinsky explained self-servingly but not entirely inaccurately. 'That, regardless of the sympathies we might have for the reforms, the mass media must inform. Traditionally, there had been a certain degree of self-censorship. Not because Gusinsky gave an order not to write bad things about Chubais, but simply because everyone understood that Chubais was honest, that he was Russia's real future. And for that reason, to write bad things about him was dishonourable. Suddenly, editors-in-chief and journalists realised that those honest people were not completely honest; that they had suddenly played by dishonest rules, that they had violated their own public codes. And then the self-censorship ended. There was no bankers' war. Just the end of self-censorship among journalists.'

Perhaps worst of all, the mud-slinging had deprived the young reformers of what was left of their popular credibility. In the rarefied world of Moscow, at first I had found it hard to take the allegations too seriously. By the yardsticks of the New Russia, the amount of money involved was relatively small and the frolicking at the Oneximbank dacha complex commonplace. But to the rest of Russia, where $150 dollars was a monthly salary and $100,000 more than a man could earn in a lifetime, the young reformers' exploits seemed decidedly less innocent. I visited the Red October coal-mine in the Kuzbas, a depressed industrial region in Siberia, in the autumn of 1997, as the bankers' war was raging. To my surprise, the miners had been following the story closely.

The Kuzbas miners' disgust with communism, and the strike action they took to express it, had been one of the forces which had thrust Yeltsin to power in 1991. But, as they pulled on their coal-blackened work-clothes, they told me that the recent revelations had extinguished their support for the young reformers.

'I don't like Chubais, I haven't since he gave our country away,' explained Ivan, a 36-year-old with sharp Slavic cheekbones and a handsome smile. 'But I liked Nemtsov and I was happy when he went to Moscow. I thought he might clean out that whorehouse. Now I see him swimming with the oligarchs' prostitutes and all the others taking their money. $100,000 for a book! That might be nothing to them, but out here in the dying Russia they've created it's a fortune.'

In a way, Ivan was right. Part of the young reformers' problem was that, in a country with an increasingly gaping divide between rich and poor, they had come to feel they belonged in the world of the New Russians they had created, rather than to the rest of the society whose support was vital if their reforms were to succeed. The distance between these two domestic worlds was vast. Jordan offered a sense of the universe the young reformers inhabited and the financial expectations they had learned to entertain when, in an attempted defence of Kokh's behaviour, he explained to me that the $100,000 book fee could not possibly have been a bribe because Kokh would never have sold himself so cheaply. 'Kokh wouldn't have given information for a hundred thousand dollars,' Jordan insisted. 'It's funny money in Russia. A hundred thousand dollars is just not serious for these people.'

Living in social circles where $100,000 was 'funny money', but earning government salaries of less than $500 a month, the young reformers faced a terrible personal dilemma. The contrast between their own thin pay packets and their extravagantly rich business friends left some of them with a sense of bitterness, or at least of entitlement. A few months after the bankers' war, I talked about the issue with Kokh and was astonished by both his candour and his anger. His children never had a country dacha to visit, he and his family lived in a cramped apartment and had to scrimp by on a salary of about $400 a month, Kokh complained. And what was his reward for all this deprivation? Only criticism, attack and police interrogations.

Would it be better, I suggested placatingly, if the cabinet followed the lead of the central bank, which paid its top executives healthy monthly salaries of more than $10,000 in an effort to prevent corruption? Kokh's answer to that question was even more surprising. 'For me, that's too little,' he said with a derisive snort. And what sort of salary would have satisfied Kokh? Nothing short of a 3 per cent cut of all the revenues he brought in to the treasury as GKI chief. It was a truly mind-blowing suggestion. Kokh, a cabinet minister in a country unable to keep the lights on in its hospitals, thought he should have been paid according to a formula which in 1997 would have netted him close to $60m. I couldn't quite believe what I was hearing, so I offered him a way out. Money was always nice, I said, but I knew that he and the other young reformers had been driven by higher things: market reforms, a commitment to the common good, a profound sense of personal honour. Kokh was unimpressed. 'What do you mean by honour?' he shot back. 'You won't get far on honour alone.'

But without honour, without their squeaky-clean reputations, the young reformers couldn't get very far either. The bankers' war stopped the second radical burst of change dead in its tracks. Over the course of just a few months, in the time that elapsed between the sale of Sviazinvest on 25 July and the sacking of Chubais' team on 15 November, the young reformers had gone from basking in the president's favour to jockeying desperately to keep their jobs. Fending off the oligarchs' attacks consumed most of the energy which should have been devoted to pushing ahead with reforms.

The split over Sviazinvest underscored just how dependent the politicians were on the businessmen to push their initiatives through the creaky machinery of the Russian state. With the oligarchs on board, when crucial but controversial bills came before parliament the young reformers could and did call on the businessmen to use their formidable lobbying muscle – a combination of favours owed, favours promised, smooth persuasion and outright bribes – to secure legislative approval. Without the oligarchs, suddenly the parliamentary wheels gummed up. The paralysis showed the young reformers, yet again, the narrowness of their own political base. Without the support of some powerful ally, be it the president or the oligarchs, they were helpless.

13

THINGS FALL APART

As COUNT GALEAZZO Ciano observed in his diaries, victory finds a hundred fathers but defeat is an orphan. The same principle applies to financial crashes; after the fact, everyone always knew the meltdown was coming. It's not just a matter of pride – in hindsight, it all starts to seem so obvious, so inevitable. Memory played these usual tricks on the survivors of Russia's August 1998 economic crisis; but, although the collapse was probably inevitable, it certainly wasn't obvious, at least not while it was happening. The Russian meltdown was no US-style economic tragedy: an impatient, forthright crash like the Great Depression, which rushed in almost overnight. Instead, Russia's financial demon was slower and more cunning, consuming the country with a salami strategy sufficiently delicate that the government didn't realise what was happening until it was too late.

The first slice came off in the autumn of 1997, almost a year before the final collapse. Investors, whose giddy optimism about Russia's prospects just a few weeks earlier had pushed share prices to record highs, began to get nervous. On 28 October, the Russian bourse plunged by almost 20 per cent, the largest one-day fall in the brief history of the country's capital markets. 'I'm not bullish for the first time in a long time,' Boris Jordan admitted to me in November. 'Russia is very fragile.'

Russia had done a reverse Cinderella thanks to a combination of external shocks and internal stumbles. At least at first, the external pressure was the greatest. Over the spring and summer of 1997, the tiger economies of east Asia had contracted a devastating economic flu. One by one Indonesia, Thailand, Malaysia and South Korea had collapsed into a crisis which Soros described as deeper than the Great Depression. The Asian crisis had a knock-on effect throughout the world, but particularly in emerging market economies such as Russia. Over the past few years, as North America and much of western Europe enjoyed a sustained economic boom, the big investors whom the *New York Times* columnist Thomas Friedman calls the Electronic Herd had started grazing further afield. Emerging markets, once the preserve of the specialist or the super-high-risk fund, became more and more mainstream. When the Asian crisis struck, the Electronic Herd suddenly become more cautious, galloping out of places like Russia. Worse yet, many of the most aggressive investors in Russia had been based in emerging markets themselves, particularly Brazil and South Korea. As their own economies began to tremble, they started pulling their money out to take it back home.

For Moscow, this newly sceptical mood was made more sour still by another global economic trend: falling commodities prices, especially for oil. Oil was a mainstay of the Russian economy, accounting for as much as 20 per cent of its exports. With prices for Urals crude (the main Russian blend) falling from $18 a barrel at the beginning of 1997 to just over $15 a barrel at the end of the year, the finances of the Russian government, and of many of Russia's leading companies, suddenly looked far more precarious.

Russia's ability to withstand these external shocks was compromised by internal problems. Distracted and weakened by the bankers' war, the dream team was making far less progress than everyone had hoped. When an IMF mission visited Russia in October, it came up with a surprisingly discouraging verdict: the young reformers simply were not delivering vital change, particularly improvement in revenue collection. Disappointed by Russia's poor performance, the IMF froze the October $700m tranche of the $10bn loan it had been steadily dripping into the Russian economy.

Yet most of the Russian leadership continued to insist that the country's problems were minor, fleeting and based solely on adverse external circumstances. Some of the young reformers even argued that the Asian crisis might actually boost the Russian economy by causing a shift in the investment funds earmarked for emerging markets from volatile Asia to the safe haven of Russia. As Chubais rashly predicted in December: 'Russia could emerge from the stock exchange and financial crises in the world with some gains, thanks to the redistribution of world financial resources.'

A few foreign investors appeared to share that confidence. In mid-November, Russia clinched its two biggest strategic investment deals since the beginning of market reforms: Royal Dutch/Shell formed an alliance with Gazprom committing to invest $1bn in a convertible bond offering by the company, and British Petroleum teamed up with Sidanco, the oil company owned by the Oneximbank group, paying $571m for a 10 per cent share. Western investors were still willing to offer Russian companies hefty loans as well. In early December, Yukos, the oil company which was part of the Menatep group, raised $1bn to help finance its purchase of Eastern Oil, a smaller Russian oil firm.

This guardedly confident mood continued into the New Year, as Moscow endured one of its periodic snaps of bitter cold with temperatures plummeting below −30 degrees Celsius. The IMF gave the Russian economy its seal of approval, and a much needed lump sum of ready cash, by releasing the frozen loan tranche and extending its Russian lending programme for an extra year. The conventional wisdom started to conclude that the Russian government had received a salutary shock at the end of 1997, but was now setting its house in order. Fitch IBCA, one of the big international rating agencies, reflected that prevailing sentiment when in early March it withdrew a warning that it might downgrade its assessment of Russia risk.

As the Asian threat appeared to subside, Moscow's leading players began to go back to business as usual. All around them, emerging market economies were collapsing and many observers were blaming crony capitalism for their demise. But in Russia, the nouveaux riches serenely continued to play by the old rules.

I caught a glimpse of how Moscow continued to operate one morning in March when I was in Kitaigorod, literally Chinatown, a comforting warren of narrow, twisting streets and elegant, refreshingly unSoviet buildings which had been the commercial quarter in medieval Muscovy. Now one of the New Russia's leading clans of merchant princes, the Menatep group had a cluster of offices here in a pretty cobbled courtyard, its entrance bristling with security. I was there for an informal briefing from one of the senior Menatep executives. As usual, our discussion was punctuated by the urgent summons of his mobile telephone and, as was quite often the case, those terse one-sided conversations were far more interesting than anything I managed to elicit with my own questions.

My eavesdropping efforts became particularly keen when I heard one of the callers addressed as Borya, a common Russian nickname for Boris, and began to suspect that Berezovsky was on the other end of the line. The rush of disjointed phrases which followed was even more intriguing: 'So, it's $200,000 each?' 'That's fine,' 'Is it all right with Gus [a nickname for Gusinsky]?' 'Another $150,000 for the plane?' 'Great, that makes it $250,000 each? No problem.' 'You take care of the inscription. Make sure it says something about the oligarchs.' 'That's great, hahaha [a series of deep chuckles followed].'

Unable to contain my curiosity, I broke my usual pose of disinterested discretion and asked what the conversation had been about. My nosiness was richly rewarded. The caller had indeed been Berezovsky and he and the Menatep executive were, of all things, arranging a birthday gift for Prime Minister Chernomyrdin who would turn 60 on 9 April. So important a man and so meaningful a milestone called for a very special present and Berezovsky, the Menatep group and Gusinsky had risen to the occasion. In addition to his well-known predilections for hunting hibernating bear-cubs and snow-mobiling, Chernomyrdin had a less publicised fondness for old cars. The troika of oligarchs had tracked down a vintage Mercedes, 'in a German museum or something', which was exactly as old as the prime minister. The car itself cost $600,000, plus an additional $150,000 to fly it to Russia, the only safe way to transport so old a vehicle. That brought the total price tag per oligarch to $250,000. As a finishing touch, the car was to be fitted with a plaque inscribed: 'To Viktor Stepanovich, from the grateful oligarchs.' 'You see,' the Menatep executive told me with a smile, 'we do have a sense of humour. We know how to laugh at ourselves.'

But, even as the oligarchs were arranging a tangible sign of their gratitude to Viktor Stepanovich, at least some of them were part of a back-room cabal agitating to have him sacked. Berezovsky, now again installed in a quasi-official government role as unpaid adviser to Yumashev, the Kremlin chief of staff, was one of the chief anti-Chernomyrdin schemers: he hoped to replace the prime minister with his own man. His machinations reinforced the president's own growing concerns. Yeltsin had always been the worst kind of boss, the sort who slapped down his subordinates the minute they seemed to grow too strong or too independent. That seemed to be what was happening with the stolid but reliable Chernomyrdin. Just as in 1996, when the Moscow elites had rallied round a sick and deeply unpopular Yeltsin, it was starting to look as if in 2000 Chernomyrdin might become the consensus candidate of the establishment.

In the third week of March, Yeltsin's simmering resentment came to a boil. As usual, the president had been feeling under the weather and Chernomyrdin had taken his place at a summit of Black Sea heads of state. The unfortunate understudy had performed his stand-in role too well and Yeltsin decided to take action. That Saturday, on 21 March, Yeltsin summoned Chernomyrdin for one of their regular meetings at the president's dacha. Chernomyrdin drove over expecting the usual – a few cups of tea, maybe a surreptitious shot of vodka, and a discussion of the main political and economic issues of the day. He was one of Yeltsin's longest-serving ministers and a comrade of more than three decades' standing; the two men had first met in the 1960s, when Yeltsin was working in provincial government in the Urals and Chernomyrdin was a Gazprom middle-manager in neighbouring western Siberia.

But this time Yeltsin had an unpleasant surprise for his old colleague: he was sacked. (For good measure, Yeltsin decided simultaneously to fire Chubais.) With Chernomyrdin gone, panic of another sort began in the presidential entourage. Who would be the next prime minister? Berezovsky – feeling invincible now that he had succeeded in forcing Chernomyrdin's ouster – felt confident that his ally, Ivan Rybkin, former speaker of the Duma, would prevail. But here, as so often, Berezovsky overreached himself. Rival Kremlin factions, including the young reformers, began their own lobbying campaign to prevent the government from falling completely under the oligarchs' sway. One candidate they started to push was Sergei Kiriyenko, the practically unknown 35-year-old businessman whom Nemtsov had brought with him to Moscow a year earlier. Kiriyenko's politics were progressive, his manner was conciliatory and, perhaps most important of all, he was insignificant and inoffensive enough to sneak in under Berezovsky's radar.

By Sunday night, Berezovsky had been outfoxed and the deal was done. Yeltsin had chosen Kiriyenko as his next prime minister; all that was left was to tell Kiriyenko himself. The fuel and energy minister, nicknamed 'Bambi' in some circles for his baby-face and gentle smile, was summoned to the Kremlin for an early morning meeting. A stunned Kiriyenko later left the hour-long audience as Russia's prime minister designate. When questioned by equally astonished journalists about his sudden elevation, he cheerfully admitted: 'I'm as surprised as you guys are.'

At least at first, plucking a new prime minister out of relative obscurity seemed to be another demonstration of Yeltsin's enduring political shrewdness. As a newcomer, Kiriyenko had not yet managed to accumulate too many political enemies in Moscow or reveal too many flaws. Both the young reformers and the oligarchs who despised them lavished Kiriyenko with praise. Headstrong regional bosses, with little affection for the central government, nodded their approval. Even the court jester of Russian politics, Vladimir Zhirinovsky, appeared to be a fan.

But Kiriyenko's emollient temper and chameleon character were not enough to tame the savage and long-standing conflicts in Russian high politics. Determined as usual to assert his supreme authority, Yeltsin presented the unknown prime minister designate to the communist-dominated parliament as a *fait accompli*, refusing to bargain with the legislators about cabinet posts or government policy. Thanks to his bespoke constitution which granted huge powers to the president, Yeltsin inevitably won the resulting month-long stand-off, but it was victory at a steep price.

The battle forever soured the initially encouraging relations between the new prime minister and the Duma. Moreover, although Kiriyenko had dozens of political friends, the parliamentary battle had shown he had no absolute allies. In the end, his only source of support had been the Kremlin. This absolute dependence of the prime minister on the president was dangerous for them both: if ever Yeltsin's favour wavered, Kiriyenko could be gone in a minute; and if ever Kiriyenko made a mistake, Yeltsin, as his first and only patron, would immediately share the blame.

Worst of all, the whole prime-ministerial drama consumed more than a month of valuable political time. At a moment when the nation should have been bracing itself for the next wave of the Asian economic crisis, Russia was absorbed in domestic politics. Only in early May, with Kiriyenko traumatically but firmly installed as prime minister, did Moscow again turn its attention to the economy.

As the new prime minister began to pick up the reins of government, the initial forecasts were almost as enthusiastic as they had been a year earlier when the young reformers were reinstalled in the cabinet. During the bruising confirmation struggle, the communists had dubbed Kiriyenko 'Gaidarchik', or 'little Gaidar'. The pro-market tendencies which had horrified the communists delighted the young reformers and Western financial analysts. Kiriyenko, everyone began to hope, would be a sort of Gaidar-lite, committed to the same principles as the young reformers but less politically abrasive and, most important of all, installed as a fully-fledged prime minister.

Better yet, Kiriyenko was free of the young reformers' greatest millstone – their controversial past. As a political newcomer, he was not part of the tortured relationship with the oligarchs and had an opportunity to cleanly and simply inaugurate a new era in which big business and government kept their distance. To the oligarchs' deep disgust, that is precisely what he set out to do. Yeltsin's sole instruction to him upon taking office was to avoid becoming entangled with the oligarchs. To begin with at least, Kiriyenko faithfully followed the president's orders.

'We tried to help him, but he decided strictly to comply with the desires of the president,' Khodorkovsky told me. 'He [Kiriyenko] said, "I will take a position of equal distance from each of the oligarchs, I will not hire your people."'

Kiriyenko decided to keep his distance from the young reformers as well. Many retained their old jobs in the new cabinet, or were given new ones. But, perhaps not surprisingly, Kiriyenko was reluctant to give himself over fully to this united, experienced team, who had a tendency to view him as a probably well-meaning but certainly naïve newcomer.

In less turbulent times, Kiriyenko might have been able to afford the luxury of independence. He could have asserted his control over the government gradually, taking a few months to discover who were the most useful allies and to learn how the machinery of state operated. But time was one thing Kiriyenko did not have. No sooner had he been confirmed in office than the fragile Russian market economy again began to tremble.

Oil prices continued to soften, weakening some of Russia's most important companies and depressing tax revenues. The political environment was growing more tense as well. Wage arrears again began to mount and Russia's normally quiescent workers finally discovered a way of getting the Kremlin's attention: they began to stage wildcat protests, blocking the nation's major railway arteries.

The most devastating omen came at the end of the month, on 26 May, when a humiliated Russian government announced that it had been unable to find a single bidder for Rosneft, the largest oil company yet to be privatised. Less than a year earlier, the contest for Sviazinvest had been fierce; the battle for Rosneft had been expected to be at least as intense – and to bring the cash-strapped treasury at least $2.1bn in revenues. But now, no one was interested in buying.

Investors pressed the panic button. The next day, which traders would dub Black Wednesday, share prices plummeted by more than 10 per cent. The crash brought the stock market down 40 per cent since the beginning of the month and to less than half its value since the start of the year. Yields on treasury bills soared above 80 per cent. The rouble, rocked by fears of devaluation, edged below the central bank's daily target corridor and the Russian authorities were forced to resort to desperate measures. Throughout the spring, interest rates had gently fallen from their January peak of 42 per cent to an almost reasonable (for Russia) 30 per cent. But in mid-May, the central bank had reluctantly hoisted them back up to 50 per cent. On 27 May, the bank was compelled to drop all semblance of business as usual and raise them again, this time to an emergency level of 150 per cent.

The collapse in investor confidence focused attention on Russia's government debt burden – a problem which dated back to 1994 when the young reformers took what I termed the Grand Debt Gamble. This was their high-risk response to a seemingly insurmountable economic challenge: to give the nascent market economy half a chance, they needed to rein in inflation and stabilise the rouble. But doing that meant balancing the budget, a politically impossible task at the time. So the young reformers took the Grand Debt Gamble: they plugged the holes in the budget by borrowing money at home and abroad. To entice investors, they offered outrageously high returns, at times even exceeding 200 per cent annually. It was a high price to pay, but they accepted it with open eyes. They took the same attitude as the Internet entrepreneur who maxes out his credit cards to keep his company running in the hungry days before its IPO. If the company turns into an iVillage or a Hotmail, paying Visa's usurious rates of interest for a few months becomes insignificant. If the company flops, it doesn't matter too much either, because our young entrepreneur will probably go bankrupt anyway.

The Grand Debt Gamble involved the same kind of all-or-nothing calculation. If the bet worked, then within a few years the Russian economy would bloom into growth. An expanding economy would bring painlessly increased tax revenues and lower interest rates, allowing Russia effortlessly to pay off the debt contracted during the lean years. But if the gamble didn't work, Russia would go broke: a weak economy would grow ever weaker under the strain of its heavy debt, forcing up interest rates and sapping government resources until, finally, investors lost confidence in the whole project and pulled out their money.

In early 1997, it had still looked as if the Grand Debt Gamble was going to pay off. But by early 1998, the bet had begun to go badly wrong. The economy wasn't growing yet, tax revenues were drying up and the debt just kept getting higher and higher. By May, the government had amassed $140bn of hard-currency debt and $60bn of domestically-traded rouble debt. The pay-back schedule was punishing: throughout the summer, Russia needed to redeem $1–$1.5bn of debt a week. With total cash tax revenues running at less than $3bn a month, even if the government devoted every kopek it collected to paying its debts, it would go bust.

The obvious solution – and the one the government had been relying on for the past few years – was to pay off maturing bonds by issuing new ones. The only catch was that, as investor confidence collapsed, Russia was finding it harder and harder, and more and more expensive, to raise new money. By the end of May, the government was paying more than 80 per cent on its rouble denominated domestic bonds. The high rates added to the government's debt burden, further depressed investor confidence and stifled prospects of economic growth. The situation had become unsustainable.

One option was to devalue the rouble. If it was willing to allow the rouble to fall, the government could print some money to clear its domestic debt. A weaker rouble might also ease the pressure on the central bank, whose reserves had fallen from more than $20bn in 1997 to $14.5bn in May 1998 in the battle to defend the faltering Russian currency. Russian exporters, whose revenues were in dollars and whose costs, including tax bills, were in roubles, also stood to benefit from a devaluation. In the spring of 1998 many of them, including those oligarchs whose principal business was oil, began to lobby the government to let the rouble slide.

Yet the risks of devaluation, as both the IMF and the young reformers warned, were tremendous. The stable rouble and relatively low inflation were among the chief achievements of seven difficult years of reform. They were also two of the only anchors of public confidence in the still fragile and unfamiliar market economy. If the Russian authorities let the rouble go, the centre might not hold.

Unable to pay its bills but terrified of devaluing its currency, the Kremlin had only one choice – to turn to the West for help. As usual Chubais, with the president's personal mandate, was dispatched to make the initial request. Just two months earlier, Chubais had lost his cabinet seat. But the Russian establishment, which still viewed the workings of Western institutions as a mysterious affair, felt that he had an almost magical knack for negotiating with the IMF and the US Treasury. So, together with Sergei Vasiliev, two days after Moscow's Black Wednesday, in the last weekend in May Chubais flew to Washington D.C.

There, the two reformers met the world's bankers of last resort: Stanley Fischer, the deputy head of the IMF, and James Wolfensohn, the head of the World Bank. On Saturday morning Chubais and Vasiliev, accompanied by a minder from the Russian embassy, had breakfast at home with Strobe Talbott, deputy secretary of state, one of Clinton's

Oxford house-mates and a lifelong Russophile. Next the three went over to the home of Larry Summers, then deputy head of the US Treasury and probably the most influential voice in shaping American economic policy towards the rest of the world. Key members of his team – including David Lipton, the Under Secretary for international affairs and a long-time supporter of Russia's market transition – were there. Over bagels and orange juice – and for Summers his trademark Diet Coke – Chubais made his pitch. He didn't ask directly for money; instead, he said Russia needed a clear and public pledge of support if things got worse. The meeting was cordial, but Summers replied with a stern caution. Western money alone would not save Russia. To win back investor confidence, the Russian government would need swiftly to formulate and implement a strong and concerted new reform plan.

The warning voiced, the Americans promised to give Chubais what he wanted and they delivered the very next day. On Sunday, President Bill Clinton promised to come to Russia's aid: 'The United States endorses additional conditional financial support from the international financial institutions, as necessary, to promote stability, structural reforms and growth in Russia.' Implicit in that statement was a pledge of hard cash. Vasiliev and Chubais left Washington confident that the IMF and the G-7 would come up with a $10bn fund to bail their country out.

Chubais' visit left his American supporters feeling very anxious. 'I was scared shitless,' admitted Lipton, who feared the Asian financial crisis was about to consume Russia. But back in Moscow, the sense of urgency seemed to abate. Kiriyenko placidly announced, 'I am absolutely certain that the situation is under control,' and he seemed to believe it. Instead of working round the clock to transform Clinton's promise into instant hard cash, the novice Kiriyenko administration took its time.

'We achieved a very big result [in Washington],' fumed the normally good-natured Vasiliev. 'But unfortunately, Chubais was not in the government and in the government there were no people who knew how to make it happen. It all stalled.'

Yeltsin's mercurial decision to appoint a new cabinet in the midst of a financial crisis was taking its toll. Horrified by the Kiriyenko administration's leisurely attitude, and worried that the Grand Debt Gamble was about to be lost, the new Russian establishment decided to act. Kiriyenko's appointment had been an effort to push the weird marriage of the oligarchs and the young reformers out of power. But by mid-June, the establishment had had enough. Everything Russia had achieved since the collapse of communism was in jeopardy, and the adults no longer trusted Kiriyenko to fend off total collapse.

On 16 June, Berezovsky called a meeting at the Logovaz Clubhouse. He invited the usual motley crew of oligarchs and their most senior executives: Khodorkovsky, Nevzlin, Shakhnovsky, and Kagalovsky from Menatep, Potanin from Oneximbank, Friedman and Aven from the Alfa group, Zverev from the Most group, and Smolensky from Stolichny. Chubais was there as well, along with Aleksandr Shokhin, an economist and politician who was part of the young reformer team but had always been at its margins.

Chubais kicked off the discussion with a pessimistic assessment of Russia's economic condition. The Grand Debt Gamble, he said, was falling apart and Russia might be forced to default on its government debt, an extreme measure which would set back the country's economic development by a decade. The only solution, he argued, was a new round of emergency talks with the IMF and the G-7. They must be persuaded immediately to grant Russia $35bn to avert economic disaster. The oligarchs agreed. The problem, they felt, was the Kiriyenko government which was, as one of the oligarchs put it, 'bloodless' – too weak and immature to cope with the mounting crisis.

A more formidable figure, someone with steely nerves, a sophisticated understanding of the economy and international stature, was needed to lead the crucial talks. Chubais proposed Gaidar, suggesting he be made first deputy prime minister and head of Russia's international negotiating team. The oligarchs were aghast. 'We said we wouldn't be able to hold back the fury of the narod [the people] if we appointed someone they hated as much as Gaidar,' Khodorkovsky told me. Someone else proposed Shokhin, leader of Our Home is Russia, the pro-government faction in the parliament. This time, it was Chubais who furiously objected. 'Chubais exploded into a savage tirade, with foul language,' Zverev said. Inevitably, Chubais himself was suggested for the job but he demurred: he had had enough of government, he was too busy with his new job as head of the national power company, Gaidar was really the right man.

To settle matters, the oligarchs held a secret ballot. Chubais was the runaway favourite and after some cajoling he agreed to become the official head of Russia's negotiations with international financial organ-isations. Berezovsky pressed the white button at the centre of the conference table to summon a lackey, and soon everyone held an elegant flute of chilled champagne. The oligarchs raised their glasses in a double toast: it was Chubais's 43rd birthday, so they wished him many happy returns. They also, with perhaps a little more passion, wished him luck in his latest mission impossible.

Having come to their own collective assessment of Russia's financial situation and appointed a man to handle it, the oligarchs now set about imposing their will on the government. The group, minus Chubais and Shokhin, went straight from Berezovsky's Logovaz Clubhouse to the Kremlin where they met with Yumashev; as they had expected, he fully backed their plan. A few hours later, the calvacade headed off to Volynskoe, a leafy government dacha complex within city limits where the prime minister often retired for more privacy and comfort than he could get in his White House office. Kiriyenko was waiting for them and he too agreed with both their general assessment of the situation and their idea of appointing Chubais as Russia's chief negotiator. Before leaving Volynskoe, the oligarchs agreed to meet Kiriyenko there again two days later. This time, they would bring a written action plan – to be drafted by Potanin – and brief the prime minister on how the govern-ment should handle the financial crisis over the next few weeks.

Politically and economically, Chubais' birthday was a turning point. Most of the players who gathered at Berezovsky's Logovaz Clubhouse that bright Tuesday morning had been mortal enemies just a few months before. Potanin and Berezovsky and the Most group had been at daggers drawn following the controversial sale of Sviazinvest. Chubais had been on even worse terms with most of the oligarchs. Now, brought together by a common danger, these old gladiators had gathered in one room to discuss how they might combine to avert the biggest disaster yet to threaten Russia's market economy. Seven years after the collapse of communism, the new Russian establishment was still painfully narrow, so small that most of it could comfortably fit around the dainty white conference table in the Logovaz mansion.

Even more strikingly, the reunited 1996 coalition was restored to kissing and advising terms with the government. Kiriyenko had come into office determined to make a break with the old, scarred and com-promised establishment but by the middle of June, the economic crisis had broken down his resolve. 'In the end, he gathered the oligarchs to himself,' Khodorkovsky told me. Once again they were walking the corridors of power, invited singly and in groups to share their views with the prime minister and his cabinet.

The young reformers were back, too. Chubais again had an official post and the Gaidar brain-trust, which had served as a sort of working centre for the government in 1997, started to play an active role. Most Russians loathed both the oligarchs and the young reformers and blamed the two tribes, with varying justification, for the country's woes. But, somehow, the Russian government seemed unable to do without them. This small, feuding, self-interested group alone seemed to possess the will, the money and the chutzpah to presume to lead Russia at its moments of greatest uncertainty.

On 13 July, Chubais and the IMF delivered. With a bit of nudging from the US Treasury, the Fund announced a massive bail-out package: Russia would get $22.6bn over the next two years from the IMF and other international financial institutions. The first tranche, a walloping $4.8bn, was dispersed in the last week of July. The money came hand-in-hand with a massive debt-restructuring deal designed to lighten the short-term financial burden on Russia. Under the complex scheme, managed by Goldman Sachs, the Russian government swapped more than $8bn worth of short-term GKOs – as Russian government rouble-denominated, short-term bonds were known – for longer-term securities, mostly 7- and 20-year eurobonds. At a stroke, the two measures significantly eased the pressure on Moscow. The IMF had bought the Kremlin precious breathing space. If the government, as it promised, acted decisively over the next few months – slashing its budget deficit, boosting tax collection and liberalising economic activity – maybe the looming financial crisis could be averted. This was, the IMF warned, Russia's last chance.

At first, it seemed to be working. When US Vice-president Al Gore came to Moscow at the end of July, the Russian leadership (including Chubais) told him the IMF money had bought the economy absolute safety until October. Middle-class Russians, a cynical lot who had only recently grown trusting enough to deposit their money in bank accounts, made the same calculation. When I spoke to sociologist Igor

Bunin a few days after the debt deal, his chief preoccupation was the security of his foundation's bank deposits. Thanks to the IMF, he was confident that the rouble would definitely hold until the end of the summer. 'Just to be safe, I'll withdraw our money at the end of August,' Bunin told me, 'but we'll pay a penalty if we take it out before August 28. Now, though, I'm sure it's all right to wait until then.'

The government was ecstatic. Russia seemed to have scraped by one more time, and its leaders had the invincible swagger of the gambler whose luck never runs out.

But not everyone was quite so cocksure. As the bail-out package was being negotiated, some of the more cynical economists in the IMF team jestingly coined a new acronym for the programme – FIEF, or Foreign Investor Exit Facility. Their in-joke was based on the one fear which haunted the plan: the idea behind the Western bail-out was to give the Kremlin enough money to overcome its short-term cash-flow problems and restore confidence in what Russia-sympathisers still saw as a basically sound economy. But what if, sceptics asked from the very start, the rescue package had exactly the opposite effect? Maybe instead of luring in new investors, the Western money would make it easier for the old investors to get out without losing their shirts.

As the first rush of euphoria subsided, the IMF team's joke turned out to be horribly prescient. Foreign investors couldn't get out fast enough. 'Everybody thought that the big announcement was going to solve Russia's big problems,' Jordan recalled. 'But that's total hogwash, because all everybody used it for was an exit out. Everybody felt like . . . Look, while we've got four billion let's get out. The first guy out is the smartest.'

By the beginning of August, the rush to the door had become a stampede and the Russian economy was being crushed. The oligarchs realised it was no longer a question of *if* the financial system would crash, but merely of *when*. Mikhail Friedman telephoned Chubais to say the game was up and to urge him to announce a controlled, intentional devaluation rather than wait for the invisible hand to come crashing down on the Russian markets. But the Russian authorities didn't want to believe that their rescue plan was not working. Chubais and Sergei Dubinin, chairman of the Central Bank, went abroad on holiday. Closer to home, Yeltsin went on vacation too. While the government's top officials relaxed, the investor exodus, a financial ebola virus, began to eat away at the soft underbelly of Russia's young market economy.

By the second week of August, the disease had turned terminal. On Tuesday morning, 11 August, I was at Renaissance Capital in one of the gleaming chrome and glass office buildings which had mushroomed in 1997. At about 11 a.m. my conversation with Stephen Jennings, one of the bank's founders, was interrupted by an anxious young trader who came racing to the door and asked for a private word with his boss. A few minutes later Jennings came back, wearing the ambivalent expression half-way between victory and defeat of a man whose bleak predictions have come true. The share prices of Russian blue-chip companies had dropped by 10–12 per cent in the first hour of trading. The stock market had had to be temporarily closed because trades could not be settled.

'I think this could be the end,' he told me. We had been talking about the loans-for-shares scheme and the strange way in which Russia's newly minted capitalist system had been created. To Jennings, the coming economic meltdown was a fitting dénouement: 'They [the oligarchs] were given these huge companies and they have shown they couldn't manage them. This is the end of that drama.'

In the afternoon, things got worse. Two major Russian banks, SBS-Agro, as the enlarged Stolichny bank had been renamed, and Inkombank, failed to meet margin calls. The pair of wobbling institutions had been founded and were controlled by two of the lesser oligarchs: Smolensky and Vinogradov, respectively. Like everyone else, in the last eighteen months the two bankers had rushed to take advantage of the new foreign enthusiasm for lending to Russia at relatively low rates. They had secured their hard-currency loans with the only collateral they had, Russian stocks and bonds. As Russia's debt and equity markets collapsed, the value of this collateral plummeted, prompting automatic margin calls from their foreign lenders. By 11 August, SBS-Agro and Inkombank could no longer keep up with the constant pressure for more money. After consulting with their foreign partners, they defaulted on the latest margin call. Two of Russia's banking giants had surrendered to the financial crisis.

On Wednesday, the situation deteriorated still further. SBS-Agro and Inkombank were two of the cornerstones of the Russian banking system, intimately connected with the other big domestic banks through a web of mutual loans. With both of them in default and a third major bank, Imperial, teetering on the brink, other players began to be pulled down as well. That morning, Nevzlin, a senior Menatep executive, told me that SBS-Agro and Imperial had defaulted on their loans from Menatep. All the other main Russian banks were also being squeezed by defaults from the crippled troika. At the same time, they were all facing margin calls of their own from their foreign creditors. It was a matter of days, if not hours, before the banking system collapsed. Menatep, Nevzlin said, was 'squeezing' the Central Bank to cover the domestic defaults, but Russia's bank of last resort was running out of money too. I asked him if he thought that, in the end, the government would bail out the biggest banks. Not this time, was the doleful reply.

By now, the panic among Russian and foreign businessmen was palpable. Some of them were frantic, struggling to make as many provisions as possible ahead of the now inevitable storm. Others had settled into a very Russian numb stoicism: there was nothing more to be done but wait for the coming beating. The pathetic fallacy had gone to work on the weather as well: it was damp, grey and brooding, almost exactly like the hours before a surly autumn squall.

Bizarrely, one place which seemed oblivious to the tension was what should have been Russia's nerve centre – the Kremlin. On Wednesday afternoon, I went in to see Aleksandr Livshits, a former minister of finance who had moved to the job of the president's economic adviser. The dark granite fortress which housed the presidential administration on Staraya Ploshchad was strangely quiet. Everyone was away on their summer holidays, Livshits' secretary explained. When Livshits invited me into his office, I apologised profusely for taking up his time on such a difficult day for the Russian economy. Yeltsin's chief economic counsellor brushed my comments aside. 'And what day is not difficult for Russia?' he asked placidly. 'Don't worry, today is no worse for us than any other day.'

By contrast, the US government was far less philosophical – particularly David Lipton, the Treasury's point-man on Russia. An intense, sturdy man, with floppy dark hair and bushy eyebrows that operated like facial exclamation marks, Lipton was one of the West's true believers in Russia's market transition. He had been involved from the very beginning, first as an academic adviser and then as part of the US administration. Since late July, Lipton had been taking worried calls from investment bankers in Moscow, London and New York warning him that the IMF package wasn't working. 'By the last day of July, people were no longer saying that Russia was going to make it to the next IMF disbursement,' he told me.

Worried, Lipton lobbied his bosses to send him to Moscow and on Wednesday afternoon he arrived at Sheremetyevo airport prepared to tell his old friends that Uncle Sam thought the game might be up. To his outrage, many of the people he had come to see were on vacation: Chubais was touring the green Irish countryside, thinking about buying himself a castle; Dubinin, chairman of the central bank, was in northern Italy. Lipton thought their absence 'was more than a little bit strange'. It set the tone for the oddest two days he had ever spent in the Russian capital, 48 hours of meetings he would later compare with his encounters with the opaque and guarded politicians of Japan. Normally querulous, warmhearted and indiscreet, this time the entire Russian economic leadership seemed to be woodenly reading from the same script.

Lipton was most disappointed by Zadornov, the minister of finance. 'He was so focused on the budget, he didn't see this coming,' Lipton told me. 'He was formulaic and wrong.' Kiriyenko and the central bank authorities had a similarly blinkered point of view. Even Gaidar, Russia's smartest economist and a man Lipton deeply respected, stuck to the party line. Over supper with Lipton on Wednesday night, Gaidar assured him that the Russians had counted their money and, thanks to the IMF support, were confident they would be able to meet their punishing weekly schedule of debt payments well into the autumn. In reply, Lipton warned his host that the Russians were looking at the wrong issue. National survival in an economic crisis was not just a simple matter of housekeeping, of having enough cash to pay the weekly bills. It was also a more elusive question of confidence, and that was vanishing fast, with devastating effects on the national currency. That afternoon, a central bank official had told Lipton that in the first eight business days of August the central bank had haemorrhaged $300m a day, depleting $2.4bn of its reserves since the beginning of the month. No one trusted the rouble any more and, with less than $18bn in gold and hard currency left, the central bank would not be able to hold out against the doubters for much longer.

By Thursday, the rouble was in even direr straits. That morning, the *Financial Times* published an explosive letter by George Soros in which this major investor in Russia described the internal rot: banks unable to meet margin calls, debt and equity prices falling precipitously, the paralysis of the stock market. The Russian financial meltdown, Soros diagnosed, had reached 'the terminal phase'. Already, a devaluation of the rouble of 15 to 25 per cent was inevitable, and an additional Western rescue package of $15bn was urgently required. Otherwise, Soros warned, Russia's nascent market economy would collapse into either massive default or hyper-inflation. The political and financial consequences would be 'devastating'.

Over the next four days, as Soros' predictions came horribly to life, some accused him of provoking the catastrophe he had foretold. And, indeed, Soros was a currency-hunter of some repute: in Britain he was still known as 'The Man Who Broke the Bank of England' for his lucrative bet against the pound in 1992. But with the rouble, Soros was more witness than assassin. By the time his piece was published, the Russian currency was already dying.

The Russian financial system went into deeper convulsions as Soros' letter hit a few select breakfast tables in Moscow and many more in Tokyo, London and New York. Share prices plunged a further 15 per cent, triggering the circuit-breakers which automatically halt trading. Short-term bond yields spiked above 100 per cent. Western investment bankers, who for the past couple of years had been delightedly mining the little-known Klondike of the Russian equity boom, realised that the party was over. Yet even as the Electronic Herd galloped off, the Russian government remained resolutely, even obstinately, calm. On Thursday afternoon I visited the office of Charlie Ryan, the young American who had established one of Moscow's leading investment banks. Ryan was convinced 'this could be the end', and his subordinates were in a controlled panic as they sought to make sure all their positions were closed and guarded against counter-party risk.

But in the middle of our conversation, when he took a telephone call from Boris Fyodorov, his former business partner and now head of the Russian tax service, Ryan learned that the Russian government was still standing firm: there would be no devaluation. Kiriyenko took the same line on television that evening. The only problem, the prime minister insisted, was 'investor psychosis'. The government was confident it would ride out the storm.

Behind closed doors, however, Kiriyenko was being told ever more urgently that the government's position was untenable. The harshest warning had come that afternoon from Lipton who, frustrated by the complacency of the Russian officials he had been talking to, was undiplomatically direct. 'I tried to be very sharp,' Lipton recalled. As he meekly submitted to the lecture from a US under-secretary, Kiriyenko suddenly seemed scared and tired. A small man dwarfed by the huge old-fashioned decor of his office, Kiriyenko looked diminished, intimidated by the faceless forces mounting a ravaging assault on his country's economy.

On the streets, things were still quiet. As usual, Moscow had emptied for the summer. The unseasonably cold, damp weather and overcast skies lent the capital a vaguely funereal air, but the mood was sleepy, not panicky. A trickle of cautious or well-informed citizens was withdrawing its money from bank accounts and changing roubles to dollars, but there was no mass exodus – yet. Changing money myself in the town centre on Thursday afternoon, there were just three people ahead of me in the queue.

On Friday morning, though, the financial crisis finally became impossible for the government or the people to ignore. Imperial, one of the three large Russian banks which had been unable to meet some of its obligations earlier in the week, defaulted on a syndicated loan, a far more serious breach than failing to meet a margin call. The bank was dead and its employees turned into vultures – packing up computers, unplugging telephones, even tearing light fixtures off the walls before leaving their offices for good.

The crisis, which on Wednesday night Gaidar had told Lipton was restricted to a narrow elite, began to spread to the rest of the country. For a few days, Russian newspapers had been carrying stories about the liquidity crunch in the banking sector. On Friday the public began to respond, with mass withdrawals from SBS-Agro and Sberbank, the state-owned savings bank. Things could only get worse. Several banks had big loan payments coming up in the next week which they would be unable to meet. The state was on the brink of bankruptcy, too. As the panic spread to the population, the central bank estimated it would have to spend $1bn on Monday alone to prop up the rouble within its official corridor of no less than Rbs 6.2 to the dollar. The weekly $1bn-plus bond payments, which the government had calculated it could meet until the autumn, were a further inexorable drain.

The oligarchs and the cabinet ministers pressed the panic button. Chubais and Dubinin were urgently summoned back to Moscow and a marathon series of meetings began. The first emergency council was on Friday evening at the central bank, a gracious cream-coloured mansion. In his high-ceilinged, chandeliered office, Dubinin met the main commercial bankers, many of them oligarchs, to consider if the banking system could be saved. The oligarchs pressed him to make a public pledge to fully redeem their GKO portfolios. If the central bank and the government did that, the businessmen argued, investor confidence might be shored up and perhaps the strongest banks would survive the liquidity crisis.

But the cash-strapped central bank refused to make a promise which it was increasingly afraid it could not keep. Unfortunately, Yeltsin had no such reservations. Never a details man, in seven torturous years of market reforms Yeltsin had been won over to a few basic principles: privatisation was good, inflation was bad and a strong and stable rouble was the only foundation upon which economic growth could be built. Once convinced, he clung to these three articles of faith with the naïve but steely conviction with which his unschooled peasant ancestors had believed in the mystical Orthodox God. Throughout the crisis, his reformist advisers had assured him that the creed to which they had converted him was truer than ever. Indeed, as a complacent Livshits had told me on Wednesday afternoon, they had argued that no matter what the pressures, the government must defend the rouble because otherwise the entire financial system would collapse.

Thus schooled, on Friday afternoon Yeltsin did what he always did in a crisis – he came out slugging. 'There will be no devaluations of the rouble,' the president declared. 'I say it firmly and clearly. It is not just my fantasy. Everything has been calculated.' In political battles, Yeltsin's take-no-prisoners aggression invariably cowed his opponents into submission; but this time the Kremlin leader was fighting an invisible opponent and one which he himself had created: the ruthlessly rational market economy. And the market, as Adam Smith had observed two hundred years earlier, could not be regulated by kings and ministers. Yeltsin's final defiant bellow had no effect but to embarrass the president. On Saturday morning, the frantic crisis meetings continued.

The crucial gathering was at noon in Kiriyenko's dacha outside Moscow. The prime minister had assembled the key government players: Dubinin and his top deputy at the Central Bank, Sergei Aleksashenko, Mikhail Zadornov, the minister of finance, and Chubais. Gaidar was there too.

Kiriyenko began the discussion by admitting that the government was broke. After a long, hard fight, central bank reserves had fallen too low to defend the rouble any further. Devaluation, which the young reformers had been insisting for months would be the death of Russia's nascent market economy, was inevitable. One of the horrible knock-on effects of devaluation would be to make it even more difficult for the government to meet its debt payments. With the rouble plummeting, it would be impossible for the government to attract new buyers into the domestic debt market. Without new money, the government would be unable to pay off its old debts.

That left Russia with just two choices, the assembled ministers and advisers agreed. One would be to print enough roubles to pay off the debt; but the Russians feared that such a huge expansion of the monetary supply would lead to hyper-inflation and an almost unstoppable collapse of the rouble. Russia's fledgling market economy would be completely undermined and the country would face a new debt crisis, this time with its foreign borrowings which would be impossible to repay with devalued roubles. The other option was simply not to pay back the domestic debt. By defaulting, the Russian government could step off the gruelling treadmill of weekly repayments; with its consequently lightened financial load, it might be able to control the rouble's fall and retain some vestige of faith in the national currency. The catch – and it was a huge one – was that a default on the domestic debt would mean robbing the very investors, both domestic and foreign, whose faith in Russian paper the government had so carefully cultivated over the past four years. Even so, with heavy hearts the men around Kiriyenko's table decided that a default and controlled devaluation were Russia's least terrible option.

'It was a bastardly, disgusting scenario,' Gaidar told me. 'But it was the tentative decision we took and which we started to work on.'

Meanwhile, the oligarchs had appeared on the scene. That morning, a group of them had met at Menatep's headquarters and then gone on to a meeting at the Central Bank. Afterwards, most of them migrated to the White House and became part of the blur of discussions and telephone calls which, over the next 36 hours, would transform the Russian economy. In the corridors of power on Saturday afternoon, for the first time the oligarchs learned that the government was seriously planning a twin devaluation and default on the domestic debt. They were outraged. Many had been pressing for devaluation for weeks if not months, but default was another matter altogether. Russian banks were among the principal holders of government paper and they would be wiped out if the state reneged. The oligarchs made a counter-threat.

'You know what we'll do? We will immediately block all the accounts of the Ministry of Finance through the Russian courts. Immediately. We are not Western banks, we won't pause for a minute,' the oligarchs warned. 'The courts would have definitely backed us,' Khodorkovsky later told me. The government 'would have had no chance'.

Desperate to appease the angry tycoons, the government – which had already been discussing ways of softening the blow for domestic banks – proposed a state-imposed moratorium on debt payments by commercial banks to their creditors. By the standards of international finance, it was a bizarre scheme but, in the pressure-cooker of the White House, it somehow made sense. The government had no choice but to stiffen its own banks; in exchange, the least it could do was to offer them an official shield against the claims of their foreign creditors. The oligarchs still didn't like it, but they at least agreed not to go to war against the government on Monday. 'In the end, bad as we might be, we won't fight our own government,' Khodorkovsky told me. 'But we knew it was the end of the Russian banks.'

The government, particularly the young reformers, still hoped against hope that there was one last chance to save the situation: more money from the West. In July, Fischer had insisted that the summer IMF package was the end of the line. On Wednesday and Thursday, Lipton had repeated that message. Even so, Chubais and Gaidar could not suppress the thought that, just maybe, if the G-7 realised how devastating a Russian financial collapse would be, a few more billion dollars could be found. 'We came to the conclusion that it [the situation] required further consultations between us and the G-7,' Gaidar told me. 'To be frank, I am convinced that if the G-7 and the IMF had fully understood what would happen after 17 August they would have helped. Just $7–10bn separated victory from defeat.'

But on Saturday night, those last tendrils of hope were firmly crushed. Gaidar had supper that evening with the IMF Russia team at the Liberal-Democratic Club in central Moscow. Over that meal, he realised there was no chance of further IMF support. Nonetheless, Gaidar outlined the government's tentative crisis plans to the fund's economists and promised to stay in touch over the weekend.

That evening, the Russians were in contact with the US Treasury as well. Lipton, who had just arrived back in Washington on Saturday morning after 'one of the worst flights in my life', took a phone call from Chubais almost as soon as he stepped through his front door. By then, Chubais, who had already been on the phone to Summers and Fischer, understood there would be no more Western money. But he wanted Lipton to know that the disaster he had predicted had struck and that the Russians were preparing to deal with it come Monday morning.

On Sunday, the Russian establishment's economic death watch in the White House continued. When they weren't frantically trying to cobble together a crisis programme, the key government officials seemed numb with shock. One young reformer walked into Chubais' office on Sunday morning to find him staring out of his wide window; he came up to his old friend's desk and launched into a monologue about what should be done. Five minutes into his spiel, a dazed Chubais turned to him, saying: 'Oh, hi, I didn't notice you were here.' Dubinin, the guardian of the rouble, was even more shattered. One Russian banker remembered walking into his office that weekend and finding the central bank chairman alone, laughing uncontrollably. Some of the oligarchs displayed a little more sangfroid: Potanin took a break from the tension at the White House that afternoon to go jet-skiing at his dacha complex.

For everyone, there was a sense of a frantic race against the clock. A huge, loose-lipped circle of government officials and businessmen now knew that Moscow planned to devalue the rouble and default on its debt. On Monday morning, the news would spread like wildfire and as soon as the markets opened everything Russian would take a horrific beating. The government had to be ready to announce its plan by 10 a.m. the next day. Cabinet ministers spent Sunday hammering out a three part plan: devaluation, default on the government's $40bn domestic debt and a moratorium on commercial debt repayment. By 6 p.m. it was time to break the news to the president, who had spent the weekend oblivious to the political drama while relaxing at the Rus, an official dacha north-west of Moscow. Chubais and Kiriyenko flew out by helicopter to see him.

The two men outlined the disastrous situation and explained their plan. But rather than present the president with a total *fait accompli*, in a clever piece of psychology they then offered him one choice. Either

they could let the devalued rouble float freely against foreign currencies, or they could establish a new, broader corridor against the dollar
to replace the band they would be breaking the next day. Yeltsin, who
had promised the nation that the rouble would not be devalued just two
days earlier, chose the second, less dramatic option. It was riskier – who
knew if the central bank would be able to keep the rouble above the
new level of Rbs 9.5 to the dollar? – but it offered the Kremlin a welcome political figleaf.

When they got back to the White House that evening, Kiriyenko and
Chubais summoned the milling oligarchs for a final meeting. It was
already past midnight when the pow-wow began, and by now there was
no time left for horse-trading. Kiriyenko was just giving the oligarchs
the courtesy of eight hours' early notice. Usually a rowdy, argumenta-
tive bunch, they listened in silence as the prime minister told them that
the Russian economy – *their* economy – was about to self-destruct.

But even as the government was informing the oligarchs of its final
plan, it was struggling to untangle a last-minute complication.
Throughout the weekend, Chubais had been in contact with the top
leadership of the IMF: Michel Camdessus, the managing director, who
was in Paris on the last day of his summer vacation, and Fischer, who
had rushed back home from a holiday on the Greek island of Mykonos.
Although Chubais understood that the IMF would not give Russia
additional financial support, he desperately wanted its seal of approval
for the Russian crisis measures. Securing the IMF's moral support now,
Chubais believed, would help the Russians to arrange new loans from
the fund in the future and might reassure Western investors. It could
also help to shield Chubais, Kiriyenko and the young reformers from
the political flak they were certain to face the next day.

Yet, at the eleventh hour, Camdessus balked. His officials in Moscow
had seen the oligarchs haunting the corridors of the White House, and
he was worried that in defaulting on its domestic debt the government
would discriminate against foreign investors while finding ways of pro-
tecting its own fat cats. He also wanted the government to take more
immediate political action to improve its public finances, which the
IMF all along had believed was the core of the problem. In July, the
Duma had failed to pass several measures on taxation and budgetary
reform which the IMF had argued were crucial to underpin its summer
bail-out package. Why not call an emergency session of the Duma

tomorrow, Camdessus asked Chubais, and get those measures passed, rather than merely stiff the foreigners? The middle-of-the-night discussion was sharp and at times acrimonious. At one point, according to a person present in the room, Camdessus threatened to expel Russia from the IMF, and at another he warned that the fund would have no choice but to publicly criticise the crisis package. The Russians were stunned by what they saw as Camdessus' last-minute U-turn.'It was a very big surprise,' Gaidar told me. 'It was very strange because everything had been worked out with them.'

But for Chubais, at this point there was no going back on the three-point plan. It had been agreed with Yeltsin and it would be impossible for him or for Kiriyenko to reopen discussions with an already furious president. After more than four hours of telephone haggling with Camdessus, Fischer, Summers and Robert Rubin, the US Secretary of the Treasury, Chubais secured the IMF's grudging support. The fund was obviously not thrilled with what the Russians were doing, but it would not openly condemn them either. By 4 a.m. the telephoning was over and the ministers and the oligarchs went home to brace themselves for disaster. A few hours later, a worn-out-looking Kiriyenko publicly announced that the government would allow the rouble to slide to Rbs 9.5 to the dollar, a fall of more than 50 per cent; would freeze all of its domestic bonds maturing to the end of the year; and would impose a moratorium on the payments of all foreign debts by Russian companies and citizens.

The impact was swift and devastating. The rouble plummeted, quickly breaking the new floor. By the end of the year it fell to below Rbls 20 to the dollar, less than a third of its value before the crisis. The banking system froze. Hundreds of thousands of middle-class Russians lost their jobs as companies slashed their work-forces. Shop shelves began to empty. Queues, that sad signature of Soviet life, returned as people lined up in a frantic effort to change roubles into dollars.

The biggest losers, and the people whose setback was the most heartbreaking, were those Russians who had found a way to prosper in the new system. These people, who had founded real, productive businesses rather than wallow in the Loophole Economy, had been Russia's future. Now they were Russia's victims. I thought the best place to see how they were faring was Luzhniki, the exuberant, grubby, cacophonous wholesale market in central Moscow. It was not yet 10 a.m. when I arrived but Lena, a pretty blonde in a polyester tracksuit who hawked cheap Italian shoes, was already changing her prices for the second time that day.

'While I went to buy a cup of tea, the rouble fell even more and now we have to raise our prices,' she told me wearily. 'One of the traders in my row has a pager and whenever the rouble falls further, he sings out like a canary. It's impossible to keep up with the rate. I've lost $3,000 in the past ten days. Soon, I will have to close my business.'

Like everything else at Luzhniki, Lena's business was a ramshackle operation; there was no cash register, not even a shop counter, just shoes and boots crudely tied to fifteen tall metal racks cheek-by-jowl with competitors' wares and dispersed at strategic locations around the vast bazaar. But until 17 August, this unpretentious marketplace had been the engine room, and perhaps even the soul, of Russia's capitalist transformation. After seven years of painful market reform, Russia had not made much progress in restructuring its industrial behemoths; but in the retail and consumer sectors, the transition had been a dazzling success. Once a country in which oranges were a rarity, Russia became a place where the inhabitant of even the most remote Siberian village had access to the full capitalist cornucopia of goods, ranging from computers to kiwi fruit. Luzhniki, which sold goods wholesale to traders from the hinterland, was one of the driving forces behind this consumer revolution.

This trash-strewn, hard-edged market was also one of the birth-places of the Russian middle class, a fragile young species whose proliferation was vital if the country's capitalist democracy was to survive. Nuclear physicists, factory engineers, teachers, doctors, lawyers – the professional classes who lost their jobs or their salaries with the Soviet Union's collapse – many had found salvation, and often even the wherewithal for a prosperous new lifestyle, in the cramped stalls of bazaars such as Luzhniki. But as the mounting economic crisis eviscerated the rouble, paralysed the financial system and ravaged the stock market, the middle-class army of Luzhniki was endangered.

'This is our death,' complained Sasha, Lena's neighbour, as the market 'canary' sang out the latest tidings of the rouble's decline. 'We work with an American businessman, he supplies us with goods, inexpensive but good-quality Taiwanese clothing. All summer long we sold them well and paid our supplier in roubles.'

'But yesterday when we brought him the roubles he said, "Why have you brought me sheets of worthless paper? The market is frozen, I can't sell roubles for dollars",' recalled Sasha, in his past life an engineer at a weapons factory outside Moscow. 'So now, he won't sell us the goods any more. And we understand him. He just sits in his office all day long and reads the newspapers and cries.'

These were the complaints of Muscovites who, just as in the Soviet era, remained a privileged class in the new Russia. Lena's customers from the provinces were even more worried. Ira and Andrei were in their early thirties. She used to be an economist; he was a police detective. Since the collapse of the Soviet Union they had earned their living by driving their dented blue Lada once a week over 800 miles of rough roads to Moscow, filling it with shoes and clothes at Luzhniki and then returning home to Orsk, a city of 275,000 in the Urals, and selling the goods there. Now, as they loaded a half-dozen boxes of winter boots into their car, they feared it could be their last trip.

'We used to stuff our car with boxes, fill up the trunk, and tie a few more to the roof,' said Ira, who had the ghost-white complexion and shabbier clothes of the Russian provinces. 'Now we're just buying a little bit, for ourselves, sort of like a bank account.'

'We are going to have to stop trading. There may be money left in Moscow, but there is no money at all left in our town,' she told me. 'Wages haven't been paid at our factories for ten months. We are just going to work in our garden and sit in our apartment and try to live until our stocks run out. And when they do run out – and our neighbours' stocks run out – then there will be a bloody revolution.'

It was a horrifying prediction; but even as Ira prophesied a bloodbath, her features were calm and her voice a soft monotone. Her eerie stoicism was due to more than just the legendary patience of the Russian people. At that moment everyone was, as Lena put it, 'in a trance, in a state of shock', since only three weeks earlier Russia's middle class had finally begun to truly believe in the Kremlin's promises of a prosperous capitalist future.

Even in the depressed provinces, some real improvements were starting to be felt, Ira recalled: 'People's standard of living was improving. At first, they would just buy any Western good they could get their hands on, and worry only about the price. Then they began to be more choosy, look for a specific heel or colour . . . Personally, our life became much better than it had been in the Soviet era. I was even thinking of having a second child.'

In Moscow, many people were beginning to feel the real beginnings of an economic boom. Three months earlier, Lena said, her modest trading operation was turning a massive monthly profit of $10,000. She could afford to take a summer holiday in Italy with her husband and two sons – their first trip abroad; she bought a car, a ten-year-old Ford; and she dreamed of building herself a house in the country and sending her children to English boarding-schools. 'We were making good money and life was full of possibilities,' she told me. 'For a while, we forgot what Russia is really like.'

Lena's solid middle-class acquisitions were part of a rising economic wave that had made parts of Russia seem like a modern-day Klondike. Perhaps even more than an end to the gulag, it was these creature comforts which were Yeltsin's most powerful promise. Russia's doughty middle class had believed him. Now it felt betrayed. 'In 1996 we all backed Yeltsin, we were terrified the communists would come back to power and shoot us just like they did in the 1920s,' Sasha admitted. 'Now Yeltsin is still president and no one is shooting us, but our business is dead.'

Battered by the hard realities of the Russian economy, most of the Luzhniki traders kept their savings in dollars and at home – 'under my pillow, close to my heart', as Lena put it. Those Russians who offered the Kremlin the ultimate gesture of confidence – holding their savings in roubles in Russian commercial banks – were even more disenchanted. 'I know I will never get my money,' Olga, a 35-year-old accountant who worked in a Western construction firm, told me as she waited outside the locked doors of her bank. 'We believed in market reforms. We trusted the promises of our government and of our Central Bank. They said: "Trust the commercial banks, put your money there, they will pay you higher interest." Now I will never trust a Russian government again. I only trust the International Monetary Fund. Why can't they send us some intelligent Western government and send our own ministers to some desert island?'

For the bright young thinkers who spearheaded Russia's market reforms, losing the faith of the middle class was profoundly depressing.

For more than a decade they had seen themselves as holy warriors, fighting a jihad against the evil communist regime. But now the truest practitioners of the new creed – the merchants and professionals of the middle class – were turning atheist and the revolution's ideologues were wondering what went wrong.

'I feel very guilty and very sad,' Mikhail Berger, the Moscow journalist, told me. 'I don't want to say that we were mindless propagandists, but especially at the beginning, I and a few other journalists totally supported the reform effort. Now we face a horrible situation where everything the leftist opposition says about the government is turning out to be true. It is a terrible thing to have to agree with [Communist Party leader Gennady] Zyuganov.'

Like the rest of Moscow's increasingly prosperous middle class, Berger had been slowly building a solidly bourgeois way of life. He had a car, he sent his son to a private school in Moscow, he was building a home in the suburbs. Now, like everyone else, he felt that his own slice of capitalism was under threat. Many of his expenses – like the wages he paid the workers building his home – were pegged to a hard currency, but his salary was paid in devalued roubles. As the crisis escalated he had to worry about more than selecting the perfect headline. Whole chunks of his day were devoted to searching frantically for an exchange point somewhere in Moscow where he could convert his swiftly collapsing roubles into dollars. 'The fundamental tragedy is that the very best, smartest people, who believed in reforms, may now become disenchanted with the liberal idea,' he warned.

Remarkably, though, many of the Russians who were impoverished by the financial collapse were not giving up on reforms – they had just lost all faith in the reformers. There was nothing wrong with a market economy, they said; the problem was that their government had been too corrupt and too incompetent to create one. They drew this lesson from their daily battles at the coal-face of the Russian economy – the stands at Luzhniki. The Luzhniki traders said that the official rent they paid for a space at the market, $5,000 per month for one of the big trucks from which business was done, was matched by a parallel $6,000 they had to pay to racketeers working in collusion with the authorities. (More savvy than the trusting professional middle class, the *mafia* had never had much faith in the rouble or Russian banks; all payments were in cash dollars.) Policemen were bandits in uniform, eating free at private food-stands and collecting pay-offs. The merchants of Luzhniki believed that their market was a microcosm for the Russian economy and that the distorted business principles of their bazaar were, ultimately, what caused the financial collapse.

'Intuitively, we knew things would collapse,' Sasha told me. 'The problem with our economy is that money always goes to the bandits with their Swiss bank accounts, not to doctors and teachers. The elite in our country stole everything. We think that the $5bn which Chubais got from the International Monetary Fund this summer could have been deposited directly in Zurich for all the good it did us.'

As the economic crisis mounted, Russia's leaders became obsessed by internal power struggles and the technical details of warring economic proposals. But their toughest battle would be one they hadn't even begun – to win back the faith of the bruised middle class. Until they did, Russia would again be a nation of dissidents: people would flee from the rouble to the dollar and dream of abandoning the country altogether.

'My deepest wish now is for my sons to live in another country,' Lena told me. 'It is God's punishment to be born here. It's a terrible thing to say about your own land, but this is a country of thieves and idiots. In Russia, it is impossible to be a patriot.'

Western investors were hit hard, too. Of the $40bn of government paper affected by the Russian default, more than a third was owned by foreigners. The restructuring deal which was eventually agreed the next year gave foreigners a paltry three to five cents on the dollar. Russian losses pulled down the profits of several leading international investment banks in 1998 and contributed to the crisis at Long-Term Capital Management, the investment fund whose near-collapse came perilously close to taking Wall Street with it.

The Western investment bankers who just a year earlier had been irrepressible Russian boosters now turned more Russophobic than the hoariest of Cold-War warriors. Adam Elstein, a friend of mine and the head of the local office of Bankers Trust, was speaking for many of his colleagues when he bitterly pronounced, 'After this, Western investors would rather eat nuclear waste than buy Russian debt.' A Russian proposal hatched in the 48 hours immediately after the crisis, to give domestic

holders of GKOs a better deal than foreigners, particularly angered the
international banking community. Camdessus, described as 'furious' by a
close Western source, warned the Russians that if they carried out their
plan, the IMF would openly condemn them. Intimidated, the Russians
backed down, but the damage to their reputuation was irreversible. As
Mikhail Friedman put it, 'You didn't steal, but you wanted to steal.'

The wisest comment I heard about the plight of Western investors
came from the band of coal-miners who had been camped outside the
White House for months in a campaign to force the government to pay
them their back wages. Two days after the crash, I went over to their
ramshackle settlement to talk to them about it, fully expecting a com-
munist-tinged anti-Western harangue. I couldn't have been more
mistaken.

'Tell the Western bankers to come down here and join us and
together we will demand that the government pay us its debts,' Ramir
Gashygalin, a gold-toothed, black-haired miner from Vorkuta told me.
'We'll give them miners' hard hats and share our vodka. They should
have asked us before they lent money to the Russian government. We
would have told them that our bastards here in Moscow never pay
their debts.'

With Yeltsin's best allies – the West and the burgeoning middle class –
so deeply betrayed, the government could not last long. On Sunday 23
August, exactly a week after he had helicoptered out to tell the president the rouble could not hold, Kiriyenko was summoned for another
private meeting with the Kremlin chief – this time at Gorki 9, a country dacha about an hour's drive from the Kremlin. Later that day, the
president's spokesman announced that Kiriyenko and his cabinet were
sacked.

Russian politics, rarely stable at the best of times, now took on a frenetic pace. Yeltsin had always enjoyed playing musical chairs with his
cabinet, but now the record was playing at double speed. First
Chernomyrdin was pulled back into the fray and made acting prime
minister. Then, in the face of a rebellious Duma, he was ditched in
favour of Yevgeny Primakov, the former foreign minister and spymaster
whose aggressive Cold War service and unknown economic views
made him the ideal compromise candidate.

Eight months later, it was all change again. Primakov had done nothing to resuscitate Russia's moribund economy, but he had been surprisingly skilled at restoring political stability to Russia's battered body-politic. So skilled, in fact, that he had to go. He had begun to overshadow Yeltsin – the same crime for which Chernomyrdin had been fired in March 1998. His place was taken by the colourless but unimpeachably loyal Sergei Stepashin, the minister of the interior. Three months after that, Stepashin too got the axe and was replaced by Vladimir Putin, an almost unknown former KGB agent who had spent most of his career in East Germany. For good measure, Yeltsin named Putin his chosen successor in the Kremlin. By then, the turn-over in Russian prime ministers had become so speedy that the rest of the world could no longer be bothered to keep track. When we discussed Putin's appointment at our morning news conference, Richard Lambert, the editor of the *FT*, turned to me and asked: 'Do I really need to remember this one's name?'

As it turned out, he did. When the faceless Putin was first presented to the world as Yeltsin's heir, the president's choice had seemed so outlandish that a few observers publicly accused the Russian leader of senility. But thanks to the bizarre alchemy that seems to rule Russian politics, Yeltsin's oddest appointment turned out to be his most enduring one. Putin not only lasted the year as prime minister, on the eve of the new millennium he got a promotion. On 31 December 1999, Yeltsin stunned the world by announcing his retirement and naming Putin acting president. That gave 'the magician without a face', as one Russian newspaper dubbed the enigmatic Putin, a tremendous advantage over the other candidates in the 26 March presidential elections. Primakov, who had been the favourite just a few months earlier, bowed out of the race in early Febuary. Yuri Luzhkov, another much-touted president-in-waiting, retreated to Moscow city hall.

Putin owed his remarkable political debut partly to the war in Chechnya, which the former spymaster prosecuted with a ferocity that won him tumultous support at home and whimpering disapprobrium in the West. The acting president's background in the shadowy security structures also helped. Not only did it provide Putin with an instant political network, but it gave him a set of skills which were particularly apt for a country whose greatest crisis was the disintegration of the state.

Mostly, though, Putin arrived at the top seat in the Kremlin thanks to the same forces which had secured it for Yeltsin in 1996. In 1999 and in 2000, the same combination of the state's machine, the oligarchs' money and the young reformers' intellect which the Davos Pact had so powerfully assembled four years earlier, now lined up again, this time behind the new Kremlin chief. As in 1996, this political juggernaut monopolised the television airwaves and dominated the public space. The revived alliance helped ensure the popularity of the new war in Chechnya by keeping stories of defeat off the nation's television screens. It also propelled the two pro-Kremlin political parties – Unity, known as Medved, or Bear, and the Union of Right-Wing Forces, the young reformers' new political umbrella – to a combined majority in the December, 1999 elections to the Duma.

Even more than in 1996, the establishment's ability to conjure political leaders and political parties out of nothing – Unity did not even exist until three months before the parliamentary ballot – raised fears that Russia had fallen under the sway of an omnipotent oligarchy. As Grigory Yavlinsky, Russia's leading independent democratic politician, scathingly put it in a Radio Liberty interview after the Duma vote: 'They declared, "We can do anything we want. We only want a few oligarchs, several TV channels and we shall do whatever we want. We can make anyone president; we can create any structure or any Duma, anything". They can choose anyone – bear, hare or wolf. Why? Because in 1991, a democratic revolution failed to take place in Russia. It happened in Poland, in the Czech Republic, but not in Russia. In Russia, we had a coup by the nomenklatura.'

Other politicians were more optimistic. The young reformers, who had been close to Putin since he and the St Petersburg gang had served together in Anatoly Sobchak's city government, were openly allied with the new acting president. They reaped the first rewards of that partnership in the Duma ballot, attracting nearly 9 per cent of the vote to their new party – a tribute to the power of Putin's televised endorsement to wipe out memories of the catastrophic crash of August, 1998. But the young reformers were still idealists and they weren't riding Putin's coat-tails merely for the dubious privilege of serving in the Russian parliament. They, like a growing group of Western business people and diplomats, believed the new Kremlin strongman would usher in a second wave of market reforms, just as soon as he had secured his political position.

These hopes were oddly reminiscent of the cheerful expectations which had welcomed a re-elected Yeltsin back into the Kremlin in 1996. Again, the young reformers and Western business people were pinning their dreams on a strongman of ambivalent or simply unknown ideological inclination; again, they were prepared to forgive him the callous abuse of human rights in Chechnya; and, again, they believed that – after all the votes had been securely counted – he would somehow prove able to shake himself free of the vested economic interests which had sponsored his rise to power.

The biggest danger was that Putin, like his predecessor, is a man driven by power, not by ideology. Yeltsin's overriding political objective was to remain in command; Putin's is almost certain to be exactly the same, for the simple reason that he was hand-picked by the Family, as Yeltsin's entourage came to be known, for precisely that quality. Yeltsin did not choose Putin out of friendship, or shared moral beliefs. He didn't pick the lack-lustre East German sleuth for his intellect, his public profile or his parliamentary finesse. Putin was selected for one quality alone: Yeltsin and his clan judged him to be the man most able to hang on to political power, and in so doing to protect the interests of the Yeltsin family, which feared poverty and prosecution the minute its patriarch left the Kremlin. Putin began to deliver at once – his first step as acting president was to sign a decree granting the president and his family immunity from prosecution.

Yeltsin's motivation in handing the Kremlin over to Putin was so nakedly personal and self-interested that even some of the cynical handlers who helped run his 1996 campaign were disgusted. As Vyacheslav Nikonov, the political consultant, told the *New York Times* at the time of the succession: 'What shocks me about the Western reaction is that this is seen as a triumph for democracy in Russia while in my mind, it is completely the opposite. In my mind it is a defeat of civil society and a victory for the Family, which I consider the most anti-democratic force in Russia.'

In the first few months after the August 1998 crash, it seemed inevitable that the oligarchs would be marginal in Russia's next phase of development. They were among the chief casualties of the crisis: their GKO portfolios were wiped out, their shares prices collapsed and the golden river of money from the West abruptly dried up. More importantly, the financial collapse seemed to have soured, perhaps for ever, the cosy relationship between them and the government.

Primakov was determined to weaken the oligarchs' grip on the levers of state and his campaign against them had more muscle than the young reformers' crusade against bandit capitalism. The wily old party hack had few personal debts to the oligarchs and, in contrast with the isolated young reformers, he could muster the full force of the shadowy security structures and the apparat. Primakov began to collect some powerful scalps, most notably that of Berezovsky: he was hounded out of his various government posts and a warrant was issued for his arrest.

There was poetic justice in the apparent end of the oligarchy. The business cabal had done much to create Russia's distorted version of capitalism, which had now collapsed under the weight of its own flaws and taken its creators with it.

However, as time went on the obituaries of the oligarchs began to seem premature. They had all been weakened and a few seemed likely to lose their empires altogether. Smolensky's SBS-Agro was forced into receivership. The banking arms of Khodorkovsky's, Potanin's and Gusinsky's conglomerates were effectively run into the ground as well. But all three managed to hold on to the industrial cores of their businesses and Gusinsky, who had been one of the first to foresee the crisis, came out relatively unscathed. The same was true of Friedman. Even Berezovsky, whose political capital began to fall so precipitously, turned out to have been a far more conservative businessman than he was a politician. Sibneft, the oil company covertly under his control, emerged from the wreckage more or less intact.

Bloodied but not broken, the oligarchs went back to their old tricks with even more ferocity. Those still standing tried to prey on their more wounded counterparts. Friedman made a muscular bid to wrest Chernogorneftegaz, a profitable oilfield, from the weakened Oneximbank group and its partner, British Petroleum. A vindicated Gusinsky made moves to acquire Sviazinvest, the original apple of contention, from Potanin who could no longer afford to own it.

The same aggression was turned on outside shareholders. Minority shareholder rights had always been paid scant attention; now, with share prices depressed as far as they could go and little chance of attracting fresh foreign investment for the next few years, most of the cash-pinched oligarchs took to even more blatantly and crudely squeezing out their minority shareholders. As one of the oligarchs confessed to me a few days after the crisis: 'Actually, this is very good for us. For the next five years no one will buy Russian shares and no one will lend Russia money. It is a chance to consolidate our share-holdings.'

Rather perversely, the collapse had confirmed rather than under-mined the oligarchs' self-image as Russia's natural-born titans, with a right to a voice in the highest councils of state. Khodorkovsky, smart-ing from one manager's decision to invest $300m in Russian treasuries despite his explicit instructions to the contrary, vowed that he would never again trust a non-oligarch to run an autonomous part of his empire. The oligarchs, he believed, were the only men who had truly proven themselves in the Hobbesian environment of Russia's young capitalism.

'If a man is not an oligarch, something is not right with him,' Khodorkovsky told me. 'It means for some reason he was unable to become an oligarch. Everyone had the same starting conditions, every-one could have done it. And today they could as well. If a man didn't do it, it means there are some sorts of problems with him. And in that case, you can't trust him with big money. This is the conclusion I have drawn. Maybe it is a mistake, but I believe it. I will manage my own business and maybe invest some money with another oligarch. It might sound a little bit arrogant but, since you are writing a book and not an article and it will not appear immediately, that is all right.'

Most observers had concluded that the oligarchs' engagement in politics was disastrous for the country. Many, particularly the young reformers, believed their machinations had been a major cause of Russia's collapse. But Khodorkovsky had come to the opposite conclu-sion. The problem, he believed, was that the oligarchs had played too small rather than too large a role in the political life of the nation. Now, he promised that that would change.

'Now we will take an active political position and fight for it until either we have been defeated or the country has become normal,' he told me. 'We will participate actively in politics and try to bring to power those people who have positions similiar to our own.'

It was tempting to dismiss this as pure braggadocio. After all, the crisis had revealed how poorly managed many of the oligarchs' empires had been, had discredited them politically and had swept their allies out of office. Yet, within a few months, they started to make a political comeback. By the beginning of 2000 Berezovsky, against whom all charges had been dropped, had a seat in parliament and was again a power in the Kremlin (his protégé, the oil trader Roman Abramovich, was even stronger). The oligarchs once more began to convene to decide affairs of state. As they lined up behind Putin, most of them quietly started to predict the new regime would be as good to them as the old one had been.

Like the oligarchs, the young reformers were left reeling by the crisis. They were widely held responsible for the crash and, by October, many analysts had consigned them to the dustbin of history, seemingly destined to live out a sort of half-life as semi-celebrities lecturing in American Ivy League universities. They would be tragic heroes abroad, but their political role in Russia appeared to be over.

'In all those years, Chubais and Gaidar did nothing to make even one sector of the national economy work. Nothing,' insisted Malashenko, the NTV boss, in October 1998. 'They lost an absolutely wonderful chance, which was given to them by history. I'm not interested in what they will do now. From my point of view, politically, they no longer exist.'

But, like the oligarchs, the young reformers were also convinced that history would give them another chance to run Russia. They believed the crisis had occurred not because their ideas had been wrong, but because they had not been given the chance properly to implement them. Convinced that they were Russia's only capable economists, they were sure they would eventually get the opportunity to try again.

'I think the reform team, in the broadest sense of the word, will inevitably again head the government,' Gaidar predicted to me two months after the August crash. 'The earliest would be 2000, the latest would be 2004.'

Audaciously – given that they had no independent power-base or economic empires of their own, had never bothered to build up their own political machine, and not only lacked widespread public support but were openly loathed by the vast majority of ordinary Russians – they assumed that Chubais would lead them, this time as president. 'Yes, Chubais is thinking about the presidency in 2004,' Sergei Vasiliev told me. 'A lot of things may change in six years.'

Their serene self-confidence was not entirely absurd. The young reformers' great political strength was that they knew exactly what they wanted and what they believed in. In a country of atheists, they were the only true believers. Moreover, most of the country, even the die-hard communists, had already been converted to the basic precepts of their faith: private property and market economics.

They began to regroup. Their tortured relationship with the oligarchs had convinced them that they needed their own economic base and Chubais started to build one. In the spring of 1998, after his ouster from government, he forced the young Nizhny Novgorod reformer, Boris Brevnov, out of UES, the national power company, and took over the job himself. As head of Russia's second-largest firm – out-muscled only by the gigantic Gazprom – Chubais began to be described as an aspirant oligarch.

Some sceptics were concerned that as the young reformers created their own economic empire, they would lose their ideological purity. Chubais might succeed all too well and become an oligarch not only in bank balance but in behaviour. What neither Chubais nor his allies worried about very much at all in these first months after the crash was how they would fare in a Russia ruled by Putin and the *siloviki*, the hardline functionaries who had been the big losers in the Yeltsin era. But by 2005, as a politically supreme Putin consolidated his second term administration, that seemed to be the country's dominant political and economic question.

14

THE OLIGARCHS, CAPITALISM AND THE KREMLIN – THE SEQUEL

Late one night in September 2003, five years after the default and devaluation, I returned to my Moscow hotel room to find an urgent telephone message. I was in Russia to profile Mikhail Khodorkovsky, at that moment the country's richest man, for the *Financial Times* and I had spent the past 14 hours with him as he travelled to and from St Petersburg. Although Khodorkovsky had gone on from the airport to an urgent meeting with Roman Abramovich, his business partner and fellow oligarch, the day of speech-making, glad-handing western CEOs and trading insults with Russian business rivals had left me worn out. But the call, from a senior American investment banker based in London, seemed too important to leave for the morning. 'I'm so glad you called,' my contact said, when his PA put me through to his mobile phone. 'I have some hot gossip for you from Russia from a very good source. Khodorkovsky and all of his senior colleagues have had to flee the country!'

As gently as I could, I explained that I was very certain this particular tip-off was not true. My American banker friend was slightly deflated, but for both of us it was a useful reminder that, more than a decade after Kremlinologists were put out of work by the collapse of the Soviet Union,

Russia remained a land of speculation, gossip and conspiracy. Yet, more often than foreigners can easily fathom, the wildest Russian stories turn out to be true. And so it was that almost exactly a month later, when I was back in London, a phone call from Moscow informed me of an even more extreme twist in the Khodorkovsky saga. On 25 October, at 5 a.m., armed government agents stormed Khodorkovsky's private jet as it was refuelling in Novosibirsk airport. According to Yukos officials they shouted, 'Weapons on the floor or we'll shoot', arrested Khodorkovsky and flew him back to Moscow. There, they took him to an 8-man prison cell in the notoriously overcrowded and tubercular Matroskaya Tishina prison and charged him with fraud and tax evasion. At the beginning of 2005 he was still in jail, with no immediate prospect of release.

The theatrical arrest was the climax of a 4-month government campaign against Khodorkovsky. For the man himself, it marked a dramatic reversal of fortune: as recently as the spring, Khodorkovsky had looked like the clear winner in Russia's primal capitalist struggle, with a personal fortune estimated at $8bn and an oil company that was pumping more barrels per day than all of Kuwait. For the oligarchs as a group, the dramatic confrontation represented a stunning escalation in the power struggle between big business and the Kremlin, now under the firm control of Vladimir Putin. The most important question in Putin's Russia – and the most entertaining Moscow parlour game in the febrile months ahead of the 2004 presidential elections – was figuring out what the exact cause of the fight between Yukos and the Kremlin was, and who was going to win.

Business nerds liked the theory that a commercial dispute between Yukos and the state oil company Rosneft was the catalyst for the battle. Political types inclined to the view that Yukos had been hit by the fall-out of an internecine Kremlin fight between the *siloviki*, hardliners from the former KGB, police and the military brought into power on Putin's coat-tails, and 'the Family', more moderate hold-overs from the Yeltsin era. Yukos executives believed that a contributing factor was the irritation of a few cabinet ministers at the company's effectiveness at blocking specific pieces of legislation, notably a production-sharing agreement that would have given favourable tax treatment to western oil companies investing in Russia. Indeed, so rampant was the speculation that, purely for fun, the local *Economist* correspondent assembled a

David Letterman-style 'Top 14 reasons for the attack on Yukos' email, which he sent out to his amused contact list.

Judged purely on entertainment value, my own favourite hypothesis, urgently confided to me that September over tea amid the murmuring fountains and sleek marble of a recently renovated Moscow hotel lobby, was that Khodorkovsky had been singled out because he alone of all of Russia's oligarchs was attractive to women. 'Mikhail Borisovich is handsome and rich and women love him,' my informant, herself a pretty, well-dressed and immaculately coiffed bluestocking in her early forties explained. 'Putin is small and grey and women don't like him. If Khodorkovsky looked like the other oligarchs, none of this would have happened.' (When I put this view to Khodorkovsky he chortled and insisted he was not a ladies' man, which seems to be the Moscow consensus. But he couldn't resist mentioning an online poll of Russian political and business leaders, TOPpolitica.ru, in which he ranked number 2 for intelligence, number 4 for strength, but number 1 for sex appeal.)

Machismo should never be discounted as a powerful factor in Russian politics, but ultimately the struggle between Khodorkovsky and the prosecutors was about something even more crucial in modern-day Russia: state power and its limits. Wary of scaring off already skittish foreign investors, the Kremlin took some pains to insist the fight was not about revisiting Russia's controversial division of property in the 1990s. What the Kremlin did not say – but what everyone else in Russia understood – was that the conflict was part of the state's wider effort to control the Russian political space ahead of the upcoming parliamentary and presidential elections. 'Yukos is part of Putin's political game,' the leader of one of Russia's liberal political parties told me. 'He is against the independent position of anyone, including business. I think Yukos is important for Putin because he wants to show business that if you want to make money, you have to be loyal. If you are not loyal, you will be in prison.'

Some observers, including Western ones, thought Putin was right. On my way to Moscow in September, I shared a flight with an old contact, Bill Browder, an American fund manager who had been based in Moscow since the early Nineties. Grandson of a general secretary of the American Communist Party, Browder had profited handsomely from Russia's capitalist revolution. He also believed it had been profoundly unjust. Only a strong state, he argued, had any chance of returning some of Russia's wealth to its impoverished people: 'A nice, well-run authoritarian regime is better than an oligarchic regime – and those are the choices on offer.'

Putin's battle with the oligarchs began as soon as he took over from Yeltsin in 2000. One of his first acts was to summon the oligarchs for a meeting and to announce a new deal: the oligarchs could keep the vast resources they had acquired during the Yeltsin era, but they would no longer be allowed to play a role in politics. When I interviewed Putin a few months after this encounter, he was all charm and twinkle, patting my pregnant belly and dutifully reciting a few statistics about Russian players in the National Hockey League (I was there with a group of Canadian journalists ahead of a state visit to Canada). But when I raised the issue of the oligarchs, Russia's new president turned steely: 'Those who have money shouldn't control society . . . The oligarchs must not, and have no right to influence government decisions. If somebody doesn't like this, if somebody has got used to anarchy, I am sorry, but they will have to agree with the new rules.'

For the next three years, that ukase governed Russian political and economic life. Two of the oligarchs – Vladimir Gusinksy and Boris Berezovsky – found it impossible to comply. As media barons, it was their business to comment on affairs of state; as human beings, doing so had become their beloved hobby. Putin forced both of them to sell their companies and flee the country. The remaining oligarchs concentrated on other sectors of the economy and became even more fabulously wealthy than they had been before. Khodorkovsky, in particular, flourished, transforming himself from the *bête noire* of Russian capitalism to its poster boy.

But then, sometime in the spring of 2003, something odd began to happen. Khodorkovsky began to drop hints that he would like to go into politics. He started to spend more time and money on Open Russia, his non-profit organisation devoted to promoting civil society. His always formidable parliamentary lobbying machine became even more active. He publicly admitted that he and other major Yukos shareholders personally contributed to three political parties, including the Communists. A Kremlin whispering campaign – which Khodorkovsky believed was orchestrated by an alliance of *siloviki* and his own business rivals – spread the rumour that Yukos had donated as much as $70m to the Communists. In conversation with me, Khodorkovsky hotly contested that number, saying that his left-leaning business colleagues may have contributed $1m at most.

Most explosively, Khodorkovsky started to suggest that he might personally get involved. In dozens of interviews, including one with me in 1998, Khodorkovsky had said he planned to retire from business when he turned 45. But in the spring of 2003, as Khodorkovsky stepped up his civic and political activities, commentators began to point out that his 45th birthday happened to fall in 2008, the year when Putin is constitutionally obliged to step down. The observation seemed to be based on more than the usual gossip. Everyone in the tight circle that forms Moscow's political and business establishment had at least one story about a conversation with a senior Yukos executive in which Khodorkovsky's ambitions to become prime minister were floated. One of the exiled oligarchs had a more extreme version, alleging Khodorkovsky told him that he had a meeting with Putin in which he suggested a change in the Russian constitutional set-up. Russia should become a parliamentary democracy, he claimed Khodorkovsky suggested, in which Khodorkovsky himself would be prime minister and Putin could have the prestigious, but more ceremonial, role of speaker. When I spoke to Khodorkovsky, he refused to say anything at all about his alleged prime-ministerial ambitions. However, he freely agreed that he was in favour of a shift in power – a legal shift in power, he was at pains to insist – from Russia's near-tsarist presidency to a system with a stronger parliament and prime minister.

Precisely who said what to whom within the high, thick, red walls of the Kremlin fortress as Khodorkovsky's political ambitions became more apparent was unclear. What was apparent, as spring turned to summer, was that Khodorkovsky and his team began to come under increasingly heavy fire from the Kremlin. The first to be imprisoned was Platon Lebedev, a major Yukos shareholder, who was arrested on 2 July. Vasily Shakhnovsky, the former high-ranking Moscow city apparatchik who had become another major Yukos shareholder, was charged with tax evasion and forbidden to leave the country. Leonid Nevzlin, one of Khodorkovsky's closest confidants and the second largest shareholder in the company, fled for Israel. A few months later, Russian prosecutors issued a warrant for his arrest, on charges of embezzlement and tax evasion. Later, they added murder charges. Police repeatedly raided the offices of Yukos and its lawyers, a PR company working for Yabloko, a liberal political party that received some funding from Yukos, and even searched an orphanage Yukos sponsored. The allegations against Yukos shareholders and employees ranged from tax evasion to legal violations during the privatisation of a fertiliser company in 1994 to five charges of murder.

Yukos robustly denied all of the accusations, in particular the murder charges. 'I can say with absolute authority that no one in our company is involved in contract killings, or was involved in them in the past,' Khodorkovsky told me during the two days we spent together. 'There were no contract killings.' One of the most lurid of the cases was the murder of the mayor of the Siberian oil town of Nefteyugansk, who was shot and killed on Khodorkovsky's birthday in 1998. For Moscow's myth-makers, the apparent coincidence was too much to resist, and the killing became whispered as a birthday gift to Khodorkovsky from a zealous underling. It hardly needs saying that Khodorkovsky disputed this charge. What was more interesting was his detailed and seemingly spontaneous recollection of what he said really happened. Khodorkovsky said his telephone rang at 8 a.m. The call was from a Yukos employee and Khodorkovsky said he remembered it vividly – 'How could I not?'. The mayor had been shot. 'Is he alive?' Khodorkovsky recalled asking. He still seemed a bit stunned by the horrific reply: 'How could he be alive! A whole glassful of his brains has spilled out.' More softly, Khodorkovsky mouthed the final phrase a second time: 'A whole glassful of brains'. It was an image, he said, he would never forget.

Denials notwithstanding, as raid followed raid and fresh offences were steadily added to the charge-sheet, it seemed inevitable that the prosecutors eventually would reach Khodorkovsky. For that reason, the question uppermost in my mind as I prepared for my September trip to Russia was whether Khodorkovsky would soon publicly capitulate – or simply leave. According to a senior Yukos executive, in early July, after the first arrests, Khodorkovsky considered doing just that. 'We discussed full, unilateral surrender,' the executive told me over supper at Shinok, a Ukrainian-themed restaurant that caters to the New Russian nostaglia for an Arcadian Slavic past. 'But we decided that it would be dangerous – it would be taken as a sign of weakness by our opponents in the Kremlin.' As of late 2004, Khodorkovsky had not looked back from that decision to stay and fight. He was sticking by the statement he released a few hours after his arrest: 'I don't regret anything I have done; nor do I regret what has happened today.'

Within the first few minutes of seeing Khodorkovsky in the flesh, it was apparent that he was not for turning. Khodorkovsky had always cut an incongruous figure for an oligarch, and even $8bn had not significantly turned up the volume of his mild-mannered persona. The stutter and occasional twitch I remembered from our first encounters in the mid-1990s were gone; his ever-present glasses were now a fancy, frameless variety, and his trademark dress-down wardrobe tended to cashmere and leather, rather than cotton and denim. He remained soft-spoken, though, with rather gentle brown eyes, extremely clean hands and a tendency to giggle when nervous.

But you didn't have to go far past his slightly nerdy exterior to reach the aggressive instincts that had made him a tycoon. We had barely sunk into the soft grey leather armchairs of the Tupolev-134 which was ferrying Khodorkovsky and a few aides to St Petersburg for a US–Russian oil conference before Khodorkovsky threw a Russian newspaper down in disgust, exclaiming: 'He [the president] is breaking the constitution again!' On the ground, as his black Mercedes SUV with tinted windows pulled away from the airport, Khodorkovsky shouted a triumphant 'Yes' into his mobile phone. It was a call from the Siberian city of Tomsk, where a court had just ruled in Yukos's favour in one of the hundreds of investigations the government was pursuing against the company at various levels. 'It won't make any difference in the long run,' Khodorkovsky admitted, 'but it is nice to win sometimes.'

Once we arrived at the Pribaltiskaya Hotel – an intimidatingly ugly building that screamed Soviet Union – Khodorkovsky used his speech to call for liberalisation of the Russian oil transport system and faster work on a pipeline to China, two issues over which Yukos had clashed with the Kremlin. At lunch afterwards, Khodorkovsky spotted the head of the Transneft, the state-oil pipeline monopoly, and gaily shouted: 'So, how did you like my loyal speech?' Red-faced and clearly very unamused, the Transneft boss bellowed back, 'If that was loyal, I am a trolleybus!' 'So, where are the headlights then?' a cheerful Khodorkovsky yelled back, miming flashing headlights with his hands in the manner of a hyperactive children's television presenter.

For much of the summer of 2003, the lobby in Yukos's Moscow skyscraper was decorated with posters that mimicked the style and some of the iconic themes of Soviet Second World War agitprop, with one crucial twist: Khodorkovsky and Yukos were the beleaguered and virtuous Soviet motherland, while the Kremlin was the would-be Nazi oppressor. When I first learned of these posters I was delighted, but dismayed. The story seemed too good to be true and almost impossible to confirm – after all, if Khodorkovsky had any sense, as the fight escalated surely he would hide all traces of rather juvenile provocations like this one? When I visited the Yukos headquarters in late September the posters were indeed gone – they were taken down after the government approved Yukos's merger with Sibneft, another major Russian oil company, in what at the time was interpreted as a step back from total war. But then I turned to page 28 of Yukos's glossy in-house quarterly magazine, and there the posters were, proudly illustrating a special section devoted to the 'Attack on Yukos'.

Like the lantern-jawed Stalinist soldiers in those retro posters, Khodorkovsky himself seemed almost proud to be in the firing line. As he walked into the conference room in St Petersburg, another Russian oil baron commented on Khodorkovsky's new, extremely short hairstyle. 'I'm getting ready for them to throw me in jail,' Khodorkovsky joked – sort of – with a steely smile.

In retrospect, Khodorkovsky's gallows humour was chilling because it was so prescient. At the time, it was jarring because it seemed so out of synch with his golden business reputation. In the autumn of 2003, there were a lot of people who hated Khodorkovsky. But everyone – the Russian business rivals who were privately delighted by his discomfiture; the Western investors who would have preferred Khodorkovsky in exile and Putin installed as modern-day tsar; even the government which was harassing his company – agreed on one thing: the Khodorkovsky of 2003 was an outstanding business manager – the best in Russia – and Yukos was Russia's most transparent, best-governed company. It even inspired a new word, 'yukosisation', the process whereby a poorly managed, opaque Russian company cleans up its act.

Having watched Khodorkovsky when he was a hate figure among Western investors like Ken Dart, and having been gobsmacked by the chutzpah of Yukos executives who in 1998 believed Western investor sentiment could be reversed in just a few years, I was a bit dubious when stories about Yukos's pioneering campaign to deliver shareholder value began to appear in the Western business press. Part of Khodorkovsky's clean-up drive included assembling a powerful PR machine, and I wondered how far beyond image the changes went. Mikhail Friedman, a rival oligarch I visited the day after my travels with Khodorkovsky, hinted as much, telling me: 'In PR, Yukos did very serious work. It is like the prodigal son. They said, we sinned, but now we will be good. This wildly pleases the society, especially the Americans.'

But even Friedman, who pointedly refrained from supporting Yukos in its fight with the Kremlin, felt obliged to concede: 'Hats off to them [the Yukos team]. They made the correct decisions.' Outside observers, even those whose political sympathies were with Putin, went further. As Browder put it: 'Yukos is head and shoulders above the rest. Everything they do is better. The company is fixed.'

Khodorkovsky did two big things to fix it: he improved the way Yukos did its work and he improved the way it treated its investors. When Russians are serious about technical reform, they have a knack for marrying imported Western know-how with home-grown ferocity – think Peter the Great or Stalin. This slightly scary combination was in evidence everywhere in Yukos, whose gleaming Moscow headquarters were crawling with keyed-up, red-eyed foreigners. The ones who lasted – and many didn't – had learned to love what Ray Leonard liked to call the 'extreme sport' of the Russian oil industry.

When Leonard, an Austin-trained geologist and Amoco veteran who ran Yukos's exploration department, first arrived at the company in 2000, he remembered being horrified to discover that a rival team would always be assigned to work on the same project he had been given: 'A western manager would look on it as a gross betrayal of trust.' By 2003, Leonard was setting up the same unforgiving internal competitions within his own department. 'Monday morning staff meetings are like internal warfare,' Leonard told me one morning in September with a tired smile – he had been in a meeting with Khodorkovsky until 2 a.m. At one of these public sessions, Leonard's boss 'got really pissed at me and called me something that related to a sexual dysfunction'. It was, Leonard said with a wistful smile, a terrific moment: 'It meant I was one of them.'

The one Russian boss who didn't do much shouting was Khodorkovsky. 'He never abuses or humiliates people,' Leonard said. 'He goes out of his way to avoid embarrassing people.' But in his quiet way, Khodorkovsky, who described his own management style to me as 'authoritarian', was reputed to be the toughest of all. During the day I spent shadowing him, I saw his disciplinarian streak flash just once. The Power Point slides for his St Petersburg presentation – to an audience that included heads of the world's oil majors, Russian cabinet ministers and the US ambassador – didn't work. In the seats around me, I heard a chorus of grumbles. Yukos prided itself on its paperless office and now its boss couldn't even produce a few humble slides. Was the Kremlin pressure finally getting to Khodorkovsky? At the time, Khodorkovsky himself seemed not to mind and ad-libbed his way through his speech confidently enough. But a few hours later, as the Yukos team sat down at a groaning table and worked its way through a ritualised set of toasts, Nikolai, the hapless aide who was responsible for the computer failure, raised his glass. 'Here's to democracy and civil society,' he said, picking up on what was very much the 'in' campaign at Yukos at the moment. 'You are just saying that because in a civil society they don't shoot you if your computer doesn't work,' Khodorkovsky retorted softly. There were a few dutiful titters, but a very white Nikolai did not join in. I was sure he would have preferred to be shouted at and accused of a sexual dysfunction; I wondered whether he was worried about keeping his job.

Within Yukos, Khodorkovsky's toughness manifested itself in other ways. He was ruthless about eliminating Soviet-era working practices, like the Russian oilman's traditional penchant for always drilling new wells rather than maximising the yield from existing ones. He systematically monitored his workforce – in the late 1990s he told me he had installed CCTV cameras in one enterprise – and was unsentimental about firing those who didn't make the grade. One example, which he called up for me on his laptop computer as we flew back to Moscow, was the weekly report his security service compiled for him on the number of Yukos employees who had been discovered drunk on the job. In the first few months after Khodorkovsky took over Yukos, he fired thousands of habitual drunks, a significant number even in Yukos's massive workforce of more than 100,000. For the week in mid-September which he clicked open on his screen, there were just 27. Of these, Khodorkovsky's rule was that 90 per cent must be sacked.

'The operating side of that business is an amazing turnaround story,' Stephen Jennings, who was still in Moscow and had become the sole head of Renaissance Capital, told me. 'Because he [Khodorkovsky] is not from the oil industry he doesn't give a toss about how things used to be done.'

Khodorkovsky's second big drive was to clean up Yukos's corporate governance and its treatment of shareholders. He did a deal with Ken Dart, the Western minority shareholder whose fierce attack did so much to besmirch Yukos's reputation in the late 1990s, brought in a Western CFO and prepared GAAP compliant company accounts. Shareholder value, that Western corporate mantra, suddenly became a religion at Yukos, too. I saw the change in 2002, when Khodorkovsky came to see me at the *FT*'s office in London. At the end of our conversation, he asked to use my computer. Within seconds, he had called up the Yukos share price and, with a whoop of joy, summoned his entourage over to take a look at how much it had risen that day. Khodorkovsky was the first oligarch officially to declare the size of his personal shareholding and that of his partners. (Before his arrest, he owned 59 per cent of the Menatep Group holding company, which in turn owned 60 per cent of Yukos.) According to Browder, there were no corporate governance issues at Yukos left to sort out: 'You can get right down to the details and see what is happening.'

Khodorkovsky's two-pronged restructuring campaign yielded measurable results. Yukos's production costs plunged by two-thirds and its share price skyrocketed. Yukos and Sibneft (the oil company with which Khodorkovsky was concluding a merger on the eve of his imprisonment) accounted for more than two-thirds of the phenomenal rise in the Russian stockmarket between early 2000 and early 2003, when the fight with the Kremlin began to hit Yukos's share price. Five days before Khodorkovsky was arrested, Yukos reported forecast-beating second quarter net profits of $955m, up 26 per cent on the previous year.

For anyone who watched him in the bad old days, the transformation of Khodorkovsky's image and conduct was breathtaking. In part, it was a testimony to what Russians, who still remember their Marx, have known all along: capitalism really does have no conscience, and yesterday's villain can become today's hero, as long as he makes money for his shareholders. As Friedman, who experienced his own metamorphosis from British Petroleum's 'thieving' nemesis in 1998 to its 'trusted' partner in 2003, explained to me: 'The thing about investors is they have a terrible memory, they are like dogs. Like all the world, they believe in success. While their shares are increasing in value, Yukos is wonderful.'

Equally surprising was the turnaround in Khodorkovsky's own behaviour. Yegor Gaidar, no longer in government but still unofficially reigning as Russia's most brilliant economist, told me it all made perfect sense: 'They [the oligarchs] were involved in the consolidation of property. They pushed out those who were not necessary to them. Then, having done that, the job was to improve management – to bring in Western managers and to clean up your accounts. Mikhail Borisovich Khodorkovsky didn't change, but the situation in the country changed. People react to incentives. Mikhail Borisovich showed that he is good at reacting both to the incentives of 1995 [when the loans-for-shares deal was done] and to those of 2000.'

The incentives of 2000 were powerful indeed. Yukos's transformation gave Khodorkovsky celebrity in Russia, and respectability in the West. At home he was treated, as Jennings put it, 'like a rock star'. Within minutes of quietly walking into the St Petersburg conference room and sitting in a back row, Khodorkovsky was mobbed by journalists as the speaker at the podium was ignored. Outside Russia, he started to become a player. In 2003, when Yukos celebrated its 10th anniversary as a company, a roll-call of global oil executives – Exxon's Lee Raymond, Chevron's David O'Reilly, British Petroleum's Lord John Browne – sent letters of congratulation. Khodorkovsky had met with George W. Bush and Condoleezza Rice and was on first-name terms with the US ambassador to Russia. When BP was searching for a Russian partner in the summer of 2002, Khodorkovsky was interested, but only if he could keep control of the company. He didn't feel he needed to sell out, because his success in turning Yukos around had inspired Khodorkovsky to set himself a new goal: he wanted to create Russia's first multinational company. 'I know how I will finish my business career,' Khodorkovsky told me. 'I will build the best company in Russia and I will strive to make it international.' 'His horizons have completely changed,' one Western investment banker told me after talks with Khodorkovsky in early 2003. 'He thinks he can be Lee Raymond. He thinks he can run Exxon, or its Russian equivalent.'

It takes a lot of chutzpah to think you can run a world-beating multinational oil company. It takes even more to think you can create one, especially if you are a 40-year-old Russian, not a lifer from the Houston oil business. But if you wanted to be a factory director at five and became an oligarch at 35, it makes a kind of egotistical sense. What is more surprising was that, sometime in 2003, Khodorkovsky decided he wanted to do something even more audacious – he wanted to be the man who brought democracy to Russia.

Part of the explanation is hubris. To outsiders, the oligarchs may have seemed to have owed their good fortune to government connections, a lack of ethical reservations, or just plain luck. But the oligarchs themselves – all of them – believed they had triumphed in the brutal Russian capitalist contest of the 1990s because they were the strongest, smartest, and most daring six men in Russia, and possibly the world. As one of the more diffident oligarchs – one who was not yet in jail or exile – explained to me: 'We all made a lot of money – and it was not just lying on the street. We all took risks to get there, and not everyone is able to take such risks. I had partners who dropped out when we made our first $10,000 and $100,000 and $1 million. But I kept going, and so did the others.'

With Khodorkovsky in jail and Berezovsky and Gusinsky in exile, this sense of invincibility is easy to mock. But, after spending even a little bit of time in the orbit of an oligarch, it is also easy to see how that feeling of monumental self-belief can take hold. These are men who had the instinct and the courage to bet against the communist system – and to win! On countless smaller questions – Is machine-building or banking the right sector to invest in? Is now the moment to court Western investors, or to stiff them? – they made the right choices, and watched their rivals make the wrong ones. They made a president – Berezovsky made two – who was to say they couldn't transform the political system? Even losers can become addicted to gambling. Imagine what it is like when you make bigger and bigger bets – and you always take home the jackpot.

I had a glimpse of that sweet adrenaline rush during the day I spent with Khodorkovsky in St Petersburg. In the early afternoon he disappeared for a private meeting with the head of one of the Western oil companies which was courting Yukos (probably Chevron's O'Reilly, but I couldn't be absolutely sure). An hour later, an exhilarated Khodorkovsky slid into the back seat of his SUV, murmuring cheerily to himself, 'Money,

money, money . . . who needs a casino when you can have this?' Here he was, negotiating a high-profile, potentially multi-billion-dollar deal with a hugely more experienced counter-party and at the same time facing the imminent prospect of arrest and incarceration. For me, just thinking about it was positively stomach-churning. For Khodorkovsky, it was purest, most glorious, boyish good fun.

A love of risk, an $8bn winning streak – it is not hard to see how these could make a man a megalomaniac. What is more complicated to judge is the difference between megalomania and courage, and whether it is even possible to harness the overweening self-confidence, and ill-gotten gains, of an oligarch to a just cause. I watched Khodorkovsky struggling to resolve these questions for himself after his secret meeting, when we zoomed off to a rather kitsch, rustic-themed restaurant in a park on the outskirts St Petersburg. Outside, the weather had turned gloomy. Inside, everyone was starting to relax after a few shots of vodka and not much to eat. As the toasts rolled on, Leonard, the ex-Amoco geologist and one of those slightly straight-laced Westerners who is attracted by the unzipped passion of Russian culture, stood up, raised his vodka glass, took a deep breath and launched into a carefully rehearsed speech: 'This is the first time I have been to St Petersburg with Mikhail Borisovich. I have been reading a biography of Peter the Great. Peter the Great invited foreigners in and had to defend them against the locals. Three hundred years later, not that much has changed. Yukos is a small microcosm of the same process and I am proud to be a small part of it.'

Khodorkovsky had the generosity to thank Leonard for his tribute, but he also had the humility to qualify it. After all, he explained, the real lesson of Peter the Great was tragic, not heroic: 'We have to remember that under Peter the Great there were 24 million Russians and 300,000 of them died building St Petersburg. There were 2 million fewer Russians when Peter the Great died than there had been when he became tsar. We have developed quickly, and we have developed slowly, but in all this time, human life in Russia has not been worth even a kopek.'

It was an admirable response and I didn't think it was particularly directed at me. The episode made me wonder which force was more powerful in shaping Khodorkovsky's conduct in his clash with Putin: the self-belief of a man surrounded by fanatically devoted workers who routinely compared him to Peter the Great, or the idealism of one who remembered that Peter the Great was a murderous autocrat? To put it another way, was Khodorkovsky's new-found commitment to politics the dangerous power-grab of a preening oligarch or the philanthropic crusade of a public-spirited billionaire?

Like many Russians, Khodorkovsky was uninterested in mining the deeper reaches of his own psyche. (After the Peter the Great toast the conversation turned to Americans and their enthusiasm for psychoanalysis. The conclusion was that they need it because they are repressed and don't drink or have sex often enough. Russians, it was agreed, don't have either problem.) Khodorkovsky's personal motives for taking on the Kremlin were therefore a mystery even to the man himself. The best I could get from him was the observation that, 'Yes, I was once absolutely different in this respect, but people change with time, they mature.' Another oligarch attributed Khodorkovsky's transformation to 'the ennui of success'. 'Once you make so much money, it becomes boring,' he explained to me. 'You are young and you don't need to work to live anymore, so you look for something else.'

Some of the oligarchs, like Khodorkovsky's on-again-off-again partner Abramovich, turned to the traditional rich man's pastimes of international celebrity and conspicuous consumption. By contrast, even before he was confined to a prison cell, Khodorkovsky was moderate in his personal tastes: he took his family on holiday to Finland, lived in a house that wouldn't be out of place in most upper-middle-class Western suburbs, and told a Russian interviewer in early 2003 that you have to be born wealthy to get much pleasure from hobbies like connoisseurship of fine wines. He thought inherited wealth was soul-destroying (he himself began working part time at 14) and told me he planned to leave only a million or so to each of his four children. Instead, Khodorkovsky decided his second career would be giving Russia back the money he made during his first.

Khodorkovsky's decision has honourable international precedents: he cited both the nineteenth-century American robber barons and modern-day philanthropists like Bill Gates and George Soros as models. Like them, through his Open Russia foundation, he started ploughing money into standard civic good works: libraries, internet access for rural communities, orphanages, summer youth camps, international exchange programmes, scholarships and universities. But in a fledgling

democracy like Russia's, civic activity inevitably has political implications. Khodorkovsky exacerbated those by becoming involved directly
in politics, openly funding political parties and supporting the decision
of some key Yukos shareholders to run in the December 2003 parliamentary elections.

It is hard to judge what Khodorkovsky and his partners were hoping
to achieve with their foray into politics. Purely as a business decision,
it was unnecessary. Like Russia's other major corporations, Yukos
already had an extremely effective lobbying operation and, on corporate issues, was good at putting its case in parliament, the cabinet and
the Kremlin. Was Khodorkovsky, as his critics allege, trying to 'buy'
parliament and, through his control of the Duma, make himself
Russia's political master? He might have been – and he certainly has
the chutzpah to have tried. But whatever Khodorkovsky's motives
were and whatever his plan had been, the arrest of Lebedev changed
everything. On 2 July, Khodorkovsky found a new project for the
second half of his life: he would not capitulate to the Kremlin hard-
liners and he would devote himself to building a political alternative to
their rule.

The mystery I kept coming back to during the time I spent with
Khodorkovsky in the autumn of 2004 was why he wouldn't simply
give up his political projects. That had been Putin's deal with the oligarchs in 2000 and it seemed to be the only way Khodorkovsky could
be sure of keeping his company and keeping out of jail. But no matter
how many different ways I put the question, his answer was always
equally adamant: 'I recall now and have often recalled our discussions
with the president, and absolutely agree that businesses cannot and
should not participate in politics. But, at the same time, according to
our constitution, I have the same civil rights [to participate in politics]
as other citizens. For me, my civil rights are even more important
than my property because I believe that civil rights guarantee private
property. As long as I have strength, I am ready to fight with the view
that I must renounce my civil rights to guarantee my private property.
I do not think that such a policy of appeasement is correct. Everyone
knows how it ends. In 1929 and in 1917 people thought, let's compromise. It ended with 5 million killed and with tens of millions
of people in prison. Our White officers fled the country, not wanting
to fight for their rights at home. And how did it end? If they had

stayed and fought, perhaps 30 million of their fellow citizens would have lived.'

Interestingly, even a rival oligarch, who was worried that Khodorkovsky's venture would hurt all big business, believed his commitment to democracy was genuine, if misguided. 'We spoke to him and said "Stop your political activity." He refused,' the oligarch told me. 'He said he was bringing democracy to Russia. He has a messianic vision. Of course, all of our dictators start with messianic visions. And you can't buy democracy. It has to mature naturally.'

The warning about Russia's bitter past experiences with power-hungry messiahs is well put. And for all his protestations, it is still hard to see Khodorkovsky as Russia's modern-day Andrei Sakharov. His commitment to civil society is relatively new found and was hardly disinterested. But on our flight back to Moscow, he told me he was ready to go to jail, if that's what it took. He was still young and rich. At some point, they would have to release him and then he would carry on his battle. Several leading Russian politicians, businessmen and Yukos executives told me Khodorkovsky had said the same thing to them. Most of them predicted that Khodorkovsky's bravado would not last many hours in a crowded, tubercular prison cell. Only one person thought Khodorkovsky would hold out. A rival oligarch told me: 'There will be no backwards step for Khodorkovsky. He will not give up . . . But for Putin, putting Khodorkovsky in jail is frightening. He is young – eventually he will get out, and then Putin will have a very rich opponent with a personal animus against him. If he puts Khodorkovsky in jail, he almost has to shoot him.'

Khodorkovsky's clash with the Kremlin showed the limits of oligarchic power under the new regime. Mikhail Friedman's fate, at least as of late 2004, showed how the oligarchs could still prosper, as long as they played by Putin's new rules. More surprisingly, it also revealed the extent to which the oligarchs' own rules continued to govern the ways in which money was made and lost in the new Russia. These rules were unwritten and unenforceable by any court; but they had a real power which even the biggest foreign investor ignored at his peril. The strange story of Friedman and the oligarchic business code begins in 1997, when British Petroleum made its first great foray into the Russian market, buying 10 per cent of Sidanco, the Siberian oil company controlled by Potanin, then the most powerful of the oligarchs. In the chaotic aftermath of the 1998 crisis, Friedman decided to prey on Sidanco, buying up the debt of Chernogorneft, its richest production subsidiary, and then using sympathetic provincial judges and bankruptcy proceedings to try to seize control. When BP cried foul, it seemed to be the standard Russian story: corrupt courts, duped Western investors, predatory local businessmen and a Russian government and public perfectly prepared to tolerate them.

But, as I learned quite by accident on a visit to Russia in January 2000, the entire saga turned out to have a vital Russian subtext. Friedman and Potanin actually were playing by a fairly well-defined set of rules; it was just that their Western partners and rivals didn't realise they existed. For the Russians, the conflict, like almost everything else in the country, dated back to the nation's primal business moment: the loans-for-shares auctions. In that fraught period, Friedman had entered into a private pact with Potanin, putting up $40m towards the purchase of Sidanco and getting a third of Potanin's stake in the company in exchange, as well as two seats on the board. Like so many Russian partnerships, however, Potanin and Friedman's relationship soon began to sour. Sensing the possibilities of a lucrative strategic alliance with a foreign oil company, Potanin took advantage of legal loopholes to push Friedman out of Sidanco. He offered Friedman $100m for his holding. That may seem to be a handsome return, but it was far short of the $571m BP would pay for a 10 per cent share in the company a few months later.

Friedman never forgave Potanin for what he saw as a betrayal. When the crash of 1998 weakened Potanin and gave Friedman an opportunity for revenge – and to make money – he seized it. As Friedman put it to me in a conversation in 2003: 'With Chernogor it was a principled issue for us because we considered that we, without meriting it and unfairly, had lost a serious asset and a business opportunity . . . We were firmly convinced that if we wanted to feel ourselves to be serious businessmen, we had to defend our rights and win.' Unfortunately for both BP and Friedman, whose reputation took a beating in the West, Potanin's foreign partners, who also included George Soros, British billionaire Joe Lewis and the Harvard University Endowment, got caught in the crossfire. 'The tragedy of the situation was that we took aggressive measures against Sidanco, wanting to go to battle against Potanin, but we ended up fighting with BP,' Friedman told me in January 2000, in Moscow. 'We never wanted to go to war with BP, we wanted to go to war with Potanin.'

Moreover, as Friedman insisted in a later conversation with me, 'All the Russian business community knew perfectly that we had a conflict and everyone knew the circumstances of that conflict. Potanin knew it perfectly well, too.' As I did the rounds of the oligarchs during my January 2000 trip, I saw for myself that Friedman was right: this inside story had been an open secret among Russia's business leaders. Khodorkovsky, a disinterested party, had known about it all along and agreed that 'Friedman had had some grounds' for launching his vendetta. Even Potanin confirmed the broad outlines of the tale, although he added another, even more bizarre, twist. According to Potanin, among the oligarchs it was a rule that if you accepted money for a business deal you lost the 'moral right' to oppose the terms of that transaction. Friedman had taken Potanin's money and thus he had lost his grounds for later seeking revenge. 'I consider that he conned me,' Potanin explained with a philosophical shrug, 'and he considers that I conned him.'

The more I learned about the secret history of the Sidanco feud, the more Byzantine the saga became, and the more revealing. For one thing, it was another instance of how profoundly the loans-for-shares deal haunted Russia still. Like the settling of the western frontier for the United States, loans-for-shares is Russia's foundation story and it will continue to exert its hold on the future for some time to come. The Sidanco episode also reminded me of a fundamental mistake we Westerners are apt to make when we think about Russia: our assumption that what seems confusing to us must in reality be confused. But even though we do not always understand them, or even realise they are there, in the 1990s Russian business evolved a rough-and-ready set of rules. Most are unwritten, many are unenforceable, and their supreme arbitrator is the court of elite opinion rather than courts of law – but they are there and even the most powerful multinational corporations need to be aware of them.

Three years later there was a further twist in the Sidanco story, and one which suggested to me that Western investors were learning to be mindful of the oligarchic rules, even if they didn't always like or understand them. In the spring of 2003, BP announced a landmark $7.6bn deal in Russia, the country's biggest foreign investment since the Bolshevik Revolution. BP's Russian partner was Mikhail Friedman.

BP's change of heart was astounding. At the height of the conflict with Friedman, BP had mounted a sustained and fierce vilification campaign against the oligarch, including prompting British prime minister Tony Blair to write a letter to Putin decrying Friedman's behaviour and lobbying the US government to block a $500m loan to TNK, Friedman's oil company, from a US state-backed bank. For Lord Browne, BP's lionised chief executive, financially the conflict was a mere 'pin-prick'. But, for him, it was about more than money. 'We were being robbed,' Browne told me in the autumn of 2003, toying with a trademark Cuban cigar, in his sleek, minimalist office suite in St James's Square. 'That was an important watershed moment. If we had lost, we would have pulled out of Russia.'

Friedman did two things to turn Browne and BP from, as one British paper put it, 'hate to love'. The companies reached a financial compromise: Friedman's TNK got back a 25 per cent stake in Sidanco and Sidanco got back Chernogorneft. Just as crucially, Friedman found a way to persuade BP that he was not simply a 'Russian bandit', as he knew they believed at one point, but was behaving honourably – according to Moscow rules. Making his case was not easy. 'It was very difficult to arrange a meeting,' Friedman told me in September 2003. 'They refused to enter into any relations with us. We wrote them letters, we phoned, but had no reply.' In his desperation, Friedman tried informal channels, too. The close relationship between Lord Browne and his mother, Paula, an Auschwitz survivor, was well known. Friedman arranged for Mrs Browne's rabbi to pass on the message that he was a trustworthy man, eager to make personal contact with her son. Eventually, Friedman broke through, and when he did, he made a point of showing senior BP executives a document signed by Mikhail Prokherev, Potanin's partner, setting out Alfa's involvement in the initial acquisition of Sidanco. The document had no legal weight, either in the Russian courts or in commercial negotiations with BP. But Friedman believed, and a senior BP manager in Moscow concurred, that 'on a human level, it was important for them to understand why we behaved as we did.'

The Sidanco story was fascinating to me because it showed the ways in which the oligarchs' rules continued to govern Russian business life.

Paradoxically, though, the BP deal with which the story concluded may have marked the beginning of the end of that era. Putin was pushing the oligarchs out of political life; the logic of international business may have been pushing them out of the economy, too.

'All of the oligarchs over the next three to five years will either sell their assets and leave Russia or they will joint venture these assets, like BP–TNK,' Stephen Jennings, the investment banker, told me in Moscow in September 2003. 'Most Russian businesses are for sale at the right price right now.' The oligarchs, he argued, had a particular set of skills and personality traits which equipped them for the crude capitalist competition of the 1990s, but were less suited to the challenges of the following decade: 'These guys had a particular advantage in stealing assets, in grabbing assets, in consolidating assets, in controlling assets and in doing the first stage of clean-up of those businesses. But they don't have the skills to manage these assets to international quality. It is not like the US, where someone gets to the top at 55 after years of hard work. It is not a marathon here, it was a lolly scramble. They don't have the personalities to want to slog their guts out year after year.'

Crucially, many Russian businessmen seemed be coming to the same conclusion. Although not known for their modesty, many oligarchs appeared to have realised that only Western managers could take their companies to the next stage. 'As managers, we can be effective at a certain place and at a certain time,' Friedman told me. 'We believe that people of my generation, we are not professional managers. There are only a few specific niches in which we as managers can add something, and after that you must clear the way for more professional people.'

Moreover, having won the struggle to control many of Russia's most valuable resources, many of the oligarchs seemed to be realising that bringing in Western strategic investors with their superior management skills would make them richer still. They were beginning to think like shareholders, rather than gladiators. As Friedman said of his deal with BP: 'We felt that as shareholders, we would win. That experience which BP has should seriously improve the quality of management in the company. It should put the management really on the level of a first-class company. We think this will change the attitude of investors. And if investor perception of BP–TNK changes, then, of course, our remaining 50 per cent will become worth much more.'

Of the original group of oligarchs who came together in the mid-1990s to re-elect Yeltsin and profit mightily from his privatisation process, by 2005 Khodorkovsky was poring over law books in his Moscow prison cell; Berezovsky and Gusinsky were offering frustrated commentaries on Russian political life from comfortable but dull exile in London and New York; and Potanin was in business, but on a reduced scale. Only Friedman was still a tycoon, but he was sharing control with foreigners, and schooling himself to maintain as humble a demeanour as his billions would allow. Some oligarchs, Friedman told me in September 2003, liked buying sports teams or becoming provincial governors. For him, going to a concert, visiting a museum or reading a book was enough. 'It is not that I don't think I'm great,' he explained. 'But it is enough for me to know it. I don't need the world to know it, too.'

15

CONCLUSION

When Gaidar sat down to write his memoirs of his time in office, a line from Pasternak came to mind: 'You yourself should not be able to distinguish between victory and defeat.' It makes the perfect epitaph for the young reformers and for Russia's fearless but flawed capitalist revolution.

So much was achieved. Russia demolished communism and laid the foundations for capitalism. Between 1998 and 2003 the battered economy finally started to grow, expanding by more than a third. Five years after the devastating default of 1998, international currency reserves were at a healthy $60bn. A radical 13 per cent flat income-tax rate reduced corruption and boosted returns.

But so much was left to be done. Russia's market economy remained trapped in a web of red tape and government intervention, which crippled entrepreneurs even as it enriched sleazy apparatchiks. Worryingly, many businessmen, especially in the regions, said that the Kremlin campaign against Khodorkovsky emboldened provincial bureaucrats to step up their own attacks on local businesses. Putin's clampdown on the independent media, and the defeat of liberal parties in the 2003 Duma elections, weakened an already feeble civil society. The arrest of

Khodorkovsky dramatically underscored the continued arbitrariness of the law. Without deep structural reform, economists warned that Russia's petro-fuelled economic performance was likely to falter. As Willem Buiter, chief economist at the EBRD, told the *Financial Times* in August 2003: 'Without serious changes, growth will peter out. In fact, I'm surprised it hasn't already.'

Does this unfinished revolution count as victory or defeat? Even in late 2004, more than ten years after the collapse of the Soviet Union, the easy answer, and probably the best one, is that, as Chinese prime minister Zhou Enlai once said of the French Revolution, it is too soon to tell. So far, the only certain consequence of Russia's capitalist revolution has been forever to change the parameters of the national debate. At the beginning of the 1990s, the question was communism or capitalism. A decade later, the question is what sort of capitalism Russia will have: an open, liberal system, with clear rules of the game and free entry to competitors, or a corrupt, crony capitalism, with a highly interventionist state and a changing cast of favoured oligarchs.

So far, the answer is not very encouraging. But compared with the other choices Russians have faced over the past century – Tsarism or Communism? Stalin or Hitler? – the question itself is something of an accomplishment.

Russia has always been a country of the extreme and the improbable. Its politics have usually been equally hyperbolic. Some countries are happy just to get by, content to trot along in their geopolitical pack, maybe no better than their neighbours but not worse either. Not Russia. For much of the past millennium, Moscow has been in the grip of a messianic vision of its own destiny. It started with Ivan IV, the medieval prince known as 'The Terrible', a word which in Russian means great as well as frightening. Like many Russian leaders, Ivan was troubled by the gap between Russia and its European neighbours. But where others saw the cultural, technological and religious differences as symptoms of Russia's backwardness, Ivan saw them as signs of superiority. During his reign, the monk Philotheus of Pskov declared Moscow to be the Third Rome, the spiritual and secular leader of the Christian world now that Rome and Byzantium had grown too weak and too corrupt to wear that crown. In Philotheus' vision, which became an integral part of official Muscovite political theory, Russia was a 'Christ among nations', a country which was fated to suffer more than the rest of Christian Europe but which would be rewarded for its trials with the heavenly kingdom, and the earthly one, too.

This messianic tendency informed much of Imperial Russian history and can be seen in the implacable march of Russia's tsarist expansion: from the days of Peter the Great to the First World War the Russian Empire expanded unremittingly. It is evident in Imperial Russia's love–hate relationships with Western technologies: the tsars were always eager to adopt foreign know-how, but intensely suspicious of the habits of mind that went with it, lest Russia lose the spiritual apartness which made it special. It can even be detected in the thinking of Imperial Russia's dissident intelligentsia, which could not shake off the view that its country's suffering – its poverty, its feudalism, its police state – was somehow ennobling.

Ironically, though, Ivan the Terrible's messianic project reached its full expression only with the Russian rulers who formally sought to make a clean break with the autocratic past: the Bolsheviks. Communism was the perfect vehicle for Russia's sense of manifest destiny. It gave Russia a global mission, made the country a global leader and offered it the reassuring belief that, whatever its shortcomings, in all the really important ways it was the best country on earth. When Nikita Khrushchev pounded his shoe on the table and announced that 'We will bury you', he was voicing Moscow's age-old dream of becoming the Third Rome.

The messianic subtext of the communist era was part of the reason that the collapse of the Soviet Union was so traumatic for so many Russians. By 1991, few Russians continued to believe in the Marxist ideology, but many of them still wanted to have faith in Russia as a Christ-nation. Now that that creed was discredited, what did Russia have left?

In 1991, the only Russians with a convincing, coherent response to that question were the young reformers, and their answer was capitalism. In one way, their project was fundamentally – and reassuringly – different from Russia's earlier messianic missions. When Moscow styled itself the Third Rome or set out to create the world's first communist system, it had been pursuing an ideological model which was emphatically different from that of the West. The young reformers believed that this insistence on a uniquely Russian 'third way' – either as a Third Rome or as the leader of the Soviet bloc – was pig-headed and crippling.

Capitalism had worked for the West, they thought, and it would work for Russia too.

But in other ways the capitalist revolution was eerily similar to Russia's previous crusades. It was fiercely ideological, it was shot through with an ends-justify-the-means urgency and it even contained something of the superior swagger which had animated Russia's earlier messianic quests. Sure, Russia had decided to play by foreign rules; but, as the capitalist revolution got going, Russia's leaders quickly came to believe that within a few years they would be beating the West at its own game. As one American investment banker told me, 'They thought that by 2001 Moscow would be New York.'

There was something exhilarating about the young reformers' capitalist messianism. Russia's past was so wretched and its immediate circumstances so impoverished that when the Soviet Union collapsed many Russians wrung their hands and sadly concluded that nothing was to be done: their country was doomed to economic decline and political chaos. The young reformers were braver and more generous; they refused to be cowed by history and insisted on hoping for a better future for their people.

Yet while the fervour with which Russia took to capitalism was certainly understandable, and may even have been laudable, it hasn't really worked. Part of the problem, I've come to think, was the age-old messianic mindset with which the young reformers launched their revolution. In saying that, I don't mean to buy into the argument – fashionable since the meltdown of 1998 – that the capitalist revolutionaries went too far or pushed too fast. Indeed, I'm convinced that the central failure of Russia's capitalist revolution was that it did not go far enough. Price liberalism was bold, but not bold enough, allowing the oil and gas barons and the rentiers of the loophole economy to get rich on the difference between world prices and domestic ones. Balancing the budget was painful, but the government should have cut even more deeply – if it had, it might have avoided the Grand Debt Gamble which triggered the financial crisis of 1998. Privatisation was a radical break with state-ownership, but Russia would have been better off if the young reformers had had the political authority to give fewer perks to the red directors.

The problem was not that the young reformers were too radical, but that they were too fanatical. They sought to impose capitalism with the same fervour as their ancestors had fought for communism or defended autocracy. And they made the classic mistakes of all fanatics. They thought their own small band of revolutionaries could transform Russia without grass-roots support – and they found themselves without a political power-base. They thought the central tenet of their faith, private property, was ultimately all that mattered – and watched helplessly as corruption, a weak state and ineffective laws made private ownership close to irrelevant. They believed the end justifies the means – and made a Faustian bargain with the oligarchs which forever corrupted their revolution. Their particular messianic creed has been discredited for some time to come.

The question for Russia now, as it slouches into a new millennium, is whether a fresh fanatical faith will seize the national imagination. The oldest and most durable one is still lurking in the national psyche, and of late it has been making a comeback. Russia's nationalist mission has always been one of the country's most powerful and successful ideologies. It was more effective than Orthodox mysticism in tsarist Russia, and at least as important as class war or the desire to unite the workers of the world was in the Soviet era. Part of Putin's appeal, and the attraction of the puppet parties he has sponsored in parliament, is that he harkens back to this notion of a great Russia, one not afraid to defy the West or menace its neighbours. Putin has used the obscene language of the barracks in his public comments about Chechnya; his campaign against the oligarchs is not without a whiff of anti-Semitism, even if the president himself has not made any anti-Semitic comments or gestures.

These ugly nationalist undertones led some Russian liberals, embittered, perhaps, by their devastating defeat in the 2003 parliamentary elections, to make dark comparisons between Putin's Russia and Weimar Germany. That is a bleak scenario, and an extreme one. What seemed more likely to me is a slide into a milder form of authoritarianism. Already, by 2004, Putin had systematically crushed many of the institutions of civil society that Gorbachev and Yeltsin had taken such pains to promote. National television, which the oligarchs had shown could make a president, had been brought back under the control of the state. Independent political parties had been defeated, elected regional governors had been neutered and outspoken businessmen exiled or imprisoned. The activists, reformers, oligarchs and wheeler-dealers who shot to prominence in the Yeltsin era gradually were being pushed out of business and political life.

In their place, Putin steadily promoted the group that was one of the big losers of the Yeltsin era – the Soviet apparat, in particular the *siloviki*, or functionaries from the 'power' ministries of the interior, army and former KGB. According to Olga Kryshtanovskaya, a leading Russian sociologist, the proportion of *siloviki* in the top echelons of power increased from 4.8 per cent under Mikhail Gorbachev, the last Soviet leader, to a walloping 58.3 per cent under Putin. Kryshtanovskaya told my *FT* colleague, Arkady Ostrovsky, that the *siloviki* had a collective enthusiasm for rebuilding the power of Russia and of the Russian state: 'The *siloviki* are a very homogeneous group in terms of their social status and mentality. They think they act in the interest of the state and their aim is for Russia to be feared again. They call it patriotism and states-manship. The trouble is that the notion of a strong state is inseparable in their mind from fear.'

Tragically, the creative chaos of the Yeltsin era proved to be the ideal preparation for the return of the *siloviki*. For one thing, the anarchy and corruption of that period left Russia with a collective yearning for order. The colossally unfair distribution of assets which the young reformers tolerated – in their urgency to destroy communism – is another resented legacy that has abetted the rise of Putin and his grey functionaries. And finally, the contradictory and incomplete legal framework, a crazy quilt of Soviet-era and free-market laws, bequeathed Putin a capitalism in which every businessman was a potential criminal. It is an ex-KGB officer's paradise and a perfect environment for imposing state control under the high-minded guise of enforcing the rule of law.

Friedman, who has proven to be one of the most adept negotiators of this perilous environment, told me that it was the continuation of a relationship between the state and the individual which dated back to the tsarist era: 'Karamzin [the eighteenth-century Russian historian] said that the severity of Russian laws is compensated by the fact that it is not obligatory to follow them. The state establishes rules of the game according to which it is impossible to live. But, somehow, everyone lives and everyone does so by breaking the rules. And so everyone feels himself to be a criminal. For that reason, it is always easy for the state.'

For Yeltsin and the young reformers, the enemy was the communist system and the economic order it imposed. They devoted themselves –

using fair means and foul ones – to discrediting the communist ideology, defeating the Communist Party, and, above all, dismantling the communist economy. But maybe the real enemy wasn't the Communist Party and its ideologues, or even the communist economic order per se. Perhaps the more dangerous opponents of Russian democracy and free markets were the communist apparatchiks, who were once tsarist chinovniks, and have now been rebranded as Putin's civil servants. For centuries, Russian liberals saw their country's essential struggle as a battle between an omnivorous, arbitrary state – and its functionaries – and a feeble civil society. Under Putin, Russia seems to have reverted to this old, unbalanced contest. And it was Yeltsin's closest allies, and Russia's most cunning oligarchs, who made the revanche of the apparatchiks possible; it all began in 1999, when they thought to secure their own legacy by plucking a mid-ranking, ex-KGB officer from obscurity and installing him in the Kremlin.

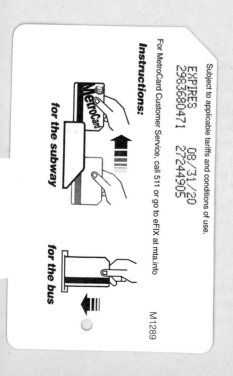

CHRONOLOGY

1991

12 June – Boris Yeltsin elected president of Russia.

19–21 August – Failed hard-line communist coup against Mikhail Gorbachev.

28 October – Yeltsin outlines his radical market-reform plans in a speech to the Russian Congress of People's Deputies.

6 November – Yegor Gaidar appointed deputy prime minister (later he would become acting prime minister). Over the next few days, many of the other young reformers join him in government.

8 December – The presidents of Ukraine, Russia and Belarus sign the Belovezh accord on dissolving the Soviet Union.

25 December – Gorbachev resigns as president of the USSR.

1992

2 January – The young reformers' radical price-liberalisation goes into effect.

30 May – Viktor Chernomyrdin named deputy prime minister.

15 June – Gaidar named acting prime minister.

19 August – On the first anniversary of the putsch, Yeltsin announces voucher privatisation.

12 December – Gaidar is ousted as acting prime minister by the Congress of People's Deputies.

14 December – Chernomyrdin appointed prime minister.

1993

25 April – National referendum unexpectedly supports Yeltsin and the young reformers' radical market reforms.

18 May – The first GKOs (short-term Russian government bonds) are auctioned off.

18 September – Gaidar returns to the government as first deputy prime minister.

21 September – Yeltsin dissolves the Congress of People's Deputies and the Supreme Soviet. Deputies refuse to leave the White House, at that time the parliament building.

3 October – Vice-president Aleksandr Rutskoi calls for an armed attack on the Ostankino television tower and the Moscow mayor's office.

4 October – The Russian army shells the White House; the rebellious parliamentarians are defeated.

12 December – Parliamentary elections and referendum on the new constitution. The constitution, which grants the president vast powers, is approved, but extreme nationalists and communists dominate the new legislature.

1994

16 January – Gaidar resigns as first deputy prime minister.

22 July – The MMM financial pyramid crashes, depriving millions of Russians of their life savings.

11 October – 'Black Tuesday' – a one-day collapse of the rouble against the dollar.

2 December – The 'faces-on-the-snow' clash between Vladimir Gusinsky, the media baron and future oligarch, and the Kremlin security service, headed by Aleksandr Korzhakov, the president's bodyguard and friend.

11 December – Russian troops enter Chechnya. The first Chechen war begins.

New Year's Eve – Russian forces launch an ill-fated campaign to storm Grozny.

1995

31 March – Vladimir Potanin, flanked by Mikhail Khodorkovsky and Aleksandr Smolensky, outlines his loans-for-shares scheme at a meeting of the Russian cabinet.

9 May – Grandiose celebrations in Moscow to commemorate the fiftieth anniversary of the Soviet victory in 'The Great Patriotic War'. More than fifty heads of state attend.

6 July – The Central Bank and government peg the rouble to the dollar, announcing a 'corridor' within the parameters of which they guarantee the Russian currency will trade.

31 August – Yeltsin signs a decree authorising the loans-for-shares programme.

17 December – Communists dominate elections to the Duma, the lower house of the Russian parliament.

1996

16 January – Chubais is sacked from the government.

February – At the annual meeting of the World Economic Forum in Switzerland, the oligarchs and Chubais form the Davos pact to ensure Yeltsin's re-election and the defeat of Gennady Zyuganov, the communist leader.

15 February – Yeltsin officially announces his candidacy on a trip to Yekaterinburg.

15–17 March – The Kremlin plans, then calls off at the last minute, the dissolution of parliament and postponement of the presidential elections.

27 May – Russian and Chechen officials sign a cease-fire.

16 June – Yeltsin comes in first, Zyuganov second and dark horse candidate Aleksandr Lebed third in the first round of presidential elections. No candidate wins the 50 per cent required for victory in the first round, so a second ballot is scheduled.

18 June – Lebed is appointed secretary of the Kremlin's Security Council.

19 June – Arkady Evstafiev and Sergei Lisovsky are detained as they leave the White House (by now the seat of the Russian government). Korzhakov's security service claims they are carrying a Xerox box containing $500,000 in cash.

20 June – After a night of frantic lobbying, the Davos pact triumphs over the party of war. Yeltsin sacks Korzhakov, Oleg Soskovets, the first deputy prime minister, and Mikhail Barsukov, the chief of the FSB.

3 July – Yeltsin overwhelmingly defeats Zyuganov in the second round of presidential elections.

15 July – Chubais is appointed Yeltsin's chief-of-staff.

7 August – A frail and stumbling Yeltsin is sworn in as president.

August – Potanin, one of the oligarchs, is named first deputy prime minister.

5 September – Yeltsin admits he has suffered a heart-attack and will undergo open-heart surgery.

October – Boris Berezovsky is appointed deputy head of the Security Council.

17 October – Lebed is sacked as head of the Security Council.

5 November – Yeltsin successfully undergoes open-heart surgery.

21 November – Russia issues its first eurobond since the Bolshevik Revolution, borrowing $1bn in the foreign capital markets.

1997

27 January – Aslan Maskhadov is elected president of Chechnya. Russia and the breakaway republic seem to settle into an uneasy peace.

March – A reinvigorated Yeltsin delivers a powerful state of the nation address, calling for a fresh wave of market reforms. He signs a series of decrees reorganising the cabinet and bringing in two powerful young reformers – Chubais and Boris Nemstov, governor of Nizhny Novgorod – as first deputy prime ministers.

1 July – The government pays off pension arrears, fulfilling the president's promise.

25 July – The Russian government sells 25 per cent of Sviazinvest, the telecomms giant, to a consortium led by Potanin's Oneximbank for $1.875bn.

13 August – Alfred Kokh, a young reformer, resigns from his job as head of the GKI, the State Property Committee. In the days following his resignation, he is accused of having been too close to Potanin.

27 October – The Asian economic crisis rocks the buoyant Russian stock market, pushing down blue-chip share prices by 19 per cent and weakening the rouble.

12 November – Journalist Aleksandr Minkin accuses a group of young reformers led by Chubais of receiving a 'veiled bribe' in the form of a $450,000 payment to write a book on market reforms.

November – Chubais' allies are fired from government one by one. Chubais keeps his job but is severely weakened.

December – Government struggles to meet Yeltsin's end-of-year deadline for paying off wage arrears.

1998

23 March – Yeltsin announces the dismissal of Viktor Chernomyrdin, his longest-serving prime minister, and appoints Sergei Kiriyenko, an unknown former businessman from Nizhny Novgorod, as his acting prime minister. After a battle with parliament, Kiriyenko is confirmed as prime minister on 17 April.

27 May – The stockmarket plummets and the rouble softens, forcing the Central Bank to raise interest rates to 150 per cent.

May – In the last week of May, Chubais and Sergei Vasiliev travel to Washington and meet with senior US officials to make the case for massive financial assistance for Russia.

15 June – The oligarchs and young reformers meet at Berezovsky's Logovaz Clubhouse and decided Chubais should negotiate on the country's behalf with the IMF.

13 July – The IMF approves a $22.6bn loan for Russia. The first $4.8bn tranche is to be disbursed in the last week of July.

14 August – Yeltsin announces the rouble will never be allowed to devalue.

15–16 August – The young reformers, the oligarchs and Russia's Western partners spend the weekend frantically calculating how to manage the – by now inevitable – crisis.

17 August – Government announces the devaluation of the rouble, default on its GKOs and a moratorium on payment of foreign debt by private companies.

23 August – Kiriyenko is sacked.

11 September – Yevgeny Primakov, the former Soviet spymaster and Russian foreign minister, is confirmed as prime minister by the parliament.

1999

12 May – Primakov is sacked. Sergei Stepashin, the minister of the interior, becomes prime minister.

9 August – Stepashin is sacked. Yeltsin appoints Vladimir Putin, an unknown former KGB chief, his prime minister and declares he will be his successor.

September – Bombs go off in Moscow and Volgodonsk. Chechen terrorists are blamed, though there is little evidence linking them to the explosions. The incidents build public support for a renewed attack on Chechnya.

19 December – Yedinstvo, the pro-government party supported by Putin, does remarkably well in parliamentary elections, coming a close second to

the communists. Riding on Putin's coat-tails, the Union of Right Wing Forces, a group dominated by the young reformers, also makes a strong showing.

31 December – Yeltsin stuns Russia and the world by resigning, automatically making Putin acting president.

2000

January/February – Russia prepares for presidential elections, scheduled for 26 March, with Putin the overwhelming favourite. The Kremlin continues aggressively to pursue its war in Chechnya.

26 March – Putin is elected president. He summons the oligarchs for a meeting and tells them they can keep their wealth as long as they stay out of politics.

June/July – The state launches an aggressive campaign against Gusinsky and the Most Group, which includes the brief arrest of Gusinsky. In late July, Gusinsky is allowed to leave the country, but eventually he loses control of Most.

12 August – The *Kursk* submarine disappears during a training exercise in the Barents Sea. It sinks and all 118 crew members are lost. Putin's initially cavalier handling of the tragedy is the first major crisis of his presidency and heightens tensions between him and the media.

September/October – Berezovsky flees Russia, fearing he would otherwise be arrested. Under duress, he sells his stakes in the ORT television network and Sibneft, which goes to rising oligarch Roman Abramovich.

2003

February – British Petroleum announces landmark deal with TNK, the oil company controlled by Mikhail Friedman and his partners.

2 July – Platon Lebedev, a senior Yukos executive, is arrested. On the same day, Roman Abramovich announces he will buy Chelsea football club for £140m.

Summer – Leonid Nevzlin and a handful of other Yukos partners flee to Israel.

September – Berezovsky is granted political asylum in Britain.

25 October – Khodorkovsky is arrested and imprisoned.

7 December – Parliamentary elections, with a huge victory for the pro-Putin bloc. The liberal democratic parties, led by the young reformers, are almost completely wiped out.

2004

24 February – Putin sacks his reformist prime minister, Mikhail Kasyanov, and the rest of the cabinet, to assert his personal authority ahead of the presidential poll. Mikhail Fradkov, a little-known diplomat, is later appointed as the new prime minister.

14 March – Putin is re-elected by an overwhelming majority.

1–3 September – Chechen terrorists attack a school in Belsan in the Russian North Caucasus. Nearly 340 die, more than half of them children.

13 September – Responding to the Belsan attack, Putin further centralises power, ending the direct election of regional governors. Instead, in the future, they are to be nominated by the president and ratified by regional parliaments. He also ends the direct election of members of the Duma. Instead, all Duma members are to be elected solely from party lists.

ACKNOWLEDGEMENTS

My Russian friends and contacts have been endlessly helpful to me and remarkably generous with their time. Dozens of people, particularly the oligarchs and the young reformers, submitted to my repeated requests for interviews both while I was reporting for the *Financial Times* and while I was working on this book. I am grateful to them for their patience and their courage. Without Yekaterina Shaverdova, herself a former journalist and the researcher at the *FT* Moscow bureau, Natalya Belova, the *FT* office manager, and Leonid Burmistrov, who worked as my researcher for this book, I would have been unable to complete this project. All three of them provided logistical and, more importantly, intellectual support, sharing the latest Moscow gossip and patiently correcting my Western misconceptions. Katya and Leonid both read the manuscript and caught many of its errors. The comradeship and ideas of my Russian journalist colleagues were invaluable. I am particularly grateful to Aleksandr (Sasha) Bekker, Mikhail Berger, Mikhail Leontiev, Dmitry Ostalsky, Sergei Parkhomenko and Dmitry Volkov. Russian analysts Andrei Piontkovsky and Sergei Karaganov were excellent sounding boards for my ideas about Russia, even though we did not always agree. Nina Golovyatenko and her husband Dimitry Alekseev, Oleg Mitaev and Olga Zharkova at the *FT* Moscow bureau provided tremendous support and encouragement, as did my friend Larissa Konyukhovskaya.

My fellow foreign correspondents and Western friends in Moscow offere invaluable insights and companionship. Foremost among them are John Lloyd, of the *Financial Times*, and David Hoffman, of the *Washington Post*. A journalist of boundless energy and analytical rigour, John was my mentor and inspiration when I first began reporting on the former Soviet Union. I have admired him, and he has supported me, ever since, including reading my manuscript with care. David was my favourite companion on my travels to war zones and remote Siberian factories, greeting me at the airport with a fat folder of research and a determination to get to the truth of every story. His tireless investigative skills and interest in ideas rather than sensation have been a model for me. David read the manuscript and made many valuable suggestions. Fred Hiatt and Margaret Shapiro, also of the *Washington Post*, gave me a job and some unforgettable instruction in how to write news stories. John Thornhill, my colleague at the *FT*'s Moscow bureau, was always ready to trade the latest market rumours and conspiracy theories. John kindly pointed out several errors in the manuscript of this book. Alan Philps of the *Daily Telegraph* and his wife Sarah plied me with wine and valuable advice on navigating the ethical quandaries of reporting in Russia. Andrew Meier, of *Time* magazine, was a neighbour and stimulating source of ideas. Carey Scott of the *Sunday Times* taught me never to take Russia, or our job in reporting on it, too seriously.

Moscow can be a lonely city for foreigners. I was lucky enough to be there with two of my closest girl-friends: Roberta Feldman and Sarah Mendelson. I am also grateful to Alan Bigman, Matthew Brzezinski, Lance Crist, Santiago Eider, Maria Kozloski, Marcia Levy, Julie Mindlin and Courtney Tuttle for their friendship and their insights on Russia.

The *Financial Times* is renowned for its intelligence, its seriousness and its generosity, but it is not always thought of as daring. Yet the *FT*, particularly Richard Lambert, the editor, and Andrew Gowers, then the deputy editor, took a great risk in sending me to Moscow as bureau chief when I was just 26. I am very grateful to them for taking that gamble and for the consistent support and guidance they offered me throughout the nine years I spent working for the *Financial Times*. Martin Wolf shaped much of my thinking about the Russian economy. Robert Thomson and Julia Cuthbertson were inspiring editors and instructors. Graham Watts is one of the best story editors and journalism teachers in the business. I was the lucky recipient of his ministrations. He also read the first draft of this book and provided vital encouragement and advice. Lionel Barber, the *FT*'s news editor and my boss after I left Moscow, was tolerant of the absences writing this book entailed and taught me most of what I know about editing. Peter Cheek, the *FT*'s finest researcher, checked and corrected hundreds of facts for me. Jeanette Owen, one of the *FT*'s best sub-editors, ruthlessly and cleverly helped me condense an earlier draft. My new employers at the *Globe and Mail*, particularly Phillip Crawley, the publisher, and Richard Addis, the editor, also generously supported my completion of this book, even though it came at the sensitive moment when I was starting a new job.

As an undergraduate I had the good fortune to be taught by Timothy Colton, Edward Kennan and Richard Pipes of Harvard University. These three pre-eminent scholars of Russia and the Soviet Union gave me a powerful intellectual framework for trying to understand the new Russia. Marshall Goldman, also of Harvard, read the manuscript and, to my relief, pointed out errors of fact and judgement. Anders Aslund, Thomas Graham and Michael McFaul of the Carnegie Endowment traded ideas with me about Russia's political and economic transition. David Lipton, formerly of the US Treasury, and Martin Gilman, of the IMF, were invaluable in helping me to understand the economics of the new Russia. Both offered helpful comments on the manuscript of this book. Graham Allison and Steve Miller of the Belfer Center for Science and International Affairs at the Kennedy School of Government at Harvard University provided me with a non-resident fellowship at their institute in 1999–2000. The stimulating environment they have created there was the perfect place to complete my book.

I am grateful for the friendship and council of Jennifer Copaken, Alison Franklin and Marci Glazer. Alison read my manuscript and offered vital encouragement during the exhausting final push to complete this book. I also want to thank my family. My mother, Halyna Freeland, and my aunts Chrystia and Natalka Chomiak and uncle John-Paul Himka all read my manuscript, caught some of my mistakes and offered moral support. My in-laws, Barbara and David Bowley, provided a loving sanctuary where much of this book was written and were sympathetic about the absences this project required. My brother Adik Freeland and my father Donald and my stepmother Carol gave me a way to begin both my Russian journey and my book. My grandmother Alexandra Chomiak, herself a talented writer, taught me Ukrainian, my first Slavic language, and she and my grandfather, the late Mykhailo Chomiak, told me the first stories I ever heard about Russia. My paternal grandparents, Helen and Wilbur Freeland, offered constant encouragement.

I have been blessed with wonderful publishers. Jon Karp of Random House, US had the rigour and the insight to force me to make difficult but valuable changes. Many of this book's virtues (but none of its defects) are thanks to him. Richard Beswick, of Little, Brown, UK, made dozens of elegant stylistic and structural suggestions and was marvellously tolerant my struggle to adapt daily-journalism skills to book-writing. John Pearce Pamela Murray of Doubleday, Canada were my biggest champions fro very beginning. They edited several versions of this book with grace and care, making countless improvements and offering endless encouragement along the way. Without my magnificent agent, Patricia Kavanagh, I would not have written this book. I am truly grateful to her for taking me on and for working with Joy Harris and Bruce Westwood, her US and Canadian associates, to find me North American publishers.

My greatest thanks are for my husband, Graham Bowley and my sister Natalka Freeland, to whom this book is dedicated. Natalka has been my confidante, counsellor and teacher all her life and her wisdom and compassion have not waned over the past two difficult years of writing this book. Graham is my first editor and closest friend. He indulged the huge amounts of time and energy this book consumed and never let me lose heart.

Notes on Sources

My main source of information was personal interviews. I am very grateful to everyone who took the time to talk with me, both when I was reporting for the *Financial Times* and in the hundreds of separate interviews I did specifically for this book. The Russian media has become a rich and intriguing mine of information. I relied most on *Izvestia*, *Segodnya*, *Vremya*, *Kommersant*, *Nezavisimaya Gazeta*, *Moskovsky Komsomolets*, the *Moscow Times* and the newsmagazine *Itogi*, as well as the radio station Ekho Moskvy and the television station NTV. The coverage of Russia in the *Washington Post* (especially the remarkable work of David Hoffman), the *New York Times* and the *Daily Telegraph*, as well as the work of my colleagues at the *Financial Times* (particularly John Lloyd and John Thornhill and the columns of Martin Wolf) was invaluable. The monthly and quarterly publications of *Russian Economic Trends*, produced by the Russian–European Centre for Economic Policy were the best source for economic data.

The translations from Russian language texts are all my own, as are the translations of the interviews, which were almost all conducted in Russian. I have tried to be consistent in transliterating Russian names in English, except in those cases where an odd spelling has become the English language standard.

Prologue

The Marquis de Custine's *Empire of the Csar: A Journey Through Eternal Russia* provided a powerful counterpoint to my trip to Moscow to collect my adopted brother Adik. Richard Pipes' magisterial *Russia Under the Old Regime* was also helpful.

Chapter 1: Everything Marx Told Us About Capitalism Was True

The most important interviews and discussions were with Sergei Zverev, the businessman and political aide who introduced me to Serebryany Vek; Ilya Kolerov, the Moscow gas-station entrepreneur; Dmitry Zimin, of telecom company Beeline; Lukoil chief Vagit Alekperov; Boris Jordan, the Russian–American investment banker; Sergei Kovalyev, the former dissident and Kakha Bendukidze, the biologist-turned-industrialist. I am also indebted to Allan Bigman, an American businessman in Moscow, for bringing me into the private lives of some New Russians, including Leonid, the St Petersburg insurer.

Boris Yeltsin's memoirs were helpful, in particular *Zapiski prezidenta*, with its vivid account of the August 1991 attempted coup. Angus McQueen's documentary film, *Gulags*, offered moving insights into Russia's damaged psyche. *Kremlin Capitalism* by Joseph Blasi, Maya Kroumova and Douglas Kruse as well as *Privatizing Russia* by Maxim Boycko, Andrei Shleifer and Robert Vishny, are useful statistical and analytical guides to the early, triumphant years of Russia's market revolution.

Chapter 2: Storming the Bastille

Interviews with the young reformers and their allies including Boris Brevnov, Yegor Gaidar, Andrei Illarionov, Konstantin Kagalovsky, Sergei Kovalyev, Alfred Kokh, Otto Latsis, Vladimir Mau, Boris Nemtsov, Aleksei Ulyukaev, Dmitry Vasiliev, Sergei Vasiliev. Frequent discussions and interviews with Russian journalists Aleksandr (Sasha) Bekker, Mikhail Berger, Mikhail Leontiev and Dmitry (Dima) Volkov and western advisers including David Lipton, Jonathan Hay, Anders Aslund and Joseph Blasi were also useful.

Yegor Gaidar's memoir, *Dni porazhenyi i pobed*, is written in beautiful prose and gives a powerful account of the acting prime minister's motivations and emotions when he launched Russia's market reforms. Boris Yeltsin's memoirs also offered valuable insights into this period. *Ekonomika perekhodnogo perioda*, a massive study of the Russian economy in the transition period produced by Gaidar's institute is an excellent guide to the economics of Russian reforms.

Aleksei Ulyukaev's *Reforming the Russian Economy, 1991–1995* and Vladimir Mau's *The Political History of Economic Reform in Russia, 1985–1994* are other useful inside accounts. Anders Aslund's *How Russia Became a Market Economy* and Richard Layard and John Parker's *The Coming Russian Boom* are two detailed and cheery Western studies of the early, optimistic years of Russia's reforms. Martin Wolf's columns about Russia and eastern Europe in the *Financial Times* and conversations with him helped me to understand Russian market reforms in a global context.

Chapter 3: The Iron General Privatises Russia

Interviews with young reformers and their allies including: Yegor Gaidar, Boris Nemtsov, Alfred Kokh, Sergei Vasiliev, Dmitry Vasiliev, Leonid Gozman, Arkady Evstafiev and Otto Latsis. I also interviewed Westerners who participated in the privatisation process as advisers or executives of Western aid organisations: Alan Bigman, Joseph Blasi, Tony Doran, Roberta Feldman, Jonathan Hay, Stephen Jennings, Boris Jordan, Charles Ryan, Leonid Rozhetskin and Gretchen Wilson. Some of the other important interviews were with: the banker and politician Boris Fyodorov; Sergei Karaganov, a political scientist and sometime Yeltsin adviser; Kremlin bodyguard Aleksandr Korzhakov; Moscow mayor Yuri Luzhkov; Vasily Shakhnovksy, the Moscow city civil servant; Sergei Kovalyev and Mikhail Berger. Stephen Jennings generously shared a two-volume report about voucher auctions he had helped to write.

In addition to the economic and business books consulted for the previous chapter, *Privatizing Russia*, by Maxim Boycko, one of the young reformers, and Andrei Shleifer and Robert Vishny, two Western economists who advised them, is a comprehensive account of the theory and practice of Russian mass privatisation and provided very useful details of the timing, legislation and statistics. Alfred Kokh's controversial book, *The Selling of the Soviet Empire*, is an inside account of Russian privatisation. *Kremlin Capitalism*, by Joseph Blasi, Maya Kroumova and Douglas Kruse is one of the most comprehensive Western accounts of the Russian privatisation process. Stephen Jennings generously shared the diary he and Boris Jordan kept for CSFB of the Bolshevik voucher auction.

Chapter 4: Who Gets the Loot?

Interviews with: prime minister Viktor Chernomyrdin; Gazprom chairman Rem Vyakhirev; Vagit Alekperov; Sergei Zverev. Kakha Bendukidze allowed me to join two of his bodyguards on a trip to Gaz-Sala. Joseph Piradashvili and Vladimir Semianiv were attentive guides to this remote settlement. Shiv Khemka, Sergei Mitirev and Perry Moi introduced me to the Perm Brewery. Aleksandr Bekker exhausted me on our trip to Novosibirsk, but only increased my admiration of his reporters' tenacity. The other players in the tin factory drama – Anna Gumerova, the economist; Yana Rogozhina, the prosecutor; Sergei Afanasiev, the policeman and Aleksandr Dugelny, the factory director – were also generous with their time. Discussions with Leonid Griaznov, a Gazprom executive; Anders Aslund; Craig Kennedy, an investment banker and Andrew Cowley, an investment banker, helped me understand the Gazprom empire.

Aslund's *How Russia Became a Market Economy* includes one of the best dissections of Gazprom's rent-seeking strategies and it was very useful. Joseph Blasi, Maya Kroumova and Douglas Kruse's *Kremlin Capitalism* is also useful in understanding this stage of Russian market reforms.

Chapter 5: The Loophole Economy

Interviews with: Mikhail Gutseriev, of Bin; Ruslan Aushev, president of Ingushetia; Sergei Aleksashenko, deputy minister of finance; Shamil Tarpishchev, Kremlin aide; Vladimir Konovalov, World Bank economist and several leaders of the Afghan war veterans charities.

Chapter 6: The Oligarchs: The Outsider, the Apparatchik, and the Blue Blood

I interviewed Mikhail Friedman, Mikhail Khodorkovsky and Vladimir Potanin, the three oligarchs described in this chapter, many times, over several years. I am grateful for their time. Others also helped me to understand these three men and their empires: Inna Khodorkovska, Mikhail's wife; Leonid Nevzlin, a Menatep executive; Konstantin Kagalovsky, a Menatep executive; Vasily Shakhnovsky, a Menatep executive; Aleksei Kandaurov, a Menatep security officer; Olga Kostina, a former Menatep press secretary; ʹotr Aven, a senior Alfa executive; Alan Bigman; Len Blavatnik, one of ʹedman's business partners; Mikhail Kozhokin, an Oneximbank execu- Larissa Zelkova, Potanin's press secretary; Oleg Boiko, one of Potanin's ʹlients; Boris Jordan; Stephen Jennings; Leonid Rozhetskin; Igor

Golembiovsky, editor of *Izvestia*; Charles Ryan; Bill Browder, an American investment banker; Mikhail Leontiev; Mikhail Berger; Aleksandr Bekker; Dmitry Volkov; sociologist Igor Bunin; liberal politician Grigory Yavlinsky; Yegor Gaidar.

Khodorkovsky and Nevzlin's book, *Chelovek s rublyem*, offers insight into their thinking in the early 1990s. Igor Bunin's study of the Russian business elite, *Biznesmeni Rossii* (*Businessmen of Russia*) was one of the first comprehensive attempts to identify and describe Russia's emerging capitalist class and it remains useful. Rose Brady writes interestingly about the oligarchs in her *Kapitalizm*.

Chapter 7: The Nomad and the Impresario

I interviewed Vladimir Gusinsky and Boris Berezovsky many times over several years. Interviews with many others also helped to understand these two oligarchs and their businesses: Lena Gusinskaya, Vladimir's wife; Sergei Zverev, a senior Most executive; Igor Malashenko, president of NTV and later a senior Most executive; Svetlana Mironiuk, a Most executive; Yevgeny Kisiliev, NTV's chief anchorman; Mikhail Leontiev; Dmitry Ostalsky, founding editor of *Segodnya*; Dmitry Volkov; Aleksandr Bekker; Yevgeny Sevastianov, the head of the Moscow FSB; Katya Berezovskaya, Boris' daughter; Eugene Shvidler, president of Sibneft; Vladimir Kadannikov, head of Avtovaz; Valery Okulov, Yeltsin's son-in-law and head of Aeroflot; Nina Golovyatenko; Boris Brevnov; Igor Bunin; political analyst Andrei Piontkovsky; Mikhail Berger; Otto Latsis; Aleksandr Korzhakov; Yuri Luzhkov; Vladimir Yevtushenkov; Viktor Chernomyrdin; Sergei Kovalyev; Grigory Yavlinsky and Yegor Gaidar.

Korzhakov's scurrilous and hugely readable account of his time in Yeltsin's court, *C rassveta do zakata*, is full of stories about Berezovsky and Gusinsky. John Lloyd's coverage of the faces-on-the-snow incident in the *Financial Times* was vivid and helpful. Bunin's book was useful. David Remnick's *Resurrection* has a beautifully written chapter about Gusinsky.

Chapter 8: The Faustian Bargain

Interviews with: Vladimir Potanin; Vladimir Gusinsky; Mikhail Khodorkovsky; Mikhail Friedman; Boris Berezovsky; Leonid Nevzlin; Konstantin Kagalovsky; Sergei Zverev; Alfred Kokh; Aleksandr Korzhakov; Mikhail Zadornov; Boris Jordan; Stephen Jennings; Anders Aslund; Yegor Gaidar; Aleksei Ulyukaev; Sergei Vasiliev; Dmitry Vasiliev; Andre'

Piontkovsky; Kakha Bendukidze; David Lipton; Boris Fyodorov; Viktor Chernomyrdin; Dmitry Volkov; Vladimir Vinogradov.

Alfred Kokh's book, *The Selling of the Soviet Empire*, is a plodding but surprisingly candid account of how the loans-for-shares auctions played out.

Chapter 9: The Davos Pact and the Fight for the Kremlin

Interviews with: Mikhail Berger; Mikhail Khodorkovsky; Sergei Zverev; Yegor Gaidar; Boris Nemtsov; Arkady Evstafiev; Vladimir Gusinsky; Boris Berezovsky; Leonid Nevzlin; Mikhail Friedman; Petr Aven; Vladimir Potanin; Igor Malashenko; Vladimir Vinogradov; Sergei Vasiliev; Mikhail Zadornov; Alfred Kokh; Yuri Luzhkov; Vasily Shakhnovsky; Aleksei Ulyukaev; Viacheslav Nikonov; Aleksandr Korzhakov; Emil Pain, a Kremlin aide; Viktor Chernomyrdin; Mikhail Gorbachev; Raisa Gorbacheva; Gennady Zyuganov, the Communist leader; Gennady Selezniov, the Communist speaker of parliament; Aleksei Podberiozkin, a Communist ideologist; Anatoly Lukianov, a Communist ideologist; Andrei Piontkovsky; Vladimir Semago, a businessman and Communist member of parliament; Grigory Yavlinsky.

Ot Yeltsina k Yeltsinu, a collection of essays, chronologies and primary source materials about the 1996 elections, is an invaluable resource. Michael McFaul's *Russia's 1996 Presidential Election* is the best English-language academic study of that political race. Lilia Shevtsova's *Yeltsin's Russia: Myths and Reality*, is an insightful account of the politics of the entire Yeltsin era. Ellen Mickiewicz's *Changing Channels* is a comprehensive analysis of the relationship between television and politics in Russia, both before and after the collapse of the Soviet Union. Zyuganov's election-year books, in particular *Veru v Rossiyu* (*I Believe in Russia*), offer some insight into the thinking of post-Soviet Communists. Carlotta Gall and Thomas de Waal's *Chechnya: A Small Victorious War* is the best description of the war which was the backdrop to the 1996 election.

Chapter 10: Dividing the Spoils

Interviews with: Arkady Evstafiev; Sergei Lisovsky; Aleksandr Korzhakov; Sergei Zverev; Viacheslav Nikonov; Georgy Satarov, the Kremlin aide; Igor Malashenko; Vladimir Gusinsky; Aleksandr Lebed, the former general and politician; Boris Berezovsky; Vasily Shakhnovsky; Mikhail Friedman; Leonid Gozman, an advisor to Chubais; Vladimir Potanin; Boris Jordan; Sergei

Kovalyev; Sergei Medvedev, Yeltsin's press secretary; Stephen Barber, a British investment banker.

NTV offered extensive coverage of the nocturnal showdown between the oligarchs and the party of war. I am grateful to Igor Malashenko for providing me with videos of many of these broadcasts. The BBC's documentary series *Tsar Boris: The Yeltsin Years* first aired in January, 1998, includes some excellent footage from that tense night. Korzhakov's memoirs offer a biased but extremely page-turning account of this period. Aleksandr Lebed's *Za derzhavu obidno* is the best introduction to the man who makes his political debut in this chapter.

Chapter 11: Champagne Too Soon: Stories from the New Russia

Interviews with: Boris Brevnov; his wife, US investment banker Gretchen Wilson Brevnov; Sergei Medvedev, the UES press secretary; Boris Nemtsov; Alan Bigman; Dmitry Zimin; Augie Fabela, the US co-founder of Beeline; Alan Apter, the American investment banker; Vladimir Yevtushenkov; Stephen Jennings; Boris Jordan; Andrei Piontkovsky; Yegor Gaidar; Martin Gilman, an IMF official; David Lipton; Arkady Novikov, the restaurateur; Vladimir Potanin; George Soros, the American financier; Valery Shantsev, deputy mayor of Moscow; Yuri Luzhkov; Kyoji Komachi, the Japanese diplomat; Gennady Koniakhin, mayor of a Kuzbas town; Vyacheslav Skvortsov, Sergei Kliukvin, and Viktor Cherepakhin and many other workers at the Zlatoust Metallurgical Factory. I also benefited from discussions during this period with the economist Andrei Illarionov; Anders Aslund; Roland Nash, an economic analyst; Henrik Piper and Julie Quist, utilities analysts.

Chapter 12: No Honour Among Thieves – The Bankers' War

Interviews with: Vladimir Potanin; Vladimir Gusinsky; Alfred Kokh; Sergei Zverev; Mikhail Friedman; Boris Jordan; Stephen Jennings; Boris Nemtsov; Leonid Rozhetskin; Igor Malashenko; Yegor Gaidar; Mikhail Berger; Arkady Evstafiev; Boris Berezovsky; Mikhail Kozhokin; Larissa Zelkova; Mikhail Khodorkovsky; Leonid Nevzlin; Vladimir Yevtushenkov; Andrei Piontkovsky; Boris Brevnov; Maxim Boiko; Lilia Shevtsova, a Russia analyst; Liuba Vlasova, a merchant in the Kuzbas; Andrei Ostalsky, a BBC journalist

Chapter 13: Things Fall Apart

Interviews with: Vladimir Potanin; Vladimir Gusinsky; Mikhail Khodorkovsky; Mikhail Friedman; Boris Berezovsky; Leonid Nevzlin; Konstanin Kagalovsky; Vasily Shakhnovsky; Sergei Zverev; Dmitry Ostalsky; Igor Malashenko; Viktor Chernomyrdin; Boris Nemtsov; Boris Brevnov; Sergei Dubinin, chairman of the central bank; Sergei Aleksashenko, deputy chairman of the central bank; Irina Yasina, spokeswoman of the central bank; Denis Kisiliev, central bank executive; Yevgeny Yasin, minister of the economy; Sergei Kiriyenko, the prime minister; Aleksandr Livshits, the Kremlin aide; Yuri Luzhkov; Vladimir Yevtushenkov; Leonid Gozman; Dmitry Zimin; Mikhail Zadornov; Aleksei Kudrin, deputy minister of finance; Sergei Kovalyev; Yegor Gaidar; Aleksei Ulyukaev; Sergei Vasiliev; Dmitry Vasiliev; Boris Fyodorov; Charles Ryan; David Lipton; Martin Gilman; Vladimir Konovalov; Boris Jordan; Stephen Jennings; Bill Browder; Allan Bigman; Len Blavatnik; investment banker Adam Elstein. Lena and the Luzhniki traders were generous with their time and insights, but asked that their surnames not be used.

George Soros' *The Crisis of Global Capitalism* includes a detailed and provocative account of the August, 1998 financial collapse. *Newsweek* published a wonderfully detailed narrative of how the crisis unfolded. Anders Aslund's article in the September/October 1999 issue of *Foreign Affairs* contains valuable, if characteristically optimistic, predictions of the longer-term economic consequences of the 1998 crash.

Chapter 14: The Oligarchs, Capitalism and the Kremlin – The Sequel

The most important source for this chapter was the full day I spent shadowing Mikhail Khodorkovsky on Monday, 22 September 2003 and the extensive sit-down interview I did with him on the next day at his office in Moscow. This may have been the last significant interview Khodorkovsky gave before his arrest. The Khodorkovsky interview was the basis of a piece I wrote for the *FT* magazine, published in November 2003. The *Financial Times* has kindly allowed me to draw on that piece for this chapter. On that trip to Moscow I also did interviews with: Ray Leonard, the Yukos geologist, Bruce Missamore, the American CFO of Yukos, Joe Mack, another American Yukos executive, Charlie Ryan, the head of United Financial Group, Boris Nemtsov, the liberal politician, Irina Yasina, the former journalist and central bank official who went to work for Khodorkovsky's Open Russia foundation, Gleb Pavlovsky, the political consultant who worked on Putin's first election campaign, Mikhail Zagin, a political consultant, Grigory Yavlinsky, the liberal politician,

Konstantin Kagalovsky, a Yukos executive, Mikhail Friedman, Yegor Gaidar, Stephen Jennings, the head of Renaissance Capital, Bill Browder, the head of Hermitage Capital, Bob Dudley, of BP–TNK, Stanislav Belkin, a pro-Putin political consultant and Evgeny Kisiliev, the former TV anchor and new editor of Khodorkovsky's *Moscow News*. In London, I spoke with business people and diplomats involved in Russia, including Lord John Browne of BP, Peter Weinberg of Goldman Sachs, Tommy Helsby of Kroll, Konstantia Kagalovsky, one of the self-exiled Yukos shareholders, Leonid Nerzlin, another self-exiled Yukos shareholder, and Alexander Vershbow, the US ambassador to Russia. I also met with Boris Berezovsky, Vladimir Gusinsky, Igor Malashenko and Pyotr Aven. In late 2000, together with a group of Canadian journalists, I interviewed Vladimir Putin. For the section in this chapter on Alfa and BP in addition to the interviews above, I also interviewed Vladimir Potanin.

A magisterial three-part series on John Browne and BP, by my colleagues Tobias Buck and David Buchan, and published in the *Financial Times* on 31 July, 1 August and 2 August 2002 is a rich source of information on the man and his company. Peter Koenig's report in the *Sunday Times* on 'BP: from hate to love in Russia', published on 5 October 2003, is a good account of BP's relationship with Alfa. David Hoffman of the *Washington Post* was a wonderful friend and partner on many reporting trips, and my favourite sounding board for new theories about Russia. His superb book, *The Oligarchs*, was published after mine, so I was unable to draw on it for this work, but I strongly recommend it to anyone interested in Russia and business.

Conclusion

Richard Pipes' three-volume work on the Russian Revolution and his *Russia Under the Old Regime* were inspiring. I also relied on Ryszard Kapuscinski's *Imperium*, Isaiah Berlin's *Russian Thinkers*, Nikolai Karamzin's *Memoir on Ancient and Modern Russia* and Zbigniew Brzezinski's books and articles about Russia's future geopolitical place in the world. Yegor Gaidar's autobiography of the early Yeltsin years remains a thoughtful reminder of what it was like to take the big decisions at the moment when Russia was still delicately poised between communism and capitalism. Interviews with the Russian business-men and politicians listed in the note for Chapter 14 informed this section, including an interview with Mikhail Friedman in September 2003 from which the quotation in the text was taken. The Russian sociologist Olga Kryshtanovskaya is a leading student both of the oligarchs and the *siloviki*; her work is an illuminating guide to Russia's new elites. This chapter also draws on the reporting of my *Financial Times* colleagues, Arkady Ostrovsky, Andrew Jack and Stefan Wagstyl, and my frequent conversations with them.

BIBLIOGRAPHY

Aslund, Anders, *How Russia Became a Market Economy* (Washington, D.C., Brooking Institution, 1995).

Blasi, Joseph, Kroumova, Maya and Kruse, Douglas, *Kremlin Capitalism: The Privatization of the Russian Economy* (Ithaca, N.Y., ILR Press, 1997).

Boycko, Maxim, Shleifer, Andrei and Vishny, Robert, *Privatizing Russia* (Cambridge, MIT Press, 1995).

Brady, Rose, *Kapitalizm: Russia's Struggle to Free its Economy* (New Haven, Yale University Press, 1999).

Brzezinski, Zbigniew, *The Grand Failure: The Birth and Death of Communism in the Twentieth Century* (London, Macdonald, 1979).

Bunin, Igor, *Biznesmeni Rossii (Businessmen of Russia)* (Moscow, AO OKO, 1994).

Clark, Bruce, *An Empire's New Clothes* (London, Vintage, 1995).

Colton, Timothy, *Moscow* (Cambridge, Mass., Harvard University Press, 1996).

Custine, Astolphe, marquis de, *Empire of the Czar: A Journey Through Eternal Russia* (New York, Doubleday, 1989).

Djilas, Milovan, *The New Class: An Analysis of the Communist System* (London, Thames & Hudson, 1957).

Dobrokhotov, L.N., *Ot Yeltsina k Yeltsinu: prezidentskaya gonka – 96 (From Yeltsin to Yeltsin, the presidential race of '96)* (Moscow, Terra, 1997).

Figes, Orlando, *A People's Tragedy* (London, Pimlico, 1996).

Gaidar, Yegor, *Dni porazheniy i pobed* (*Days of defeats and victories*) (Moscow, Vagrius, 1997).

Gaidar, Yegor (ed.), *Ekonomika perekhodnogo perioda* (*Economy of the Transition Period*) (Moscow, Institut ekonimicheskikh problem perekhodnogo perioda, 1998).

Gall, Carlotta and de Waal, Thomas, *Chechnya: A Small Victorious War* (London, Pan Books, 1997).

Handelman, Stephen, *Comrade Criminal: Russia's New Mafiya* (New Haven, Yale University Press, 1995).

Hosking, Geoffrey, *A History of the Soviet Union* (London, Fontana Press, 1992).

Josephson, Matthew, *The Robber Barons: The Great American Capitalists* (New York, Harcourt Brace, 1962).

Kapuscinski, Ryszard, *Imperium* (New York, Knopf, 1994).

Karamzin, Nikolai, *Karamzin's Memoir on Ancient and Modern Russia: A Translation and Analysis* (ed. Richard Pipes) (New York, Atheneum, 1966).

Khodorkovsky, Mikhail and Nevzlin, Leonid, *Chelovek s rublyem* (*A Man with a Rouble*) (Moscow, Menatep-Inform, 1992).

Kokh, Alfred, *The Selling of the Soviet Empire* (New York, SPI Books, 1998).

Korzhakov, Aleksandr, *Boris Yeltsin: C rassveta do zakata* (*Boris Yeltsin: From Dawn till Dusk*) (Moscow, Interbuk, 1997).

Kostikov, Vyacheslav, *Roman s prezidentom* (Moscow, Vagrius, 1997).

Layard, Richard and Parker, John, *The Coming Russian Boom* (New York, Free Press, 1996).

Lebed, Aleksandr, *Za derzhavu obidno* (*I am ashamed for my nation*) (Moscow, Moskovskaya Pravda, 1995).

Lloyd, John, *Rebirth of a Nation: The Anatomy of Russia* (London, Michael Joseph, 1998).

Mau, Vladimir, *The Political History of Economic Reform in Russia, 1985–1994* (London, The Centre for Research into Communist Economies, 1996).

McFaul, Michael, *Russia's 1996 Presidential Election: The End of Polarized Politics* (Stanford, California, Hoover Institution Press, 1997).

Mickiewicz, Ellen, *Changing Channels: Television and the Struggle for Power in Russia* (New York, Oxford University Press, 1997).

O'Rourke, P.J., *Eat the Rich* (New York, Atlantic Monthly Press, 1998).

Pipes, Richard, *Communism the Vanished Specter* (Oslo, Scandinavian University Press, 1994).

Pipes, Richard, *The Russian Revolution* (New York, Knopf, 1990).

Pipes, Richard, *Russia Under the Old Regime* (London, Penguin Books, 1974`

Remnick, David, *Lenin's Tomb: The Last Days of the Soviet Empire* (New Yo~ Random House, 1993).

Remnick, David, *Resurrection: The Struggle for a New Russia* (New York, Random House, 1997).

Rogger, Hans, *Russia in the Age of Modernism and Revolution 1881–1917* (London, Longman, 1983).

Sakwa, Richard, *Russian Politics and Society* (London, Routledge, 1993).

Saunders, David, *Russia in the Age of Reaction and Reform 1801–1881* (London, Longman, 1992).

Shevtsova, Lilia, *Yeltsin's Russia: Myths and Reality* (Washington, D.C., Carnegie Endowment for International Peace, 1999).

Simes, Dimitri, *After the Collapse: Russia Seeks Its Place as a Great Power* (New York, Simon and Schuster, 1999).

Soros, George, *The Crisis of Global Capitalism* (London, Little, Brown, 1998).

Ulyukaev, Aleksei, *Reforming the Russian Economy, 1991–1995* (London, The Centre for Research into Post-Communist Economies, 1996).

Yeltsin, Boris, *Zapiski prezidenta* (*Notes of a president*) (Moscow, Ogonyok, 1994).

Zyuganov, Gennady, *Veru v Rossiyu* (*I Believe in Russia*) (Voronezh, Voronezh Publishers, 1996).

INDEX